Literature After Euclid

HANEY FOUNDATION SERIES

A volume in the Haney Foundation Series, established in 1961 with the generous support of Dr. John Louis Haney

Literature After Euclid

The Geometric Imagination in the Long Scottish Enlightenment

Matthew Wickman

PENN

UNIVERSITY OF PENNSYLVANIA PRESS

PHILADELPHIA

Published by
University of Pennsylvania Press
Philadelphia, Pennsylvania 19104-4112
www.upenn.edu/pennpress

Printed in the United States of America on acid-free paper
1 3 5 7 9 10 8 6 4 2

Library of Congress Cataloging-in-Publication Data

Wickman, Matthew, author.
Literature after Euclid : the geometric imagination in the long Scottish Enlightenment / Matthew Wickman.
pages cm. — (Haney Foundation series)
Includes bibliographical references and index.
ISBN 978-0-8122-4795-4 (alk. paper)
1. Scottish literature—18th century—History and criticism. 2. English literature—Scottish authors—History and criticism. 3. Geometry in literature. 4. Enlightenment—Scotland. 5. Scotland—Intellectual life—18th century. I. Title. II. Series: Haney Foundation series.
PR8547.W53 2016
820.9'9411—dc23

2015022963

For Kerry, Hadley, and Elena: adventurers on all my tangents

CONTENTS

Introduction

Always visualize! Increasingly, this revision of Fredric Jameson's famous opening salvo in his 1981 study *The Political Unconscious*—"Always historicize!"—seems to be acquiring the status of an imperative in an age of big data, when traditional distinctions of canon and period seem ever less satisfying, ever more the product of historiographical accident.[1] Visualization, the graphical display of information, accompanies a new method of historicist engagement: distant reading. As Franco Moretti puts it in his collection bearing that title, "The trouble with close reading," the method of much of the "new"—that is, old—historicism, "is that it necessarily depends on an extremely small canon. . . . [Y]ou invest so much in individual texts *only* if you think that very few of them really matter. Otherwise, it doesn't make sense."[2] And in an era when digital archives make vast corpuses available online, a diminishing number of scholars, it seems, find close reading sensible. "Close reading is not only impractical as a means of gathering evidence in the digital library," Matthew Jockers argues, "but big data render it totally inappropriate as a method of studying literary history."[3] In part, this is because the exponential increase in the amount of information at our disposal and the capacity to scale that information to sizes ranging from the virtually infinite to the infinitesimal will inexorably exert an influence on the kinds of historical questions we are able to pose. These are stories we must *show* as much as *tell.* And so, digital humanists make the case that scholars of literary history "have increasingly become involved in what is often referred to as the 'visual turn' . . . sometimes correlated with the 'spatial turn' that has favored mapping."[4]

If we ask the question, as digital humanists often do, of how our tools for engaging the past reflect the tools *of* that past, then we may find ourselves considering "models of statistical expression, such as bar and pie charts, [that] came from the world of 18th century 'political arithmetic' and provided a rich and much developed legacy that extended the vocabulary of much older visual forms of diagrams, grids, and trees."[5] Or, we may undertake a more elemental encounter with a discipline that underwrote many of these older models. I am speaking here of geometry, a mathematical practice in which visual display has traditionally been a matter of course. It is geometry that lured Moretti, who professed in his landmark 2005 book *Graphs, Maps, Trees* that the patterns of history revealed by distant reading provoked him. A "geometrical pattern is too orderly a shape to be the product of chance. It is the sign that something," some force of history, "is at work here—that something has made the pattern the way it is."[6] This is, indeed, a compelling thought. But geometry is not a static or homogeneous discipline, however much we may associate it with ideal objects. Modern geometry comes in a multitude of varieties—differential, projective, non-Euclidean, and more. Even classical geometry bears a history; its triangles, circles, and squares contain crevices of human complexity that may not always appear at first glance. In the eighteenth century, for example, the earlier half of the period on which Moretti turns sustained attention, geometry was in some circles (excuse the pun) a fraught philosophical exercise whose controversies spilled into exercises in literary form. In some cases, these are the very forms Moretti analyzes through distant reading, though without probing the wrinkles that introduce alternative meanings into those forms—nuances that only the supplementation of one (heuristic) geometry with another (historical) reveals.[7]

This book explores at closer view those shapes that, today, we idealize from a "distance"; that is, it examines the interface between literature and geometry in a place—Scotland—and during an extended moment—a (very) long eighteenth century (extending into the nineteenth and even the twentieth centuries)—when certain mathematico-philosophical paradigms came under increasing pressure without yet yielding to entirely new formations. To the extent that these older models informed the humanities, as we will see they did, this book might thus be said to discuss a kind of "crisis in the humanities" some two centuries prior to its irruption in the modern university. But what most interests me are the creative forms, literary and conceptual, that this crisis spawned. In examining them, I make no pretension that this is a book *of mathematics*; instead, I analyze literary experiments in what Arkady Plotnitsky calls "mathematical thinking" as the recrudescence of mathematical ideas in areas of culture that are not formally mathematical.[8] The literature I analyze, for example, may not have directly intervened in mathematical debates during the (long) Scottish Enlightenment, but it creatively adopted and distorted mathematical ideas—or, as I will call them, *figures* of thought.

To explain what these figures are and what they might mean, let me resort to the familiar historicist device of the anecdote. Sometime around 1789 or 1790, when she was in her late twenties, Joanna Baillie assigned herself a peculiar task:

> I heard a friend of ours, a mathematician, talking one day about squaring the circle as a discovery which had been often attempted but never found out[.] . . . I very simply set my wits to find it out. . . . "But surely" thought I "it will be found in Euclid," so I borrowed from my friend Miss Fordyce, now Lady Bentham, an old copy of Euclid. . . . I went through it by myself as well as I could, though in no very plodding way, being only intent on this one purpose. . . . But my disappointment & mortification may easily be guessed, when on arriving at the apendix of the book . . . I found my own discovery . . . proved in a different manner. "So I have mistaken what is meant by squaring the circle" said I bitterly to myself, and thus ended my mathematical pursuits. I had by this time written Basil & De Monfort and very soon consoled myself for such a wild goose chace.[9]

Baillie's experience—in some ways repeating an idyll from her childhood when, "without any teacher, [she went] through a good part of Euclid for her own amusement"[10]—seems familiar, even a little self-reflexive. Not only did she turn to the arts, specifically the theater, as a failed mathematician (the lot of many a student of literature), but the problem she addressed possessed an evocatively literary aspect. Contrary to her claims, the riddle of how to construct a square with the same area as a given circle using only ruler and compass had not already been solved (indeed, it would be proven insoluble later in the nineteenth century), but the equation of dissimilar properties—*square* is *circle*, *this* is *that*—corresponds with the structure of metaphor, the archetypal poetic trope. For Baillie, to square the circle was to craft the ultimate figure, to make romance a reality, to bring fancy to fruition.[11]

But failing in mathematics—that is, in a "literary" aspect of geometry—she turned to literature—or to a "geometric" dimension of drama. I say this not because Baillie's *Plays of the Passions*, as she later called them and for which she is best known, are overtly mathematical but rather because they reveal the workings of a "methodical mind" that remained evocatively Euclidean.[12] Baillie was fascinated, for instance, by idealized constructs or by what Plato called the geometric "knowledge of the eternally existent."[13] In her "Introductory Discourse" to her published *Series of Plays* (1798), she professed her desire to distill the perfect shapes, as it were, of natural passions from the "decoration and ornament, all [the inflated] loftiness and refinement" of orotund poetry.[14] Her early play *De Monfort* presents a kind of Platonic abstraction in the character of Lady Jane de Monfort, "[s]o stately and so graceful [in] her form" that other characters "shr[i]nk at first in awe."[15] But Lady Janes are not ubiquitous presences in Baillie's *Plays of the Passions*; indeed, she tempered such archetypes with a dramatist's taste for mixed forms.[16] The propensity to have "all tragic characters drawn very good or very bad . . . arises from a nobleness in our nature; but the general prevalence of [such designs] would be the bane of all useful and natural delineation of character."[17] Hence, Michael Gamer observes, Baillie's theater "demonstrate[s] a doubleness of perspective" between the ideal shapes of the fancy and the contingent forms they take in everyday life.[18] It's a case not of squared circles, two idealized constructs, but of conflicting dramatic imperatives.

Baillie's example speaks to the larger subject of this book, which concerns the relationship between literature and mathematics, especially geometry, in Scotland's long eighteenth century. I make the case for a kind of disjunctive union between these disciplines that causes them not so much (or not only) to inform or reflect as to supplement and provoke one another. In the chapters that follow, for example, historical fiction will be seen to evoke and disfigure calculus, and poems enacting the formation and breakdown of community will conjure the specter of irrational numbers. But to what effect, we might ask? How might the indication of a mathematical unconscious in these texts—or, more simply, a balky and bedimmed, though conscientious, engagement of mathematical ideas in them—expand the scope of implication of these texts and possibly reconfigure literary form and history? And how might the transmediation from one (mathematical) context to another (a literary one) expand our vision not only of what literary texts are but also of what they do—of how they intervene in knowledge creation?

While I focus primarily on some key literary exhibits from the early eighteenth through early nineteenth centuries (essentially, from poems by James Thomson to novels by Walter Scott), the backdrop for my study is the wider quarter-millennium between the analytic geometry of René Descartes and the self-conscious appeal to non-Euclidean geometry in the work of the European avant-garde. As different as the seventeenth and twentieth centuries are from one another, they represent historical bookends of an era in which mathematicians sought in various ways to circumvent the perceived limitations of classical geometry. For Descartes and his followers, this meant creating a coordinate system that affixed numerical or algebraic values to, for example, a given point along a plane, making it easier to calculate values; for avant-garde artists, it meant incorporating postclassical theories about the shape of the universe and the nature of reality into the visual and narrative arts, changing ideas about the nature of truth and the realm of the possible. The geometric thinking of Scottish Enlightenment literati—and I refer principally here to poets, novelists, and philosophers—falls literally and figuratively, I argue, between these two positions. Arriving two-plus generations after Descartes and a full century or more prior to, say, Marcel Duchamp, Scottish writers of the long eighteenth century, outwardly eschewing Cartesian innovation, often employed the language and constructs of classical geometry to creative ends that were neither expressly Euclidean nor manifestly non-Euclidean. I call it a culture of late Euclideanism, a phrase that means little in mathematical-historical terms but indicates the deployment of a language of classically conceived nature to strange new ends. The book's title, *Literature After Euclid*, highlights the ambiguity of a literature imagined, at once, in the manner of and as a successor to Euclidean norms.

Therefore, like Baillie's tale of a dashed geometric fantasy, the story I am telling is only elliptically mathematical. It concerns less the history of mathematics in eighteenth-century Scotland—a history recounted elsewhere by George Davie, Richard Olson, Helena M. Pycior, Alex D. D. Craik, Niccolò Guicciardini, and others—than an analysis of how mathematics inflects or even revises our understanding of the literary and intellectual history of the Scottish Enlightenment. At the same time, it also takes up ways in which Enlightenment writers drew upon mathematical ideas as fuel for literary flights of fancy. And while this study will anchor itself in the long eighteenth century, it will occasionally extend its analysis into the later nineteenth and twentieth centuries before circling back (in post-Euclidean fashion) to its historical point of origin. Call it the study of a long, looping eighteenth century.

Such recursions have become an important part of Scottish literary history. This is largely because the latter's evolution as a discipline has involved both the shadowing and occasional subversion of grand narratives that help explain other branches of English literature. Today, for example, the Scottish Enlightenment, popularly recognized for its broad influence on later modernity, is seen by many scholars as contemporaneous with a Romantic movement that, in traditional "English," supposedly succeeds it.[19] Scottish modernism, meanwhile, when it is identified as such at all, represents less a violent break from the "classical" past than the reformulated perpetuation of deep Scottish traditions.[20] I will discuss these dynamics in greater detail in later chapters; the point worth underscoring here is simply that Scottish literary history has tended to downplay or even deny the types of constitutive ruptures that help explain some of the prominent categories—"enlightenment," "romanticism," and "modernism"—we use to organize literary history in other national or even international traditions.[21] In Scotland's case, it is especially difficult to say when one period leaves off and another begins, and connections between them often wind around themselves, fashioning strange and sometimes contorted designs from the imagined flow of time.

One could analyze such puzzles without reference to mathematics, but the latter brings powerful and provocative elements to it. This is especially the case relative to literature and the arts, where mathematics explains but then skews or even collapses period distinctions on a grand scale. Take, for example, one of modernism's credos that new conceptions of non-Euclidean space, mathematically conceived during the nineteenth century, transformed cultural consciousness.[22] Max Weber, Henri Lefebvre, Anthony Giddens, and other social theorists, reprising the credos of modern*ism*, say that modern*ity* involves a widespread "ability to critically estrange or reflexively engage the contemporary arrangement of the world." Such zones of discrepancy, they contend, heighten our sense of difference from the past: "The spatial practices of modernity . . . create the conditions of possibility for practicing, conceiving, and living temporality and history in new ways."[23] Modernity's novelty, the idea of history made "new," consists of an ethos of spatiotemporal rearrangement, a reconfiguration of the traditional dimensions of experience. Such experience takes perhaps its most iconic aesthetic form in Cubist painting and stream-of-consciousness narrative. And yet, these latter forms operate on principles of recursion, with the presumed sweep of the eye across a canvas or the movement of a narrative from one episode to the next doubling back on itself (as angles onto an object converge with each other or as the train of a story's associations or a character's thoughts collapses distant moments or locales). Paradoxically, then, it is the muddle of nominal distinctions, the circling of viewpoints around themselves, that announces an aesthetic departure from traditional habits of representation: the "space" of the artwork declares its modernity by challenging the idea of straightforward succession on which it is predicated.

In the arts, then, mathematical concepts thus accentuate *and* challenge revisionist histories, undercutting the very presumptions of progress (from one period to another) on which, for example, a certain narrative of modernism is founded. And so, what are we to make of the fact that Scottish mathematics of the eighteenth century traditionally carries the association—even the stigma—of an entrenched, antimodern classicism? The seventeenth and nineteenth centuries are remembered as more innovative centuries in mathematical history—the seventeenth for analytic geometry and the geometric calculus, for instance, and the nineteenth for a variety of non-Euclidean geometries. During the eighteenth century, Scotland's signal contribution to mathematics was in traditional, Euclidean geometry, most evidently in the internationally esteemed work of Colin Maclaurin, Matthew Stewart, and Robert Simson. Simson especially is noteworthy for the half-century duration of his career as professor of mathematics at the University of Glasgow (1711–61) and for the massive influence he exerted over other scholars in that field, including Maclaurin and Stewart. But the sheer force of this influence and the insistence of all three on retaining and even, in Simson's case, "restoring" Euclidean geometry tend to obscure the role Scots played in experimenting within (and often at or across the limits of) Euclid. The richest illustration here may belong to Thomas Reid, best known as the founder of Common Sense philosophy, who devised a dynamic thought experiment that expressly involves non-Euclidean space. Reid's example, which I discuss below and then take up again in later chapters, is especially important to this book, for his innovation in a work of philosophy speaks to the degree to which mathematics permeated Scottish thought and culture during the long eighteenth century.

Such provocative convergences between geometry and the humanities allow us to reimagine literary and intellectual history, both substantively and formally (that is, in terms of what-led-to-what and also of what history even "is" as a figure—a shape—of thought). But these encounters, I claim, could only happen in a society where geometry suffused popular consciousness, however much or little particular writers may have engaged or grasped it in its fine details. Geometry, in other words, was not only a rigorous discipline but also a cultural medium, a trope.

In his memorable 1962 study *The Democratic Intellect*, George Davie explains why this was the case in eighteenth-century Scotland, remarking that geometry constituted a centerpiece of a Scottish university curriculum that impacted numerous corners of Scottish society. The nation's disproportionately high number of universities (five, compared with only two in England) meant that a greater percentage of Scots received some advanced training. And yet, in most cases, this was not higher education as we know it today, consisting less of intensive specialization than of broad exposure to a variety of subjects. The unifying link between these subjects, Davie argues, was philosophy, or metaphysics, which inculcated what we would call critical thinking. Geometric reasoning, with its emphasis on precision and logical exposition, featured prominently there. But "[t]he national habit was to treat mathematics as a cultural subject, not as a technical one, and it was found generally that the best way to maintain the students' interest in the subject was to give courses in which . . . elementary mathematics was discussed with special reference to its philosophy and its history." In this regard, mathematics functioned "as one of the 'humanities.'"[24] This is why a number of distinguished Scottish Enlightenment literati remembered today for their contributions to philosophy and the arts were also mathematicians, particularly geometers.

Examples here are plentiful and impressive. We might begin with Reid, who eventually published his most famous book, *An Inquiry into the Human Mind on the Principles of Common Sense*, in 1764 after assuming the professorship of moral philosophy vacated by Adam Smith at the University of Glasgow. However, Reid composed most of this work while holding a professorship at King's College, Aberdeen, where his lectures "ranged across Euclidean geometry, algebra, fluxions [or Newtonian calculus], applied mathematics, mechanics, astronomy, electricity, magnetism, hydrostatics, pneumatics, physical optics, catoptics and the theory of vision," many facets of which found their way into the *Inquiry*.[25] We might consider also the case of Adam Ferguson, author of *An Essay on the History of Civil Society* (1767) and hailed as "the father of modern sociology."[26] Ferguson was named professor of mathematics at the University of Edinburgh in 1785 after serving (from 1759) as professor of natural philosophy and then (from 1764) as professor of pneumatics and moral philosophy. His *Essay* does not take up mathematics directly, but the latter informs Ferguson's philosophy in subtle but substantive ways, as when Ferguson explains the course of civilization by formulating astronomical analogies that were themselves the province of applied mathematics ("Where states have stopped short in their progress . . . we may suspect, that however disposed to advance, they have found a *limit*, beyond which they could not proceed. . . . On this supposition, from being stationary, they may begin to relapse, and by a *retrograde motion* . . . arrive at a state of greater weakness").[27] Newton introduced the notion of limits in his fluxional calculus, which was a conceptual apparatus used to calculate rates of motion and change. To cite another example (to which we will return below), Dugald Stewart, the son of the geometer Matthew Stewart and eventually Ferguson's successor as the chair of moral philosophy, also lectured on mathematics at the University of Edinburgh. John Playfair, meanwhile, was professor of mathematics there until assuming the position of chair of natural philosophy.

The migration of Scottish philosophers into and out of mathematical chairs in Scottish universities illustrates Davie's point. Unsurprisingly, then, mathematics informed diverse areas of the curriculum. The poet James Thomson, for instance, was taught the moral-philosophical implications of Newtonian philosophy while a student at the University of Edinburgh from 1715 to 1719. After making his way to London to seek his fortune, he took up a position at Watt's Academy, a school that emphasized Newtonian science. Eventually, Newtonian thought and tropes would suffuse Thomson's influential poem *The Seasons*, as we will discuss in Chapter 5. Or consider the very different case of Robert Burns, who had no university education but was tutored in geometry as a boy and later received further training in applied geometry when he began working for the excise. Geometric tropes and riddles crop up throughout Burns's work, as we will see in Chapter 4. They do so as well in the work of James Macpherson (see Chapter 1) and Walter Scott (see Chapter 2). We have already discussed Joanna Baillie's familiarity with mathematics. And the list goes on, as one would expect in a nation where geometry functioned as a lingua franca, or as what Regina Hewitt would call a source of "symbolic interaction" among disciplines as well as people.[28]

But consistently with any language, which traffics in idioms, colloquialisms, figures of speech, and even slang, geometry took a variety of discursive and material forms in Enlightenment Scotland. Reid, for example, devised his thought experiment in non-Euclidean geometry not as a response to Euclid (the founder of the problematic parallel postulate), Galileo (the first person, according to Edmund Husserl, to "mathematize nature"[29]), or Colin Maclaurin (Reid's teacher at Marischal College) but rather to David Hume. Hume's *Treatise of Human Nature* (1739–40), which purported "to introduce the experimental method of reasoning into moral subjects," asserted that all understanding, even geometric reasoning, finds its origin somewhere in our experience. On this basis, Hume had called into question the parallel postulate and, with it, the province of reason itself: "How can [a mathematician] prove to me . . . that two right lines cannot have one common segment? . . . [S]upposing these two lines to approach at the rate of an inch in twenty leagues, I perceive no absurdity in asserting, that upon their contact they become one."[30] Geometry was not the object of Hume's critique, either, as much as an occasion for him to undercut pretensions to pure rationality, the supposed foundations of geometric reasoning. Reid's rejoinder took aim at Hume's reference by positing an apparently straight line traced around the surface of a sphere. If an observer were placed at the center of that sphere (and were nothing more than an instrument of vision, devoid of the sense of touch, for instance), she would not be able to recognize any curvature in the line.[31] The "straight" streak across the sky would eventually simply appear, inexplicably, to rejoin itself. Reid's example purports to undercut Hume's notion that experience alone is adequate to the subversion of reason. His non-Euclidean experiment, predicated on the possibility of curved space, was born from the practical aim of justifying the quotidian, commonsense reliability of our rational faculties.

Notwithstanding the force of Reid's rebuttal, Hume's argument, which precariously perches human knowledge on "fictions of the understanding," would reemerge in the work of Walter Scott, whose historical novels employ such fictions in order to reconstruct plausible explanations for the course of human affairs.[32] (I take up the creatively geometric qualities of these "fictions" in Chapter 2.) Equally influential on Scott was Dugald Stewart, who incorporated "the mathematical sciences" into his famous model of conjectural or theoretical history. Conjectural history accounts for the course of historical events beyond the reach of memory or historical record. Stewart formulated these ideas partly on the basis of an analogy with mathematics, discerning there "a better opportunity than in any other instance whatever, of comparing the natural advances of the mind with the actual succession of hypothetical systems."[33] Mathematics, in other words, provided Stewart with a mode of reasoning and also with a series of examples of historical reconstruction that were the very essence of conjectural history. (His father, Matthew Stewart, in concert with Robert Simson, had vigorously attempted such reconstructions or "restorations" of supposedly lost portions of Euclid's oeuvre.) Hence, while Scott claimed, perhaps demurely, to be "an utter stranger to geometry," his fiction imported sophisticated (if residual) geometric paradigms into its representational structure and then, as we will see, dynamically reconfigured them in accordance with the demands of "history" as he envisioned it.[34]

So, was Scott a geometer? No. But can geometry and its place in Scottish Enlightenment and Romantic culture enhance and in some ways revise our understanding of Scott's work? Yes, absolutely. And in pursuing a line of thinking that discloses the intersection of the humanities with so-called STEM fields (science, technology, engineering, and mathematics), this book supplements and enters into conversation with recent studies of the "long" Scottish eighteenth and nineteenth centuries that reveal Scottish literature's meaningful intersections with geography (Penny Fielding, Eric Gidal), geology (Adelene Buckland), and the sciences of man (Ian Duncan), to say nothing of books that divulge its relations to psychology (Juliet Shields, Evan Gottlieb) and media studies (Maureen McLane).[35]

At a more general level, this book might be considered part of a modest but nevertheless noticeable "mathematical turn" in literary studies. Literary scholars from a variety of fields, interested in a wide range of subjects, are drawing upon mathematics as a way of reconfiguring periods, authors, texts—even the concepts of writing and history. This is true even (if not especially) for books that are by no means *stricto sensu* mathematical, like Moretti's *Graphs, Maps, Trees* or Wai Chee Dimock's *Through Other Continents*, which invokes fractals. But here, let me mention two other studies that address in a more rigorous fashion the integral relationship between mathematics and culture during the eighteenth and nineteenth centuries, for they touch upon a phenomenological difference between geometry and algebra that is important to my argument. In the first of these, Leon Chai traces the origins of the most universalizing schools of theory (for example, structuralism) to the Romantic era and accords special attention to the theoretical algebra of Évariste Galois. Around 1830, Galois had posed the question of "whether any equation . . . was solvable without [anybody] actually solving it."[36] This was a hypothetical or theoretical query whose technicalities exceed the boundaries of our study here. More pertinent is what Chai perceives as the chief contribution of Galois's algebra to Romantic theory in "the spatial perspective" it accorded to problems: "What Galois offered Romantic theory, first of all, was a new way to look at concepts. Specifically, Galois theory attempted to describe concepts spatially," at least after a fashion, "in the notions of a field or group. . . . In particular, he saw how a spatial description of concepts might yield a new kind of insight into various problems or questions even if you didn't know exactly what elements were involved. Precisely because you lacked that knowledge, you focused on a simple question: whether they might collectively be said to form a set of some kind."[37] As Chai sees it, these operations connected Galois's theory to other spatializing abstractions of the Romantic era, like Hegel's ideas concerning the stratified and dialectical arrangement of social phenomena and their stages of history. But as Alain Badiou has argued, the mathematical medium enabled Galois to address these questions of organization even more schematically, with dynamic consequences—theoretical and poetic—for thought.[38]

Chai's disclosure of the shared spatial dimensions of the new algebra with other Romantic-era formations leads us to Alice Jenkins's compelling work on the meaning of spatiality in early nineteenth-century Britain. Similarly to Chai, "[t]he kind of space discussed in [Jenkins's] book . . . is the immaterial, conceptual space . . . that allows us to perceive and compare distances, sizes, and locations."[39] But here, it is geometry and not algebra that serves as the focal point, for "geometry carried profound significance for the early nineteenth century by representing space in its purest form."[40] Geometry represented a theory (or even a metatheory) of space in everyday life. That said, it is precisely where such spatiality was *not* pure or not strictly theoretical—that is, where it breached the boundaries of geometry proper—that it operates most powerfully in Jenkins's book, informing such cultural phenomena as the rhetoric of landscape in gardening, painting, and Wordsworthian poetry as well as a host of innovations in the physical and social sciences. If Chai's point is that Galois delineates Romantic theory at its highest level, Jenkins reminds us that geometry informs the metaphorics of spatiality on which such theory was implicitly, even if only figuratively, predicated.

Jenkins's work is crucial to my own, for I too focus on the cultural inscriptions of "geometry." And I too am interested in the interface between literature and geometry, a zone of imagination defamiliarizing each discipline. As a literary scholar, I am most intrigued (like Moretti and Dimock) by the way geometry helps us reimagine literary form and history. Hence, while I draw necessarily from important work in mathematical history, geometry is most significant to my study when it ceases to be purely geometrical and becomes something *figurative*—metaphorically and, after a fashion, diagrammatically. I borrow here from the illuminating discussion by John Bender and Michael Marrinan of a "culture of diagram" in the eighteenth century. As they see it, the diagrams employed in the French *Encyclopédie* illustrated not only particular objects but also the mental processes whereby we arrive at understanding. Modeled after geometry, the "virtual space[s]" of these figurative objects made possible "an imagined, tactile manipulation of things"; encyclopedic diagrams functioned as a heuristic mode of representation connecting mind and world.[41] And the encyclopedists were not unique: Domenico Bertolini Meli observes that "[d]espite the growth of algebra," which acquired tremendous significance both mathematically and philosophically during the seventeenth and eighteenth centuries, "the geometrical diagram was a key tool of investigation. Mathematicians from Galileo to Newton worked and reasoned with the help of geometrical figures."[42] (And indeed, the philosophical tension between algebra and geometry is a recurrent subject in this book, with the debates over calculus a particularly fruitful locus of discussion.)

One of my book's contentions, if I may put it this way, is that geometry in eighteenth-century Scotland possessed a meta-diagrammatic quality. That is, in addition to providing thinkers with useful sketches of the pathways of thought, geometry functioned as a medium through which literati reasoned across disciplines. A discrete science, geometry also served then as a common language connecting disparate fields: mathematics and philosophy, the natural and moral sciences, history and literature. (So it was that Henry Home, Lord Kames imagined his voluminous *Elements of Criticism* [1762], an exemplary work in literary studies, after the virtually universal [and, in Scotland, widely disseminated] *Elements* of Euclid.) I discuss several such examples of geometrically mediated works of literature in this book. The book's aim, however, is not simply to catalog such examples and create a broad cross section of geometry's permeation of Scottish literary culture in the long eighteenth century but rather to attend to particular cases that reveal something at play in the workings of literary form. I take this approach for three reasons. First, the Scottish Enlightenment is widely seen as a key moment in the development of modern literature and literary studies, both relative to the elaboration of literary discourse as creative or fictive writing and to the institutionalization of English literature as a discipline.[43] And geometry's presence in Scottish literary culture helps us better understand how that culture's exponents imagined literary form (even, in ways, as a kind of *shape*) and its place among the incipient disciplines. Second, the relationship between literature and geometry, as well as the latter's relation in Scottish universities to the metaphysical tradition, makes literature a compelling discursive site for the explication, expression, and revision of tradition and hence a powerful vehicle not only of metaphysics but also of historiography. But third, and reflecting now on the first two, geometry's relation to literary texts and culture also modifies how we understand such categories as *literature* and *history* and thus "literary history," which is why the enigmatic status of Scotland's long, looping eighteenth century—at once classical and romantic, enlightened and modern—becomes important not only to Scotland or even to literary history itself but also to how we tell the broader story of literature's emergent place in the world of the sciences and, more expansively, the modern disciplines.

The book divides its study into three parts, each consisting of two chapters. The first part constitutes a theoretical overview of the subject, the second addresses iconic exhibits of the geometric imagination in Scottish culture, and the third probes the historical limits—the origins and aftermaths—of eccentric Euclideanism in Scottish Enlightenment culture. Chapter 1 sets forth what I call the late rather than non-Euclidean poetics of the Scottish Enlightenment, particularly as they pertain to literature and culture. I then turn in Chapter 2 to their illustration through a peculiar but telling manipulation of space in Walter Scott's second novel, *Guy Mannering*. There, at a key moment in the plot when the young protagonist returns from abroad to a Scottish estate that once belonged to his family but of whose origins he is oblivious, Scott enfolds a classical, Euclidean shape into a larger, non-Euclidean one. He does so as a self-reflexive literary rather than mathematical exercise, but the complex design of his narrative at this moment reveals Scott's sophisticated manner of navigating between "history" and "romance," the understanding and the imagination. The intersection of narrative and geometry in Scott's work proves to be uncanny, revealing how literature was capable not only of representing intellectual conflict but also of operating at the frontiers of available paradigms. This becomes especially important when we consider how critics have implicitly and in some cases expressly articulated a vision of Scott as an apologist for a modernity that operates on algebraic principles—that is, on a series of substitutions and displacements of a world reduced to a sequence of numbers. This chapter analyzes the differences between the geometric and algebraic interpretations of Scott, arguing that the geometric picture presented in *Guy Mannering* opens us to different formal and even ethical dimensions of Scott's work. Indeed, what critics have long recognized of Scott's novels, namely that their generic imbrication of fiction, history, and romance overdetermines Scott's narrower political convictions, intensifies when we reflect on the implications of the complex shapes embedded within them.

One way in which the subject of shape has long informed criticism of Scott is through the language and imagery of the picturesque, an aesthetic mode that influenced Scott and that has come to define the iconography of modern—and, seemingly, perpetually ancient—Scotland. In Chapter 3, I take up important ways in which theorists of the picturesque (and travel writers who adopted its conventions in the late eighteenth and early nineteenth centuries) effectively negotiated the limits of classical geometry in the scenic visual and verbal ways they arranged the Scottish landscape. Travelers did so partly by representing bizarre forms of nature that seemed opposed to the regular shapes of Euclid and partly by calling attention to the exigencies and inadequacies of traditional (Euclidean) perspective. The picturesque thus became a language of artistic abstraction that redounded upon and experimented with the geometric medium of its exposition. And while this describes picturesque aesthetics generally, its status as a late Euclidean scene of writing becomes especially representative of the interstitial status of late eighteenth- and early nineteenth-century Scottish culture, for which the categories of "Enlightenment" and "Romanticism" are notoriously labile.

One of the most distinctive figures associated with the Scottish landscape (albeit in its pastoral rather than Highland settings) is Robert Burns, whose status as national poet represents a fusion of place and people. His poetry, to which I turn in Chapter 4, also represents a merger of languages (English and Scots), forms (satire, description, elegy, epistle), eras (classical and modern), and national spaces (Scottish, British, and internationalist). But his work also negotiates relationships between the arts and sciences, as well as between classical and more expressly experimental forms of each. My aim in this chapter is to explain how this is so and, by extension, what Burns means to literary history. As we will see, Burns brings into relief the complex dynamics at play in key humanistic and literary concepts that were implicated in the logic of geometry, like Adam Smith's concept of sympathy (which fashioned individual and group psychology around a spatial relationship between subjects, objects, and "impartial spectators"). His poems "To a Louse" and "To a Mouse," for example, enact failures of sympathy and install beings characterized by their irreducible irrationality—an ontology of more and less than "one," the classical geometric idea of unity. For that matter, the very concept of a national poet, which is how Burns styled himself, rests on a border between a unified concept of the people and a fragmentation of that unit into a chaos of self-interested individuals—in effect, between a metaphysical idea of form and the dispersal of that ideal into a morass of modern numbers, which is precisely where some of the period's key philosophical debates involving geometry irrupted.

The conflict between form and number, we will see, comprises not only the intuitive nexus of the Burnsian legacy but also the more literal origins of calculus, whose practitioners derived in the place of whole numbers a malleable panoply of incremental units that made for more precise (albeit imaginary) systems of calculation. Having already discussed the historical and philosophical rudiments of the calculus in earlier chapters, I turn in Chapter 5 to a more rigorous examination of the conflict in Newton's fluxional calculus between its practical efficacy and its theoretical riddles and implications. Crucially, it was not only Scottish geometers who took up these conundrums and rushed to Newton's aid; so did poets like James Thomson. And it is Thomson's freighted poetic defense of Newton that I take up here. Thomson envisioned the Newtonian system as an imaginative poetics whose effects were both beneficial and mortifying to conventional poetry. In *The Seasons*, therefore, Thomson tacked a course between Newton and Milton that both accommodated and undercut the natural philosophy it purported to describe. As Thomson enacts it, to make like Newton is also to diverge from Newton; hence, in attempting to emulate Newton's calculus in explaining nature's universals, Thomson actually distorts and displaces it. The poem thus effectively foreshadows the twentieth century's "two cultures" debate between science and literature, speaking eloquently to an ambivalence toward the Newtonian project that permeated the Scottish Enlightenment, including in the work of some of Newton's most fervent defenders.

Readers will notice that, from Chapters 2 through 5, my argument unfolds through a backward chronology: beginning with Scott in the 1810s, I move to a consideration of the picturesque near the turn of the nineteenth century, then to Burnsian poems of the 1780s before jumping back a half-century to Thomson's poetry of the 1720s and 1730s (which was conceived during the era when Scottish Enlightenment geometry was beginning to arrive at its most forceful articulation). While each chapter cuts a broad historical swath (Chapter 4, for instance, brings Smith's moral philosophy from the 1750s and 1760s into contact with Burns's poems and then traces the logic of Burns's revisionist model of sympathy into nineteenth-century theories of topology that inform present-day practices in the [post]humanities), I proceed generally through a reverse chronological trajectory as a way of undertaking with literary readers unfamiliar with geometry a kind of journey into the heart of mathematical darkness—which is to say, into a set of ideas that has exerted a powerful but rarely recognized force on literary studies. Taking this path also enables me to clarify the relationship between geometry and its creative adaptation in later, more familiar (but now defamiliarized) literary and artistic contexts, not only in Burns and the picturesque and Scott but also in modernist works that reprised those earlier, innovative "forms."

Chapter 6 is the lone exception to this reverse chronological movement, taking stock of the long history of Scottish geometry by examining its recrudescence in later modernity. Beginning where Chapter 5 leaves off, with Thomson's poetry, it takes up the vestiges of Newtonian thought in Thomas Reid's Common Sense philosophy, then moves into Reid's legacy in Poe's 1848 cosmological essay *Eureka* before tracing the echoes of that legacy into the avant-garde. I show, for example, how Poe's essay became a key theoretical text for Charles Baudelaire and the Symbolists and how Walter Benjamin, drawing upon these various influences, adopted Poe's portraits of Newton and Johannes Kepler and brought them into his own work. I discuss Benjamin's well-known circuit of thought alongside Patrick Geddes's efforts to link modernist experimentation with Celtic traditions in his 1890s-era Scottish art journal, *The Evergreen*, and conclude by analyzing one of the key exhibits from the tradition of Scottish modernism that followed Geddes's line of thought, Hugh MacDiarmid's poem "On a Raised Beach." MacDiarmid's poem asserts the durability but also the radical quality of certain natural forms through time and thus represents a Scottish movement that drew, on one hand, upon national traditions and, on the other, upon a set of wider European ideas that had themselves been inflected by those same traditions—hence, upon developments that were both "new" *and* atavistic. MacDiarmid gazed at primordial Shetland rocks and beheld not only the cosmos and a set of cosmopolitan ideas but also the image of his own national inheritance refracted through those objects. This concluding chapter thus lights on the elliptical as well as the more overt presence of Scottish geometry in a late—an even later—Euclidean moment.

At its core, this is a book about the allure of form at an especially provocative and extended moment in literary history. I attend particularly to fortuitous instances of shape that reveal, first, how seemingly divergent disciplines intersect in works of literature and, second, how these convergences help us remap literary history. I am thinking less of Gaston Bachelard's evocative "poetics of space" than of the types of designs Moretti, for example, has taken to sketching as a way of illustrating—diagrammatically—the flow of time and its impact on genre.[44] Increasingly evident in the humanities in the form of data visualizations, these shapes that so inspire digital humanists also appear occasionally in particular works—say, in the way a poem or narrative delineates (and implicitly spaces) its objects. But ultimately, I am less intrigued by the status of visual forms as data than I am by the effect of their appearance or by the supplement that shape adds to (literary) form. It conjures a unique intellectual constellation in the Scottish Enlightenment, beginning with David Gregory in the late seventeenth century and concluding with Scott in the early nineteenth, when the very idea of such figures arrives at an especially compelling degree of imaginative and self-reflexive exposition. This is a moment when literati dynamically explored the manifold possibilities and implications of forms, and their striking variants in the period's literature enable us to pose a set of simple but far-reaching questions, to wit: What would it mean to imagine a poem or any work of literature not only as a puzzle of signs (the [post]structuralist reflex) but also as a constellation of shapes—that is, to think of it not only by way of algebra, with its linguistic logic of symbolic substitution, but also through geometry, with its model of spatial relations? Indeed, what might it mean to conceive of a *line* of poetry? To answer these questions is to better grasp a world whose contours (as "visualizations") are increasingly familiar to us but whose history, in the work of an influential group of Scottish writers, risks perpetual obscurity.

PART I

Theorem: Shapes of Time

Theorem: 1. A universal or general proposition
or statement, not self-evident (thus distinguished
from an axiom), but demonstrable by argument.
2. In Mathematics and Physics; *spec.* in Geometry,
a proposition embodying merely something to be
proved, as distinguished from a problem, which
embodies something to be done.

—*Oxford English Dictionary*

CHAPTER 1

Scotland's Age of Union: Toward an Elongated Eighteenth Century

This Enlightenment Which Is Not One

Modernism, defining itself against the past, bears a notoriously ambivalent relationship to the history that accords the "modern" its sense of distinction. And no chapter from that history is more problematic to modernism than the Enlightenment. In 1909, the Italian Futurist F. T. Marinetti proclaimed that "[w]e are on the extreme promontory of ages! . . . Time and Space died yesterday," supposedly taking with them Newtonian physics and Kantian ideas concerning cognition, each of which had elevated classical theories of time and space to the status of absolutes.[1] And yet, however monumental the concepts of, say, relativity and the unconscious may have been in reshaping our understanding of mentality and the universe, the Enlightenment left an indelible imprint on the modernist idea. For one thing, Newtonian science helped spawn the very machines that fueled industrial progress and, with it, the modernist ideology of innovation.[2] For another, the modernist propensity toward autonomous rather than strictly mimetic artworks—the spawning, for example, of abstract expressionism—was actually born with Galileo and the "astrophysical world view." At least, this is the inference drawn by Hannah Arendt: the astronomic imperative of Enlightenment science, the process of abstraction whereby we contemplate celestial motion from some Archimedean position above the earth, challenges "the adequacy of the senses to reveal reality" and eventually bequeaths "us a universe of whose qualities we know no more than the way they affect our measuring instruments."[3] As

Clement Greenberg already recognized in 1939, the avant-garde replicated this logic by "creating something valid on its own terms," a " 'nonobjective' art" that aspired less to capture reality than to fashion a new world from someplace beyond it.[4] Indeed, Louis Menand argues, "[t]he 'It' in" Ezra Pound's " 'Make It New' is the Old—what is valuable in the culture of the past."[5] In this respect, Futurism represented less a departure from history than a retooling of the classical, Newtonian philosophy it purported to spurn.

Then again, we might invert this assertion by recognizing that the very concept of the Enlightenment was a modernist invention—or, at least, that the early twentieth century was the period when the Enlightenment fully emerged as a historical category. So claims Nicholas Hudson, who explains that Kant's famous 1785 essay, "Answer to the Question: What Is Enlightenment?" arose not as an age-defining credo but rather as a local response to a banal appeal to revoke the clergy's authority to perform marriages.[6] For that matter, the term "the Enlightenment" (or its German and French equivalents: *der Aufklärung* and *Les Lumières*) appeared rarely in the eighteenth or even the nineteenth centuries. One finds it in the historical philosophy of G. W. F. Hegel, who invoked it, Hudson says, "to describe a bounded period of time characterized by rational thought, the decline of superstition, and the rise of political liberties" (166). But the concept really came of age early in the twentieth century, especially in Germany, where it acquired ideological significance as a commentary on liberalism. In 1932, for example, the Jewish scholar Ernst Cassirer published his landmark book *The Philosophy of the Enlightenment* defending the proclivity of eighteenth-century philosophers toward self-criticism, thus issuing a tacit plea for greater self-reflection in an increasingly boorish and anti-Semitic public sphere. A decade later, however, in *The Dialectic of Enlightenment* (1944), Max Horkheimer and Theodor W. Adorno indicted all reflective processes as part of a systemic tendency toward domination—reason become mastery become violence.[7] The Enlightenment would retain this status as an ideological bellwether throughout the remainder of the century, stirring debate during the Cold War era of the 1950s, the culture wars of the 1980s, and then again after 9/11.[8] Today, Hudson remarks, the category has become an institution by virtue of "the sheer power of the American academic industry," which has "chiseled" the Enlightenment "into the canonical language of historians throughout the English-speaking world, and even in France" (172).

And yet, as prominent a role as America has played in sponsoring "the" Enlightenment (even making a diasporic home for Cassirer, Horkheimer,

Adorno, and other German Jewish intellectuals in the aftermath of World War II), perhaps no nation bears a more intimate or curious relationship to the Enlightenment than Scotland. The category first entered the English-speaking world through Scotland, specifically through the nineteenth-century commentaries on German thought by the Scottish philosophers James Hutchison Stirling (in *The Secret of Hegel* [1865]) and Edward Caird (in *The Critical Philosophy of Immanuel Kant* [1889]).[9] Shortly thereafter, the Enlightenment became an identifiable feature of Scotland's own eighteenth century, to the point that today it functions as a virtual national icon, Scotland's greatest contribution to the modern world.[10] Consistently with the emergence of Enlightenments elsewhere, the term "Scottish Enlightenment" was born retrospectively, in this case with William Robert Scott in 1900. And commensurately with what Hudson notes of the Enlightenment generally, interest in this *Scottish* Enlightenment did not really reach a critical level until the 1960s or even the 1980s, when it became the subject of university courses and scholarly books.[11]

Oddly, however, and as Cairns Craig persuasively argues, the story of Scotland's Enlightenment has often been attached to a larger narrative not of progress—the standard line in Enlightenment historiographies—but rather of the nation's alleged nineteenth-century decline. Evidence for this national decay consists, variously, of Scotland's failure to accommodate rapid industrialization, its deteriorating university system (or at least that system's diminished autonomy in its increasing approximation to the English curriculum), its "brain drain" to London and the far reaches of the British Empire, and the absence of subsequent luminaries equal to Adam Smith and Walter Scott.[12] This makes the story of enlightenment in Scotland something of a gothic tale, comprising less a saga of national becoming than a foreboding picture of ruin.

Scotland's, in other words, is not simply one Enlightenment among others. As such, it throws something of a wrench into the grand narratives about modernity into which the Enlightenment often figures. Typically, the Scottish Enlightenment is heralded by scholars and politicians alike as a period in Scottish history associated with influential advancements in moral and natural philosophy, medicine, political economy, literature, and other fields (not the least of which is historiography, which represents the discipline in which such questions arrive at self-consciousness). But Craig reveals that enlightenment's coming of age in Scotland was a belated, discontinuous, and altogether more modern phenomenon. For starters, the era of Scotland's most meaningful contribution to the modern world may not have been the eighteenth century but rather the latter half of the nineteenth, when the new science of energy developed by William Thomson (Lord Kelvin) and James Clerk Maxwell initiated "nothing less than the overturning of Newtonian physics"—the achievement of which Marinetti dreamed.[13] What is more, the machines heralded by Futurism as the agents of innovation descended from Scotland's development of those Enlightenment technologies (such as James Watt's perfection of the steam engine) that modernized Western societies with unparalleled rapidity, replete with all the booms and busts of progress. Such advancements bore mixed fruit in Scotland, promoting the nation's reputation as an "Athens of the north" but also eventually making it a home to some of Europe's most appalling industrial slums.[14]

But while Marinetti's evocation of brave new worlds pertains aptly to Scotland's nineteenth century, it also redounds onto the nation in the eighteenth century, whose literati knew less about the long history of "the" Enlightenment than scholars in subsequent eras and who therefore may have been the least enlightened of all. I say "least enlightened," but we also, paradoxically, might call them the most modern(ist). For one thing, eighteenth-century Scotland was a Futurist (or, in its own terminology, an "improving") nation, inventing or "making new" a state and its constituent societies, especially in the Highlands with the forced modernization of a feudal culture.[15] But for another, the Enlightenment features in an influential trend in twentieth-century Scottish thought that projected modernity and specifically modern*ism* back onto the past. For example, in assessing the "enormous genius" but equally unseemly "blemish[es]" of Walter Scott's work, the disillusioned Scottish expatriate Edwin Muir concluded in 1936 that Scottish culture had propagated an evocatively modern brand of alienation, a T. S. Eliotic "dissociation of sensibility" between thought and feeling beginning with the Protestant Reformation in the late sixteenth century.[16] Muir's book *Scott and Scotland* essentially inverted a position staked out in anthropology (in the work of James George Frazer and Emile Durkheim), psychology (especially in Freud's theories), and the arts (for instance, in Paul Gauguin's fascination with the tropics), all of which catalogued modernity's extensive inheritances from the past and asserted the lineaments of primitive societies in modern civilization.[17] Muir, by contrast, did not discern the vestiges of primitive society in the present as much as he gazed into history and intuited the grim visage of the modern world already staring back at him.

This projection of dissociated sensibility onto the past actually echoes two essays by Eliot—"The Metaphysical Poets," which enunciates the idea of such dissociation, and "Tradition and the Individual Talent." In that latter essay, Eliot declares that a new work (or, with respect to modernism, a new *Zeitgeist*) modifies the existing order of all that came before—that, in Muir's case, his traumatic experience in industrial Glasgow as a youth projects modernist alienation onto all of Scottish history, particularly that of industrial modernity and its Enlightenment roots.[18] And yet, Muir's Eliotic image of Scotland grows more complicated when we recall that Eliot notoriously dismissed the idea of a Scottish literary tradition in a 1919 review essay, concluding that it had long since faded into a "provincial literature."[19] Strangely, then, Muir's cooptation of Eliot's theories becomes an oddly patriotic assertion of national culture: taking Eliot's claim at face value, Muir presents Scotland as the quintessential modernist wasteland, a nation so alienated from its own past that it exemplifies the modern condition Eliot struggled to explain in his poetry and criticism. Muir's image of Enlightenment Scotland as a primordial locus of modernist sensibility thus provides a mythic complement to the material emergence of the Enlightenment as a historical category during the early decades of the twentieth century: modernism was born during that earlier era whose ethos it subsequently distilled. Hence, in Muir's narrative of the Scottish Enlightenment and in the mode of the autonomous, autotelic art that (according to Greenberg) his age fetishized, modernism gives birth to itself.

The self-reflexive and oddly nationalist dimension of Muir's essay ("how Scots invented the modern*ist* world") has proven plenty durable: versions of it reappeared from the 1940s into the 1980s and beyond in the work of John Speirs, David Craig, David Daiches, Kenneth Simpson, and others.[20] Its most venerable defense may have come in the guise of its repudiation in Tom Nairn's *The Break-Up of Britain* (1977). Nairn vehemently disagreed with Muir over the cause of Scotland's nationalist anomie: instead of tracing the seed of the nation's decay to the Reformation, Nairn attributed it to Scotland's precocious prosperity in the eighteenth century, a phenomenon that would wed the nation to the British Empire and thus retard a specifically *Scottish* self-consciousness a century later, when nationalist sensibilities began taking radical political form (including, notably in Nairn's view, in Ireland). But this makes Scotland a special case in Nairn's account, an exemplum of the global dynamics of uneven development: reaping the early benefits of union, the nation cultivated little more than the hollow tokens of its own past, making Scott's innovations in the genre of historical fiction an arch irony, the literary equivalent of a junk bond—the imparting of a cultural asset whose value the nation had long since liquidated. "History" and "national culture" in Scott's fiction thus served to foreshadow modernist alienation or, better still, postmodernism's junkyard late capitalism, commoditizing Scottish consciousness into such marketable stereotypes as kilts and Kailyard fiction.[21] Nairn's view is compelling in light of Muir's thesis, for the a priori reduction of Scottish history to a set of cultural tropes or to swatches of tartan discarded from the body of lived experience fashions the landscape of Scottish representation into an Eliotic wasteland of recycled images, a region of fertile decay in which writing and ecology are one.[22]

Scottish studies have come a long way from Muir and Nairn; so, after a fashion, has Nairn himself.[23] And yet, while arguments for Scotland as a nation that either fell from enlightened grace or was already corrupted at the outset have certainly not gone undisputed over the past two or three decades, they have not exactly disappeared, either. For instance, they took a revised form in Cairns Craig's Preface to the 1990s-era "Determinations" book series at Polygon, which was conceived during a period of cultural resurgence with momentous political consequences.[24] As Craig observed, "Scotland's history is often presented as punctuated by disasters which overwhelm the nation, break its continuity and produce a fragmented culture. Through the 1980s such conceptions have been challenged by a wide range of critical and analytical works that have shown just how profound the tradition of Scottish culture has been, and how dynamic the debates within it have remained—even in those periods (like the period after 1830) which cultural history usually looks upon as blanks in the nation's achievement."[25]

Craig identifies the wave of revisionist historicism that swept through Scottish studies in the decades following Nairn's book (and, more important, the failed Devolution referendum of 1979).[26] His manifesto all but denounces Muir and Nairn by name. However, it does not dispel the darkness of the Scottish past as much as it displaces it from the mid-nineteenth century to the mid-twentieth. But this means that narratives of Scotland's modernist Enlightenment, like Muir's and Nairn's, not only provide the impetus for the revisionist histories that refute them but also uncannily inform the logic of their own refutation. At this new moment in Scottish studies, that is, *Scott and Scotland* and *The Break-Up of Britain* have become the image of the past they once renounced: while Nairn, for example, imagines Scott flattening

Scottish history (as a literary precursor to the compression of perspective one associates with the paintings of Édouard Manet or Paul Cézanne), Craig sees Nairn doing the same thing. Past and present, enlightenment and modernism, enter into a mimetic relationship with each other.

A Modernism of Other Times?

This strangely mimetic relationship is the subject of this book. In it, I analyze what it means for past and present to circle around and reflect each other, not only as a historical dimension of the Scottish Enlightenment (in which such doubling has become a recurring theme) but also as a principle of form. I make two interdependent claims—first, that the (non)linear nature of these forms modifies our understanding of literary history (with the eighteenth century becoming alternately instigative and derivative of paradigms one usually associates with later periods), and second, that these forms acquire peculiar and in some ways exemplary historical force in Scotland.

I do not, however, concern myself with modernism per se. Or, for that matter, with the Enlightenment. Instead, I am invoking a set of features corresponding in Scotland with what we might call an Age of Union (a phrase for which I am indebted to Ian Duncan). This "age" begins with the Union of Parliaments that formed Great Britain in 1707 and extends into the early decades of the twentieth century, when World Wars I and II frayed the British Empire and called the longstanding logic of union into question.[27] I focus primarily on the late eighteenth and early nineteenth centuries, though the early twentieth century sketches an important horizon that places the earlier period in context. This is because a variety of circuitous forms emerged in the 1910s and 1920s, underscoring, with Muir, the simultaneity of perspectives and points in time. Cubist painting, for example, purported to capture objects from multiple angles; Proustian narrative folded time over itself in its evocation of tangible objects dense with memory, much as Molly Bloom's stream-of-consciousness reveries in James Joyce's *Ulysses* crafted bizarre chronotopes in the sprawl of its endlessly looping sentences. In 1945, Joseph Frank published a landmark essay on this subject entitled "Spatial Form in Modern Literature." Taking as his starting point the philosophy of Wilhelm Worringer and T. E. Hulme, Frank consolidated his theory of literary form through Pound's notion of the image as "an intellectual and emotional complex in an instant of time," a spatial apprehension of disparate moments and impressions.[28] Proust's *À la Recherche du Temps Perdu*, for example, "was to be at once the vehicle through which [the novelist] conveyed his vision and the *concrete experience* of that vision expressed in a form" (24, Frank's emphases), and Joyce's *Ulysses*, for all its playful engagement of the Western literary canon, was "to build up in the reader's mind a sense of Dublin as a totality" (20). Frank likened these achievements to those of Cézanne, whose work blended "a self-enclosed unity of form-and-color harmonies" with "the recognizable depiction of natural objects" (30). And literature, he argued, presented a radically reimagined mimesis distilled into the form of an image.

To be sure, Frank's theory inspired critics—Roger Shattuck, Richard Poirier, Frank Kermode—who insisted on the temporal horizon of spatial form.[29] *Ulysses*, for example, represents less an *image* of complexity than a gradualist experience of reading. Joycean "form" is thus an exercise in deferral as it only coalesces over time; it is never wholly present. But in another sense, the dichotomy between space and time is a red herring. From the seventeenth century forward (if not earlier), geometric shapes became most compelling when they were conceived genetically—that is, as products of motion through time. Of greater interest to me, then, than Frank's defense of Pound's Imagism is, first, his tracing of the modernist aesthetic back to the eighteenth century in G. E. Lessing's *Laocoön* (which introduced "a new approach to aesthetic form" as "the relation between the sensuous nature of the medium and the conditions of human perception" [*The Idea of Spatial Form* 8, 9]) and, second, Frank's inspiration for that return to Lessing "in Edwin Muir's [1929] classic *Structure of the Novel*" (xiv). Muir does not mention Lessing in that book, but he conducts an extended discussion of time and space as they pertain to literature.[30] It was Muir, then, who prompted Frank to read Lessing, and Lessing in turn enunciated a theory that struck Frank as both classical and modern—a hallmark of the Age of Union (as Muir's *Scott and Scotland* symptomatically attests).[31]

Hence, while many modern artists interpreted innovations as radical departures from the past ("In or about 1910, human character changed," Virginia Woolf famously declared[32]), the contemporary perspectives of Muir, Frank, and Worringer cast these modern developments in a different light. The Age of Union, a long or elongated Scottish Enlightenment, I argue (turning now to the second of my two claims), vividly illustrates this formal principle. Muir's notions (and Nairn's, Craig's, and numerous others') concerning Scotland's asynchronous cultural history are key to my argument, in part because they distend—in the mode of Frank's Cézanne, almost—what we usually take historical periods to be. It has become fashionable to hate periodization (literary history's disco in an era of deep time), though in Scottish literary studies, that contempt has occasionally expressed itself as an earnest case for Bloomian misprision. Susan Manning, for example, has ascribed modernism's origins to the literature of the Scottish Enlightenment (through the conceit of the "fragment"), and, indeed, more than most of its peers, Scotland's Enlightenment is about the transformative state of the modern world and the latter's curious and often distortional relation to its own past.[33] Scott gave eloquent expression to the notion of uneven development (and the compression of time and the distortion of national space) in his postscript to *Waverley* when he remarked that, by the early nineteenth century, there was "no European nation which, within the course of half a century or little more, [had] undergone so complete a change as this kingdom of Scotland."[34] Modernization had so transformed the nation, Scott implied, that in gazing at Scotland, one saw modernity itself.

Scottish Enlightenment literati imagined this modernity as a product of immanent as well as serial change—that is, and in rudimentary mathematical terms, as a function of "shape" as well as "number." I employ these terms metaphorically, but they possessed a vividly analogical and evocatively literal quality for these writers. Take, for example, the popular "four-stages" theory of social progress associated with Adam Smith's *Lectures on Jurisprudence* (1762), William Robertson's "A View of the Progress of Society" (1769), John Millar's *Origin of the Distinction of Ranks* (1776), and other key texts of Scottish Enlightenment historiography. The stadial model segmented development into a series of steps—numerical sequences, if you will—but the logic there is subtler and more geometric than at first appears. Often said to derive from an empirical, statistical impetus rooted in the accumulation of firsthand accounts and the compilation of data, conjectural or theoretical history, as this method was called, might more accurately be said to have blended such techniques of information gathering with a process of geometric deduction, synthesizing ideal forms as the normative ground through which to interpret accidental deviations.[35] This at least is how Dugald Stewart, the principal theorist of conjectural history and the son of the geometer Matthew Stewart, seemed to envision the practice, expressly invoking the analogy of the "mathematical sciences," which, he says, afford "a better opportunity than in any other instance whatever, of comparing the natural advances of the mind with the actual succession of hypothetical systems."[36] Mathematics, in other words, prospectively unifies theory and observation, making it a compelling model for the practice of conjectural history, which in turn became a key mode for articulating the relationship between past and present. Indeed, conjectural history permeated disciplines from history and philosophy to literature, reconciling the uncanny effects of strange and inexplicable historical forms.

Stewart's appeal to the *analogy* of mathematics was itself predicated on a deeper analogy concerning the relationship of mind and world. A precursor to Stewart, the mathematician Colin Maclaurin, addressed this principle in the Introduction to his voluminous *A Treatise of Fluxions* (1742), remarking that since classical times, geometry "has been most admired for its evidence."[37] Evidence in this context designated demonstration, but the word also bore the etymological connotation of "clarity"; "evidence" enabled one "to see clearly the truth" of a proposition through the soundness of its logic but also, by implication, the illustrative nature of its claims.[38] Geometry was doubly "evident" because of its rational proofs *and* because it might illustrate such ratiocination in the form of diagrams: one might "see" its proofs both figuratively and literally. It was thus an imaginative art as much as a science, which I say with an eye to the eighteenth-century definition of imagination as the power to conceive of images. Geometry would make for a powerful analogical basis of conjectural history because it would enable one hypothetically to illustrate or imagine the progress of society through a series of stages—the evidential steps of an equation, as it were.

But other cultural forms employed geometric reasoning in asserting continuity. One of these, romance, has received a great deal of attention in literary studies as a medium of recovery synchronizing disparate eras by configuring as imaginative, as *merely* hypothetical or diagrammatic, what earlier generations had viewed as factual. As Scott put it, "Romance and real history have the same common origin," the latter being an outgrowth of the former. "Thus the definition we [give] of Romance, as a fictitious narrative turning upon the marvellous or the supernatural, might . . . be said to embrace, in a large sense, the mythological and fabulous history of all early nations."[39] Scott's novels exemplified this principle, synthesizing complex historical forces into a credible array of circumstances through media ranging from ballad culture (as voices of the past) to David Hume's philosophy of the imagination (as the power to rearrange "the materials afforded us by the senses," a kind of cognitive *bricolage*).[40]

These ideas concerning romance actually help us cast geometry in a different light. Those who pursued geometry often did so on account of its "elegance" as well as its accuracy, its aesthetic quality as much as its usefulness.[41] And in the Scottish Enlightenment as, later, in the avant-garde, geometry underwrote some of the movement's most dynamic imaginative ventures. These broadly "literary" experiments with spatial form—their impetus, articulation, and historical residues—are my book's focus; I argue that they revise our understanding not only of such conventional literary forms as, say, historical fiction and descriptive poetry (where linear movements through time and across space acquire new meaning) but also of literature's interventions into the cultural narratives of other disciplines (such as the status of the non-Euclidean turn in the arts and sciences in the late nineteenth century). Scottish geometry was a deeply humanistic science; it entailed the formal engagement of modes of perception and understanding, experience and being, reading and writing. Prior to the formal separation of the disciplines in the nineteenth century, geometry served a poetic (indeed, a virtually epic) function in linking, through metaphor or evocative association, history and nature.

Classical though it may have seemed, geometry also opened new avenues of literary expression in the eighteenth century, as James Macpherson's controversial but hugely influential *Poems of Ossian* attests. Iconic as portraits of noble savagery and bardic tradition in ancient Scotland, evocatively modern in their lyrical sentiments, and dense with vivid (if ethereal) natural description, the Ossian poems set an important precedent for the gothic fiction of Walpole and Radcliffe, the poetry of Blake and Coleridge, and even the philosophy of Goethe and Herder.[42] But their structure of affect was wholly in keeping with Scottish Enlightenment geometry, which nourished most branches of learning in eighteenth-century Scotland. Bailey Saunders, Macpherson's first substantive biographer, remarked in 1894 that Ossianic imagery "betrays the study of classical models rather than any capacity for direct observation," characterizing the poetry as a deductive operation.[43] Fiona Stafford, Macpherson's more recent biographer, situates this classicism in the context of Macpherson's education at King's College, Aberdeen in the 1750s, when the "University . . . could boast among the teaching staff many of the leading Scottish academics . . . such as Thomas Blackwell, Thomas Reid, Alexander Gerard, James Beattie, John Gregory, and George Campbell. Many of the lecturers were also members of the vigorous Aberdeen Philosophical Society," which "contributed to the strong emphasis on philosophy in the degree course" Macpherson followed. This course "began with History, Geography, Mathematics and Natural Philosophy and moved on to

Logic and Metaphysics only in the final year"; literary criticism "was completely left out until the third year," when it was only partly integrated. University staff were especially keen on the study of Latin and Greek: "The classics were by no means seen as obscure, academic pursuits, but as an essential part of a proper education and invaluable to the future."[44] Extended exposure to geometry, including a study of conic sections, was part of the training.[45] This was the broadly humanistic, cross-disciplinary curriculum that Macpherson assimilated.

In pursuing this course of study, Macpherson was emulating Thomas Blackwell, his influential tutor at Marischal College, Aberdeen (where Macpherson continued his studies after leaving King's College). Blackwell was the author of the popular *Enquiry into the Life and Writings of Homer* (1735), a pioneering work consisting less of criticism of *The Iliad* and *The Odyssey*, Stafford remarks, than of a philosophical investigation of "the causes which had resulted in Homer's extraordinary ability."[46] And when Blackwell himself, twenty years prior to the Ossian controversy, was assailed for failing to provide documentation for his theory of Homer, he responded with a second book bearing a quasi-mathematical title: *Proofs of the Enquiry into Homer's Life and Writings* (1747). Claiming to adduce the classical sources of his study, the aim of this later book, Blackwell professed, was comparative, enabling readers "to make out the Connection" between his sources and his interpretations. It amounted to a kind of measuring exercise similar to the one undertaken by poets who, Blackwell claimed, had "borrowed, in one *Shape* or other" from Homer.[47] Geometry thus provided Blackwell with a set of analogies and metaphors through which to imagine and defend his reconstruction of the Homeric past.

The geometric valences of thought were even clearer in the work of Thomas Reid, the founder of Common Sense philosophy and Macpherson's regent during his second year at King's College. As a regent, Reid led his pupils "across Euclidean geometry, algebra, fluxions, applied mathematics, mechanics, astronomy, electricity, engineering, magnetism, hydrostatics, pneumatics, physical optics, catoptics and the theory of vision."[48] He also emphasized the relationship between feeling and language by the same associative logic that Blackwell used to connect his *Enquiry* to their *Proofs*. Reid's language, however, was expressly, vividly mathematical:

> Is it not pity that the refinements of a civilized life, instead of supplying the defects of natural language, should root it out and plant in

> its stead dull and lifeless articulations of unmeaning sounds, or the scrawling of insignificant characters? The perfection of human language is commonly thought to be, to express human thoughts and sentiments distinctly by these dull signs; but if this is the perfection of artificial language, it is surely the corruption of the natural.
>
> Artificial signs signify, but they do not express; they speak to the understanding, as algebraical characters may do, but the passions, the affections, and the will, hear them not.[49]

Geometry, consisting of the clear relation between signs and their objects, served for Reid as the language of nature, unlike algebra, predicated on arbitrary principles of signification. Years later, in 1783, Hugh Blair, Macpherson's most powerful early defender, differentiated between "figures" and "tropes" on this same basis. Tropes, he said, "consist in a word's being employed to signify something that is different from its original and primitive meaning," whereas figures, a more primitive and natural use of language, denote words "in their proper and literal meaning . . . where, though you vary the words that are used . . . you may, nevertheless still preserve the same Figure in the thought." Tropes modify words, whereas figures alter expression in order to divulge the shape of a thought; tropes, essentially, are algebraic, while figures are geometric.[50]

Macpherson imported these sensibilities into his "classical" appreciation of Gaelic as a "primitive" but natural language, unlike English, which was "the more suitable medium for philosophy." "The use of letters," Macpherson asserted in his *Dissertation concerning the Antiquity, &c. of the Poems of Ossian, the Son of Fingal,* "was not known in the north of Europe till long after the institution of the bards." Hence, poetry proceeded according to the perfect correspondence of sound, a Platonic harmony of the spheres: "Each verse was so connected with those which preceded or followed it, that if one line had been remembered in a stanza, it was almost impossible to forget the rest." Indeed, "it was almost impossible . . . to substitute one word for another. This excellence is peculiar to the Celtic tongue, and is perhaps to be met with in no other language."[51]

The "voice of the echoing heath" and poetry of "other times" for which *Ossian* became so well known was thus modeled on a geometric analogy—which is to say, on the (geometric) ideal of "evidence." And, in fact, geometry informs Macpherson's conception of the poems at multiple levels. Elsewhere in his *Dissertation*, Macpherson describes a process of bardic initiation and idealization that reflects his own university training:

> The bards who were originally the disciples of the Druids, had their minds opened, and their ideas enlarged, by being initiated in the learning of that celebrated order. They could form a perfect hero in their own minds, and ascribe that character to their prince. The inferior chiefs made this ideal character the model of their conduct, and by degrees brought their minds to that generous spirit which breathes in all the poetry of the times. . . . This emulation continuing, formed at last the general character of the nation, happily compounded of what is noble in barbarity, and virtuous and generous in a polished people.[52]

Highland culture, a virtual retrojection of Macpherson's university course, consisted of the emulation—"by degrees"—of heroic figures adopted from the (Pythagorean) Druids and subsequently traced by the (classically trained, Reid- and Blackwell-like) bards. This is a process, Blair noted, that applies to the experience of reading *Ossian*: "Few poets are more interesting. . . . The characters, the manners, the face of the country become familiar; we even think we could draw the figures of his ghosts: In a word, whilst reading him, we are transported as into a new region, and dwell among his objects as if they were all real."[53] In the poems, these intersections of sound and figure (the "ghosts" to which Blair refers: the traces of nature in the artifice of allegory) take the form of poetic visions dense with what Ian Duncan calls "the pathos of abstraction":

> I sit by the mossy fountain; on the top of the hill of winds. One tree is rustling above me. Dark waves roll over the heath. . . . It is midday: but all is silent. Sad are my thoughts alone. Didst thou but appear, O my love, a wanderer on the heath!
>
> But is it she that there appears, like a beam of light on the heath? . . . She speaks: but how weak her voice! like the breeze in the reeds of the pool. Hark! . . .
>
> Alone I am, O Shilric! alone in the winter-house. With grief for thee I expired. Shilric, I am pale in the tomb.[54]

The elegiac structure of such passages is complex, Duncan remarks; "we read the past mourning itself" as already absent, a compound *figure* (or, in Blair's terms, a literal rendering) of a set of "original" poems whose existence was tenuous at best. In their "mute apparition" as "printed text," Macpherson's translations, the marks on the page, graphically illustrate their own evanescence and the alienation of their host language, the Gaelic.[55] Imagined on the model of Reid's distinction between nature and artifice, or geometry and algebra, the Ossian poems throw the classical world into shadow in the very process of making it new.[56]

Reid and Macpherson were actually relative latecomers to the primitivist party. From the 1720s (or perhaps earlier—from the time of his appointment in 1711), Robert Simson, professor of mathematics at the University of Glasgow, had been envisioning Euclid along similar lines. In the preface to his 1756 translation of Euclid's *Elements*, which became the standard edition in British schools through the middle of the nineteenth century, Simson lamented the decline of classical geometry due to the omissions and apocryphal embellishments of Euclid's ancient editors. Simson thus attempted "to remove such blemishes, and restore the principal Books of the Elements to their original Accuracy"—a geometric (indeed, bardic) task of translation.[57] He had undertaken a similar project in 1723 relative to Euclid's doctrine of porisms, a concept I will discuss below. The moderns, Simson argued, no longer understood Euclid's invention "or only guessed at what [it was]." Transmitted primarily through the *Collection* compiled by Pappus of Alexandria (whose life span from c. 290 to c. 350 made him a rough contemporary of Ossian) and transcribed only as a series of lemmas (or received propositions), the porisms had become a mystery by the time of "the celebrated David Gregory," the famous late seventeenth-century Scottish mathematician. Gregory professed that he was able to make little headway in restoring the porisms due in part to the fact that Pappus's description consisted in large measure of "many right lines . . . without any alphabetical marks," making it difficult "to guess what Pappus meant." Shorn of explicative apparatus, Pappus's Euclid was almost too geometric for Gregory. But not for Simson:

> After I had read in Pappus that the Porisms of Euclid were a most curious collection of many things which related to the analysis of the more difficult and general problems, I was earnestly desirous of knowing something about them; wherefore often and by various ways I endeavoured to understand and to restore as well Pappus's general proposition, lame and imperfect as it was, as also the first

> Porism of the first book, which, as was said before, is the only one out of the three books which remains entire; but my labour was in vain for I made no proficiency. And when these thoughts had consumed much of my time, and at length had become very troublesome, I firmly resolved never to make any further enquiry for the future, especially as that best of geometers Halley had given up all hopes of understanding them. Therefore as often as they occurred to my mind I endeavoured to put them by. Yet afterwards it happened that they seized me unawares, forgetful of my resolution, and detained me so long till some light broke in which gave me hopes of at least finding out Pappus's general proposition, which indeed not without much investigation I at length restored.[58]

Simson's vatic experience—"seiz[ing him] unawares" through a "light [breaking] in"—enabled him to see (with quintessentially geometric clarity) what Gregory had failed to perceive. And yet, Simson's supplementary explanation, expanded from Pappus's minimalist sketches, effectively does to those fragments (themselves the residues of a lost Euclidean original) what Macpherson's published poems eventually did to Ossian's oral epics. That is, Simson's *Treatise Concerning Porisms* geometrically configures Euclid's disappearance, substituting in place of an absent original a classical edifice that is less a straight translation than a creative adaptation. It is a new geometry dressed up—poetically—in the "figures" of the old.

Simson's primitivist project becomes even more interesting and resonant with a wide-ranging body of Scottish literature when we reflect on what porisms were. Technically, the porism was a proposition that occupied a place between a theorem and a problem, linking the proofs of the former with the constructive principles of the latter. The late eighteenth-century Scottish mathematician John Playfair defined the porism as a "proposition affirming the possibility of finding such conditions as will render a certain problem indeterminate, or capable of innumerable solutions."[59] One theorem, "innumerable" problems: in one respect, the porism opened geometric constructs to virtually limitless articulations, not unlike Maurice Blanchot's meditations on writing as an interminable exercise or "infinite conversation."[60] But in another sense, porisms enabled their users to ascertain the broader limits of a specific problem, thus compressing multiple theorems around a single (concrete) instance, after the manner of historiography. A mathematical construct with literary and historical resonances, porisms amounted to a geometric portent of the process of historical deduction that Scott later revisits (and revises) in his fiction. In effect, *Waverley* was itself something of a porism, comprising a *theory* of Scottish modernization motivated by the specific *problem* of the Jacobite Rebellion.

Compared with the complex Scottish Enlightenment "figures" of geometry and romance that I am describing, the Futurist paradox—that history does not cease but rather begins with the proclamation of its death, with its consignment to the dustbin ("Time and Space died—*yesterday*")—appears thoroughly conventional, even staid. More than that, it suppresses the history (say, the Newtonian elements) it purports to surpass. Contrast that with the situation of the "long" Scottish Enlightenment that Nairn and Craig (and Simson, Macpherson, and Scott) delineate wherein history doubles as its own future—that is, in which the distortional effects of a changing society eventually impact the way we narrate its history. In that latter instance, figures of historical self-reflection (in geometry as well as narrative) take the form of an ecosystem in which nothing is laid waste or in which the past is always present, forever *evident.*

On the Poetics of Late Euclideanism

This book is not about ecology per se, although it does trace the lines of history as they curve back on themselves, weave their way, emergently, into a burgeoning network of texts and ideas, and stimulate new ways of configuring the passage of time. Indeed, it takes the contortions of Scottish cultural history literally by addressing the challenges its eighteenth- and early nineteenth-century literati faced in negotiating Newton's theories of space and time, especially the beguiling forms these theories took in literary practice. However, and this is a crucial part of my argument, the cultural meaning of these eighteenth-century experiments with space and time differed from the form they would eventually take in the early twentieth. To avant-gardists like Duchamp, bizarre geometric forms enacted a radical break from the past. But in the "long" Scottish Enlightenment, such forms served as a medium of connection to the past (as a neo- or modified classicism) even as they also enabled literati to imagine the past in new ways. In that respect, the contortions of Scottish Enlightenment literati were more radical than those of later ages, which imagined themselves rupturing as much as resolving the problematic relations of past and present and thus dividing as much as bending the lines of history around each other.

The basic contention here is that Scottish Enlightenment thought so entangled itself in webs of epistemic and illustrative complexity that it challenges the notion of the "classical" that it sought to conjure (for example, in the moniker "the Athens of the North"). On this score, Murray Pittock insightfully remarks that "[t]he paradox of the Scottish Enlightenment was that so many autonomous ideas rose from [a] paradigm of conformity," a formulation that aptly describes what I am calling the poetics of late Euclideanism.[61] While these poetics were hardly "modernist" after the manner of Marinetti or Joyce, the Age of Union was not simply an eighteenth-century phenomenon, either—even, to a degree, during the eighteenth century. For that reason, modernism is useful as a point of reference for defining three principal traits of late Euclideanism: a series of experimental departures from the status quo (in the arts as well as the sciences), a self-conscious negotiation of tradition and innovation, and the distillation of history as a principle of form rather than succession. Intellectuals from this Age of Union, I argue, confronted a set of geometrical and cultural quandaries that compelled them to experiment with new modes of mathematical and literary representation (trait 1), attempt a reconciliation of new practices with those from the past (trait 2), and account for the formal dimensions of the history they were both living and making (trait 3).[62]

But deconstructing the differences between classical Scotland and post-classical Europe and restoring a measure of the history that links them, although important to our understanding of the long (long . . . long) eighteenth century, are not the sole ends of my project. Rather, my aim is to reflect on literary form, particularly those aspects that often go overlooked in discussions of form relative to genre and rhetoric. My interests here, for example, do not concern novels versus tales or odes compared with elegies but rather involve literary experiments with linearity as a connective activity across space and time—that is, with *figures* in the diagrammatic as well as rhetorical sense.[63] Such diagrammatic figures played an important role in the explication of calculus in the early eighteenth century, when the practice had yet to achieve its formal grounding. John Colson, one of the first to publicize Newton's method of fluxions, invoked geometric figures as illustrations of moving points, hoping to engage not only "the Understanding, and . . . the Imagination . . . but even [the] Sense."[64] These diagrams were thus part of a multimediated approach that effectively functioned metaphorically by creating images that superseded simple deduction. Geometric figures were (also) figurative.

Late Euclidean poetics were thus an art as much as a science—a fact that is both underscored and forgotten in literary studies. Take, for example, the well-known "poetics of relation" to which the French Caribbean writer Édouard Glissant implicitly appeals as a way of asserting "the linked histories of peoples."[65] For Glissant, this is more a geographic than a geometric enterprise and understandably so: Galileo's idea of geometry as a language of nature exerted a major influence on how Enlightenment thinkers organized their understanding of the globe in an age of expansive imperialist activity. Glissant's poetic geography linking France to the Caribbean thus articulates the connection between mathematical abstraction, colonial history, and a globalized cultural sphere. In doing so, it resonates with a powerful tradition in twentieth-century criticism that reached something of an apotheosis in the 1980s and 1990s. Fueled by Heidegger's discussion of technological "enframing," Lacan's analysis of the gaze, Foucault's image of the panopticon, and other tropes of observation, scholars began widely associating Enlightenment geometry with dogmatic rationalism, big-brotherly power, and an inhumane "quantifying spirit."[66] "For modernity," writes Thomas R. Flynn, "vision has become supervision."[67] Wai Chee Dimock still invokes this vaguely geometric model—one in which time is spatialized and measured, period to period, and in which "[s]tandardization reigns"—as the paradigm against which she presents a more putatively nonlinear version of "deep time."[68]

But in some cultural contexts, classical geometry was less rigid—more ductile—than this. The geometry that some intellectual historians demonize today often devolves on the idea of abstract grids: Newton's "geometrization of space" into "homogeneous and abstract" quadrants, say, or the "table of signs," which for Michel Foucault constituted the dimensions and limits of Enlightenment epistemology.[69] But such taxonomic exercises actually (or also) correspond with an *algebraization* of space, a conversion of line segments and curves into a system of coordinates and formulae that revolutionized mathematical practices in the seventeenth and eighteenth centuries, enabling measurements that were far more intricate than those of earlier eras. These new methods found a home in Scottish universities and in a variety of applied contexts, making the sustained devotion to Euclidean geometry by Simson and others something more akin to the cultivation of tradition than the modern specter of a dehumanization of everyday life. The geometers' aim, as George Davie has remarked, was to unify thought with perception along phenomenological lines, as I will discuss below. Hence, the place of geometry across the disciplines and in quotidian practices undercut as much as embellished the presumptions of rational quantification; as Barbara Maria Stafford would have it, geometry accommodated aesthetic as well as scientific impulses.[70]

Returning to Glissant, then, my book does not examine the applications of geometry as a globalizing agent as much as it takes a closer look at the history and form of the very idea of the "relations" Glissant evokes metaphorically and at the role that Scotland's Age of Union, particularly its long eighteenth century, plays in the elaboration of this idea.[71] The spatial dynamics of relation may partly explain why a more elastic, elongated field is necessary in the way we conceive of literary history, particularly in an era of distant reading and quantitative interpretations—numerical approaches that employ spatial configurations as conceits.

Scotland's Geometric Imagination: A Historical Overview

Before pursuing this argument in the remaining chapters, it may be useful briefly to delineate the mathematical and cultural history that will serve as these chapters' horizon. I will begin, unconventionally although for useful illustrative purposes, with the mathematical poetics that (mostly) exceed the parameters of my study. I am referring here to the non-Euclidean paradigms that came to inform, if not the literal design of literature and art in the early twentieth century, then at least their idea. I call my approach an unconventional one, illustrating as it does the intellectual backdrop to the experiments within classical form by way of what those experiments were not. But we might be better advised to begin from a more conventional position—literally. I am referring here to the late nineteenth-and early twentieth-century French mathematician Henri Poincaré's "conventionalist" mathematics (which is the title Poincaré bestowed on his critique of Galileo's conception of mathematics as the language of nature and to the corresponding disclosure of geometry, algebra, and arithmetic as contingent ways of framing the world) and to the influence of these ideas on Duchamp, who imported them into the visual arts. Art historians tell of how non-Euclidean and *n*-dimensional geometries began insinuating themselves into the creative work of Lewis Carroll and Edwin A. Abbott (the author of *Flatland*)—and into the poetic forays of the mathematicians James Clerk Maxwell and James Joseph Sylvester—after 1850, before bursting into artistic consciousness in the early decades of the twentieth century. Linda Dalrymple Henderson remarks that Poincaré, who, with E. Jouffret and Maurice Boucher, helped disseminate the new mathematics, "was to become a popular intellectual hero for the French during the early years of the twentieth century. His three major books on his philosophy of science, published in 1902, 1904, and 1908, were widely read and served as major vehicles in the dispersion of knowledge about the new geometries."[72]

These "new geometries lent themselves to wonderful and even mystical excesses of the imagination," Gerald Holton notes, "not least by literary and figurative artists and musicians. These included Dostoyevsky, H.G. Wells, the science-fiction writer Gaston de Pawlowski, Alfred Jarry of pata-physics, Marcel Proust, the poet Paul Valéry, Gertrude Stein, Edgar Varèse, George Antheil, the influential Cubists Albert Gleizes and Jean Metzinger, and so on—not to speak of Ouspensky and the Theosophists."[73]

In the case of Wells, for example, "the idea of the fourth dimension as a place or as a temporal means of reaching another era provided a position from which to comment on contemporary society. This was clearly [his] purpose in his 1895 tale *The Time Machine*," in which "Wells treats time . . . as the fourth dimension."[74] Duchamp, for his part, was among the first to become enraptured by these new mathematical ideas, importing them not only into specific works like *The Bride Stripped Bare by Her Bachelors, Even* (1915–23), a complex effort to represent (at least) four dimensions within a three-dimensional grid, but also into his very conception of the "conventionality" of art. Hence, his readymades, like the famous *Fountain* (the urinal he signed and placed in an exhibit), although perfectly decipherable within three-dimensional, Euclidean space, bespoke the influence of Poincaré's mathematics.[75]

We risk misperceiving the nature of these modernist innovations if we interpret them simply as extensions of the new geometry. For example, T. J. Clark argues that Cubism corresponded less with "a new description of the world—one in which . . . the terms of space and time were recast in a way which responded to changes out there in physics or philosophy. It was [rather] a counterfeit of such a description," an aesthetic mimicry of these world-changing paradigms within the forms available to the arts.[76] And yet, the galactic implications of the new mathematics (for example, in the theory of relativity) became a language in which the avant-garde trafficked, and the cultural as well as conceptual implications of the new geometry may explain Marinetti's vehemence in pronouncing the death of time and space—categories of cognition that were associatively Euclidean and that had been reduced to mere conventions, mere cultural artifacts, by the early twentieth century. As Poincaré put it (with Kant clearly in mind), "Geometrical axioms are . . . neither synthetic *à priori* intuitions nor experimental facts. They are conventions."[77] Kant, by contrast, interpreted geometry as "a science which determines the properties of space synthetically, and yet *à priori*." That is, geometry presents to the mind pure intuitions of time and space "before any perception of objects" and hence prior to all experience. Such thought is at once formal and natural, Kant believed, with the mind reflecting the workings of nature: "Geometrical principles are always apodictic, that is, united with the consciousness of their necessity, as, 'Space has only three dimensions.'"[78] This is precisely the "necessity" that *n*-dimensional geometry disproved, explaining Poincaré's divergence from Kant. Poincaré did meet Kant halfway, however, by agreeing that Euclid's geometry is, if not the truest, then at least the most resonant with quotidian experience: "One geometry cannot be more true than another; it can only be more convenient. Now, Euclidean geometry is and will remain the most convenient" because it is the simplest, "just as a polynomial of the first degree is simpler than a polynomial of the second degree."[79]

We should underscore here that, although nominally making a different point, Poincaré effectively reproduces Kant's reasoning: Euclidean geometry may be conventional, but it is *necessarily* the simplest of all geometric conventions and thus most closely resembles the mind's own tendencies (after the manner of the Kantian categories). Therefore, *n*-dimensionality acquires a counterintuitive—indeed, a surreal—quality, a kind of baroque status in the service of higher-order operations, making it appropriate for science fiction like that of Wells (or, for that matter, a new science like Einstein's). This alone lends Poincaré's conventionalism an air of avant-garde edginess.

When Marinetti fêted the avant-garde, he was thus taking aim not only at Euclid but also, and more important, at the inscription of Euclid in more recent Western history, especially the intellectual legacy of the Enlightenment. His celebration of machines as the vehicles of the new poetics ("A race-automobile adorned with great pipes like serpents with explosive breath . . . is more beautiful than the *Victory of Samothrace*"[80]) lends his manifesto a dialectical quality with a distinctively Marxist flavor: Enlightenment mechanical science (thoroughly informed by the applied geometrics of pulleys and weights and levers) enables the development of industrial machinery, but such tools eventually turn against the hands that created them, liberating their operators from the delusions holding recalcitrant Euclideans like Kant and Newton in thrall. Hence, while Newtonian mathematics evokes a classical aesthetic in its ratification of a harmoniously orchestrated universe, it also helped motivate a logic of progress that eventually installed a post-Euclidean, postclassical set of mathematical practices. Crucially, however, as I will discuss below, Newton affected a kind of classicism in full consciousness of the attempted circumvention of Euclid in key areas of seventeenth-century mathematics, making him something of a kindred spirit to Poincaré in his tacit recognition of the conventional quality of classical geometry. But to this extent, the experimental Duchamp also begins to appear as the avatar of a much older intellectual tradition.

Indeed, one could trace the conventionalists' disgruntlement with Euclid at least as far back as 1580, when Petrus Ramus in France adopted "a critical attitude toward Euclid as a geometrical text-book for beginners."[81] Geometry literally signifies "earth measurement," and the doubts expressed by Ramus regarding Euclid's effectiveness in imparting such instruction would only increase over the next two centuries. As Katherine Neal explains, this skepticism was partly a product of mathematical syncretism: England in the late 1500s employed mathematics in a wide variety of labors—"ballistics, navigation . . . surveying . . . and increased mercantile activity"—that collectively inspired ingenuity. Hence, "[m]athematics was not a unified discipline in this period. . . . At least three different approaches existed," belonging to the algebraists, the formulators of logarithms (like John Napier), and "university mathematicians [like] Isaac Barrow" who believed that all of mathematics should be based on geometry.[82] René Descartes exhibited one of the most portentous manifestations of this mosaic of mathematical approaches in 1637 when he devised a set of algebraic procedures designed to free geometry from the use of diagrams. Called coordinate (or, more properly, analytic) geometry, these methods allowed geometric constructs to take the more precise form of algebraic and numerical equations—an operation, observes the historian Morris Kline, that "revolutionized mathematical methodology."[83] During the Enlightenment, tentative explorations of non-Euclidean space also began to appear, particularly from mathematicians looking to bolster the weakness of the parallel postulate (which famously asserts that parallel lines never intersect). As reasonable as this postulate may appear at face value, it is not empirically evident. (Indeed, this is what "vanishing points" in perspective painting are all about: parallel lines appear to intersect at a distance even though we "know" that they do not.) What is more, and simply from a formal standpoint, Euclid's articulation of this postulate seemed uncharacteristically contorted and problematic: "[I]f a straight line falling on two straight lines make the interior angles on the same side less than two right angles, the two straight lines, if produced indefinitely, meet on that side on which are the angles less than the two right angles."[84] Could this be proved? If so, wasn't there a simpler, more lucid way to enunciate this idea?[85]

While the broadly innovative attitude toward geometry made the critique of the parallel postulate seem newly urgent, this was not, in itself, an utterly new line of inquiry. It had been undertaken by Ibn al-Haytham, the eleventh-century Islamic mathematician, and by the later Persian mathematicians Omar Khayyám and Nasīr al-Dīn al-Tūsī in the twelfth and thirteenth centuries, respectively.[86] Then, in 1733, the Italian mathematician Giovanni Girolamo Saccheri published a work entitled *Euclides ab omni naevo vindicatus* ("Euclid freed from every flaw"), attempting to prove Euclid right by demonstrating the absurdity of any contrary assertion, specifically that the sum of a triangle's internal angles adds up to more or less than 180 degrees. He was actually unable to prove that these angles cannot add up to less than that number; picture what happens, for example, if we trace a triangle across a saddle, bending its three sides and their corresponding angles inward. Instead, he could only lay claim to traditional sensibilities, arguing that such acute angles "are repugnant to the nature of the straight line!"[87] But in stating his case in this particular way, Saccheri inadvertently laid the foundation for what is now called hyperbolic geometry, a non-Euclidean model later espoused and explained by Eugenio Beltrami in 1868. In the 1770s, Saccheri's prototype for hyperbolic geometry found a natural counterpart in the elliptical model propounded by the Swiss mathematician Johann Heinrich Lambert. (Elliptical triangles are triangles in which the sum of the angles is greater than 180 degrees, as we would find if we drew a triangle across the exterior of a sphere.)

Together, Saccheri and Lambert are important to mathematical and intellectual history because they reveal that when János Bolyai and Nikolai Ivanovich Lobachevsky enunciated non-Euclidean theories from Hungary and Russia, respectively, in the early nineteenth century (and some scholars would add Carl Friedrich Gauss, from Germany), they were essentially expounding upon a longstanding project of revisionist geometry, admitting and extending the demonstrable if counterintuitive axioms that Saccheri deemed "repugnant." Then, of course, there were pursuits of these axioms in nonmathematical venues, including perhaps the most ingenious geometrical construct of the eighteenth century, a theory of non-Euclidean space from *within* a notionally Euclidean paradigm. I am referring to Thomas Reid's "geometry of visibles," a section of his treatise *An Inquiry into the Human Mind, on the Principles of Common Sense* (1764). We discussed Reid's invention briefly in the Introduction. Responding to David Hume's attachment of understanding to the visual sense (through the etymology of the Greek word for "idea," *idein*, meaning "to see"), an equation that Hume employs to deconstruct causal reasoning (since causality demands conclusions based partly on extrapolations of our experience), Reid creates a scenario that reveals our visual sensibility—and thus our "ideas" and, therefore, our skepticism on that basis—to be, in Poincaré's words, merely "conventional." If, Reid imagines, we placed the eye "in the centre of a sphere," then "every great circle of the sphere [would] have the same appearance to the eye as if it [were] a straight line; for the curvature of the circle being turned directly toward the eye, [would not be] perceived by it. And, for the same reason, any line which" we drew "in the plane of a great circle of the sphere, whether it be in reality straight or curve, [would] appear straight to the eye." What appears straight may actually be curved, contrary to empiricist assumptions. And such a scenario of spatial curvature, Reid argues, would be "not less true nor less evident than the propositions of Euclid."[88]

That may be true, but that does not mean that Reid was exactly giving us Euclid. Indeed, Alexander Broadie observes "[s]omething utterly non-Euclidean [had] happened. According to Euclid, however far a straight line is projected it will never return to its starting point. But a visible straight line," Reid had shown, might well "return to itself. So visible straight lines are not like tangible straight lines, that is, they are not like the straight lines of Euclidean geometry."[89] Hence, the parallel postulate only partly holds in Reid's spatial experiment: "If two lines be parallel—that is, every where equally distant from each other—they cannot both be straight," they simply bend around the sphere beside each other before joining with themselves and confounding the Euclidean ideas of nature. Reid further employs this logic in evoking the possibility of a fourth dimension, an idea that would rise to prominence in the late nineteenth century. While he believed we could have no experience of such a dimension (along the lines of Poincaré's argument that Euclidean dimensions are most intuitive to us), its existence was, with the curvature of space, a startling feature of the logic of "common sense."[90] This was a mode of reasoning that would find powerful new expression in the avant-garde, whose exponents insisted that the world as it is may be radically different from how it appears.

I will return to Reid's model and its implications and legacy at the conclusion of Chapter 5 and then in greater detail in Chapter 6. The point worth emphasizing here is that Reid's ingenuity was the product of sustained adherence to Euclidean precepts by Scottish intellectuals who continued to evoke geometry as a kind of ur-discipline, or critical ground of thought uniting diverse branches of inquiry. For these intellectuals, geometry was a poetic or creative language during a time when many dynamic advancements in mathematics were algebraic; this is what made quirky but also startlingly prophetic thought experiments like Reid's possible, not only in mathematics proper but also in other areas of study and expression. In Chapter 2, for example, we will see how historical fiction represented a non-Euclidean extension of the geometric calculus (which itself was the formal expression of the relationship of space and time); in Chapter 3, we will discuss the dynamics of the picturesque as the introduction of complexity into the façade of the classical.

All this transpires, I argue, as a function of uneven development: the devotion of Scottish geometers to Euclid made Scotland an intellectual backwater *and* a place of innovation—made it "primitive" *and* "modern"—all at once. Indeed, geometry comprised something of an eddy in the general algebraic flow of mathematics in the eighteenth century. The turn toward algebra had commenced in earnest in the previous century, when, as we discussed above, astronomers, political economists, and natural and moral philosophers throughout Europe became increasingly concerned with problems of measurement in applied mathematics and with the limitations of geometry in accommodating a growing range of mathematical operations. For example, it was a precept of ancient metaphysics that objects found their measure in whole numbers: to exist was to be "one" thing or else a countable assembly or fractional mass of 1. But the Pythagoreans recognized that not all shapes possessed ratios reducible to whole numbers: isosceles triangles with two equal sides each measuring 1 will have a hypotenuse measuring $\sqrt{2}$, which cannot be expressed as a simple fraction. Irrational numbers, as these fragments were called, bore a problematic philosophical existence, and yet they figured into a host of calculations, including velocities, distances, rates of accumulation, and more. Scottish geometers, following the Greeks, expressed irrationals by way of ratios and thus avoided the infelicities of (metaphysical) nonexistence. But as Neal has shown, many mathematicians saw no need for such delicacy. "[T]he purpose and goal of mathematical research for practitioners [of the logarithms] such as Napier and [Henry] Briggs lay in its practical applications" to such ends as navigation and equations of probability. Hence, Neal says, most practitioners "were more than willing to violate the canons of Greek mathematical philosophy."[91]

Hence, if geometry retained its reputation as "the queen of the sciences" well into the nineteenth century, as Joan Richards argues, this is not because it represented "binding truths about real space" but rather because its demonstrable certainties were seen as a model of how the mind arrives at truth.[92] In terms we outlined above, geometric reasoning was "evident" and thus appealing even given its empirical and theoretical shortcomings. It is to this conceptual allure that scholars usually refer when they conjure the "geometrical spirit" of the Enlightenment. Linnaeus evoked it in his system of botanical classifications, for example, and this system then migrated into mineralogy, chemistry, medicine, linguistics, and other disciplines.[93] In the nineteenth century, geometry so popularly symbolized the inculcation of rational thought that Charles Dickens in *Hard Times* made it a characterizing feature of his soul-crushing headmaster, Thomas Gradgrind.[94]

For such Scottish geometers as John Keill, Robert Simson, Colin Maclaurin, and Matthew Stewart, geometry signified the modern era's link to the "classical" past as well as the mind's ability to sketch its own thought processes and thus more fully connect reflection with perception. Intensifying their devotion to geometry was the geometric turn in Newtonian thought. Newton, an expert algebraist, was something of a convert to geometry, his early ventures in mathematics being largely Cartesian. In his eulogy of Newton, Bernard le Bovier de Fontanelle observed that Newton had found Euclid "too clear, too simple, too unworthy of taking up his time" and had "leapt at once to such books as Descartes's *Géométrie* and Kepler's optics."[95] But Newton later expressed regret at "his mistake at the beginning of his mathematical studies, in applying himself to the work of *Descartes* and other algebraic writers."[96] The source of this regret may well have been his dispute with Wilhelm Gottfried Leibniz over priority in the invention of calculus and also a subtle but important difference between the Leibnizian model and his own. It is difficult to overstate the impact of calculus. The wide scope of applications of calculus—charting rates of movement and degrees of differentiation (for example, in the slope of a curve) over time and thus measuring change in phenomena ranging from the motion of planets and the impact of artillery fire to the progress of financial markets—has led some scholars to declare it the most important mathematical innovation in modern history.[97] Philosophically speaking, however, the Leibnizian and Newtonian methods differed somewhat. The Leibnizian differential calculus divided curves into a series of minutely spaced points, calculating the rate of change by measuring the difference between these points. But Newton's fluxional calculus foregrounded the element of time by conceptualizing a point in motion in the creation of a line; the aim here was to calculate the speed of linear movement. For Newton, this calculation involved two steps—an "analytical" conversion of the geometric line into algebraic terms and a second, "synthetic" step "deliver[ing] a geometrical demonstration" of the analytical result.[98] In essence, Newton translated geometry into algebra, then retranslated algebra back into geometry. The first step surpassed the simple operation of geometry, but the second relied on the "evidence," or clarity, of geometry to justify its operations.

This justification was important, Niccolò Guicciardini observes, inasmuch as calculus incorporated "infinitesimals," algebraic numbers greater than zero but smaller than any measurable quantity, "in its demonstrations" (216). I discuss the logical and ontological challenges posed by infinitesimals in later chapters; here, suffice it to say that Newton was never able to resolve the conundrums they posed (for instance, of how an infinite number of infinitely small numbers might nevertheless amount to less than any measurable number) except through recourse to "geometrical and kinematic intuition" (222). This means that his method worked not because he had solved the mystery of infinitely small numbers (that is, how a unit might possess immeasurable quantity) but rather because "the continuity observed in physical motions" or in the kinematics of nature's curves made "it possible to conceive of mathematics as a language applicable to the study of the natural world" (223). And this, in turn, means that the geometric figures that were supposed merely to illustrate algebraic calculations actually became "graphic aid[s]" that helped Newton justify and even purport to solve them. For this reason, Guicciardini explains, Newton's calculus was "a matter of art rather than science" (210).

The geometric figures in Newton's fluxions were thus distortional mirrors held to nature. Unlike the static depiction of figures on Cartesian grids, fluxions adduced lines "not by any apposition of Parts, but by a continual motion of Points." There, "Surfaces are generated by the motion of Lines, Solids by the motion of Surfaces, Angles by the Rotation of their Legs, Time by a continual flux. . . . These *Geneses* are founded upon Nature, and are every Day seen in the motion of Bodies."[99] Leibniz, by contrast, pioneered a model known as "differential" calculus. While it too charted the motion of points along a graph, Leibniz emphasized the algebraic articulation of the infinitesimal differences between these points and thus made little attempt to square "analysis" with traditional geometry. His was an art for art's sake rather than one pretending to the status of "nature." The differential calculus enjoyed wider currency on the Continent, where such prominent mathematicians as Leonhard Euler, Joseph-Louis Lagrange, and others refined its operations such that later advancements in the field (including, significantly, those by Augustin-Louis Cauchy in 1823 in situating the calculus on more rigorous foundations) tended to build on Leibniz's system.

These later developments were anything but evident in the seventeenth and eighteenth centuries, when the quarrel between Newton and Leibniz devolved into a national conflict. Scots played a key role in its escalation. According to Rupert Hall, "Nearly all the [renowned British] mathematicians of this time," and "nearly all the ardent Newtonians . . . were Scots: David Gregory, [John] Craige, [Archibald] Pitcairne, [George] Cheyne, the Keill brothers [John and James], James Stirling, Matthew Stewart, [and] Colin Maclaurin."[100] History has not always—or even often—been kind to these intellectuals. Newton's biographer, Richard S. Westfall, labels John Keill, for instance, "a crude and abusive man who did Newton's cause much harm before the learned world, which quickly learned to despise him."[101] More generally, Scottish mathematicians are seen to have presided over an era in which "British mathematics fell behind that of Continental Europe," precisely on account of their collective adherence to geometry.[102]

And yet, this latter truism bears closer inspection. Helena M. Pycior observes that there were two basic schools of thought in eighteenth-century Scotland regarding algebraic innovation. The first, spearheaded by Simson, professor of mathematics at the University of Glasgow for a full half-century (from 1711 to 1761), was generally inimical, while the other, headed by Maclaurin, professor of mathematics at Marischal College in Aberdeen and then at the University of Edinburgh (and the author of the important *Account of Sir Isaac Newton's Philosophical Discoveries* [1748] and the rigorous *Treatise of Fluxions* [1742]), embraced geometry but also engaged readily with algebra.[103] In the former instance, the resistance to algebra was motivated in large part by the conviction that "many Propositions, which appear conspicuous in [Euclid, are] knotty . . . and scarcely intelligible to Learners by [the] Algebraical Way of Demonstration." This was because geometry shows "Evidence by the Contemplations of Figures," as opposed to the "Symbols, Notes, or obscure Principles" one finds in algebra.[104] Maclaurin, meanwhile, aimed to defend Newton's own ambivalent (that is, geometric *and* algebraic) mathematical enterprise against such detractors as George Berkeley (who wrote a scathing treatise, *The Analyst* [1734], denouncing fluxions) and the disciples of Leibniz on the Continent. In neither instance, crucially, was the debate over geometry really about geometry per se. For Simson, the anxiety over symbols amounted to a phenomenological argument about experience or about the relationship between reflection and perception. But geometry also touched on a national ontology, specifically concerning the "being" of Scottish identity—"British" in declaring solidarity with Newton and "Scottish" in retaining a connection with a classical (that is, a premodern, pre-Unionized) past and its intellectual and institutional traditions in metaphysics.[105] Geometry in eighteenth-century Scotland, in other words, was a philosophical and cultural rather than simply a mathematical battleground, and the mistake in perceiving it as retrograde is a function of seeing it too narrowly.

This last point becomes especially important when we consider the legacy of Scottish geometry in literary history. Whether in attempting to restore a pure Euclidean program and thereby admitting its erosion (which is what Simson did, both by providing a new translation of the *Elements* and by reconstructing "lost" aspects of Euclidean geometry), in proffering bizarrely refashioned (and even non-) Euclidean constructs (in the form of Reid's "geometry of visibles"), or simply in revising traditional Euclidean practices (which John Playfair did in presenting a new version of Euclid's parallel postulate[106]), Scottish mathematicians widely attested to the limitations of the very tradition they (also) defended. Theirs was a *late* Euclidean era; as such, they were working at the *limits* of classical paradigms. Indeed, even a cursory overview reveals that Euclid and "nature" were less the hegemonic centers of Enlightenment orthodoxy (against which, *pace* Marinetti, a radical aesthetic could only rebel) than problems with which mathematicians and philosophers—and, as we shall see, poets and artists—wrangled.

One illustrative area where this struggle played out was in Scottish Enlightenment theories of language. Above, we cited Blair's geometric notion of "figure" and the concerns Simson had with the opacity of algebraic symbols. Alison Lumsden argues that this was a wide and recurring subject in Scottish thought. She cites, for example, the attention Henry Home, Lord Kames pays to matters of linguistic "relation" and "abstraction" (for example, of signs to things or else to other signs) and then comments that "the relationship between words and what they mean . . . haunts much of the Scottish Enlightenment's discussion of language, raising far more complex epistemological questions than common perceptions of the period may imply."[107] Her examples include Kames, Blair, Hume, Lord Monboddo (who notoriously linked the communicative capacities of humans to primates), and George Campbell. The latter, in *The Philosophy of Rhetoric* (1776), makes the implicitly geometric assertion that "it is of the utmost consequence to ascertain, with precision, the meanings of words, and as nearly as the genius of the language in which one writes will permit, to make them correspond to the boundaries assigned by Nature to the things signified."[108] Hence, in the terms we cited above, one should employ "Evidence by the Contemplations of Figures" rather than the "Symbols, Notes, or obscure Principles" of algebra. Hume, however, seemed to subscribe to the algebraic view that language, consisting of conventions, is auto-referential and bears an uncertain relation to the world outside itself.[109] And yet, even here, Hume's assertion is part of a larger argument about "the connexion or association of ideas" that links our thought together—a concept suggestive not only of equations but also of the delineations of mind that his peers identified with the logic of geometry.[110]

I will address Hume in greater detail in Chapter 2. The point I wish to underscore here is that the tensions between geometry and algebra that exercised Newton and helped shape his legacy also pervaded eighteenth-century Scottish thought across a range of disciplines. And while this study will mostly restrict itself to an examination of the "long" Scottish Enlightenment, it seems worth noting that in some ways, the sustained (and even belated) attention to geometry during this period amounted to an exploration of issues that had yet to resolve themselves in the Western world in the early twentieth century. This is what we may infer given the residual presence—even the prominence—during that era of a modified (or "late") brand of classical Newtonianism. For instance, the Cubist figures created by Picasso and Georges Braque purportedly shattered linear perspective, but when the "Orphic" artist František Kupka introduced the first truly nonrepresentational paintings into Western art in 1911, he did so via a color theory he adapted from Newton, replete with a series of paintings he called "Newton's discs."[111] In the 1920s and 1930s, when André Breton and Louis Aragon began emulating the chaotic, nonlinear motions of the mind through the technique of "automatic writing" (which they imagined to be the inscription of the unconscious), they did so via the medium of the machine, a technology that, in the early twentieth century, was thoroughly informed by the principles of Newtonian mechanics. In this respect, avant-gardists essentially reprised and modified the (distortional) tactics and (creative) techniques of eighteenth-century Scottish literati. And to that degree, the Scottish Enlightenment provides us with a curious but vitally illuminating window onto later modernity. And, more pertinently for my purposes, it expands our appreciation for the long and multidisciplinary history of the complexity of form—a subject that prompts us to reconceive of the dimensions of literary history.

CHAPTER 2

Scott's Shapes

I begin by referring back to Cairns Craig's argument, which we cited in Chapter 1, that we may situate the Scottish Enlightenment in either the eighteenth or the nineteenth century and that our cumulative consciousness of that phenomenon derives from a later period still (for example, from 1900, when William Robert Scott coined the phrase, or from the 1960s, when courses on the Scottish Enlightenment began to feature more prominently in university curricula). If we accept Craig's revisionist history as true, then how are we to historicize Walter Scott, who helped commemorate (and seemed to personify) the Enlightenment in Scotland through his historical fiction? In essence, "when was Scott?"

In one respect, Scott's soaring popularity in the early nineteenth century—first as ballad collector and editor, then as poet, then as novelist—makes this an easy question to answer, as few literary figures appear so fully to have captured the spirit of their age. Indeed, Scott lorded over an Edinburgh publishing empire that bequeathed to us the print culture of Romanticism and the genre of historical fiction.[1] And yet, Scott's renowned "Tory skepticism" attests to his own discomfort with some of his era's circumstances (like political reform and the specters of revolution) and has encouraged the view of Scott as a product of the Enlightenment, the period in which Scott set several novels and whose ethos of moderate progress he seemed to embrace. As it happens, Scott's death in 1832 practically bookends the "first" and "second" Scottish Enlightenments, marking a conclusion (for scholars like George Davie) of the era of the "Scotch metaphysics" and its cultivation of a "democratic intellect"—an era of relative harmony between Scotland's traditional institutions and society—and a commencement (for Craig) of an epoch of unprecedented Scottish influence in, for example, energy physics and its aesthetic avatars (Futurism and Vorticism, for example).[2] Set in relation to these latter time frames, Scott becomes something of an anachronistic monument to "enlightenment" and "modernism" all at once.

This is where things grow more complicated still. After his star dimmed in the late nineteenth century, Scott began his reascension up the canonical ladder in 1937 when Georg Lukács devoted a substantial chapter of his landmark book, *The Historical Novel*, to Scott. The influence of this book was felt most widely after 1962, when it was translated into English. Lukács credits Scott with a precociously "modern" appreciation of the differences between distinct historical eras—praise that Fredric Jameson would reiterate in the 1980s and 1990s as he contrasted Scott's sensibilities with the erosion of historical consciousness in postmodernity.[3] However, in the late 1990s, Jerome McGann would argue that Scott is prototypically postmodern to the extent that he makes "the subject of tale-telling an explicit and governing preoccupation of [his] fiction."[4] The shift of emphasis here from "modern" to "postmodern" is significant as, for McGann, what is crucial about Scott is less his awareness of historical change per se than his consciousness of the *medium* of narrative in conditioning our perception of it.

Celeste Langan has elaborated on precisely this point, contending that Scott's evolution from ballad collector to poet to novelist reveals important things about the state of media in literature in the early nineteenth century. She shadowboxes here with Friedrich Kittler, who famously asserts that the media's meteoric impact was not felt until the turn of the twentieth century with the emergence of film, the typewriter, and the gramophone. As Kittler has it, the twentieth century differs not only technically but also conceptually from the previous age, Scott's age, in which writing ostensibly promoted the illusion of presence, or human mastery, via print's supposed transcription of the voice; it is only in later periods that the tools of mechanical reproduction turn against this self-inflating humanism, to say nothing of the humans who wield them. Langan, however, asserts that the print medium that Scott so expertly manipulated was already generating the type of sensory overload we associate with more sophisticated machines, visually encrypting the affect of voice and thus inscribing the "poetic" within the "virtual."[5] As her primary exhibit, she cites the multiple inversions of voice and text informing the genre of the imitative ballad, most notably in Scott's 1805 *Lay of the Last Minstrel*. Commenting on the romantic idea that print preserved but thus transmogrified the oral literatures of dying cultures and that "voice" accordingly disappeared into "text" as the past fades into the present, Langan remarks that for this very reason, voice became "the ostensible content of the broadcast medium of print" (70). Literature, with Scott at its helm, thus conjured a sense of history, or the deep past, less by pointing to it or exhibiting its tensions within the structure of its own narrative (as Lukács and Jameson suggest) than by functioning as the medium of its transmission. With Scott, literature "becomes" the past that in turn goes futuristic or high-tech.

So when was Scott, exactly? Langan's answer, as well as McGann's, is that Scott is "now"—less as a function of his (rediscovered) popularity than of the means, the media, by which the past is known or by which Scott presents that past to us. But this also suggests new directions for scholarship on Scott, who becomes not only (or not always) the object of criticism but also (or rather) the medium through which to illuminate or "enlighten" other phenomena. This recapitulates, in its way, the phenomenological directive of the eighteenth-century Scottish geometers, who purported to illustrate the motions of the mind as well as, for example, the planets. Langan gestures toward this process by observing how, in "capturing" the voice, the printed page converts verbal figures into "a sculptural or pictorial form" (53). Such "forms," McGann adds, reveal important clues about how we arrive at meaning. Citing the lessons the digital humanities teach us about our quotidian reading practices, he argues for a "broadly 'semiotic' rather than narrowly 'linguistic'" theory of interpretation that would heighten our appreciation of the visual, diagrammatic dimensions of texts. Taking the position that a page's "[m]ark[s], space[s, and] direction[s]" bear a figural logic of their own, he claims that the geometric lines we decipher and trace as we read may "help us grasp and invent the shapes of thought."[6] The name McGann assigns to the computer program that divulges these "shapes" or mini-histories of reading seems only too appropriate: "Ivanhoe," after Scott's famous novel.

The point I wish to underscore here is that in coming to date or place Scott "now," we may discern a provocative transformation in the governing concept of history, from Lukács's inferences concerning dates and differences—a logic of sequential progress—to the disclosure (via media and reading practices) of emergent folds and parallels—a temporality of form. The story of late or postmodernity thus finds itself inscribed in Scott's *shapes* as much as in what Ian Duncan calls Scott's *shadow*. Hence, we recover the doubly anachronistic structure of thought embedded within the Scottish Enlightenment. I call it doubly anachronistic because, as we discussed in Chapter 1, it describes the coeval belatedness and precocity of Scottish geometry during this period, its lateness with respect to the "new" algebraic mathematics of the eighteenth century and its earliness compared with the "newer," non-Euclidean paradigms of the nineteenth century. At once classical and modern, these Scottish forays in spatial form thus provide us with alternative ways of measuring history. We might call them exercises in uneven development undertaken with ruler and compass.

I discuss one such exercise here—one of Scott's. I do not focus on Scott's work as a whole or even on one whole work as much as on a particularly rich fragment in *Guy Mannering; or, The Astrologer*, his second novel (1815). This excerpt functions as an emblem of structures I discuss throughout this book that illustrate what it means to read (or "see") geometrically as well as algebraically, or to think in terms of shape as well as symbol, or by way of "nature" (as an ecology of relations) and not simply "history" (as a series of displacements). I will supplement my reading of this excerpt by reference to other Scott novels, especially *Waverley*. My aim, however, is less to create a sweeping survey across Scott's substantial corpus of work than to take up, self-reflexively, the logic of what such a survey implies. In other words, Scott is less the object of criticism here than its medium—an inversion that modifies our sense of his place in literary history as well as the very meaning of such history.

Literary History in Three Shapes

At a pivotal moment in *Guy Mannering*, Scott sends his young protagonist, a soldier recently serving in the British army in India, northward across the Solway Firth, the arm of the Irish Sea dividing England from Scotland. Harry Bertram's journey is significant to the narrative's ideological framework as well as to its plot: hoping to reunite with his beloved, Julia Mannering, the daughter of his former general, Harry will providentially discover and reestablish his family's rights to an ancient Scottish estate, thus unifying the Scottish past with the British present via the mechanism of literary romance. Such moments are typical of Scott's fiction, whose genius largely consists of its navigation of temporal, national, and generic categories like these.

But this passage in *Guy Mannering* redirects our understanding of Scott's narrative current in ways that have almost entirely eluded critical commentary:

> At length, after spending the whole night upon the firth, [Harry and the ship's crew] were at morning within sight of a beautiful bay

> upon the Scottish coast. The weather was now more mild. The snow, which had been for some time waning, had given way entirely under the fresh gale of the preceding night. The more distant hills, indeed, retained their snowy mantle, but all the open country was cleared, unless where a few white patches indicated that it had been drifted to an uncommon depth. Even under its wintry appearance, the shore was highly interesting. The line of sea-coast, with all its varied curves, indentures, and embayments, swept away from the sight on either hand, in that varied, intricate, and yet graceful and easy line, which the eye loves so well to pursue.[7]

The scene is at once grand and elegant, beautiful and sublime, and, under its wintry canopy, it seems literally frozen in time. But more meets the eye here than a picturesque Scottish bay. For modern readers, a British coastline's "indentures" may evoke Benoit Mandelbrot's famous 1977 analysis of the fractal properties of seashores (which beguilingly reproduce formal regularities while appearing random).[8] Scott himself appears to allude self-consciously to the famous S-shaped curve or "line of beauty" that the painter William Hogarth had extolled as art's most beautiful form.[9] Indeed, in *The Antiquary* (1816), the novel that followed *Guy Mannering*, Scott reprises this image. He does so, conspicuously, during an episode in which Sir Arthur Wardour and his daughter, Isabella, walking along a rugged coastline at the onset of a storm, risk drowning in the onrushing tide. It is here, at this moment of danger, that Scott pauses to comment on "the easy curving line" of the sinuous bay along whose edge Arthur and Isabella are walking, a stretch of coastline "conformable to the line of beauty."[10] The power of the image takes precedence, for Scott, over the plight of his characters.

Still, there is more in play here than aesthetics. Indeed, the most provocative echo in the passage in *Guy Mannering* may be of Scott's countryman Colin Maclaurin, the important intellectual of the first half of the eighteenth century who tacked a middle course, we might say, between Hogarth and Mandelbrot, art and nature. The "line" that Harry beholds is a genetic or moving one, "swe[eping] away from the sight" as the ship moves along the coast; it thus conforms with the image of the fluxional calculus of which Maclaurin became Europe's leading expert in the 1740s. Calculus (in its fluxional and differential iterations) is, as we discussed in Chapter 1, an invention whose significance is difficult to overstate, given how important measurement over time is to modern thought and science. Maclaurin, whom Newton knew and admired (helping Maclaurin secure a post at the University of Edinburgh in 1725), became the key spokesperson for Newtonian fluxions. Indeed, he grasped the fluxions more fully than did Newton himself, making him Newton's most powerful advocate in the face of the criticism heaped on Newton by continental devotees of the differential calculus propounded by Gottfried Wilhelm Leibniz.[11]

But Maclaurin's defense was not a simple matter of expertise. As we discussed in Chapter 1, Newton not only devised a system of calculus but also translated its algebraic procedures—its calculations and strings of variables—back into the form of Euclidean geometry, most notably in the *Principia*, his monumental theory of celestial motion.[12] In Newton's mind, the virtues of this system, the fluxions, consisted largely of the latter's verisimilitude: "Lines are described . . . by a continual motion of Points. Surfaces are generated by the motion of Lines, Solids by the motion of Surfaces, Angles by the Rotation of their Legs, Time by a continual flux, and so [on]." Fluxional shapes are thus ubiquitous, "founded upon Nature, and . . . every Day seen in the motion of Bodies."[13] Algebraic constructs, by contrast, defy our powers of perception by abstracting natural shapes into a series of symbols, which is one reason why Newton, late in his life, expressed regret at "his mistake at the beginning of his mathematical studies, in applying himself to the work of *Descartes* and other algebraic writers."[14]

It was this idea of clarity, of "evidence" and its associations of visibility, that Scottish intellectuals embraced, partly out of political expediency. To defend Newton's method from the criticisms of the Leibnizians was to demonstrate allegiance to "Britain" in the wake of the 1707 Union with England while also upholding "Scottish" mathematical and philosophical traditions (in which "geometry" was a virtual synonym for "metaphysics") in the face of the pressure applied to those traditions by the circumstances of the fledgling British state. (This dynamic reversed itself in the early nineteenth century, when the Scottish mathematicians James Ivory and William Wallace introduced continental "analysis," or calculus, into Scottish universities several decades prior to its adoption at Cambridge.[15]) And then, as we also discussed in Chapter 1, there were phenomenological and even ontological reasons for the affirmation of geometry. While many Scottish mathematicians were thoroughly conversant in the new "analysis," Maclaurin and such peers as John Keill and Robert Simson clung to geometry in an effort to circumvent the semiotic infelicities of algebraic figures (that is, of signs for things: *this* variable for *that* quantity), appealing instead to the "evidence" of putatively diagrammatic proportions.[16] In dramatic illustration of the difference between the mathematical orientations, Maclaurin's *Treatise on Fluxions* (1742), the eighteenth century's most sophisticated exposition of Newton's calculus, devoted its first volume to a geometric exposition of the theory before reconstructing the fluxions algebraically in Volume II, thus suggesting that algebra was an extension of geometry rather than the converse. Tellingly, the distinguished Scottish mathematician John Playfair, Scott's friend, made a similar case under the auspices of defending the methods of algebra from what he viewed as the conservative practices of his peers: "In the algebraic expression . . . so much meaning is concentrated into a narrow space, and the impression made by all the parts is so simultaneous, that nothing can be more favourable to the exertion of the reasoning powers, to the continuance of their action, and their security against error." Algebra begets clarity, Playfair reasoned; almost anticipating Walter Pater's later argument concerning aesthetic criticism and essentially reiterating Maclaurin's view of geometry, Playfair imagined algebraic equations condensing the circumference of our impressions and thus intensifying the quality of our experience.[17]

The appeal to nature and experience enabled Newton and, later, Maclaurin to present fluxions as an amalgamation of the systematic elegance of Euclid with newer methods for measuring the external world. Fluxions thus portrayed the flow of time and, with the rise and fall of its sweeping lines, the evolving face of nature: it captured the space of modernity by way of its perceptible shapes.[18] In this way, fluxions amounted to a mathematical anticipation of historical fiction (an equation I will take up more directly at the conclusion of this chapter, with a review of the competing visions of Scott's work proffered by Georg Lukács and Edwin Muir). However, precisely because fluxions did not purport to trace the development of nations but simply the progress of points and the circuit of lines, it more abstractly schematized the formal logic of progress and hence of the "varied curves, indentures, and embayments" through which narrative unfolds, the "rising" and "falling" action of plot.[19] To this extent, the passage in *Guy Mannering* is doubly historical: Harry Bertram "returns" to his Scottish familial estate *and* Scott revisits an earlier, mathematical version of literary romance. It is a brilliantly self-reflexive moment—a hallmark of Scott's work.[20]

But this same reflexive quality also helps explain why *Guy Mannering* does not simply imitate the calculus whose logic it partly exhibits, however much the "media" of fluxions and historical fiction may share. Indeed, in some ways, Scott's project diverges from Maclaurin's as much as Scott's vantage point as narrator differs from Harry Bertram's. The "synthetic" method of the fluxions (where analysis was translated back into the form of geometric demonstration, often with corresponding diagrams) found a place in Newton's *Principia*, the Enlightenment's preeminent work on astronomy and its most powerful tool for reading the cosmos.[21] The full title of Scott's novel, meanwhile—*Guy Mannering; or, The Astrologer*—bespeaks the implications of stargazing on young Harry's fate, first foretelling the downfall of his family and then, later, inspiring the astrologer (that is, Mannering) himself to act as a beneficiary in restoring the family's birthright. Early in the novel, when the Bertram family tutor Dominie Sampson opposes astrology by contrasting it with Newtonian science, the still-callow Mannering, a half-(or romantic) believer in the old, mystical ways, juxtaposes Newton's "modern . . . [and] vernacular name" with a list of "grave and sonorous" astrological authorities from the weird science of the past—luminaries (pun intended) like "Dariot, Bonatus, Ptolemy, Haly, Etzler, Dieterick, Naibod, Hasfurt, Zael, Tanstettor, Agrippa, Duretus, Maginus, Origan, and Argol" (16). The novel's astrological conceit (which, like its title character, the narrator neither fully embraces nor disavows) thus clearly plays off the stellar paradigm to which Newton gave mathematical expression. What is more, Harry's trip across the Solway Firth all but expressly evokes Maclaurin, whose later insights into Newton's mathematics had actually helped pioneer new methods of coastal surveillance in the early 1740s.[22] This makes Harry's landward gaze the descendant of a more meticulous process of scrutiny and therefore a trope in its own right. And so, in ways that are nearly as opaque to us as they are to Scott's protagonist, Harry Bertram's maritime trek along the Scottish shoreline marks a voyage into a set of cross-disciplinary (that is, mathematical and literary) as well as familial and national pasts. Scott effectively builds tropes, or rhetorical figures, around (synthetic) fluxions, or geometric figures.

And yet, in doing so, Scott actually takes the Newton/Maclaurin model a step further. Indeed, what we read in the fluxional circuit of Scott's narrative is a subtler and more historically resonant iteration of the digression in *Tristram Shandy*, in which the title character pauses to reflect on the squiggly "lines" his narrative traces in the book's first several volumes. I call Scott's episode *subtler* than Laurence Sterne's because, unlike the excursive *Shandy*, Scott embeds fluxional figures within his narrative, melding them into Harry's gaze (consonant with Newton's and, later, the Scottish geometers' claims that fluxions represented a kind of portrait of nature). And it is *more historically resonant* in the dual sense, first, of uniting a mode of perception with historiographical form (in Harry's—and the reader's—fluxional journey across the firth and into the Scottish past) and, second, of eliciting an even more sophisticated mathematical scheme than fluxions at a particularly significant moment in time. *Guy Mannering* was published in 1815, which is roughly the period when mathematicians began experimenting with non-Euclidean geometries—shapes undreamt of by Newton. These new systems, enunciated initially by János Bolyai and Nikolai Ivanovich Lobachevsky and then, over the course of the nineteenth century, by Bernhard Riemann and Henri Poincaré, played an important role in modernist experiments in the arts, as we discussed in Chapter 1.

While nobody will confuse *Guy Mannering*'s coastal imagery with Picasso's *Les Desmoiselles d'Avignon*, the logic of linear distortion that Scott's work exhibits bears closer scrutiny. We might locate a better point of comparison between Scott and the visual arts in the formal experimentation that artists like Édouard Manet began undertaking in the nineteenth century. Manet's famous 1882 painting, *Bar at the Folies-Bergère*, for example, which depicts a barmaid gazing directly at a viewer who also catches a glimpse of himself in a corner of the mirror behind the woman, literally distorts the space of reflection by displacing the objects in the mirror to a position suggesting the motion of the viewer. In effect, the painting bends the instantaneity of vision—the shared gaze of barmaid and viewer—into a process of perception: the viewer sees, reflects on himself seeing, and beholds that reflection in the space of representation.[23] The painting depicts a historical phenomenon, Paul de Man would say, not by portraying a series of incidents but rather by lighting on a transformative event at the moment of its occurrence—the moment when perception gives way to reflection and reflection catches sight of itself. On that basis, de Man's logic would suggest, it constitutes an act of reading.[24]

Manet's painting presents a different picture, to be sure, from the "curves, indentures, and embayments" of *Guy Mannering*. But one important thing the two works share is the subtle play they instigate with their subject matter. In the case of the *Bar at the Folies-Bergère*, the centrality of the barmaid slightly diverts our attention from the viewer's own image in the mirror. In *Guy Mannering*, the attention to the striking curves along the coastline both underscores and yet distracts us from noticing the *spatial* curvature that accords the episode its narrative significance. For this is the episode in which Harry begins to intuit his family's ancestral seat as Scott's narrative instills in its readers a sense of their own moment in history. If Harry's voyage across the firth reflects the fluxional history (the wavering line through time) in which it is inscribed, then Scott's narrative, in reflecting *on* that history, becomes a kind of vision of the act—the historical event—of reading. To this extent, Scott's novel both evokes and surpasses the philosophical concept of fluxional calculus; it operates both within and outside its frame of representation.[25]

The work of other nineteenth-century painters may provide comparisons that seem more apt, for Scott exerted a considerable impact on visual culture. In a biography of the painter John Pettie (1839–93), Martin Hardie relates that "it has been said of Scottish art of the middle of the [nineteenth] century that 'every artist seemed to find a mission in illustrating Sir Walter Scott: never perhaps in the world's history was a country's art so completely subjected to the sway of one man.' In his boyhood Pettie fell under the wizard's power."[26] That power is manifest in *Disbanded* (1877; see Figure 1), an image memorialized for modern readers by its appearance on the cover of a Penguin edition of *Waverley*. It shows a Highland Jacobite soldier retreating from a scene of battle and heading into a murky future (illustrated by the mists that engulf land and sky in a general haze). As the soldier walks, he gazes at a point behind the viewer, suggestive of a place in the past—the implicit origin of his departure—which, unperceived by us, is as indeterminate as the prospects lying ahead of him. What Pettie depicts here is less a Wordsworthian spot of time, less a moment that distills a historical process, than the resolution of time as figure, converging past and future into a forward-moving, backward-glancing national symbol: the retreating soldier. History becomes timelessness that in turn expresses the national being, the "nature," of Scotland. This is, in some respects, a more "Euclidean" picture than Manet's, portraying as it does a kind of national archetype held in timeless suspension.

Although by no means adequate as a diagnosis of national essence, Pettie's painting does capture the paradoxical moment in Scottish history when history itself became bound up within the sphere of the image—when the primacy of the visible (including geometry) became the modality of the "Scottish" nation within a "British" state.[27] This is Tom Nairn's argument, which we discussed in Chapter 1—that the nation, inspired largely by Scott, reduced itself to a set of visual tropes, a "great tartan monster."[28] In *Guy Mannering*, Harry Bertram himself is arrested by the power of primordial, unwhole images, not only of the coastline's jagged curves but also of the specter of the ruined, half-recognized family estate, Ellangowan, that sits atop them. Along these lines, what *Disbanded* exhibits, similarly to the decrepit

FIGURE 1. John Pettie, *Disbanded*. The University of Edinburgh Corson Collection. Reproduced by permission of the University of Edinburgh.

Ellangowan, is an image of history-become-form. This was the cultural logic of geometry, George Davie asserts, as it was (to a degree) of the genre of the gothic, with whose hallmarks *Guy Mannering* abounds. One thinks here of how Scott's novel ventures into supernatural prophecy (via astrology and fortunetelling), portraits of ruin (in the place of Ellangowan as well as the person of Harry's beaten-down father), foul deeds conducted in gloomy caves (in the form of Dirk Hattaraick—smuggler, kidnapper, and murderer), and literally bewitching characters (in the figure of the gypsy Meg Merrilies, who helps Bertram obtain his birthright). Characteristically, and conjuring the spirit of gothic romances by Ann Radcliffe and Matthew Lewis, Scott expresses ambivalence about the course of progress, especially as it takes up residence in the institution of the law (which is the instrument of the villainous Glossin, a local "writer" or glosser on the law who cheats Harry of his estate, before it becomes the means by which Harry eventually secures it).[29] The point here is not that the gothic "is" geometric but rather that it also in its way distills history as a series of images—or rather, that it equates history with images and with the layering of moments, of histories, upon one another.

What I wish to underscore here is that *Guy Mannering* conveys history through a kind of visual logic and that it assumes several shapes simultaneously. It takes the form of a ray in presenting the more or less straightforward flow of historical progress (from "ancient" Scotland to "modern" Britain), a fluxional curve as its agents enact that progress (for example, the circuitous path pursued by Harry Bertram and by all of Scott's protagonists in the twists and turns of the novels' plots), and a non-Euclidean design as that curve loops around and reflects on itself through the mediating technology of its own narrative. If the ray represents the idea of successive stages of development and fluxions the design of the plot, then non-Euclidean dynamics help explain the space of reading.

I say "non-Euclidean" to capture the effect less of a curved line, like a circle or spiral, than of a spatial curvature in which even putatively straight lines bend around on themselves. It is less the technicalities of non-Euclidean geometry that matter here than the aesthetic associations of that geometry, for while self-reflexivity of this nature is rarely imputed to Scott, it often informs Scott's narratives as his protagonists become conscious of the history they are living (beginning, perhaps, with Edward Waverley's reflections on the moment "that the romance of his life . . . ended, and that its real history . . . commenced"[30]). This particular episode in *Guy Mannering* is important to the extent that it accentuates what we might call the geometrics of Scott's literary genius—a play of narrative trajectories that expands our sense of literary *form*. Here, such form lends expression to one of the Enlightenment's most forceful innovations, calculus, even as it circumscribes the latter within a more complex (that is, a non-Euclidean) scheme of interpretation. If we were to sketch Scott's literary program on a graph, tracing the course of the narrative in the way we chart Harry's progress—that is, if we were to try to portray ourselves seeing Harry seeing—then we would eventually cease drawing lines and find ourselves bending the paper or curving the "space" of its plane and touching its corners. Doing so would enable us to capture the reading experience of being simultaneously with Harry aboard the ship and also in some other reflective location gazing back on ourselves. This is a conventional narrative device whose complex morphology Scott here renders more apparent. He gives us, essentially, a fluxional figure within an Escher-like diagram, forming a composite of the Enlightenment history *Guy Mannering* represents, the Romantic narrative it employs, and the avant-garde aesthetic it anticipates (inasmuch as it was with the avant-garde that non-Euclidean poetics most forcefully enter the sphere of representation).

How are we to understand the significance of narrative dynamics like these to literary history? I say *to* and not merely *in* literary history, for the intersection of literature and geometry in *Guy Mannering* makes up an even more radical chronotope than scholars already widely appreciate in Scott's work, one that not only captures but also collapses space and time.[31] Typically, critics perceive in Scott's fiction a process of displacement, an evocation of the past for the purpose of its exorcism (as with the case of Jacobitism in *Waverley*, for instance, or of the Covenanters in *Old Mortality*). I will analyze this view of Scott in greater detail below. But the condensation of time in this passage in *Guy Mannering*, the way it folds eras one over the other, paints a different picture of Scott's work and seems to present a different set of implications for the way we read and understand his novels. Indeed, we cannot stop our story of Scott's spatial legerdemain here, not without first taking a detour that will help us get a fuller perspective onto the nature of his literary innovation, one that connects the late Euclidean poetics of Maclaurin and Playfair with the later, post-Euclidean dynamics that became more prominent later in the nineteenth century (with such mathematician-poets as James Clerk Maxwell and James Joseph Sylvester, to say nothing of Poincaré and those, like Marcel Duchamp, who drew inspiration from him at the turn of the twentieth century). The passage in *Guy Mannering* marks a point, we might say, at which Euclidean space begins to fold over on itself, sketching the beginning and end of history—the moment when the "classical" worldview yields to something "postclassical" but hence also when the "history" of that transition folds over and reasserts itself as something like nature or a dynamic system, something reflexive across its ongoing evolutions.

To illustrate this principle, I will take up work that measures Scott's impact on history in very different terms. I devote particular attention to Ian

Baucom's exemplary *Specters of the Atlantic*, a book of massive scope that attempts a critique of an even longer modernity than the one I address. A deeply moral work, Baucom's book is also, and this is the second point, an implicitly and at times self-consciously mathematical one, although the calculus it analyzes and proliferates is mostly algebraic—more Leibnizian than Newtonian. In other words, and in step with the logic that displaced geometry with algebra, Baucom's argument remains committed to the compulsive logic of the modernity it criticizes. Scott occupies a key place in Baucom's constellation as the architect of an instrumental and implicitly algebraic historicism. To claim as much, however, is to overlook the late Euclideanism that informed Scottish thought and culture in the "long" eighteenth century and thus those aspects of Scott's work that evoke a very different sense of modernity and of the way we might imagine ourselves in it.

Walter Scott: Algebraist?

Baucom's *Specters of the Atlantic* is an extended, thoughtful analysis of a notorious 1781 incident in which a slave ship, the *Zong*, jettisoned its human cargo into the open sea. The ship had taken out insurance prior to its voyage, and when it began to run out of drinking water, its crew cast 133 slaves overboard. Afterward, the ship's owner entered a claim against the loss. This led to a famous court case that ultimately ruled against the owners while upholding the logic of finance capital that, Baucom observes, reduces humans to numbers or that divulges how any entity may be translated into capitalized, numerical form. Significantly, as we will see, historicism—one of modernity's principal modes for categorizing experience—bears the imprint of the logic that Baucom criticizes. And as part of his diagnosis of modernity's historicist impulses, Baucom attends not only to Scott but also (in the manner of Scott revisiting Maclaurin) to scholars who, like himself, have reflected on historicism by way of Scott. He focuses particularly on Lukács, Jameson, and James Chandler, three important literary historians who present, as it were, three stages of Scott-inspired historicist self-reflection. Lukács lauds Scott for rendering vivid characters who seem representative of their era, Jameson extols Lukács-on-Scott less for capturing characters per se than for identifying what is "typical" in them and thus for distilling the "larger and more meaningful" templates of historical change, and Chandler evaluates Jameson-on-Lukács-on-Scott as part of a long Romantic (and eminently modern) tendency to attribute historical value to what is typical or representative as such and therefore to reduce history to a function of *type* and *representation*.[32]

The "type" is a curious and, Baucom reiterates, distinctively modern phenomenon. To be sure, earlier eras invoked exemplary figures who embodied social ideals (one thinks of the "character" of Socrates in Plato's dialogues, for example), but the *type* is a rather different device. It implies not so much the thing that is best but rather the thing that is most ordinary, most representative, most *probable* in a manner evocative of both aesthetic verisimilitude and statistical normativity. Geometric shapes may be "types" or representations of processes in the natural world: this is how Newton portrayed fluxions, for example, in claiming they were "founded upon" and thus differentiated from "Nature." A fluxional curve amounts to a geometric type of figures "every Day seen in [and distilled from] the motion of Bodies."

But it is numerical rather than geometric types that intrigue and concern Baucom. They emerge, he contends, over the course of the long eighteenth century, during the generative era of high finance that promulgated such numerical fictions as credit.[33] Just as the latter designated an imaginary quantity of capital, so types, entering the domain of modern narrative in the genre of the novel, functioned as the empty or strictly figurative bodies—"nobodies," in Catherine Gallagher's memorable formulation—which provided a method for organizing and explaining mounds of factual detail.[34] Moll Flanders, for example, consolidated myriad minute details into an image of early eighteenth-century London, much as, for Scott, Highlanders like *Waverley*'s Evan Dhu MacCombich "inhabit Scott's texts not as the representative types of a contemporary Scotland but as the typical representatives of a lost time" (*Specters* 46). In their trueness to life and the spirit of their age, types promoted a kind of historicist faith, inspiring readerly belief, identification, and emotional investment.

It is this animating, inspiriting quality of "investment" at which Baucom takes aim. It attests, he argues, to a formal link between modern human "being" and speculative finance and hence to an insidious relationship between social norms and human exploitation in what he calls our "long twentieth century," a period whose origins he traces to the Enlightenment.[35] In punching a hole in this financial and representational mirror of speculation, Baucom adopts a generally deconstructive strategy: from a long history of (financial) number, he strives to elicit that which is irreducible to number. But the "other" in this matrix is not that which presents an expressive alternative to number within mathematics (for example, geometric figure) but rather that which purports to be beyond all mathematical calculation in its insistent, uncanny humanism. Specifically, Baucom presents the subjects of the slave trade as the real "nobodies" in the modern economy of high finance. Slaves are "specters of the Atlantic" who, he suggests, function as the Real in the Symbolic matrix of modern being, the true (and hence forgotten, because largely unrepresentable) victims in what Walter Benjamin calls the barbaric record of civilization.[36] What Baucom thus attempts is a redemptive history that doubles as a critique of number: we have failed to *count* as human those who were essentially ciphers in the speculative system of human ontology.

This is a compelling analysis, to be sure, although its implicit opposition of the human and the numerical risks reintroducing number in the very gesture of negating or voiding it, as we will see below. That said, Baucom's inclination to try to think beyond number may help explain, albeit through a rather different logic, the allure of the "curves, indentures, and embayments" in *Guy Mannering* or of those geometric forms that, in the Scottish Enlightenment, purported less to illustrate number than to circumvent "counting" altogether. Geometric quantification, though in many instances translatable into numerical form, implied measurement of a different variety, with a different set of associations.

Scott will thus lead us down a road less traveled. Baucom also initially appears to take this path, enlisting Scott in building his case against what he calls the "actuarial" mode of historicist representation, the cultural poetics of finance capital (42–43). He does so because Scott enunciates a "romantic historicism" that appears to subsist not on abstract types but rather on actual scenes of history (like the 1745 Jacobite Rebellion in *Waverley*) that animate "something that no longer exists, something that once existed but, by the moment it enters historicist awareness, is now lost" (46). On the surface, then, Scott's work would seem to provide a fulcrum for the meaningful critique of speculative "types" (along the lines of a romantic or "negative" dialectic—the refusal to be at home in the present). In the place of animated numbers, Scott gives us material artifacts.

However, as Baucom recognizes, things are not that simple; the contrast between actuarial and romantic historicism is a tenuous one. Both models conjure representative substitutes or types: actuarial historicism evokes "average abstraction[s]," *likely* or true-to-life characters whose genealogy is tied to the statistical calculations—the numerical probabilities—of the emergent insurance industry, whereas romantic historicism elicits metonymic figures (like *Waverley*'s Evan Dhu, the noble but endangered Highlander who so bewilders and enchants Edward Waverley, the novel's protagonist) in the place of entire eras. But this is a distinction without a difference inasmuch as both actuarial and romantic types devolve on processes of exchange. The former "endorses the exchange of the 'real' for the 'theoretical' [or 'probable'] life of things" (46), whereas Scott's romantic types inspire a compounded and displaced exchange of sentiments, of sympathy. They do so, first, by presenting a character (like Edward Waverley) who stands in for the reader (and who, like the reader, encounters the "strange" Evan Dhu). This subtle act of substitution diverts sympathy from "history" (that is, from the synecdochic Evan Dhu) back to this "ideal reader" (that is, to Edward). Hence, we effectively "exchange" the compassion we might feel for singular instances of suffering (for example, "*this* experience of the Highlanders, *this* slave-trade massacre" [281]) for a sympathy we experience instead for ourselves (that is, for the Edwards whose struggles, presumably mirroring ours, demand that they, and we, *come to terms* with the present). This is the devilish genius—and, for Baucom, the devil's bargain—of Scott's fiction: we "see" history only at the cost of seeing it as "history," as what is past, thus emptying or voiding it of force in the here-and-now.

This is a powerful and influential argument. It certainly influenced Baucom, who attributes it to Ian Duncan (see *Specters* 280–82), who in turn devised it through a careful reading not only of Scott but also of theorists of romance like Jameson and Northrop Frye.[37] It marks a different way of framing the self-reflexive aspect of Scott's fiction: what we described above as "non-Euclidean poetics" in *Guy Mannering*—the novel's circuitous accounting for its own narrative process—here takes the form of "sympathetic exchange" as a species of algebraic epistemology. The equation looks something like this: $a\ (b + c) = d$: Edward Waverley's experience (a) (intensified by its confrontation with the "strange" Evan Dhu [b] and the past that that character represents [c]) "is" (or personifies) the structure of modern romance (d). In other words, romance is the product of the sympathetic attachment of reader to character and of character to history. Without undercutting this argument—for it is true, after all, that algebraic innovations served as key tools in the development of speculative finance, a detail that certainly strengthens Baucom's contentions concerning the broad reach of "typical," "actuarial" humanism in modernity—we might nevertheless remark that a sympathetic equation of this sort makes for a very different image of Scott's fiction from the geometrics of Harry's landward gaze in *Guy Mannering*.

Or does it? We discussed in Chapter 1 how mathematics in England and Scotland (and, indeed, throughout much of Europe) had acquired a syncretic character since at least the sixteenth century, fusing geometric, algebraic, and arithmetical techniques in the pursuit of solutions to a host of practical problems. The difference, then, between geometry and algebra on which Simson insisted, following Newton, may have been less mathematical than phenomenological—which is to say, it may have devolved less on the imagined properties of space than on the way we experience and represent it. Schematically speaking, and as Baucom presents it, algebra calculates what the eye cannot see (like rates of change in movement over time), whereas geometry, Simson suggests, reenacts and rationalizes perception, showing us what change looks like (for example, on a graph). Hence, geometry served what we might describe as a supplementary or aesthetic purpose, an illustrative purpose. More literally, it enacted the cognitive role of the imagination, the power to produce images.[38]

That is the purport of a 1788 entry in the *Transactions of the Royal Society of Edinburgh*, which describes how the Scottish geometer Matthew Stewart, father of the philosopher and "conjectural historian" Dugald Stewart, acquired his reputation from the way he determined "the relation between the disturbing force of the sun, and the motion of the apsides [or apsis, 'circumference'] of the lunar orbit." Stewart's solution, the entry asserts, is "deserving of the greatest praise, since it resolves, by Geometry alone, a problem which had eluded the efforts of some of the ablest Mathematicians even when they availed themselves of the utmost resources of the integral calculus."[39] The entry applauds not only Stewart's discovery but also its degree of difficulty; the interest lies as much with its "art" as with its "science." Indeed, the entry sets up Stewart's discovery by first explaining "the *arcana* of the ancient geometry," the "degree of mystery" its undertakings involved, and the way that Stewart and his teacher, Simson, "resist[ed] the encroachments . . . the modern analysis," or algebraic calculus, "made upon the ancient" or geometric method.[40] The implication here is especially noteworthy: Stewart's geometry, arcane and mysterious, is a *romantic* enterprise, communicating in a different, almost primordial language equivalent in its way to Mannering's astrology but at variance with the idiom Baucom imputes to Scott. Unlike Baucom's Scott, Stewart's geometry does not accommodate us to the "necessity" of mathematical modernity—that is, to algebra—as much as it diagrams a way of envisioning heaven and earth, physics and metaphysics, after the pattern of the ancients. It does so, moreover, at the historical moment when that range of vision appears to be passing from view. Hence, we might say, Scottish geometry and Harry's coastal gaze—and Scott's narrative reflexivity—not only illustrate particularly complex scenes but also underscore the experience of the visible at the receding horizons of the conceivable.

Scottish geometry thus performed a kind of conjuring trick: it brought the past into the present without converting that past into the representative type of a bygone era. Indeed, if the type was a species of "history," geometric shape belonged to the order of "nature" (or at least a redemptive history) in unifying rather than truncating eras, in fostering a vital relationship between present and past, and in awakening in subjects like Harry Bertram a set of immemorial forms of perception. Shapes acquire this almost magical quality in *Guy Mannering* in the episode following Harry's voyage, when the unwitting heir returns to Ellangowan castle, the ruined portion of his family estate. Pausing over "the massive and picturesque effect of the [ruin's] huge round towers," the narrator tells of how the scene worked upon its protagonist. "[P]ursuing the usual train of ideas which flows upon the mind at such scenes," and thus following a mental track not unlike the physical path of his journey, Harry begins to wonder whether the "posterity" of the ruin's family may be "wanderers, ignorant perhaps even of the fame or power of their forefathers, while their hereditary possessions are held by a race of strangers" (244). This, of course, is Harry's exact situation given that the usurping attorney Gilbert Glossin currently holds the title of the estate. But Harry intuits his deep connection to the place, asking how it is that "some scenes awaken thoughts, which belong as it were to dreams of early and shadowy recollection. . . . How often we find ourselves in society which we have never before met, and yet feel impressed with a mysterious and ill-defined consciousness, that neither the scene, the speakers, nor the subject are entirely new; nay, feel as if we could anticipate that part of the conversation which has not yet taken place! It is even so with [Harry himself] while [he] gaze[s] upon that ruin" (244).

More specifically, it is the *shape* of that ruin that serves as the medium of coincidence between Harry's intuition, his rightful place in the estate, and Scott's narrative: it is the "huge round[ness]" and "high yet gloomy arch" of the towers that lend the structure—and its impression on Harry—"a double portion of depth and majesty" (244). The language here of "portion" and "depth" is geometric, as is that which describes the family escutcheon of "three wolves' heads" that hangs "*diagonally* beneath the helmet and crest." It is these figures, if not the full import of their contents, that "have been familiar to [Henry] in infancy." They contradict the fictitious family narrative with which Harry was raised, wherein he was reportedly "brought off from the eastern coast, after a skirmish in which [his] father was killed" (244–45). In fact, the novel here sets itself against the conventional logic of historical fiction as a narrative strategy dividing human subjects from the past. *Guy Mannering* is a historical novel that brings its own generative structure into question, taking the form of an organic system of variable shapes.[41]

This organic component reveals that, as incongruous as Euclid may appear from, say, Coleridge's Eolian harp, geometry in Enlightenment Scotland was nevertheless what later history would label a romantic phenomenon. As Harry's episode at the ruin exemplifies, geometry connected thought to the experience of the world, and it forged links between current practices and the deep past. Shape—nature's morphology—brings elements as diverse as Harry's fictional and actual histories, and Scott's overlapping (fluxional and non-Euclidean) narratives, into the same frame of representation.

This is not to say that Baucom and the historicist tradition he cites are incorrect in the way they read Scott's historical fiction; certainly, algebra informed "actuarial" and "romantic" historicism as much as it did the fluxional calculus. But when we consider the geometric customs that permeated the Scottish Enlightenment about which—and out of which—Scott wrote (from metaphysics to the practical or "improving" sciences), and if we try to think along with Scottish Enlightenment literati, then we must ask ourselves what it might mean to think about literary history by way of shapes as well as symbols or via visual as well as rhetorical figures. This is a challenging thought and one with its own powerful history in the West. It bore radical and even revolutionary connotations early in the twentieth century, when proponents of the avant-garde became disenchanted with what T. J. Clark calls the "blankness" of the modern world, its conformity to a mathematical "calculus of large-scale statistical chances" made possible through Enlightenment-era innovations in algebra (not least, in the very form of calculus itself). In this new society, Clark continues, everybody "accept[ed] (or resent[ed]) a high level of risk," which may be why modernism "dreamed of turning the sign," or the linguistic *and algebraic* mechanism of this new world order "back to a bedrock of World/Nature/Sensation/Subjectivity," which is where the avant-gardes derived their fascination with the new, non-Euclidean geometry and, by extension, with a world that might be imagined—or seen—otherwise.[42] My point is not that Scott belongs with the (*avant-*) avant-garde but rather that Clark's argument about the critique of modernity already resonated, and was already taking mathematico-cultural form, in the Scottish Enlightenment that Scott himself inherited. In fact, this prompts a closer look at what the consideration of mathematics does to the dimensions of modernity.

Three Philosophical Crises Involving Number

Geometric thinking by no means disappeared after Scott's era, but its Euclidean variant became less synonymous with nature, which may be one reason why its shapes appealed to Wassily Kandinsky, Piet Mondrian, and others as a fragile ideal, a token of what is "spiritual" in art.[43] Baucom's analysis becomes especially valuable here in mounting a persuasive critique of analytical forces that decomposed nature and suppressed important chapters of history. This is a critique taken up even more expansively and with great bravado by Alain Badiou. "[W]e live in the era of number's despotism," he proclaims. "What counts in the sense of what is valued—is that which is counted." Politics operates according to polls, turnouts, majorities; "[s]tatistics invades the entire domain" of the human sciences; we expect citizens "to be cognisant of foreign trade figures, of the flexibility of the exchange rate, [and] of fluctuations in stock prices." Indeed, "[n]umber informs our [very] souls. What is it to exist, if not to give a *favourable account of oneself*?" Essentially, we live a paradox: number dominates our lives, and yet "we don't know what a number is, so we don't know what we are."[44] The sheer diversity of numbers (separated as they are into whole numbers, negative numbers, rational numbers, real numbers, complex numbers, etc.) only compounds the problem, undermining any coherence we would assign to this system that dominates our political, economic, cultural, and even personal states of being.

These fatal rifts within the concept of number emerged, Badiou argues, in conjunction with three crises that infiltrated the metaphysics of unity during the seventeenth and eighteenth centuries. The classical Greeks always related "number . . . back to the One" (7), such that they might govern the diversity of phenomena through a single principle (as in the formula of "unity amidst variety," the classical definition of beauty that persisted into the Enlightenment). This is why geometric figure and arithmetical number were easily convertible into one another in classical mathematics. But, according to Badiou, this schema broke apart when it confronted three seemingly unthinkable conundrums—the concept of infinite series in the calculus, the notion of the void (or the "zero"), and the sheer force of difference.

Of the three crises Badiou lists, the plight of difference, or multiplicity, is perhaps the easiest to grasp for anybody familiar with the basic premises of cultural studies. Difference as Badiou invokes it here speaks to a growing sense (really, from the sixteenth century forward) of the irreconcilable diversity of human experience in an expanding global sphere, a conviction hastened by transcontinental exploration. Indeed, the Enlightenment "science of man" might be (and has been) interpreted as a reaction to the sheer heterogeneity of men and, crucially, *women* in a world irreducible to "one."[45]

The difficulty posed by the concept of the void, meanwhile, is more complex, but it also pertains more directly to Baucom's argument. Baucom invokes Brian Rotman, who unfolds a Foucaultian genealogy of the void, displaying it in some of its numerical, perspectival, and economic guises since the sixteenth century (for instance, as "zero," as the painterly convention of "vanishing points," and as "currency"—both paper and credit). Rotman tells of how these variations on the notion of the void came to unsettle traditional ideas concerning the independent reality of objects. As a rule, he notes, we tend to believe that sets of mathematical variables (or signifiers) correspond with signifieds (or with actual properties), that paintings employing vanishing points depict "scenes from some supposedly pre-existing [even if only imaginary] visible world," and that currency applies to goods that have a material existence.[46] But such "reality" is a mirage: "zero," after all, can anchor algebraic sequences that have no real-world referent; vanishing points—the place at which lines of perspective seem to disappear—can imbue a sense of actuality upon scenes that are literally impossible (as in Escher's *trompe l'oeil* paintings); and imaginary money (in its paper and credit forms) obscures and potentially detaches itself from the quantity of gold it supposedly represents. What the void therefore does, Rotman says, is displace us from a universe of objects to one of systems or to virtual realities—to things that *might be* and whose actuality is a function not of our experience in the world but rather of the cognitive processes that organize our experience. These mediating systems, detachable (or voidable) from the materiality of objects and sensations, explain and estrange the world all at once. It is precisely this mediating process that Gallagher divulges as the mechanism of modern narrative (that is, of "nobody's story") and that Baucom extends to the "typifying" mechanism of historicist discourse.[47]

For his part, Badiou expands Rotman's argument by converting the void into the ground of "being," specifically as the logical extension of numerical systems but also as the fulcrum of their critique. While Badiou's conceptual apparatus is more complex than I can summarize here, Peter Hallward explains that, for Badiou, "[t]he nothing *is*; it is not mere nonbeing." Indeed, it is "the unpresentable link that connects . . . any situation to its be-ing."[48] Consider, as Badiou does, the axiom of set theory that no set simply equals itself. The mathematical historian Morris Kline gives the example of a set of four elements—the number 4—and explains that "if one has 4 objects, one can form 4 different sets of 1 object (e.g., 1,2,3,4), 6 different sets of 2 objects (1,2; 1,3; 1,4; etc.), 4 different sets of 3 objects, and 1 set of 4 objects. If we add the empty set," or the set with nothing in it, which is part of every set—a set of four *and nothing else* also "contains" the void—then "we find that the number of all subsets can be compactly stated as [two to the fourth], which of course is larger than four."[49] "Four" equals something other than 4. This subverts the principle of identity (that a thing is equivalent to itself); it also means that the void is "present" even when and where it should not be, confounding the systems it underwrites. But, for Badiou, this also means that "being" cannot be the simple product of any numerical set of circumstances, since no set theoretically defined number ("4," for example) "is" wholly itself. Instead, being always involves some decision of ours as to its meaning.[50] We *decide* that a set consisting of the elements 1, 2, 3, and 4 contains (merely) four elements, or rather, we install sets and systems that, organizing elements, nevertheless cannot contain the event of their own installation. This supplementary relationship reveals the role of agency in modern being, Badiou argues: to "be" in the modern era of zero is necessarily to "act." And such action, Badiou explains, born by the void, exceeds the equation of extant possibilities in which we would place it; it falls outside any set of given elements and so is irreducible to any normative "type."

But it is actually the third of the crises involving number that is most pertinent to Scott and the legacy of Scottish Enlightenment geometry. This quandary was intrinsic to calculus, and it devolves, Badiou remarks, on the paradoxical status of infinity or on "series of numbers which, although we may consider their limit, cannot be assigned any terminus."[51] Calculus, that is, involves a relationship between the presumed limitlessness of numbers and an imposed limit that allows discrete sequences of increments to converge at a single point. How calculus does so comprises a puzzle that Kline labels "the most subtle subject in all of mathematics."[52] And it marks the point at which Baucom's critique of Scott—or rather, of modernity by way of number, implicating Scott—gives way to a different, more evocatively geometric rationale.

Number, Line, and the Problem of History

No Enlightenment intellectual exhibited more subtlety in negotiating the problems associated with calculus than Colin Maclaurin. Harry Bertram's trek along the Scottish coastline effectively retraces the coastal surveillance that Maclaurin's innovations in calculus had made possible. Scott himself only addresses calculus elliptically (although, as we will see at the conclusion of the chapter, quite pointedly), and he declares himself "an utter stranger to geometry" even though, as Adelene Buckland shows, Scott spent a great deal of time around John Playfair and incorporated facets of Playfair's work into his own prose.[53] And the reference in *Guy Mannering* to the shapes or "curves" that Harry perceives is a suggestive metaphor if not an outright allusion to Maclaurin (and to coastal surveillance). To understand why this is important, let us return to Baucom's insightful analysis of what I have called the "algebraic" facets of Scott's historical fiction. Unlike "actuarial" fiction, which "substitutes an average abstraction for a variegated array of actually existing things (. . . 'Moll Flanders' for all the pickpockets roaming the streets of London)," Scott's historical simulacra instead invoke "a representative phantom for an entity which once existed but is now lost" (*Specters* 46). Moll Flanders is a (mere) type, but the Jacobite Rebellion really took place. Baucom discerns a testimonial logic at work here, one that Scott adapts from Adam Smith's *Theory of Moral Sentiments*, the great eighteenth-century treatise on sympathy. Smith's "testimony" takes the form of specific traces of lived experience in, for instance, its "recurrent fascination with scenes of torture and death" (like how, "[w]hen we see a stroke aimed and just ready to fall upon the leg or arm of another person, we naturally shrink and draw back our own leg or our own arm"[54]). Such scenes, Baucom says, recall the Jacobite Rebellion of 1745 and attest to their traumatic effects in Scottish culture. Accordingly, they inscribe a constitutional ambivalence into Smith's model of sympathy: we feel for the sufferer if not for his cause. Sympathetic witnessing thus "passes on to . . . inheritor texts the unresolved contradiction of its own dual relation to a singular historical occasion of address and a universalizing dehistoricized grammar of thought" (*Specters* 247). Witness testimony thus transmits a material record of history *and* the cultural translation of that history into a generic type. This makes sympathy deconstructive as well as speculative: its types divulge the raw, experiential matter from which they are formed.

One of Smith's "inheritor texts" is Hegel's *Phenomenology of Spirit*, a tome that, in Derrida's early work, represents the West's monument of metaphysics, its zenith of systematic philosophy—Blake's crushing mill.[55] Baucom educes a "witness" figure in Smith and, by extension, Hegel, by which he suggests that we may deconstruct the Western tradition of capital (that is, Smith) and speculation (that is, Hegel) and thus uncover the material bases of the "types" of modern being. However, Baucom does not extend this deconstructive principle to the systematizing tendencies of Scott's historical fiction, despite Scott's overt integration of Smith's theory in its readerly economy of sympathetic exchange. Instead, Scott, supposedly more Hegelian than Hegel, reveals the limitations of Smith's *moral* philosophy: *Waverley*, Scott's novel about the Jacobite Rebellion, converts testimonial difference into the "fateful" historicism we discussed above (see *Specters* 276–82). Scott's romance, imagined here as impenetrable to deconstruction, thus serves a kind of scapegoat function, becoming a "type" for Baucom of the mathematically fueled market forces that converted particular human subjects into slaves but also that underscore Badiou's point about our inability to think outside the auspices of number, even in attempting its critique.

This situation conjures the controversy over Newton's fluxions. Specifically, Baucom's contention that the romantic "type substitutes a representative phantom for an entity which once existed but is now lost" evokes George Berkeley's famous condemnation of Newton's model. In 1734, Berkeley had mounted a vigorous attack on the paradox Badiou identifies regarding the confusion of limits and limitlessness. Berkeley was addled at the method whereby the calculus reduced tiny (in the language of calculus, "infinitesimally small") quantities to zero. What are these "evanescent increments," Berkeley wondered? "They are neither finite Quantities, nor Quantities infinitely small, nor yet nothing. May we not call them the Ghosts of departed Quantities?"[56] If fluxions charted history by reducing these quanta to zero and then graphing them into the diagrammatic shape of moving lines, then Berkeley's concern, we might say, was with the casualties or "specters" of history whose departure makes the progress of points and lines possible. This was an injustice of signs, Berkeley believed, a war of the imagination: "Men

. . . often impose on themselves and others, as if they conceived and understood things expressed by Signs, when in truth they have no Idea, save only of the Signs themselves."[57] For Berkeley, the fluxional calculus was a chimera of psychedelic semiosis, a mechanism of erasure under the auspice of memory, an algebraic romance speciously accorded the imprimatur of Euclid.

The precept Berkeley espoused here—commensurate with the idea for which he is probably most widely remembered—is that mathematical entities like geometric figures are objects of perception, however "immaterial" such objects may be.[58] Alas, he observed, in concocting "evanescent increments," practitioners of calculus leap from ideal perceptions to fantastical romances, creating unprovable theories to maintain the illusion of reality. Berkeley enunciated this gripe as a Catholic bishop as well as a philosopher; his complaint with fluxions was not solely that calculus was illogical but also that its operations required a kind of faith—the same sort of faith, he claimed, that calculus-loving free-thinkers—natural philosophers—were denouncing in religion.[59]

This is not to say that Newton ever imagined himself becoming the patron saint of atheists. He believed that fluxions enabled one to chart not only the motion of the planets but also the designs of deity in interacting with the universal creation.[60] However, Newton formulated these ideas at a historical moment when such "designs" were beginning to accommodate not only metaphysical and religious speculation but also secular schemes pertaining to natural science and, Baucom reminds us, high finance. Calculus, that is, unveiled the hand of God and also projected the "invisible hand" of the market—an unintended consequence of Newton's mathematical theodicy.

In key ways, then, Berkeley's critique of Newton resonates with Baucom's of Scott: at stake are the abuses of faith, or narrative, in obscuring unresolved irrational sequences (in fluxions) and actual lived history (in Scott's historical fiction and, more generally, in the history of economic speculation). Indeed, and in conformity with what Baucom calls Scott's "romantic historicism," Newton's geometric points—the reduction of numbers to coordinates—amounted to "types" of what *should be* actual positions on a graph. Fluxions, Baucom and Berkeley might say, thus attempted a recuperative or "redemptive" geometry but instead gave us mere "romance," a fiction. (In that respect, Maclaurin's elaborate defense of the geometry of fluxions was as quixotic as Matthew Stewart's geometric calculus of the moon's apsis.)

But fluxions were romantic for a reason, Maclaurin implied. They made movement through time—history—seem "evident" at a moment when the past seemed increasingly to be receding. And while it is true that Newton never fully resolved the quandaries fluxions entailed (of limits and infinitesimals—problems that would only arrive at full resolution with Cauchy in the early nineteenth century), the interpretive path of geometric calculus still opened onto a "romantic" outcome other than representational untruth. I say "romantic" because Maclaurin differentiated fluxional geometry from the vulgar realism of "tangible magnitude[s]," a reductive appeal to the senses exemplified, he argued, by Berkeley's theory of vision.[61] Such materialism incurred the specter of infinitesimals, those "ghosts of departed quantities," by floundering over the logical existence of quantities that diminish beyond the power of perception. In fluxions, by contrast, "a surface is not considered . . . as a body of the least sensible magnitude, but as the termination or boundary of a body"; the same may be said of lines relative to breadth and of points relative to lines (1:245). In this way, Maclaurin asserts, fluxions evade the aporetic logic of number and infinitude; in their stead, "we conceive . . . quantit[y] to be increased and diminished, or to be wholly generated by motion," or by the tracing of lines and figures. And yet, precisely because fluxions purportedly capture nature's forms in their representational character, they also obviate the perils of mere signification. Hence, where Baucom essentially deconstructs narrative, pointing out the discrepancy between *this* sign and *that* referent (that is, between *this* narrative and *that* group of slaves; *this* mathematical system and *that* lived experience), Maclaurin effectively transposes the medium of historical reflection from symbol (for example, from the correspondence between *this* and *that*) and number (for example, the sequentiality of one period after another) to shape. He thus resolves phenomena into the form of their appearance, which in turn implies duration—in Maclaurin's words, a "motion," a coming-to-be. History in this model is a medium of connection rather than displacement. Its intrinsic logic involves contiguity, not succession: a curve consists of the unity of its relations, not its decomposition into a sequence of points (*pace* the Leibnizian differentials). Symbols involve absence and displacement; shapes imply inclusion and presence. Signs yield "history"; shapes give us "nature."[62]

This was a favorite contention of Newton's Scottish defenders, including Maclaurin in his denunciation of Berkeley: Newton's fluxions provided us with an image of nature and, therefore, with a way to imagine ourselves in it.[63] Relative to Scott and the implicit algebraism of a vein of Scott criticism, fluxions provide a subtle but substantive difference in how we imagine the purport of Scott's work. To understand it through geometric figures (that is, through "curves, indentures, and embayments" rather than, or at least alongside, representative "types") is thus to imagine history as "present"; it is to "see" spots on the globe and moments in time as fields of relation, as parts of a complex system. It is to revise history, literally to see it differently—by seeing it.

It seems significant on this score that *Guy Mannering* dramatizes the subdivision of the landed estate of Ellangowan. Early in the narrative, we are informed that Harry's ancestors "had made war, raised rebellions, been defeated, beheaded, and hanged, as became a family of importance, for many centuries. But they had gradually lost ground in the world, and, from being themselves the heads of treason and traitorous conspiracies, the Bertrams . . . of Ellangowan[] had sunk into subordinate accomplices" (8). This process describes not only the transformations of feudal and class structures in eighteenth-century Scotland but also the evermore constricted angles of modern perception, the diminishing ability of human subjects to comprehend the complexity of everyday life.[64] That this tapering of perspective occurs, paradoxically, during an era when increasing global exploration and new mathematical theories were expanding the general knowledge of the universe suggests that historical consciousness and the attendant historicist amnesia that Baucom analyzes—history, that is, as a model of serial displacements—is itself a kind of traumatic symptom, a defensive retreat from a world overwhelming our powers of comprehension.[65]

The plot of *Guy Mannering* accounts for such lacunae in consciousness. It works its way, Jane Millgate observes, through "a sixteen-year time gap at its centre," the period when the infant Harry is whisked away by the smugglers until the time when he returns to claim his family's estate. Mannering himself "is counterpointed against both Bertrams, father and son."[66] What the novel recounts, therefore, is the conversion of stargazing (which Ian Duncan calls the novel's self-conscious engagement of romance: "No longer having faith in the truth of [astrology, Mannering] engages it . . . as a fiction. Yet—not despite but because of that mode of engagement—all is true"[67]) into material reality, suturing over a void through the line of its narrative. The novel thus reprises the ideological structure of Maclaurin's fluxions, navigating across an imponderable quantum (the purgatory of irrational numbers—metaphysical nonexistence) through the motion of its protagonist.

This is where literary and mathematical history intersect. Think again of the different shapes of Scott's historical fiction: ray, curved line, and curved space. While curved space would introduce unforeseen avenues of inquiry into nineteenth-century mathematics, the fluxional line presented the most nuanced mathematical picture of nature during the long eighteenth century. And this picture was redrawn, strangely, in the early twentieth century, by those for whom the drama intrinsic to the fluxional line (smooth or segmented? representative of or supplementary to nature?) would configure Scott's legacy. I am referring here to Georg Lukàcs and Edwin Muir, critics whose impact on Scott's modern reputation extends the cultural legacy of fluxions into literary history and the twenty-first century. And it is to this broader intellectual history—of fluxions for Scott and of Scott for others—that I turn in the concluding section of this chapter.

Connecting the Dots, or Points: Hume, Scott, Lukács

The fluxional line that Harry beholds as he gazes at the coast of Scotland serves, in *Guy Mannering*, to connect Bertram's familial past to his present and future circumstances, at once *capturing* and *representing* the flow of time. What is more, fluxions here evocatively connect earlier and later chapters of intellectual history, employing Euclid to lay the foundations for postclassical theories of space. On this basis, we might characterize Scott as a writer of historical fiction situated at a threshold moment in history.

To what extent has this morphological-geometric dimension of intellectual history informed Scott's legacy in literary history? That is what I wish to discuss in this last section. The answer in one respect is quite simple: it hasn't, not really. But upon reflection, that answer proves too simple. Because the corollary to *geometric* here is not *literary* but rather *algebraic*, and what I have argued earlier in this chapter is that the algebraic view of Scott, the vision of Scott as an agent of modern dehumanization, has permeated studies of Scott and of the histories in which Scott figures. Baucom's critique here is exemplary but by no means exceptional. And fluxions, I argue, predicated both mathematically and philosophically on the ambiguity and rift between algebra and geometry, present us with a different way to understand Scott's place and possibilities within literary history.

Ian Duncan's analysis of Scott's fiction helps us frame this alternative image of Scott's legacy. While Duncan does not explore the mathematical subtext or ramifications of Scott's work, he does venture onto a philosophical trajectory that eventually leads to the history we have reviewed in this chapter. The immediate backdrop for Scott's fiction, Duncan argues (reprising a virtual consensus among scholars) is the French Revolution, an event that "opened the possibility . . . of a counterhistoriography of violent discontinuity, perpetual crisis: recasting the outline of history from [what Walter Benjamin calls] 'homogeneous, empty time,' the even (if rubble-strewn) gradient of improvement, to the jagged peaks and gulfs of *Jetztzeit*, 'time filled by the presence of the now.'" Scott wrote, Duncan observes, "in the shadow" of this event, seeking "to contain revolution's apocalyptic potential" by "displacing it into the past" and "investing it with the tropes of fiction."[68] That begs the question of the status of fiction in Scott's work, particularly since the category bore such acute ideological importance. And Duncan alerts us to precisely this question. "*Waverley* and its successors do not just fictionalize history—representing the events, figures, forms, and forces that constitute history in the medium of the novel. They historicize fiction as an institution, a set of forms and social practices, which includes as its paradigmatic modern case the novel itself and our act of reading it" (136). Scott's novels "coordinate[] different developmental narratives into a complex whole" (137), presenting their readers with a suite of sensations. These begin with "romantic absorption" in the narrative, then proceed to "disillusioning reflection" on the greater forces of history that constrain romance, and conclude with "a sentimental return to common life that at once reaffirms its historical necessity" but also "recognizes its fictionality." *Waverley* thus imparts a conviction of "the authority as well as the inauthenticity" of the present, "parsed as the authority of custom" (138).

While the novel is "the paradigmatic modern case" of this critical arrangement, it is not that case's conceptual provenance. Duncan shifts the responsibility for Scott's idea of fiction to philosophy and specifically to Hume, who initiates a "crucial dialectic between absorption and reflection," the "double consciousness" that leads to the dubious ratification of custom (131). In *A Treatise of Human Nature*, Duncan argues, Hume elaborates a modern concept of fiction as what "designate[s] a cognitive engagement with reality rather than, as in Platonic or Christian conceptions, the falsification of a reality guaranteed by metaphysical forms of truth" (124). Fiction, for Hume, is an operation of mind of such wide reach that "an opinion or belief is nothing but an idea, that is different from a fiction, not in the nature, or the order of its parts, but in the *manner* of its being conceiv'd."[69] Belief simply invests fictions—cognition's organizing of experience into coherent patterns—with "more force and influence; makes them appear of greater importance; infixes them in the mind; and renders them the governing principles of all our actions" (146–47).

Fiction is therefore, for Hume—as, later, for Scott—what Fredric Jameson calls "the central function or *instance* of the human mind," the coming-to-form of all thought.[70] But fiction in Hume's *Treatise* devolves on a larger discussion of space and time, which returns us once again to the debate surrounding fluxions. This is not to say that Hume takes up fluxions directly in the *Treatise* or that they comprise the immediate context for Hume's discussion of fiction. The connection to fluxions is rather more elliptical, unfolding by way of philosophy rather than mathematics. And that discussion helps explain the logic of Hume's appeal to fiction in Part III of Book I of the *Treatise*, "Of knowledge and probability." The larger design of Book I, "Of the Understanding," is important to bear in mind: it begins, in Part I, with "Of ideas, their origin, composition, connexion, abstraction, &c" before shifting, in Part II, to "Of the ideas of space and time." It is the unit on space and time, in other words, that links Hume's analysis of the mind's building blocks to its organization of them, in Part III, by way of fiction. The unit on space and time, then, operates at a kind of meta-fictional level: in lending shape (in Part III) to the elements of cognition (outlined in Part I), it does for fiction what fiction does for belief or for any intellectual system: it at once absorbs us into a larger system and allows us to reflect on that system. For Hume, space and time help convert experience into meaning.

How do they do this? Hume provides a clue in the titles of the first two sections of the unit, each of which pertains to divisibility: "Of the infinite divisibility of our ideas of space and time" and "Of the infinite divisibility of space and time." Hume's aim in each chapter is to attack the idea of infinite divisibility, which is to say, of the infinite. He explains how, experientially, we reach a point beyond which it no longer makes sense to divide an entity: "Put a spot of ink upon a paper, fix your eye upon that spot, and retire to such a distance, that at last you lose sight of it; 'tis plain, that the moment before it vanish'd the image or impression was perfectly indivisible" (76). A detailed exposition of Hume's arguments on this subject exceeds our purposes here, but his aim, consistently with other sections of the *Treatise*, is to leverage experience against both realist and idealist conceptions of nature, thus situating cognition on the uncertain footing of fiction (and, therefore, of custom).[71] But three points deserve particular mention.

First, it is in these sections of the *Treatise* that Hume first begins making use of the terms "fiction" and "fictitious." In discussing the paradox obtaining between the metaphysical idea of unity as an indivisible whole and the elements of which such wholes may nevertheless be made, Hume observes that the "term of unity is merely a fictitious denomination, which the mind may apply to any quantity of objects it collects together" (79). (For instance, "'Tis evident, that existence in itself belongs only to unity, and is never applicable to number, but on account of the unites [or 'units'], of which the number is compos'd. Twenty men may be said to exist; but 'tis only because one, two, three, four, &c. are existent; and if you deny the existence of the latter, that of the former falls of course" [79].) The following section takes up the subject of duration, the temporal corollary to (spatial) extension. There, Hume addresses those "who pretend, that the idea of duration is applicable in a proper sense to objects, which are perfectly unchangeable." But duration, Hume argues, "is always deriv'd from a succession of changeable objects." Therefore, we "can never without a fiction" apply the idea of duration to, or derive it from, any object we imagine as unchanging (86). Fiction in this section is an explicit synonym of "falsehood" rather than of the more nuanced cognitive process Duncan describes. But Hume's analysis of space and time lays the groundwork for the later, more widely discussed passages in Book I that pertain to identity—specifically, identity's extension and duration (identity being "nothing but a bundle or collection of different perceptions, which succeed each other with an inconceivable rapidity" [300])—where fiction comes more dynamically into play. In other words, when Hume arrives at his most eloquent exposition of fiction, it is as a derivative of his analysis of space and time. Fiction, in the narrow sense of falsehood, informs metaphysical ideas about space and time, but fiction in the broader sense of dialectical engagement is little more than space and time properly understood.

Second, Hume frequently returns in these sections on space and time to the example of geometry. This is partly due to geometry's reputation for reconciling reason and experience and partly because of its status as a battlefield where discussions over divisibility and infinitude played out, as we discussed above relative to Berkeley's intervention in the calculus debate. Hume had Berkeley very much in mind in composing these sections of the *Treatise*, and his implicit foil here, at least in part, was Maclaurin. Geometry therefore provided Hume with an especially fertile soil for the discussion of metaphysics (that is, philosophical tradition) as well as new theories, like his own, about the workings of the mind.

These subtexts become apparent when we review some of the ways that Hume engages geometry. In one representative passage, he evokes the definitions of point, line, and surface and then denounces the strictly rational definition of these imagined objects as "mere ideas in the mind" that "not only never did, but never can exist in nature." To the contrary, Hume contends, "[w]hatever can be conceiv'd by a clear and distinct idea necessarily implies the possibility of existence" (91). This does not mean, however, that geometry is an entirely accurate science. "When geometry decides any thing concerning the proportions of quantity, we ought not to look for the utmost *precision* and exactness. None of its proofs extend so far" (93, Hume's emphasis). For example, Hume addresses the geometric precept that we may measure equality by determining proportions—"that any two figures are equal when upon the placing of one upon the other, all their parts correspond to and touch each other" (94). The problem with this procedure, Hume argues, is that "this imaginary application and mutual contact of parts" presupposes some perception of them, but such perception implies the capacity to distinguish "parts to the greatest minuteness," which we cannot do (94–95). Hence, rather than leverage the rigor of proportions against the metaphysical paradox of irrational numbers, Hume contends that the appeal to geometry is as irrational as the resort to (ontologically) baseless numerical quantities.

Hume's further references to geometry work toward this same end. He effectively deconstructs the difference between curved and straight lines (a well-known geometric puzzle: if lines consist of points, aren't curves merely a series of connected dots—straight lines—too minute for us to discern?) by claiming "that we form the loose idea of a perfect standard to these figures, without being able to explain or comprehend it" (98). He takes on Euclid's famed parallel postulate by asking how it might be proved "that two right lines cannot have one common segment" or a point at which they eventually meet (99). "Or that 'tis impossible to draw more than one right line betwixt two points" (99). (Cannot we place one line on top of another or wrap it around the outside of a sphere, as Reid would later suggest?) He concludes that such assertions are contrary to our experience in nature. And this means they also are, or should be, contrary to geometry, whose "first principles are founded on the imagination and the senses" (101). He returns to this argument at the beginning of Part III, where he formally raises the problematic of fiction, remarking that while geometry "much excels both in universality and exactness, the loose judgments of the senses and imagination[, it] never attains a perfect precision and exactness." This is because "[i]ts first principles are still drawn from the general appearance of objects" (118). Algebra and arithmetic are a little different, for there "we may carry on a chain of reasoning" with a "degree of intricacy, and yet preserve a perfect exactness and certainty" (119). But geometry is ultimately more illustrative of the workings of the mind, for its genesis in perception underscores Hume's argument "that all our ideas are copy'd from our impressions" (120, emphases deleted). And so it is little use pretending, as some mathematicians are wont to do, "that those ideas, which are their objects, are of so refin'd and spiritual a nature, that they fall not under the conception of the fancy" (120). All mathematics involves the extrapolation of ideas from experience. All geometric constructs are therefore fictions of the imagination; indeed, they provide the very model of such fictions.

Hume recapitulated here a common tendency of the "Scotch metaphysics" to probe the "intellectual foundations" of experience.[72] But rather than anchor those foundations in geometry, he tectonically shifted geometry to the unstable platform of fiction. His foil here was Maclaurin. George Davie argues that Maclaurin and other Scottish philosophers like George Turnbull were "just as much taken as Hume was with the notion of introducing the method of experimental reasoning into moral subjects, and of thereby doing for the problem of mind what Newton had done for the problem of matter."[73] Maclaurin, already familiar with *The Analyst*, was critical of Berkeley's philosophical project generally, and he saw Hume's work "merely as an attempt to continue and improve on Berkeley," specifically in "the tendency to explain away common sense as a fiction" (Davie 19).

And this leads us, after our discussion of fiction and geometry, to the third point we wished to underscore in the sections on space and time. And that point concerns the presence of the calculus debate as a backdrop to Hume's *Treatise*. We have already seen how Hume lights on topics that figured prominently in that debate—the problem of succession, the nature of the line, the viability of geometry and algebra alongside each other, and so on. In the final section on space and time, Hume also takes on a subject that Maclaurin would feature a decade later in his 1748 *An Account of Sir Isaac Newton's Philosophical Discoveries*, namely the squabble over whether space consisted of a vacuum or a plenum (see *Treatise* 102ff.). Maclaurin devotes extensive attention to this subject because it had featured in the dispute between Leibniz and Newton (and their followers)—a disagreement that concerned not only space but also the Cartesian legacy in mathematics. I will briefly discuss that subject in Chapter 5. Here, I will remark simply that while Hume does not defend Newton with the same vigor as Maclaurin, he essentially justifies Newton on different grounds, observing, Davie says, "that Newton's system works quite well without the sort of" metaphysical vacuum Maclaurin and Leibniz have in mind (Davie 24). Hume's larger aim, as Maclaurin correctly intuited, was to refashion thinking about common sense, and yet, he did not wish to dispense with it altogether: "Hume would seem to be sometimes siding with those who prefer . . . common sense to Berkeley, sometimes with those who prefer Berkeley to common sense" (Davie 25). What seems most important in all this, at least for our discussion here, is that Hume appears to have assimilated the philosophical implications of the dispute between Newton and Leibniz to the extent that he could turn questions about motion and infinitesimals to the movement not only of points but also of thoughts and the segmenting not only of lines but also of identities. Hence, in the place of a full mathematical disquisition of the subject, such as Maclaurin gives with his *Treatise of Fluxions*, Hume provides instead a theory of fiction—of the motions of mind that are grounded no more firmly on solid reason than fluxional equations are on an adequate concept of number. It is this legacy, Duncan says, that Hume bequeaths to Scott. And at the core of Scott's Humean concept of fiction, I am arguing, is an embedded history surrounding geometry.

This forms an important backdrop to Duncan's argument about the Humean-philosophical valences of Scott's theory of fiction, and it complicates the implicitly algebraic tenets that have inscribed themselves into the criticism of Scott's role in literary history. The geometric facets of the philosophy of fiction that Scott inherited—and modified—also figure crucially into Scott's own distillation of his theory of fiction in the famous "Postscript, which should have been a Preface" that concludes *Waverley*. There, Scott reflects memorably on how "no European nation . . . within the course of half a century or little more, has undergone so complete a change as [the] kingdom of Scotland" after the defeat of the Jacobite Rebellion at Culloden in April 1746 and how it was "for the purpose of preserving some idea of the ancient manners of which [he] had witnessed almost the total extinction" that he crafted his novel.[74] Scott also elicits here the dialectic between romance and history that he adapted and then, for later authors of the nineteenth century, virtually came to personify: "the most romantic parts of this narrative," this history, "are precisely those which have a foundation in fact" (340).

But another, usually overlooked passage sits amid that larger discussion of Scotland and social change, history and romance. And this passage is especially important to our understanding of Scott's concept of fiction:

> The gradual influx of wealth, and extension of commerce, have since united to render the present people of Scotland a class of beings as different from their grandfathers, as the existing English are from those of Queen Elizabeth's time. . . . [This] change, though steadily and rapidly progressive, has, nevertheless, been gradual; and, like those who drift down the stream of a deep and smooth river, we are not aware of the progress we have made until we fix our eye on the now-distant point from which we set out. Such of the present generation as can recollect the last twenty or twenty-five years of the eighteenth century, will be fully sensible of the truth of this statement. (340)[75]

One of Scott's key points here is that change happens almost imperceptibly even when, in retrospect, it seems extraordinarily—unprecedentedly—rapid. Uneven development acquires here a phenomenological as much as a historical cast—and we may not perceive it at all. While "the abolition of the heritable jurisdictions of the Lowland nobility and barons," the "total eradication of the Jacobite party," and the "gradual influx of wealth, and extension of commerce" have drastically transformed the character of the nation (340), these dramatic revolutions of culture and custom bestow a feeling of torpor when taken as incidents or when mediated through the grind of daily life. It is only in hindsight or in narrative that they leave an impression. Change occurs, then, but never to us or never in a way that unites reflection with experience. This is why the signs of change—the "habits, manners, and feelings" of cultures more primitive than our own—seem so uncanny in addition to being so "romantic."

Most central to this passage, however, certainly in light of our discussion earlier in this chapter, is the analogy to a ship-born perspective of the landscape, the "drift[ing] down the stream of a deep and smooth river" that allows us to chart our course through history. The image not only foreshadows the climactic moment in *Guy Mannering* when a similar perspective awakens Harry, and the reader, to an awareness of the history in which they are implicated, but the reference to the "gradual *influx* of wealth" in *Waverley* vividly evokes, first, Hume's assertion of the "perpetual *flux* and movement" that constitutes human identity (see *Treatise* 300) and, second, the mathematics of fluxions whose philosophical dimensions motivated those ideas. At the core of Scott's passage, in other words, is Hume, and at the core of Hume's thought are fluxions. And this makes for a slightly vertiginous but brilliantly indicative rhetorical construct. For, bearing in mind Duncan's distillation of the dialectic intrinsic to Scott's concept of fiction, Scott's explanatory passage on the nature of fiction comments *reflectively* rather than *absorptively*—self-reflexively, we would say, given the virtues of fiction as a reflective exercise—on the genealogy of this concept. Here, and significantly complicating traditional views about Scott's work, fiction bears as its origin not romance only but also philosophy and mathematics. Specifically, it assembles itself on the terrain of the metaphysical dispute surrounding calculus or on the fault line between geometry and algebra.

Note, however, that Scott not only appropriates Hume's concept of fiction but also extends its conceptual reach. For Hume, identity devolves directly on the "flux" of successive impressions: "I never can catch *myself* at any time without a perception, and never can observe any thing but the perception. . . . [S]o long [as I am] insensible of *myself*, [I] may truly be said not to exist" (300, Hume's emphasis). In Scott's "Postscript" in *Waverley*, however, the flux we experience is not born by impressions alone or even primarily (since, as we discussed above, we barely perceive even rapid historical change as it occurs); instead, our identity founds itself on fiction or on the abstraction of experience into narrative. Only in fiction do we truly "drift down the stream of a deep and smooth river . . . [unaware] of the progress we have made until we fix our eye on the now-distant point from which we set out" (*Waverley* 340). Scott thus renders fiction even more central to cognition than does Hume, rendering the fluxional figure at the heart of that concept even more important. Not only, then, is the fluxional line central to the narrative of *Guy Mannering*, but it is axial to Scott's fictive and therefore cognitive imaginary.

This formulation becomes especially compelling when we supplement Scott's concept of fiction with the reception of that fiction in the twentieth century. I mentioned earlier in the chapter that a key text in Scott's resurgence was the 1962 translation of Georg Lukács's landmark book *The Historical Novel*.[76] Lukács undertook "a theoretical examination of the interaction between the historical spirit and the great genres of literature which portray the totality of history," aiming to demonstrate "the actual historical process" in the life of fiction.[77] The historical novel, he argued, is a unique creation—in both literary and historical terms—in that it is a product of history that bears the trace of that history in its very design, not only reflecting but also reflecting *on* that history. It empowers readers to perceive in their own circumstances the grand design of progress. And Scott, Lukács argued, is seminal to our understanding of the form. Tracing the origins of the historical novel to the publication of *Waverley*, Lukács portrays Scott as a happy historical accident, a Tory whose contingencies of taste and judgment enabled him to endorse the British Union and the Hanoverian regime even as he felt a deep sympathy for the mortality of tradition. But Lukács also labeled Scott "a great poet of history," the virtual personification of the historical novel, because he shaped these sensibilities into a narrative form that vividly captured both moments in time and the "necess[ary]" transition of one moment to another (58). Presumably, this sweep of time would implicate even the historical novel itself, rendering Scott at once immortal and ephemeral, the progenitor of a form that captures the history by which it is consumed.

Lukács's portrait of Scott contrasts sharply with the one painted by Edwin Muir at virtually the same time in Muir's 1936 study *Scott and Scotland*. We discussed Muir's argument in Chapter 1, and I return to it here only to indicate a telling contrast between these two critics. Like Lukács, Muir characterized Scott as a figure caught between conflicting aesthetic tendencies. But instead of synthesizing local details with historical necessity, Muir's Scott failed to effectuate such unions, presenting in their place tentative "picture[s] of [historical] life . . . half flesh and blood and half pasteboard."[78] The unevenness of Scott's work could be explained, Muir reasoned, by the "superposition of a complex and exact body of knowledge," cultivated by Scott's legal training, "upon a riotous imagination. . . . It was a superposition," Muir insists, "not a reconciliation such as might have been found in a whole body of experience radiating from a centre in an autonomous society" (127). It was such a "centre," Muir reminds us, that Scotland, and hence Scott, lacked, prompting Muir to turn repeatedly to the image of gaps in Scott's artistic vision: "The hiatus in Scott's novels, the imperviousness of his heroes to the consequences of their actions, cannot be explained," Muir elaborated, "except by the fact that he was brought up in a sort of vacuum, a country without a centre which could gather up within itself and give meaning to all the actions of the people who composed it" (171).

Like Muir, Lukács also acknowledged gaps between the grand design of history and the conceptions held by Scott's characters. But for Lukács, these were "necessary anachronism[s]" that bestowed a "colourful and varied richness" to Scott's work, the "consequence of the multiplicity of . . . interactions between individuals and the unity of [their] social existence. . . . Scott's great art," he contended, "consists precisely in individualizing his historical heroes in such a way that certain, purely individual traits of character . . . are brought into a very complex, lively relationship with the age in which they live" (*Historical Novel* 45, 47). The totality of these actions lends Scott's fiction an "atmosphere of the whole" or spirit of the age (55).

I underscore the disparity between Muir and Lukács, the fragmentary and the whole, because it uncannily resets the mathematical conceits we have been examining in this chapter. Such conceits attend Lukács's insistence on the historical novel's conversion of "quantity into quality"—of political upheaval, for example, into a shared sense of modern life. What Lukács describes through these "conversions" is the emergence of something like historical design from out of the welter of historical details, something like *form* or *shape*, the character of the present, gleaned from its mass.[79] For Lukács, the historical novel deduces such figures, Scott deduces such figures, from the flux of the passage of time, and geometry is the figure, if not the explicit logic, that lends form to Lukács's argument. This makes it easier to understand what Muir, by contrast, is intimating when he explains Scott's failings by citing, twice, Yeats's famous line from "The Second Coming"—"Things fall apart; the centre cannot hold" (*Scott and Scotland* 74, 139)—and when he writes of the "hiatus" in Scott's poetic imagination and of the "blank[ness]" of the nation in which he lived. For Muir, close scrutiny of Scott's work reveals gaps in its conception: shape is an abstraction that obscures a more profound process of decomposition.

This dialectic of form and formlessness between Lukács and Muir evokes the episode in *Waverley* when the Jacobite forces march on Edinburgh. Edward initially views the scene from a distance, the narrator remarking that while the "motions" of the Jacobites "appeared spontaneous and confused, the result was order and regularity; so that a general must have praised the conclusion, though a martinet might have ridiculed the method by which it was attained" (*Waverley* 212). However, "[a] nearer view," which Waverley gains when he descends from his perch on St. Leonard's Hill, "rather diminished the effect impressed on the mind by the more distant appearance of the army" (*Waverley* 213). From this new vantage point, it is that army's *irregularity*, a word Scott repeats several times to indicate the *failure* of the scene to yield an elegant geometric design, that becomes most apparent to Edward, both in the virtual chaos of that army's undirected attacks on the British infantry and in the "half naked, st[u]nted . . . and miserable" spectacle of the individual soldiers. From a distance, Waverley thus beholds the Jacobite cause after the manner of Lukács reading history, but from up close, his view resembles Muir's of the Waverley novels themselves.

To a certain extent, then, the image of the Jacobites in Scott's 1814 novel imparts to both Lukács and Muir the figure by which they would read Scott. But this figure, of course, was not Scott's alone. It belonged more properly to mathematics, where the difference between the continuous line and the dissolution of lines into segments had most vividly animated the dramas surrounding calculus. While I would not argue that Lukács or Muir self-consciously appeals to calculus, it seems significant that calculus furnished perhaps the most compelling historical forum for questions concerning the conversion of quantity into quality, which is to say, of the possibility, interpretation, and meaning of form.

Given how vigorously several of Scott's peers and predecessors (John Playfair, Dugald Stewart, and John Robison; more concertedly, Maclaurin, Robert Simson, and Stewart's father, Matthew) had entered into the calculus debate, the recrudescence of that language in the tacit dialectic between Lukács and Muir over Scott's legacy only lends more depth to the passage from Scott's "Postscript." When one gazes, with Scott's narrator (or, a year later, with Harry Bertram), at the shore while adrift on a body of water—when one confronts such images of abstract motion as a curve along a geometric axis or a figurative passage down the river of history—what exactly is one seeing? A smooth, Lukácsian conversion of differences into a picture of time? Or a Muir-like decomposition of trajectories into a jumble of points reconciled only by their relative contiguity? Hume had set the terms for this debate in his *Treatise of Human Nature* (even arguing there for the dissolution of identities into constellations of contiguous impressions before resolving those impressions, in Book II, back into a fuzzy-mathematical—Lukácsian—version of whole objects). But Hume did so by articulating a theory of fiction. And at the root of that theory were the language and dilemmas surrounding calculus. It was Scott who gave Hume's concept its fullest expression in the long, looping eighteenth century. And in doing so, he brought calculus into literary history. Or, better said, he rendered literary history legible on (mathematical) terms other than its own even as he employed literary history to surpass, or at least evocatively disfigure, the conceptual limits of fluxions. This is what we see in the *Waverley* "Postscript" and in the "curves, indentures, and embayments" in *Guy Mannering*. Those passages change, potentially, how we see Scott's place in literary history. And perhaps they expand the ways we see literary history itself.

PART II

Scholium: Scenes of Writing

Scholium: 1a. An explanatory note or comment. . . . 1b. In certain mathematical works (e.g. Newton's *Principia*): A note added by the author illustrating or further developing some point treated in the text.

—*Oxford English Dictionary*

CHAPTER 3

"Wild Geometry" and the Picturesque

I return again to Edwin Muir, a touchstone in this book. In the summer of 1934, Muir embarked on a commissioned tour through Scotland in an old car loaned to him by Stanley Cursiter. Then serving as director of the Scottish National Gallery, Cursiter was a one-time painter in the Futurist style, and while he had turned more toward traditional landscape forms over the previous two decades, his work still flashed occasional traces of modern influences (Impressionist, Cubist, etc.). Muir would largely follow this lead in his *Scottish Journey*, making a series of straightforwardly realistic observations empirically documenting his excursion with stylistically modernist inflections creeping in at its edges. One such example is found as his narrative nears its conclusion: "I did not find anything which I could call Scotland; anything, that is to say, beyond the vague and wandering image already impressed upon me by memory: the net result of my having been brought up in it, and of living in it until I was nearly thirty, and lastly of belonging to it." But despite this abstract sense of attachment, Muir's "deepest impression," he confided, "was one of emptiness."[1]

Muir published his travel narrative in 1935. The following year, he completed the lengthy essay *Scott and Scotland*, the piece for which he is perhaps best remembered. There, as we have discussed in previous chapters, Muir inflated his feelings of emptiness into the historical and even ontological condition of the nation he had claimed he could not find, and he attributed them to Walter Scott, the writer best known for recounting the types of Scottish journeys Muir himself had undertaken. The passage bears citing one last time: "The riddle which confronted me in approaching" Scott, Muir related, and as we discussed in Chapter 1, "was to account for a very curious emptiness which I felt behind the wealth of his imagination. . . . I was forced to account for the hiatus in Scott's endowment by considering the environment in which he lived, by invoking the fact . . . that he spent most of his days in a hiatus, in a country, that is to say, which was neither a nation nor a province, and had, instead of a centre, a blank, an Edinburgh, in the middle of it."[2]

What makes this "emptiness" most "curious" is the fact that it is not exactly the "blank" Muir declares it to be. It comprises a substantive, a common noun—"*an* Edinburgh"—which consists of a series of negations: Muir calls it "a community which was not a community . . . a tradition which was not a tradition" (12). The structure of Muir's locution thus resembles his description of Scott's work in presenting form without content, circumference without center. Muir was drawn to such paradoxes. In his 1920 book *We Moderns*, for example, he writes of the bidirectionality of time: "We have still, then, to go back—or, rather, forward—to Goethe, Ibsen and Nietzsche," whose dispositions were more modern than our own. Later in that same book, he remarks that literary masterpieces elude literary standards inasmuch as the former create the latter; hence, great works exist outside themselves or outside the category by which we eventually know them.[3]

Forward and back, inside and outside—in *Scott and Scotland*, centrality and emptiness: Muir's criticism identifies a peculiar conjuncture of vitiation and innovation, a desolate national culture made perpetually new—newly desolate. And it does so by tracing a series of recursive lines and polymorphic figures that more closely resemble topological structures, perhaps, or Möbius strips than classical shapes. "Scott" and "Scotland" for Muir were thus less "empty" than geometrically uncanny. And the year prior to his dour assessment of Scott, Muir had more enthusiastically employed similar language in describing the Highland landscape on his Scottish journey. "The ordinary sensations which mountains arouse do not fit these extraordinary rock shapes," Muir lyrically observed,

> and yet they are not terrifying in any way, but merely strange beyond the power of the mind to fathom. Part of their strangeness may, no doubt, be explained by the abruptness with which they start up out of places which seem to have no connection with them. The movement of wild mountain scenery is generally a tossing movement as of waves. . . . [T]he summits of which I have been speaking rise out of these billows like rocks out of a sea and seem to . . .

> belong to a different order. They are bold and regular and yet unexpected in their shape, as if they were the result of a wild kind of geometry. One sees huge cones with their tops smoothly sliced off to form a circular plateau, gigantic pyramids, and even shapes that seem top-heavy, so that one cannot understand on what principle they remain upright. . . . The thoughts they evoke are neither heavenly nor terrifying, but have a sort of objective strangeness and give one the same feeling one might have if one could have a glimpse of an eternal world, such as the world of mathematics, which had no relation to our human feelings, but was composed of certain shapes which existed in complete changeless autonomy. (*Scottish Journey* 212–13)

Here, anticipating Scott's centerless circumferences, we behold a landscape of morphological abstraction evocative not only of a long history of Highland travel writing (one thinks of Samuel Johnson's observations concerning the unnerving, treeless sterility of the region, which I will discuss below) but also of the types of autonomous forms with which such critics as Clement Greenberg identified the work of the avant-garde, those "wild geometries" of Cubism, Futurism, and Expressionism. As Greenberg remarked in his famous 1939 essay "Avant-Garde and Kitsch," "It has been in search of the absolute that the avant-garde has arrived at 'abstract' or 'non-objective' art. . . . The avant-garde poet or artist tries . . . to imitate God by creating something valid solely on its own terms, in the way nature itself is valid, in the way a landscape—not its picture—is aesthetically valid; [that is, as] something given . . . [something] independent of meanings, similars or originals."[4] For Muir, this is what nature itself had done in shaping Highland topography.

Greenberg's pictureless and Muir's nationless landscapes share a common expository logic, down to the mutual affirmation of their converse assertions: for Muir, it is the abstraction of Scottish scenery from Scotland that makes Scotland the historical emblem of "wild . . . geometr[ies]" and abstract forms—those same forms, for Greenberg, whose "valid[ity]" as land- (or art-) scapes derives from their status as pure images, as pictures of nothing other than themselves. Muir's Scott, the purveyor of strange shapes (those centerless circumferences), thus becomes the laureate of modernism.[5] However, and employing Muir's terminology from *We Moderns*, this is a modernism set not forward, in the twentieth century, but backward to a time even before Scott began writing his fiction, specifically to the period of the late eighteenth century. I say this because Muir's portrait of rugged scenery and wild geometry provokes "thoughts . . . neither heavenly nor terrifying," neither beautiful nor sublime. Historically speaking, this median position marks the place of the picturesque, which emerged as an aesthetic category over the course of the eighteenth century and most vividly in the 1780s and 1790s.

What I wish here is less to evoke a teleology that culminates in modernism than to instill an appreciation, prompted by recalcitrant traces of the picturesque in Muir's thinking *about* modernism, of the complex ideas and associations accruing to shape in the late eighteenth century. To be sure, the picturesque has attracted a great deal of scholarly attention in recent decades. And yet, because the mathematical (particularly the geometric) aspects of that movement have gone relatively unremarked, its range of intellectual, cultural, and literary implications has been somewhat restricted. Or so I hope to reveal. This is not to say that the geometrics of picturesque representation have gone entirely overlooked: scholars habitually call attention to the perspective of the painter, the idealized status (the careful proportions) of the "middle distance" in picturesque paintings, and the movement's departure from the neatly delineated gardens that were so fashionable earlier in the eighteenth century. Matthew H. Edney has taken the additional step of showing how the picturesque emerged in conformity with cartography, for which geometry served as a privileged mode of abstraction.[6] But even here, geometry retains its stereotype as a rational, instrumentalizing discipline when, as we have seen and as becomes more apparent in the aesthetics of the picturesque, late Euclidean thought and expression were anxiously indeterminate and even experimental exercises. In them, as Scott shows in *Guy Mannering*, reflection begins literally to turn around and gaze at itself—a non-Euclidean reflex that has become a virtual second "nature" in modern art.

The shapes of the modern world are matters about which Scottish Enlightenment literati thought theoretically and self-consciously. Geometry permeated Scottish intellectual life, from the "mathematical cosmography" informing ventures in astronomy and mapmaking to such projects in urban planning as Edinburgh's New Town, designed according to classically geometric grids.[7] So pervasive was "the geometrical tradition in Scotland in the eighteenth and nineteenth centuries," Murdo Macdonald observes, that it made up a significant "part of the intellectual heritage of every Scottish artist" as well as that of the nation's "architect[s] and engineer[s]."[8] Geometry was a language of science and art, and of the science *of* art: aesthetics.

But this "intellectual heritage" was an increasingly vexed subject in the later eighteenth century. This helps explain why Uvedale Price, who helped articulate a distinctive idea of the picturesque, distinguished the latter's images from the smooth curves one associates with geometric calculus: "the neglect . . . of all that is picturesque, is owing to . . . exclusive attention to high polish and flowing lines," whereas "the two opposite qualities of roughness, and of sudden variation, joined to that of irregularity, are the most efficient causes of the picturesque."[9] And yet, Price still drew upon geometry in delineating this new category:

> Formerly, every thing was in squares and parallelograms; now every thing is in segments of circles, and ellipses: the formality still remains; the character of that formality alone is changed. The old canal, for instance, has lost, indeed, its straitness and its angles; but it is become regularly serpentine, and the edges remain as naked, and as uniform as before: avenues, vistas, and strait ridings through woods, are exchanged, for clumps, belts, and circular roads and plantations of every kind: strait alleys in gardens, and the platform of the old terrace, for the curves of the gravel walk. (247, original spelling retained)

The old geometry is passing from view, but we perceive new shapes in its place: "regularly serpentine" canals, "segments . . . and ellipses"—in the words of Scott's *Guy Mannering*, "curves, indentures, and embayments."[10]

What Price tried to capture here was a visceral aesthetic, one of perception rather than reflective ratiocination. Hence, he remarked, the picturesque "hold[s] a station between beauty and sublimity; and, on that account, perhaps, is more frequently, and more happily blended with them both, than they are with each other" (82). The picturesque melded what might be *seen* with what must be *felt*. Price influenced Scott, who would recapitulate Price's idea concerning the new geometry of the picturesque in an 1827 essay on the cultivation of wastelands published in *The Quarterly Review*. There, Scott expressed disdain for the gardening principles of "straight lines and sharp angles" as fit only for types like "Uncle Toby" from Laurence Sterne's *Tristram Shandy*. For "it is as impossible to draw straight lines of wood . . . as it would be to draw a correct diagram on a crumpled sheet of paper. . . . Such," Scott concludes, is "as much at variance with Euclid as with nature."[11] Thirteen years earlier, Scott had undertaken a picturesque tour of Shetland, the Orkneys, and the Hebrides in the late summer months of 1814, after completing *Waverley* and before commencing *Guy Mannering*, and much of the language of that tour works its way into Scott's second novel.[12]

And so, when Scott's protagonist Harry Bertram gazes at the shoreline, as we discussed in Chapter 2, he was beholding a picturesque scene whose striking features consisted not only of Price's "clumps" and "belts" but also, and trailing outwardly from them, the mathematical conundrums that accorded these visceral shapes a heightened sense of meaning and mystery. This complicates a stubbornly enduring image of the picturesque as a relatively tame (indeed, instrumentalizing) aesthetic that converted nature's wildness into a resource fit for the consumption of an urban, middle-class viewer. In the mathematically inflected philosophy of the Scottish Enlightenment, for example, geometry did not "tame" algebra (or suppress mathematical innovation) as much as stage a drama of appearance, a drama *about* appearance. My aim in this chapter is to unpack this logic—to show how the "wild geometry" that so beguiled Muir and that Scott seemed to propagate was less a product of remote genius than a feature of the intellectual landscape in Scotland's long, looping eighteenth century, its Age of Union.

Presenting the Unpresentable

In a chapter of *Waverley* entitled "Highland Minstrelsy," Scott leads his protagonist out of a Highland castle, through a "wild, bleak, and narrow valley," past two brooks (one "placid," the other "all foam and uproar"), and into a "land of romance." This *locus amoenus* consists of rocks of "a thousand . . . varied forms," a "forbid[ding]" crag, and a dizzying chasm with "a rustic bridge" made of two overlaid pines, all of which form a kind of "sylvan amphitheatre" in which the ravishing Flora Mac-Ivor charms young Edward Waverley into temporarily taking up the Jacobite cause.[13] The scene is "roman[tic]" for it exists nowhere as such but is instead composed of commonplaces from the growing body of eighteenth- and early nineteenth-century travel literature about Scotland. Accordingly, the scene is in some ways thoroughly typical. It unites such reputed antitheses as Highland and Lowland (in labeling Flora's bardic, Ossianic song a "minstrel" production), Celtic and Saxon (in the "fur[y]" of the one stream and the "sullen" character of the other), and Jacobite and Whig (in the prospective merger of Flora and

Edward). What is more, by 1814, when *Waverley* was published, these romantic features already characterized Scott's own work, representing something of a command performance of the imagery of his popular 1810 poem *The Lady of the Lake*. Indeed, Scott's work operated here in something of a feedback loop: John Glendening remarks that it "helped make Scotland not merely acceptable to England but powerfully desirable," fueling a tourist industry from whose literature Scott's own poetry and fiction had initially drawn sustenance.[14]

This recursive loop between Scott's work and the picturesque is interesting not because it is unique—many texts from the romantic period abound in striking natural imagery—but rather because the discursive structure of this imagery, this "*scene* of *writing*" (to borrow an expression from Jacques Derrida), has come to inform the very concept of Scottish Romanticism itself.[15] Scott's chapter on "Highland Minstrelsy" provides a fortuitous template here, for it exhibits a curious hallmark of travel writing in the picturesque mode, teeming with topographical types—in visual tropes, as it were—but also imparting a sense that we behold more than meets the eye. Or rather, in this instance and arguably in Scottish Romanticism generally, the "more" is precisely what the eye beholds. As Murray Pittock argues, while Scott appears to present a "union landscape," melding diverse historical elements with the strokes of a pen, and while he thus succeeds in suppressing certain refractory political and cultural elements of this history, it is also true that the visual features Scott describes possess a logic—and even "voices"—of their own. "One can suppress the terrible, sublime, threatening, alien, and Gaelic qualities of Jacobitism with relief and sympathy, but how does one suppress" the Scottish landscape itself?[16] By the time Scott was writing, the Scottish Highlands especially conjured associations less of beauty—and of the harmonizing, unionizing poetics Scott mapped onto it—than of sublimity. Sublime imagery, however, was a virtual oxymoron inasmuch as sublimity designated the putative limits of visual conception, an excess of stimuli reprocessed as sentiment but also, notably, as sound. In Part Five of *A Philosophical Enquiry*, Edmund Burke associated sublimity with Milton's resonant blank verse; in Scottish writing, sublime Highland scenery—its assemblage of mountains, heaths, winds, and waters—accorded topographical atmosphere to numerous texts, perhaps most famously the orotund *Ossian* of James Macpherson.[17] Flora's theatrical song in Scott's "Highland Minstrelsy" episode, for example, draws upon Macpherson as well as travel literature references to Ossian's Hall, a viewing room over the dramatic Falls of the

Bran on the estate of the Duke of Athol.[18] Within the context of *Waverley*, then, Flora's performance amounts to Scott's illustration of a web of sensual and cultural associations that can be neither narrated nor illustrated, not fully: it is a presentation, Jean-François Lyotard would say, of the fact that the unpresentable exists.[19]

This is one of Lyotard's formulations of postmodernism (consubstantial for Lyotard with the experimental school of modernism), which he portrays as an extension of the eighteenth-century category of the sublime, connecting Burke and Kant to the white squares of the Suprematist painter K. S. Malevitch.[20] What most interests me here is less Lyotard's specific argument than the mottled nature of his category: it seems less descriptive of the sublime than the picturesque, which in the romantic period expressly concerned itself with the challenges of representation. "In the early decades of the eighteenth century," Walter John Hipple observed in his half-century-old landmark study, the term "picturesque" "usually bore one of two meanings: when applied to literary style, it meant 'vivid' or 'graphic,' by an obvious metaphor; when applied to scenes in nature, and sometimes when applied to imitations of these on canvas or in words, it meant 'eminently suitable for pictorial representation,' as affording a well-composed picture."[21] Later in the century, in the treatises on landscape and travel that brought the picturesque into the lexicon of aesthetic discourse, the term increasingly occupied a philosophical position between the beautiful and the sublime. William Gilpin, whose tours across Britain helped affix the language and customs of travel through Scotland, sought to carve an autonomous niche for the picturesque by distinguishing those objects "illustrated in painting" from those "which please the eye in their natural state," assigning the picturesque to the province of art.[22] His touchstone for making this case, however, was beauty—beautiful objects *versus* beautiful representations—whereas for Price, who also forged a distinct place for the picturesque, the category tended more toward the sublime. "A temple or palace of Grecian architecture in its perfect entire state, and its surface and colour smooth and even, either in painting or reality, is beautiful; in ruin it is picturesque." The latter involves roughness, irregularity, and "intricacy," which denotes "a partial and uncertain concealment" rather than classic hallmarks of the beautiful like "high polish and flowing lines."[23] Hence, for Price, what we behold in the picturesque is concealment made manifest, a vivid rendering of gloom—which is to say, in Lyotard's terminology, a presentation of the otherwise unpresentable.[24]

The "clumps, belts and circular roads" to which Price refers thus represent shapes we behold in nature but not in traditional geometry; they represent objects we perceive without being able fully to conceptualize. For Price, picturesque forms evoke the sublime as much as or more than the beautiful. Gilpin adopts similar language in the term "roughness," but since "roughness relates only to the surfaces of bodies[,] when we speak of their delineation," or geometric properties, "we use the word *ruggedness.*" We confront rough or rugged objects in the "bark of a tree, as in the rude summit, and craggy sides of a mountain" (*Three Essays* 6–7, Gilpin's emphasis). But to the degree that these characteristics evoke the sense of touch as well as sight, they evade or at least complicate the logic of classical geometric observation. This leads Michel Foucault, alluding to Diderot's *Letter on Blindness*, to quip that "the blind man in the eighteenth century can perfectly well be a geometrician, but he cannot be a naturalist."[25]

Price and Foucault generally take the same line of argument as Benoit Mandelbrot, who began outlining his theory of fractal geometry in the 1950s by asserting that Euclidean practice is "cold" and "dry" inasmuch as it fails "to describe the shape of a cloud, a mountain, a coastline, or a tree." This is because "[c]louds are not spheres, mountains are not cones, coastlines are not circles, and bark is not smooth, nor does lightning travel in a straight line."[26] Simply put, nature surpasses artifice in its design and complexity. Gilpin, however, inverts this hierarchy. It may be, he says, that smooth, Euclidean shapes exist in nature; one finds them in gardens, for example. And, when we behold them, "[t]he shape is pleasing; the combination of the objects, harmonious; and the winding of the walk in [conformity with the Hogarthian, serpentine] line of beauty" (to which Scott also alludes, as we discussed in Chapter 2). And yet, "the smoothness of the whole, tho right *and as it should be in nature*, offends in picture" (*Three Essays* 8, my emphases). Euclid may be natural, but art supersedes nature. Hence, Gilpin's conception of the picturesque is, after a fashion, non-Euclidean. Or rather, it is late Euclidean: without formulating new paradigms, it breaches the limits of the old geometry in its practice if not, yet, in its theory.

This is an important part of the historical process of abstraction, with art detaching itself from the object (in this case, the "nature") it otherwise purports to imitate. Sidney K. Robinson accordingly describes the picturesque as "a mode of composition that stands next to nature, but does not imagine [itself as] natural."[27] This is the logic of the "effect" in Gilpin's work, Kim Ian Michasiw argues, the effect representing the "contingent, non-self-identical conception of the object's identity" or the power of picturesque representations to move us *as art*.[28] While Greenberg, we saw, discerned an embryonic stage of the avant-garde in these abstractive, quasi-natural effects (thus expressing interest in what they would eventually become), Michasiw highlights the late Euclidean view that these effects "trace . . . the object's flight," revealing the irreducibility of nature to representation. The picturesque highlights the interaction between art and nature, which is why Scott, in Michasiw's eyes, is such a brilliant literary expositor of the movement. Scott structured his novels around "the interrelations between his English heroes' picturesque discourse and their capacity to be drawn out of themselves and into complicity . . . with another, oppositional cultural form."[29] In essence, Scott mastered the purportedly unresolved dialectic of object and effect, the play between presentation and unpresentability that characterized the late Euclidean techniques of the picturesque.

But we might also invert that proposition and assert that "late" Euclideanism presented itself in almost picturesque terms. Consider the case of John Leslie, who assumed the chair of mathematics at the University of Edinburgh in 1805. His signature early publication was an 1809 edition of (and an expansion upon) Euclid's *Elements* in which Leslie acknowledged both the belatedness and the aesthetic qualities of his science: "We should form a wrong estimate . . . did we consider the Elements of Euclid, with all its merits, as a finished production. That admirable work was composed at the period when geometry was making its most rapid advances, and new prospects were opening on every side. No wonder that its structure should now seem loose and defective."[30] More than his contemporary John Playfair, whom he replaced as chair of mathematics and who invoked the limitations of Euclidean geometry in order to promote new algebraic techniques in Scottish geometric practice, Leslie strove to wed modern innovations (in his case, regarding the presentation of proportionals and ratios) to "the spirit of the original" (vii), however much the latter may have fallen into a state of comparative ruin.[31] "The study of Mathematics holds forth two capital objects:—While it traces the beautiful relations of figure and quantity, it likewise accustoms the mind to the invaluable exercise of patient attention and accurate reasoning" (v–vi). Geometry "bear[s] the stamp" of the classical civilization that excelled at such practices and whose desuetude had rendered it newly fashionable in the form of (a necessarily) *neo*classicism. For Leslie, a modernized (or what I am calling a late) Euclid merges natural beauty—"the beautiful relations of figure and quantity"—with technique. There is, therefore, something of Gilpin's logic in Leslie's conception. Leslie declares that "[o]ur knowledge respecting external objects is grounded entirely on the information received through the medium of the senses." This includes geometry, which "is that branch of natural science which treats of figured space" (1). But where "[t]he science of physics considers bodies as they actually exist," geometry "contemplates merely the forms which bodies present, and the spaces which they occupy" (1–2). Geometry is thus "founded on external observation" but in an abstracted, beautified way. Geometry, Gilpin would say, is an "effect" of nature.

Playfair disputed Leslie's contention that geometry is empirical at root, but Leslie's views represent, if anything, less a divergence from than an embellishment of widely held Scottish Enlightenment beliefs that geometry squared perception with thought and mind with world.[32] (George Davie, for example, discusses how Robert Simson argued that from bodies, one derives surfaces, from surfaces lines, and from lines points. In other words, geometric categories represent a series of ever-more refined abstractions of our experience of material objects.[33]) For Leslie, we might say, geometry was thus to experience what landscape was to land. So W. J. T. Mitchell prompts us to think in reminding us that the dialectic of nature and artifice, experience and "effect," was implicit in the very idea of landscape, which forms "a medium of exchange between the human and the natural, the self and the other."[34] Picturesque aesthetics effectively "geometrize" the landscape in subjecting the latter to a further, self-reflexive degree of representation (including, in some instances, caricature[35]). As Leslie might have put it, the picturesque "contemplates merely the forms which bodies present, and the spaces which they occupy" (1–2). It converts the *process* of reflection (in the cultivation of nature, its fashioning to meet human needs) into an *object* of reflection, manipulating (and thereby "presenting") the very self-consciousness that was the vehicle of nature's conversion (and which would otherwise be "unpresentable"). The picturesque gives us "nature" as "art" and art as *criticism*, even *theory*.

This phenomenon was perhaps most evident in the technique of perspective, which the picturesque rendered an object of thematic concern by emphasizing the privileged position of the spectator. Artful arrangements of tree and rock, ruin and rustic directed attention to the center of the picture and to the optimal "middle distance" between fore- and background, making nature a *theatron* or "seeing-place" whose end was essentially the viewing experience itself. Picturesque representation was thus an aesthetic corollary to contemporary theories of knowledge that drew upon similar geometric metaphors. Alice Jenkins has written extensively about the "hub-and-ray" model, a metaphor employed by Samuel Taylor Coleridge and Novalis "structur[ing] information . . . in a circular pattern around a central point at which the observer stands." This figure made knowledge seem "accessible, but accessible in a quasi-mystical, visionary way" expressive "of the unity of the human mind"; it resolved a "range of 'multiple viewpoints' . . . into one single, ideal point by arranging the items into a geometric pattern . . . subsumed by symmetry and perspective."[36] The metaphor crafted a "middle distance," as it were, of the understanding.

But as Jenkins recognizes, aesthetic deployments of this trope complicated it. For example, in his *Guide to the Lakes* (1810), William Wordsworth added a third dimension to the "hub-and-ray" by adding height to the plane of vision, compromising the adequacy of geometric abstraction and emphasizing the concrete position of the spectator.[37] And in picturesque representation more generally, the self-reflexivity of the images—the artful arrangement of seeing as an end in itself—rendered the gaze visible, as it were, by objectifying it in the orchestration of natural elements, thus revealing the symbolic properties of perspective. This is how the art historian Erwin Panofsky invoked perspective in a landmark essay of 1924–25, during the period when viewpoint had become the subject of widespread debate and experimentation (in the sciences as well as the arts—hence, for quantum physics and psychoanalysis as much as for Cubism and literary streams of consciousness). Taking the neo-Kantian line that perspective undercuts the objectivist ideal of things-in-themselves (which become the partial products of how we perceive them), Panofsky turned a critical lens onto the geometrics of perspective. Renaissance artists and mathematicians like Albrecht Dürer, who employed Euclidean principles in fashioning the illusion of spatial depth on flat surfaces, understood perspective in its Latin etymology as a "seeing-through," Panofsky remarked, making the appearance of nature in their work the outcome of a process of abstraction. But this in turn involved an insurmountable paradox, which is that this process, which reduces objects to a set of homogeneous points and relations, demands "that from every point in space it must be possible to draw similar figures in all directions and magnitudes."[38] In Jenkins's terms, every ray implies a multitude of hubs. Hence, to "see" through the aid of geometry is not only to apprehend the object but also to catch sight of the apparatus of perception, the structure of any perceptual field. One vantage point thus implies a multitude of others, such that any single (or one-point) perspective is necessarily something more or other than itself. Here, the imitation of nature divulges its own artifice, and classicism opens a window onto the ludic, postclassical manipulation of the conditions of representational possibility. By Panofsky's argument, Dürer confronts Duchamp and Euclid foreshadows all that would come after.[39]

Panofsky thus uncovered the paradox wherein traditional geometry precipitates its own undoing, disclosing itself as a mere "effect." Kant, who set the parameters of Panofsky's argument, invoked a similar paradox in his theory of the mathematical sublime, which pits the imagination, "our power of estimating the magnitude of things" or of placing them in their proper perspective, against reason, which "demands absolute totality as a real idea" or the realization of all perspectives simultaneously. But instead of Panofsky's "play," Kant emphasized the "negative pleasure" we experience in measuring the distance between these exigencies.[40] In this respect, the Kantian sublime was essentially a picturesque "effect": it registered the flight of nature from reason without fully accounting for the difference between them. This in turn may help explain both the presence and the peculiar quality of the sublime in turn-of-the-century treatises on the picturesque. Price, we discussed above, appealed to the sublime as a way of complicating the space of representation, and even Gilpin, whose template was beauty rather than sublimity, identified the agreeable effects of the picturesque with a residual "'irritation' of the senses" or with an inassimilable remainder evocative of the sublime.[41]

Hence, while the language of the picturesque did not really factor into Panofsky's study of perspective, its principles were nevertheless implicit. The mathematization of painting (or the latter's sublimation through mathematics) meant that "the subjective visual impression . . . could itself become the foundation for a solidly grounded and yet, in an entirely modern sense, 'infinite' experiential world" (66). Accordingly, once "perspective ceased to be a technical mathematical problem"—once its principles were understood and incorporated—"it was bound to become all that much more of an artistic problem" (67). Euclidean thought became, in Gilpin's terms, its own "irritant." This is because classical perspective simultaneously asserted and abolished the distance between objects and viewers by "drawing . . . this autonomous world confronting the individual into the eye" (67): nature receded into perception and from there into representation. But instead of simplifying representation by purifying it of extraneous matter (in the manner, Leslie says, of geometric objects), the system began turning on itself.

This is because "the perspectival view of space [could] be contested from two quite different sides: Plato condemned it already in its modest beginnings because it distorted the 'true proportions' of things, and replaced reality . . . with subjective appearance and arbitrariness; whereas the most modern aesthetic thinking accuses it, on the contrary, of being the tool of a limited and limiting rationalism" (71).

Too empirical on the one end, too abstract on the other, perspective itself came to represent a half-formulated perceptual idea (neither wholly sensuous nor cognitive) as well as an uncanny historical artifact (neither wholly classical nor modern). It was late Euclidean in both the phenomenological and chronological senses of that term, involving not only "squares and parallelograms," as Price puts it, but also "segments of circles, and ellipses . . . [and] clumps, belts, and . . . plantations of every kind." Perspective, the hallmark of the picturesque, thus registered the "irritation" of art, its engagement of the world and of thought as a contingent set of "effects."

In the picturesque, then, the objective semblance of the painter's viewpoint discloses the contingency and labor of its own installation: nature reveals itself as artifice. But Scottish Enlightenment literati—moral and Common Sense philosophers, poets, and geometers—subscribed to the belief that artifice is natural to humankind.[42] Each category opens recursively onto the other. This relationship is implicit in the idea of late Euclideanism, which notionally presents traditional geometry at a later or transformed stage of self-reflection (when perspective, Panofsky would say, dissolves into play). But this is also where Scottish geometry and its cultural avatars diverge from the more straightforwardly historical and, in their way, linear exhibits of conventional progress. In Scotland, we have seen, the practice of geometry in an era of algebra required a creative adaptation of old concepts (like of the parallel postulate to yield Thomas Reid's "geometry of visibles"). But this also meant that geometry linked new sciences to old traditions (which helps account for the proto-Ossianic affect of Robert Simson's translations of Euclid: novelty dressed up as ancient Greece). And so, unlike the grand narrative one usually associates with postclassical mathematics (in which Einstein, for example, surpasses Newton), which reverts to a linear model of first-this-then-that, Scottish geometry is characterized by provocative involutions and recursions. "First-this" and "then-that" occupy the same representational field.

Take, for example, the Scottish architect Robert Adam, leader of the neoclassical movement that eventually resulted in Edinburgh's geometrically designed New Town. Alistair Rowan writes that "Adam was fascinated by geometry," particularly its "purity and . . . potential for perfection." But Adam also drew in the picturesque style (and enlisted other well-known artists to help him[43]) and was doing so from the 1750s onward in imitation of Salvator Rosa and Claude Lorrain. In fact, Rowan argues, geometry for Adam designated "a visually rich interrelationship of spaces, a picturesque . . . aesthetic."[44] However, as the art historian A. A. Tait elaborates, "Adam's picturesque drawings were poles apart from those of Gilpin. To Gilpin the use of the castle, abbey, or tower, inevitably well ruined, was for its emotive power—to give the scene a sense of history. This was never the case with Adam. The classic-Gothic castle though old and partially ruined was used and lived in and represented not a romantic past life but the continuation of old traditions into the present."[45]

In the undated *Mountainous Landscape with a Town and Castle by the River*, for instance (see Figure 2), one finds clear hallmarks of the picturesque—framing foliage, peasantry, and so on. But the castle accentuated in the middle distance not only is not ruinous, but Adam has attached it to the adjoining town as an emblem of modern life. Past and present, nature and culture fit seamlessly into the scene of presentation.

Another work even more dramatically illustrates the late Euclidean logic of the Scottish picturesque (see Figure 3). Here, Tait says, the "austere, vertical castle of the middle ground is balanced further up the river by a small city dominated by domes and campanile, showing the twin and equal sources of western architecture," gothic and classical.[46] Of equal interest here are the masses of rock and cloud that hover over these buildings and whose shadows create optical illusions thrusting the one and then the other from the background into the middle distance (that is, into the image's focal center). This effect in Adam's painting initiates a subtle but almost Escher-like play of perspective that highlights Panofsky's point that the construction of any one vantage point entails all others—that to craft a Euclidean model is simultaneously to surpass it.

To that extent, the link to the past in Adam's work (with the castle in the first drawing and the contrasting architectural styles in the second) also establishes a connection between "earlier" and "later" iterations of Euclid, when the problematics of perspective—and of the Euclidean system generally—became more fully apparent. While Adam, as a renowned architect, would have been more conscious than most of the technicalities involved in applied geometry, the picturesque ambiguities of time and perspective in his

FIGURE 2. Robert Adam, *Mountainous Landscape with a Town and Castle by a River.* © Ashmolean Museum, University of Oxford.

work speak to a larger field of cultural concern. I have been calling this field "late Euclideanism," but in the name of perspectival play, it may be fruitful to consider it briefly under the auspice of the related title of Scottish Romanticism.

Late Euclideanism Without Euclid? A Few Thoughts on Scottish Romanticism

Historical categories are typically the invention of later periods; the "Scottish Enlightenment," as we discussed in Chapter 1, was an invention of the twentieth century. But Scottish Romanticism is of even more recent vintage. Ian Duncan, Leith Davis, and Janet Sorensen describe it as the dark spot in the

FIGURE 3. Robert Adam, *Capriccio of a Romantic Landscape Showing a Castle with a Distant City Set on the Banks of a River*. Reproduced by permission of the RIBA Library Photographs Collection.

mirror of romantic self-reflection: while Edinburgh's early nineteenth-century publishing empire, including the influential periodicals *The Edinburgh Review* and *Blackwood's Edinburgh Magazine*, galvanized a wide public consciousness of new writing (including poetry by Wordsworth and Byron) and "established the main medium of nineteenth-century public discussion," Scottish literary culture remained a "shadowy anachronism."[47] Murray Pittock makes the compelling case that the so-called Romantic Ideology involving "the fetishization of creative subjectivity" and an "anglopetal literary history" emerged in the 1930s.[48] When it did, it revalidated Wordsworth's "egotistical sublime" and pushed a demotic oracle like Burns to the margins where Scott had already been relegated in the late nineteenth century.

Pittock has gone a long ways toward widening our sense of what Romanticism is and of restoring Scotland's place in it, identifying several positive criteria by which to distinguish the Scottish contribution to the field.[49] But for the purpose of our analysis here, and in keeping with Pittock's own observations concerning the uncanny qualities of the landscape in Scott's *Waverley*, it is the "shadowy," "anachronistic" features of Scottish Romanticism that are of greatest interest here. They suggest a play of perspective and time that corresponds with the logic of the picturesque and the late Euclidean principles with which we might associate it. We saw above how the oscillation of viewpoints attended the play of light and shade in Adam's work, and what I wish to discuss in this section is how such multiplicity not only characterizes Scottish Romanticism in its ludic intractability but also emerges more generally from the strange features of the landscape in narratives about journeys to Scotland during the Romantic period. These narratives underscore what is comparatively "unpresentable" about Scotland as an aesthetic and literary-historical locale.

As Gilpin's work demonstrates, the provocations of perspective and the concomitantly strange features of the Scottish landscape informed travel narratives of Scotland, especially the Highlands, long before Scott. In fact, they became something of a fixture in the 1770s. This was the decade when a number of influential travelers made their way through Scotland, from Gilpin (1776) and Thomas Pennant (1772) to Samuel Johnson (1773) and Tobias Smollett's fictive party in *The Expedition of Humphry Clinker* (1771). In that latter work, the irascible but articulate Matthew Bramble composes a letter describing the Highlands as a transcendent region "beyond imagination," which strikes the gaze as though it were "a vast fantastic vision in the clouds."[50] Bramble professes the virtual ineffability of the scene, evoking "fantastic[al] vision[s]" "beyond imagination," which, therefore, are substantive only in part, thus correlating them with Gilpin's logic of the "effect." They illustrate a broader feature of eighteenth-century Highland travel narratives, which often attested to how gloom, or a degree of inveterate secrecy or incommunicability, proceeded from expression itself and not only from what the (itinerant) artist failed (verbally) to paint. Bramble's Highlands thus reflected both the external world and the sensorium of the observer: this was a landscape in which art and nature commingled.

Vivid obscurity, eloquent stammering: these were key features of picturesque Scottish travel narratives and often the manner in which they were articulated. In some of them, the exigencies of description pushed their authors to catachresis, like when the Reverend Charles Cordiner wrote to Pennant and assured him that "[t]he antiquities and scenery of the North,

[to] which [Pennant had made] mention as such excellent subjects for drawing," would "be faithfully copied in some of their most expressive views."[51] Cordiner's "expressive views," or "speaking scenery" we might call it, exhibited the synesthesia (or sensual confusion) that was a common feature of Highland travel accounts. James Cririe employed it as a poetic strategy in a work entitled *Scottish Scenery: or, Sketches in Verse*, which took after James Thomson's influential paeans to nature in *The Seasons*, though adding a more overtly fanciful component:

> Entrenchments deep, and haunts of heroes old,
> The warlike champions of those barren wilds;
> The grave of Ossian, and the ruin'd halls
> Of dauntless Fingal, Morven's mighty Chief,
> Amid these mountains, now are wrapt in mist.[52]

Here the poet and the "barren wilds" alike envelop us in a kind of vatic gloom inasmuch as the "heroes old" materialize out of a landscape that is the vehicle rather than the object of vision; indeed, the "solitary pine" and "lofty shelving banks," to which the poem refers in its preceding lines, recede from view once the "grave of Ossian" enters the scene. William Wordsworth later and more famously performed a similar operation in the poems he wrote about his experience in Scotland, in one instance converting a "solitary Highland lass" into a muse for his own auratic fantasy "Of travellers in some shady haunt"—not in a Scottish glen but rather "among Arabian sands."[53]

Admittedly, Wordsworth's aesthetic was different from Gilpin's; Michasiw identifies the latter's with "an Enlightenment game—a sequence of decomposings and recomposings that amuse according to an arbitrary set of rules," unlike the fanciful poetics that Wordsworth invokes here.[54] However, Wordsworth's abstraction of his "Highland lass" from the Highlands to Arabia (an imaginative operation similar to Scott's later, non-"Scotch" novels, which project recurrent themes of nationhood and history into exotic and often bizarre settings) displays similarly picturesque tendencies in its displacement of the Highlands from a realm of nature to one of artifice. His is an encounter with obscurity, a vision at the moment of its disappearance (here, as it washes away in waves of music: "O listen! for the Vale profound / Is overflowing with the sound" [ll. 7–8]).

The fact that Wordsworth's muse is a laborer only makes his poem more picturesque, as rural peasantry makes up an important feature of many of the narratives and paintings of the genre. Several of Gilpin's iconic sketches display peasants at their margins, providing local color as well as perspective for the scale of the mountains and distances. This is an important point, as it underscores the close relationship between locale and the formal, geometric properties of its aesthetic composition. Later travelers who invoked Gilpin's aesthetics assimilated this relationship with varying degrees of self-consciousness. We find one such instance in Thomas Garnett's 1800 account of a tour through the Highlands, in which he asserts that the ruins of the fort of Dunglass "are low and inconsiderable, and by no means so picturesque an object as represented by Gilpin," although Gilpin "justly remarks" on the magnificence of Dumbarton Castle. Garnett then proceeds one step further, commenting that "a grotesque piece of rock" at the top of a mountain over Loch Long bears some "resemblance to the figure of a cobler in a working attitude upon his stall."[55] Garnett's observations here actually duplicated those of John Lettice in his 1792 tour through the region: the "lofty crag, on the summit of [this] mountain . . . presents a grotesque piece of rock, so exactly like the figure of a cobler, in his working attitude upon his stall, that it never fails to suggest that resemblance to every traveller, who sees it." Lettice's account may also have been instrumental to Wordsworth, for Lettice later relates a conversation he had with "a young female Highlander," who rehearsed poetry and music of a "melancholy, and highly elegant" air. "Hey-day! said [Lettice] to [him]self, who knows, but [he] may have been listening to a descendant of one of the old bards? long may have been the line of her fathers, and old Ossian himself, her great progenitor!"[56]

The relationship between place and form in Gilpin's work is thus further naturalized in Lettice's and Garnett's and then almost mystified in Wordsworth's. The "cobler" in particular is interesting because it essentially naturalizes labor—not only that of the peasantry (or, here, a working class) but also the task of picturesque representation, which underscores the work of the artist (the "effect" of the image) as well as the status of the objects. It seems fitting in that respect to find the "cobler . . . in [a] working attitude" rather than in a moment of leisure, as it becomes a self-reflexive emblem of the painterly labor of representation.

That said, a longstanding criticism holds that picturesque paintings display laborers as window dressing. Contrast the peasants in Gilpin's sketches, for example, with those in David Wilkie's, who was highly attentive to the working class, illustrating in elegant and often poignant detail the lives of subjects reduced elsewhere to mere symbols.[57] Critics in the 1980s, following

John Barrell's lead, appeared to share Wilkie's sensibilities more than Gilpin's, remarking on how, for example, the aesthetics of the picturesque ran counter to the agricultural revolution of the late eighteenth century and thus ratified rural poverty on account of its agreeable effects.[58] In his memorable 1989 analysis of Highland romance, Peter Womack inflated the picturesque into a symbol of bourgeois complacency: the "mountains of Lochaber or Assynt, the rocks of the west coast, and the treeless Hebrides, seemed to most eighteenth-century visitors to pose . . . a choice between abandoning the country to its hopeless sterility and intervening in vigorous and visible ways." Proponents of the picturesque and of Highland romance more generally reportedly took the latter position and so promoted an "aesthetics of Improvement," a rationale for modernizing agricultural practices and the backward habitudes of rural societies. "[S]terility," by contrast, implied an aura of sublimity, which, because it was allegedly "unimprovable," also elicited a politics of resistance, of social critique.[59]

Womack's dialectical categories—"improvement" and the picturesque, on one hand, and "sterility" and the sublime, on the other—echo texts that bear an important historical relationship with Scottish Romanticism and late Euclideanism. But together, these texts tell a rather different story from Womack's. The first comes from Edmund Burt, an engineer contracted by General George Wade to build military roads in the Scottish Highlands after the 1715 Jacobite Rebellion and who in the early 1720s composed a series of letters to a "friend in London." The letters are remembered primarily for the contempt they express for the poverty of the inhabitants and the desolation of the landscape. Writing almost a half-century prior to Macpherson, Burt finds the mountains "rude and offensive" to the sight, characterized by "stupendous bulk, frightful irregularity, and horrid gloom."[60] But roughly a century and a half later, and more than fifty years after Scott's *Waverley*, Highland desolation imparted a very different message. In 1867, Karl Marx asserted that "what 'clearing of estates' really and properly signifies, we learn only in the Highlands of Scotland, the promised land of modern romantic novels. There the process is distinguished by its systematic character, by the magnitude of the scale on which it is carried out at one blow . . . and finally by the peculiar form of property under which the embezzled lands were held."[61]

For Marx, Highland barrenness was a function less of the landscape than of a social process of depletion exemplified by the notorious Highland Clearances of the early nineteenth century.[62] However, in large part because of Scott's influence, Marx finds this relative bleakness almost typologically romantic and thus derives meaning even from the absence of society. Staking a position somewhere between Scott and Muir, Marx imagines the Highlands as visibly empty but, as a result, filled with history and therefore with meaning. Or, to make a different comparison, a more readerly analogy, the Highland "gloom" that Burt perceives has the quality of a blank page on which the marks of legible (or "improved") society have yet to appear, whereas Marx finds himself contemplating a topographical palimpsest that has fallen into a comparative state of ruin and that bears the marks of multiple erasures. And, after the visionary manner of Cririe or Wordsworth, what we can no longer "read" in Highland scenery becomes for Marx the basis whereby we may prophetically discern the imminent doom of Western capital.[63]

If Burt's view of the Highlands is "sublime," then Marx's is more "picturesque." But each, significantly, is "improved." And this reiterates the point we made above concerning the self-consciousness of picturesque representation. Improvement, which adds a labor quotient (Garnett's and Lettice's "cobler") to the landscape, was the basis of Highland romance, as Womack rightly argues, and it provided the framework for much of the literature of travel through Scotland in the eighteenth and early nineteenth centuries. Ironically, however, Womack's critique is more Marxist than Marx's, for Marx not only perceives in the "romantic" Highlands an allegory of London and Manchester but also grounds this vision in a picturesque conceit of eloquent ruin. Marx, in other words, does not juxtapose the sublime and the ideological, at least not in talking about the Highlands, but rather portrays the region as a "sublime object *of* ideology."

This phrase names a well-known range of work by Slavoj Žižek, which I invoke here because of the difference that Žižek levels between ideology and its critique. The rudiments of this line of thought will be familiar to many readers. For Žižek, ideology is less a mistake to which others (e.g., Scottish travelers or picturesque painters) are prone than a reflex of thought that habitually confounds the difference between nature and history, converting its own perspective into a concept of what universally "is." Because thought relies on such apparatuses, "ideology" inflects all consciousness, critical and otherwise. Indeed, we might say, this is why Burke differentiates the sublime from "the terrible": whereas the latter denotes "danger or pain [which] press[es] too nearly," the sublime *sublimates* these dangers into digestible, conceptual forms; in mastering our fears, we convert them into pleasure (which Burke calls "delight"). Essentially, the process of sublimation marks the difference between a fall off a cliff and a precipitous descent down the track of a rollercoaster: the sublime signifies fear that is always already contained, always already ideologized.[64] This is because the sublime is subject to the mechanics of representation, which is the special province of the picturesque. But this also means that our representations divulge more than they intend—namely, the system that mediates our experience—and that even the clearest images carry with them the "gloom" or trace of what falls outside the mirror of self-reflection.

As an example, recall Scott's "Highland Minstrelsy" episode. At one level, it enlists Edward in a romantic military campaign for the ultimate purpose of validating state power. And yet, as Pittock points out, *Waverley*'s conclusion, depicting a portrait of Fergus and Edward in Highland dress, "illegal in Scotland after the failure of the 1745 Rising," and situating them amid "a wild, rocky, and mountainous pass"—a quintessentially picturesque setting—amounts to a return of the repressed.[65] This is essentially an instance of an ideologically inflected perspective gazing back on itself, with *Waverley*'s landscape effectively testifying to undigested, unideologized remnants of Scott's British Union. Or, in the terms we employed above, it is the residual effect of the conversion of the Scottish landscape into "art," with the latter's representation acquiring a degree of self-reflexivity otherwise denied a more straightforwardly "ideological" situation.

In short, if we identify romance and the Romantic Ideology with a divergence from quotidian reality or with a "promise of happiness" that remains unfulfilled—and hence, if we establish a connection between romantic narrative and what does *not* appear or is lacking—then the picturesque and *Scottish* Romanticism, by contrast, imply the freighted negotiation of all that *does* appear or of what challenges the imagination by the sheer force of its presence. The picturesque and Scottish Romanticism, we may say, present the obtrusion of the visible upon the comprehensible or of the matter of experience upon the cognitive channels through which we mediate it. This is what makes these categories geometric in the terms employed in Scotland at the turn of the nineteenth century. Leslie's assertion that geometry "is grounded entirely on the information received through . . . the senses" makes even the most abstract and refined Euclidean shapes the residue of prior perceptions, the trace of unassimilated remainders.[66] At the same time, the phenomenological complexity of many of the discursive and visual representations of

Scotland during this period unsettled the straightforwardly Euclidean dimensions of geometric practice, less by venturing into wholly non-Euclidean territory than by fixating, in Uvedale Price's words, on the "clumps" and "belts" of tenuous perspective and the uncanny experience of landscape. In that respect, the picturesque exemplified the late Euclidean philosophy embedded into the conceptual justifications, by Leslie and others, of a supposedly traditional geometry. Or, stated inversely, Scottish geometry theorized the space of the picturesque.

The Highlands in particular delineated an experiential threshold in the late Euclidean age. Most travelers there commented on the grandeur of the scenery and the comparative strangeness of its inhabitants, but even writers *from* Highland regions (like "Ossian" Macpherson, the philosopher Adam Ferguson, and the poet Duncan Bàn Macintyre) invoked the area as a counterpoint to a comparatively normative state of existence (for example, to British commercial society or to Highland life in ages past).[67] Picturesque sketches and accounts of Highland Scotland thus framed and at least partly illustrated phenomena of otherwise inconceivable strangeness, bringing diverse "stages" of history into contact with one another (e.g., commercial and feudal societies) and also alternating between perspectives (now here, now there) and experiences (first "nature," then its "effect"). In doing so, the picturesque essentially reified eighteenth-century conceptions of the imagination as the cognitive agent mediating mind and world; indeed, in their way, travelers to Scotland embodied dominant conceptions of the imagination at work.

I say this with an eye to the etymology of the word "imagination." While today the word often designates a force of conception removed from reality (making it a correlative of "romance"—hence, the Romantic Imagination), Samuel Johnson's 1755 *Dictionary of the English Language* labels the imagination "the power of forming ideal pictures," which was the logic of geometry and the picturesque.[68] In the eighteenth century, Johnson implies, to think about the world was necessarily to imagine it, to create mental pictures of it, and when those pictures partly modify our understanding—when, through a process of abstraction, they "compound, transpose, augment . . . diminish" and generally rearrange "the materials afforded us by the senses," as David Hume says—then they function geometrically.[69]

The history of the concept of the imagination is important because it reveals how geometrically inflected travel narratives essentially personified the operations of the mind. (This, recall, is how Leslie portrayed geometry itself:

"The study of Mathematics . . . traces the beautiful relations of figure and quantity, [and] it likewise accustoms the mind to the invaluable exercise of patient attention and accurate reasoning." It amounts to an aesthetic education.) Indeed, the genre established itself as a key medium of *bildung*, of formative experience that yields a kind of enlightenment. But for many travelers, there was something almost gothic about Scotland generally, and hence something evocative less of understanding than desire—less of clarity than (algebraic) obscurity. It was in Scotland that Ann Radcliffe set her first novel, *The Castles of Athlin and Dunbayne*, and it was this type of fiction that many travel narratives seemed to elicit:

> A most ravishing scene, unparalleled in Britain, opens suddenly upon you. A cold and fearful shuddering seizes upon your frame. Your ears are stunned. Your organs of vision, hurried along by the incessant tumult of . . . roaring waters, seem to participate in their turbulence, and to carry you along with them into the gulph below. Your powers of action and recollection are suspended. Though eager to be gone you become rivetted to the spot; and it is not till after a considerable time, that you begin to regain sufficient composure to contemplate, with any degree of satisfaction, the grand and awful objects here presented to your view.[70]

This is how James M'Nayr, in 1797, described the falls of Corra Linn near New Lanark, roughly twenty miles southeast of Glasgow. This is a striking and in some ways strange formulation, with the eyeballs detaching themselves from the body and "hurr[ying themselves] along" downstream (in some ways a figure of his readers' eyes moving compulsively across the page of his account).[71] But M'Nayr's rhetoric of "shuddering," "suspen[se,]" and "rivetted" attention is also in some ways thoroughly conventional, eliciting the horrified discovery of "the most revolting objects; Skulls, Bones, Graves, and Images" in Matthew Lewis's *The Monk* (1796).[72] Given later conceptions of the unconscious, we can appreciate how especially the Scottish Highlands came to operate within Britain as an emblem of the mind's dusky, nether regions. Rugged topography there evoked ("sublime") delight as a function of its superficial difference from georgic Britain, to say nothing of its cultural and political differences, conjuring an aura of danger that the dulling effects of improvement simultaneously contained. And yet, the hallmarks of improvement—the replacement of peasant farms with sheep pastures, the blazing of rough tracks of land via military roads, the substitution of country retreats and fishing villages for feudal estates—acquired the virtual status of a language in that they provided travelers with access to these remote locations while also furnishing them with sufficient tokens of civilization to render their experience legible. Hence, when Johnson noted in 1773 that tourists to the Highlands arrived "too late" to see what many of them were expecting, namely, "a people of peculiar appearance, and a system of antiquated life," he actually gave utterance to the conditions—belatedness and mediation—that made the Highlands visible in the first place.[73]

Johnson's paradoxical observation—they did not find what they were expecting, which means they had already discovered it before they left—is characteristic of the genre of picturesque travel narratives. Malcolm Andrews identifies two paradoxes that were particularly prominent: picturesque accounts appealed to an untouched but already somehow improved nature, and they exalted the native (that is, "Britain") by reference to the foreign (usually France or Italy).[74] In each case, preexisting forms (agricultural societies, on one hand, and the work of Claude Lorrain, on the other) mediated travelers' experience of the unknown. Not coincidentally, the very routes most travelers took were also preestablished. While the Highlands, Andrews remarks, "were nowhere near as congested as the Lake District" during this period, there were nevertheless two Scottish tours on which most adventurers embarked—a "Long Tour," which went up the east coast "to Aberdeen and round to Inverness" before sweeping across to the west and then looping back to Edinburgh, and a shorter tour, which passed from Glasgow up to Loch Lomond and Inveraray.[75] Correlatively, travelers themselves fell into prearranged types, or so claims Richard Joseph Sulivan in his cheeky *Observations Made during a Tour through Parts of England, Scotland, and Wales* (1780), which "range[d] the several classes which are daily whirling round the world." First, he said, "come your men of science": "[c]hemists and musicians, [n]aturalists and tooth-drawers, [a]stronomers and quacks, [p]hilosophers and tailors, [p]oets and frizieurs, and in short a thousand others coupled in as ludicrous a manner." The list does not necessarily grow more coherent as it expands to include adventurers of high fashion, "[c]hildren of wealthy families, [h]eirs apparent of diseases, titles, and distinction, [w]adlers astray from the courses of Newmarket, Almanack's, and St. James's, [s]pendthrifts, laughing at their creditors" and "Dilettanti, skimming the shores of knowledge for a gaping world." Last come visitors in search of health, those seeking happiness, and, at the end of the queue, those who, like Sulivan himself, "cheerfully skip along the borders of the fair field; stop where [their] fancy leads [them] to expatiate, and wander as [their] faculties and imagination may uphold [them] for the moment."[76]

There is at least one significant group Sulivan fails to mention: women. Mary Ann Hanway, for example, was one of the first voyagers to chastise Johnson for his purported Scotophobia; Janet Schaw provided one of the most moving early accounts of Highland emigration; Sarah Murray produced an influential guidebook for subsequent travelers; and Anne Grant's seminal essay on the superstitions of the Highlanders comprises an early classic of what we might call Highland (or perhaps internal colonial) ethnography.[77] But for the purpose of drawing some general conclusions about the relationship of late Euclideanism and the picturesque to Scottish Romanticism, let us take Sulivan's satirical, proto-Borgesian list at face value. Its point, seemingly, is to underscore that what tourists saw (indeed, in large measure who they were) was less natural than artificial. Each represented a "perspective" that was also, as Panofsky reminds us, an artifice. The grand scenery they expressed was already part of a tourist industry, which, for that reason, was discursively if not geographically mass-produced. The frontier Highland landscape was a priori commoditized, cluttered with literary and aesthetic conventions. Scott's "Highland Minstrelsy" was thus a relatively late arrival in a field that was literally well traveled.

That said, and in accordance with their late Euclidean logic, picturesque travel narratives were irreducible to the sum total of their conventions, not because the Highlands defied expression per se but rather because narrative itself—representation—enunciated gloom under the auspice of dispelling it. This is why *Waverley* is interesting in this context: without reducing nature to artifice, it made artifice appear uncanny. It seems fitting, then, that Scott and the picturesque should have been memorialized in literary and intellectual history through largely the same language. In 1927, for example, Christopher Hussey invoked the picturesque as a historical category occupying a transitional phase between "classical" and "romantic" eras.[78] His historical schema strikes us as perhaps too pat, although when Georg Lukács revivified Scott's reputation just a few years later, he adopted a similar set of terms and sense of proportions (as we discussed in Chapter 2). Scott's work, he said, represented a "continuation of the great realistic social novel of the eighteenth century," amounting to "a higher development of the realist literary traditions of the Enlightenment in keeping up with the new times."[79] As Hussey might put it, Scott retained a "classical" pose in a "romantic" age and thus became a kind of expressive and compelling anachronism, articulating the forces of history that he simultaneously resisted, placing him at the vanguard of an era whose sweeping changes also rendered him a relic. Forty years later, Tom Nairn would essentially recapitulate this argument (albeit in a deprecatory way), calling Scott a "valedictory realist" who portrayed "the past . . . [as] gone, beyond recall," and who therefore "cut off the future from the past," employing in place of an authentic *Volksgeist* a garish assemblage of empty national forms, a menagerie of (mere) representations.[80] It was on this basis that Jerome McGann proclaimed Scott a romantic postmodernist, as we also discussed in Chapter 2—pushing the boundaries of anachronism considerably further than Lukács.[81]

But in the same volume in which McGann's essay was published, Duncan, Davis, and Sorensen argued more broadly that it is Scottish Romanticism, and not just Scott's work, that "describes rhythms of continuity, change, and disjunction quite different from the English model to which it has been subordinated" (including by Lukács, who repeatedly refers to Scott as an "English" novelist).[82] In figures like Macpherson, a translator/poet of romantic "fragments" a full generation prior to their appearance in the influential writings of Friedrich Schlegel, and in Scott, a devotee of "enlightenment" a full generation too late, one beholds a romanticism of the always already and the never quite yet. We encounter, that is, a *picturesque* patchwork of divergent aesthetic qualities and historical types, a late Euclidean assemblage of outlived and emergent forms.

Distant Reading and Scottish Romanticism Redivivus

Romanticism, like Enlightenment, is a retroactive construct: it generalizes a spirit of the age after the fact. The picturesque, however, I am suggesting, captures the experience of history (for example, of Scottish Romanticism) at the moment of its occurrence precisely because it merges the "too early" with the "too late" and presents—makes present—the otherwise unpresentable. For Samuel Johnson, this experience was more unsettling than illuminating. In his *Journey to the Western Islands of Scotland*, Johnson explained his adverse reaction to the Highlands as a function of what he called the region's "wide extent of hopeless sterility," resulting, he believed, from depletions of population and culture that reduced the locale to the austere forms of its landscape. "An eye accustomed to flowery pastures and waving harvests is astonished and repelled" by the stark appearance of the Highland terrain, its reduction to a set of barren figures, mere shapes (60). What Johnson bemoaned, essentially, was the unchecked abstraction of Highland life, its reduction to the sum total of its naked appearance. The landscape had reverted, or evolved, into an arrangement of seemingly inhuman forms, exemplifying Theodor Adorno's later theory of "[a]rtworks [as] afterimages of empirical life."[83] "Wild . . . geometry" was thus no more a novelty with Edwin Muir than minstrelsy was with Walter Scott.

For both Johnson and Muir, the geometric features of the landscape served as uncanny emblems of ideological abstractions—an "early stage" of society (now vanished) in Johnson's case, the Scottish "nation" (professedly inconceivable) in Muir's. For Johnson in particular, the perplexing land masses he could not help beholding in all their aridity formed a counterpart to the Ossianic manuscripts he thought he should see but were nowhere evident.[84] What beguiled Johnson, in other words, was the strange status of the classical in an otherwise modern world where it seemed no longer to belong. This was, we recall, one of the problems with Newton's fluxional calculus, which suspended the problem of infinitesimals by tracing lines and figures, thus rendering geometric shapes as the index of puzzles that would remain unsolved until the time of Louis Augustin Cauchy in the early nineteenth century. Coincidentally, perhaps, it was the fluxional problem of change over time on which both Johnson and Muir implicitly commented. For each, the unnervingly blank quality of the Highland landscape was the product of nominally enlightened but more deeply pernicious workings of capital—of "improvement" in Johnson's era and industrialization in Muir's. And the shapes these processes produced were no longer the smooth and flowing figures preferred by Newton and Maclaurin but rather the rougher forms of the picturesque—the "clumps" and "belts" of history that Muir, as we discussed in Chapter 2, associated with Scott's fiction.

These rough, picturesque surfaces are still with us, in concept if not always in name. Provocatively, they mediate, or at least significantly inform, our relationship with digital technology, especially the "big data" that are purporting to redesign not only how we interpret literary history but even how we read. Franco Moretti (whom we discussed briefly in the Introduction) has famously called the new hermeneutical practice of data visualization "distant reading"—a concept that more aptly fits some forms of visualization than others. Digital tools, we are told, enable us to process vastly greater amounts of information than the most diligent traditional historian ever could, and the interpretive operations we may undertake with them grow ever more sophisticated, from word frequencies and genre mutations to morphological, semantic, and even conceptual tracking systems that capture subtle evolutions of thought over multiple centuries through text mining. Digital instruments promise to change how we see history.

And that emphasis on *how* we see is precisely what connects data visualization to aesthetics. For Moretti, whose extended essay *Graphs, Maps, Trees* has helped stoke interest in the digital humanities, the quantitative analyses enabled by new technology are valuable both for what they teach us about particular historical constellations and also for how they help us rethink the very nature of historical change. What Moretti values here, recall, is not information alone but rather mathematics, specifically geometry: a "geometrical pattern is too orderly a shape to be the product of chance. It is the sign that something is at work here—that something has made the pattern the way it is."[85] As an example, Moretti presents graphs (and maps and trees) revealing uncannily similar trends of novelistic production across diverse chronotopes with no clear relation to one another (for example, "in Britain, Japan, Italy, Spain, and Nigeria . . . : five countries, three continents, over two centuries apart, [with] really the same pattern" [5]). Such visual models purportedly generate "a type of data which is ideally independent of interpretations" (9), data for which we have as yet no conceivable explanation. And it is on this basis that these models reproduce the effect of Kant's mathematical sublime, overwhelming our imagination and understanding while instilling in us a rational conviction that we may, someday, through these instruments, remake the literary-historical world.[86]

One of the provocative and perplexing things about Moretti's approach is the recrudescence there of eighteenth-century aesthetic modes to describe the effects of purportedly revolutionary twenty-first-century technologies. New technology has long conjured associations of the sublime, of course, but there is a peculiarity to distant reading that compels perhaps a different course of reflection.[87] In reviewing Moretti's graphs (of, say, the statistical rise and fall of novel forms in Britain [see Figure 4]), we may discern a relationship between the shapes taken by distant reading and the signifiers of distance, the mountain- and cloudscapes, in picturesque paintings of the late eighteenth century by Gilpin, Adam, and others (see Figure 5). This relationship is partly visual—Moretti's graphs reproduce little of the texture or imagined loco-specificity of the paintings—but the geometry in each instance is almost self-consciously uncanny, composed of rough irregularities in the

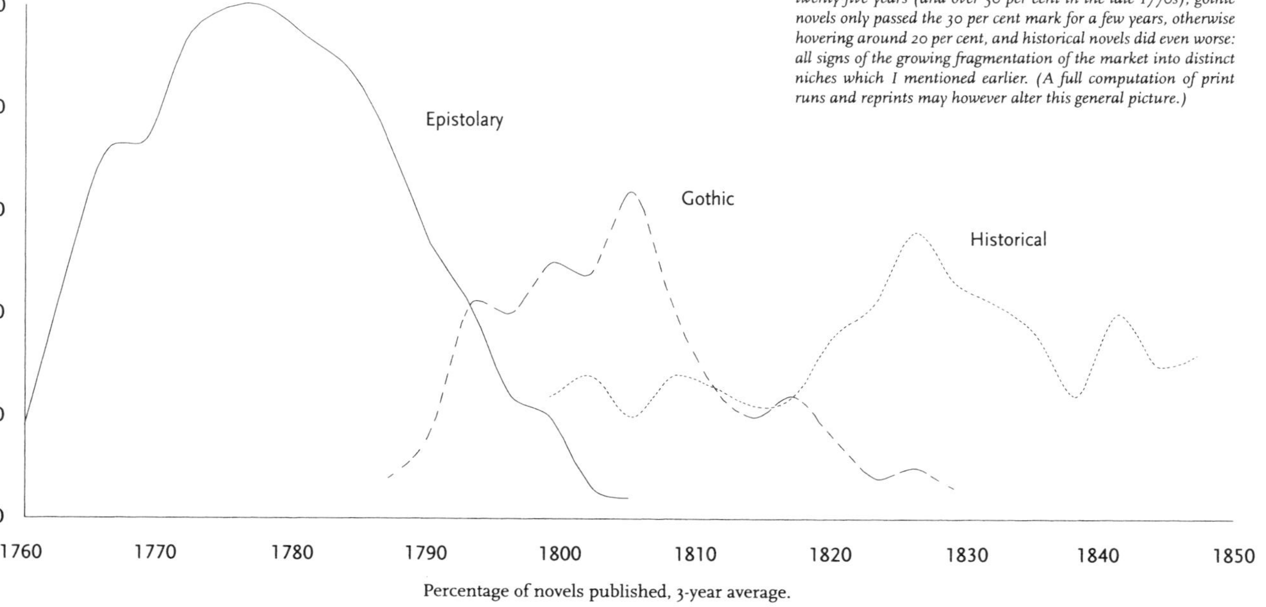

FIGURE 4. From Franco Moretti, *Graphs, Maps, Trees: Abstract Models for Literary History* (London: Verso, 2005), Figure 8.

Figure 5. William Gilpin, from *Observations, Relative Chiefly to Picturesque Beauty, Made in the Year 1776*, 2 vols., 2nd ed. (London: Printed for R. Blamire, 1792). L. Tom Perry Special Collections, Harold B. Lee Library, Brigham Young University, Provo, Utah.

prints and of the alleged flow of history in the graphs. Note, too, a kind of middle distance implied in Moretti's graphs inasmuch as distant reading invites a close reading of its data in order to deduce "from the *form* of an object," as Moretti puts it, "the *forces* that have been at work" in creating it (57). Distant reading, that is, produces historical shapes that close reading must then interpret, such that quantitative analyses consist of a picturesque play of fore- and background that establishes a kind of optimal perspective point between near and far as the idealized place of critical judgment, the putative position of the canny reader.

To conclude somewhere near the place where this chapter began, this is the type of position Muir sought as he attempted, and failed, to discern the outlines not of literary history but of a coherent Scottish nation. Some of the most famous passages in the *Scottish Journey* detail Muir's horror at the shapes of change in the industrial wasteland of modern Glasgow, whose inhabitants struck Muir as "sad and incomprehensible distortions of nature."[88] And yet, while Muir would later condemn Scott for his precocious modern "emptiness," there was a strong Enlightenment component to Muir's conception of the all-too-modern world. In 1938, three years after the publication of his *Scottish Journey* and two years after his seminal essay on Scott, Muir began composing his autobiography. First published in 1940 before undergoing some revision several years later, the volume included a famous diary extract from 1939 in which Muir addresses a primal rupture he felt had defined his existence:

> I was born before the Industrial Revolution, and am now about two hundred years old. But I have skipped a hundred and fifty of them. I was really born in 1737 [instead of 1887, as listed on his birth certificate], and till I was fourteen no time-accidents happened to me. Then in 1751 I set out from Orkney for Glasgow. When I arrived I found that it was not 1751, but 1901, and that a hundred and fifty years had been burned up in my two days' journey. But I myself was still in 1751, and remained there for a long time. All my life since I have been trying to overhaul that invisible leeway. No wonder I am obsessed with Time.[89]

This profession immediately follows an extensive citation of the *Upanishads* on the nature of the undivided soul, something Muir professes not to enjoy. He is riven, making him, in relation to the images of bifurcation he had introduced in *Scott and Scotland*, Scott's heir. Or, stated otherwise, Scott becomes the laureate of modern Glasgow while Muir doubles as the Last Man of the eighteenth century.[90] The passages and its precedents involve a play of perspectives ("I myself was still in 1751, and I remained there for a long time"), which, we have seen, conjures the long history of the picturesque. Consistently with Panofsky's observations and our own analysis of the picturesque, Muir's passage asserts the breakdown of a single, classical viewpoint and the recursion of history—the folding of space—onto itself. It presents a case of distant reading minus the graphs.

Considered in light of a wider swathe of his work, Muir's late Euclidean experience of landscape in *Scottish Journey* would thus seem to distill a serial view of history, which it reduces to the "wild" shapes of the Highland landscape. And, while the sight lines of the mountainscapes possess a "continuity of rhythm" "moulded by time," they also appear abstracted from their own setting, "start[ing] up out of places which seem to have no connection with them" (212). In this respect, the landscape is both "new" and timeless, artificial and natural. It brings past and present together—uncannily so—making them complementary to Muir's experience of traveling through Scotland by car:

> During all my way [into the Highlands] from Edinburgh my mind had been slightly but pleasantly troubled in the evening, but especially at bedtime, by a sort of illusion, partly optical and partly temporal, which must be known to everyone who covers a good stretch of country in an open car. The place I started from in the morning seemed suddenly to have dropped an immeasurable distance behind and to be almost in a different world. All the impressions of the day, all the landscapes that had followed so fast on one another, seemed to have built up an impregnable barrier between me and the place where that morning I had eaten a quite ordinary breakfast, and to have clothed it in the atmosphere of landscapes seen many years before. (224)

According to Paul Virilio, this is the archetypal effect of velocity: "With speed, the world keeps on coming at us, to the detriment of the object." Modern experience exacerbates a condition Virilio coins as picnolepsy, denoting those blanks in consciousness that result from our inability to assimilate the rush of sensory information. "[T]he rapid tour," like Muir's, "the accelerated transport of people, signs or things, reproduce[s]—by aggravating them—the effects of picnolepsy, since they provoke a perpetually repeated hijacking of the subject from any spatial-temporal context."[91] In Muir, this condition produced a "double sensation of time" that "was confusing and yet pleasant." It

> evoked in [his] imagination an unusually vivid sense of the simultaneity of the many lives and towns and landscapes scattered all over the world, the countless human and animal and material things coexisting . . . contemporaneously in a thousand forms, unaware of the life beyond their horizons and yet following the same laws as it. From this indistinct and yet vivid image [he] tried to extract a picture of Scotland as an entity, but [he] did not succeed: [he] could envisage the world in these terms, though [he] had seen very little

> of it . . . but [he] could not think of any modification of the law of being that fitted Scotland and Scotland alone. (224–25)

Muir imagines an exalted perspective that his local experience refutes by dissolving that viewpoint into the complexity, the multiplicity, of its own construction. This helps explain why the mountains in Muir's travel narrative seem to belong at once to "the world of mathematics . . . in complete changeless autonomy" (213) *and* to an avant-garde world of "wild" geometry. His is a picturesque setting between—or, rather, juxtaposing—epochs, amounting to a vividly experiential but all-but-unthinkable present.[92]

"Scotland" in Muir's *Journey* thus prompts erasure and animation; it is a nation of the undead. "I had seen a great number of things, but no thing" essentially or unproblematically Scottish, Muir writes, inciting him "to fall back on the conclusion that nationality is real and yet indefinable, and that it can be grasped at most in history, which means that it cannot really be grasped at all" (225). By Muir's logic, nations are both ineffably singular forms ("real and yet indefinable") and also something akin to fluxional constructs or entities crafted from their own movement in time. This renders them elusive to the degree that "history is continuous and unbreakable, extending in its written state behind us and in its unwritten state before us." And yet, it is precisely these types of shapes that Maclaurin had explicated and that Scott had evoked (and partly surpassed) in his fiction. Indeed, Scott was in some ways the first writer to theorize Muir's position, though he arrived at the conclusion that history is possible, if also an artifice of romance. Hence, Muir's declaration of futility in conceptualizing Scotland bears a national imprimatur. Scotland "is" to the degree that it also "is not." It is, as Muir would say of Scott, an "empty" and thus a fulsome place. And that is why *Scottish Journey* represents a late chapter in a late Euclidean story about the strange literary-historical place of Scottish Romanticism—a picturesque category that, until recently, was deemed barely to exist and whose virtual unpresentability now seems linked to its historical presentation of precisely those types of enigmas.

CHAPTER 4

Burns After Reading, or, On the Poetic Fold Between Shape and Number

I begin this chapter by returning to Franco Moretti's model of distant reading, which has caused no small stir (and, in many quarters, displeasure) among literary scholars. Part of this comes from the purported reducibility of shapes to quantities and hence of literature to number. For Alain Badiou, the real problem with numbers concerns less their applicability to literature than their unintelligibility: we no longer know what they mean, or rather, there is no longer a master concept of "number."[1] Instead, one finds divergent numerical systems—whole, negative, rational, real, complex, and so on—and different modalities of being implied by each. If we do not know what numbers are, he reasons, we do not know who we are: we do not know what it means to exist as a "whole" being or else what it means to exist in a rational, real, or complex state—which is to say, as some composite of (potentially fragmentary) selves or impulses correspondent with different numerical classifications. To read literature in terms of quantity is thus to raise some perplexing questions that the practice of distant reading alone cannot answer.

That being, like number, is multiple introduces complexity not only into such obvious ontological fictions as the square roots of negative numbers (aptly called "imaginary numbers") but even into seemingly bedrock propositions like $2 + 2 = 4$. While such numbers seem to possess the properties of what Locke called "simple ideas" like "motion" or "light," constituting the foundation for more complex structures (in the case of algebraic numbers, polynomials like $x^2 - 2x + 3$; in the case of language, concepts like "enlightenment"), they are themselves susceptible to multiple definitions.[2] As with language, then, so with numbers: even the most rudimentary designations decompose the difference between the literal and the figurative, the concrete and the chimerical.[3] (Relative to Moretti, for example, consider the ambiguity of classifying and counting a novel of multiple generic strands—the historical, epistolary, and gothic *Guy Mannering*, say—under a single delimiting category.)

Hence, it is no accident that figurative language became an acute crisis for philosophy (for example, in the work of Locke and others) precisely when number itself fell from the perch of "wholeness" into an abyss of negativity and irrationality in the seventeenth century.[4] During this period, numbers began posing especially challenging ontological as well as metrical puzzles. Take the case of negative numbers: how can existence be less than nothing? Or, consider the problem of infinitesimals, numbers greater than zero but less than any measurable quantity, in the burgeoning theory of calculus: how can nothing count as something? But negatives, infinitesimals, and other virtual numbers were immensely useful in systems of measurement, whether of celestial bodies or artillery systems, which is why they acquired a functional validity that availed them to our use even as they defied our ability to explain them. What emerged was a dialectic of mathematical enlightenment in which numbers began using us as much as we used them. This is why Badiou argues that we now find ourselves bound to "the blind despotism of the numerical unthought" (13), incapable of succeeding to some new phase of our being.

This is where Moretti's appeal to geometry as a historical propaedeutic becomes most poignant—not as the implementation of a new model but rather as the tacit expression of a wish to circumvent the limitations of number and hence, to a degree, the ontology of modernity itself as the frustrated compulsion toward succession: 1, 2, 3 . . . ; industrialization, commercialization, globalization. . . . But "geometry" imposes its own curious conditions: "To make sense of quantitative data," Moretti says, he "had to abandon the quantitative universe, and turn to morphology: evoke form, in order to explain figures" (24). To "see" the past, that is, he had to amalgamate statistics into an ensemble, designate a boundary, and assign a character to the mass of informational minutiae. In other words, he had to reprise the bare outlines of the categories he was purportedly displacing: "high and low" (by valuing "distant" over "close" reading), "canon and archive" (by antiquating "metaphysics" or theory while favoring "the natural and social sciences"), and "this or that national literature" (in the segregation of "French and German" thought from a more global—but therefore boundary-conscious—

community).[5] And this opens Moretti's project onto a slightly different historical path from the one he tries to explain.

Whose path is this? It is not Badiou's, whose rigorous efforts to redress the problems of number and modernity propel him down the path of set theory and topology with the aim of redefining how we organize and exceed the historical categories through which we articulate our being.[6] Nor is this path strictly mathematical, as "geometry" in this instance reflects primarily a literary-historical situation. In answering our question, we might begin by observing that *form* and *number*, the objects of Moretti's and Badiou's analyses, are also ways of talking about poetry. Classical metaphysics, elaborating on Plato's idea that "the qualities of number . . . lead to the apprehension of truth," portrayed astronomy as the resolution of number in space, music as the exposition of number in time, and poetry, therefore, as an expression of universal harmony.[7] Early modern poets like Robert Henryson employed complex numerological schemes of primes, squares, ratios, and series in demonstration of that principle.[8]

So what might happen, we might ask, if we were to imagine, with Moretti, the shape of modern being by way of a poet like Robert Burns instead of through the Romantic novel? Writing during the period that Moretti examines, Burns is remembered today as perhaps the first great poet of "the people" taken as a mass (a term that, like "infinity," signifies a vague numerical aggregate), and yet, in speaking as a national oracle, Burns also embodies the geometrical tradition of unity amid multiplicity (that is, many points, one shape—one harmonious whole: one nation), which differentiates the classical metaphysics of form from the modern regime of number. Badiou sketches this line of demarcation between the old and new worlds in the long eighteenth century, when innovative concepts pertaining to the infinite (for example, in calculus, using infinite series $n + 1/2n + 1/4n + 1/8n$ . . . to arrive at a number smaller than but infinitely close to $2n$) confounded the notions of simple wholeness that the Greeks had always categorized in terms of proportion and relation (which displace the problem of irrational numbers inasmuch as the latter are not expressible as quotients of integers, that is, as simple fractions). This leads Badiou to formulate the proposition that for us moderns, "the one *is not.* . . . [T]he one . . . solely exists as [an] *operation*" or as a component in a system of ordering. Hence, in the place of (the) one, we designate a "count-as-one," making whole or substantive being seem less the product of nature or experience than of the systems we deploy to articulate it.

Yet Burns's case is in some ways more complex, for the logic animating him as a national poet makes him both the emblem of a seemingly metaphysical wholeness *and also* a count-as-one element in a modern mass of national cultures, whose porous borders render them irreducible to one. Burns's reputation as a bard of the people complicates the situation further, for he thus presents literary history with two conflicting postulates: as national poet, he speaks *for* the people, and as token of the common man, he speaks *as one of* the people. According to Badiou's schematic, if the first postulate holds, then the people "are not" to the degree that they subordinate themselves to the singular Word, much as unity amid variety represents an extension of (the) one (in this instance, of Burns as *the* "heaven-taught ploughman" or as *the* oracle of the Scottish nation[9]). But if the second postulate is true—if, that is, the poet speaks *as one of* the people or as their mouthpiece—then he himself "is not," at least not as a unique subject, since his absorption into the mass means he merely "counts-as-one" when gaining utterance. Who speaks, then? The poet, the "one," or the people, the "mass"? But if the "one" and the "mass," the prophet and the populist, coexists, as they do in the image and legacy of Burns, then we essentially uncover a fold between the metaphysics of unified form and the modern hegemony of number—basically, between two moments and modes of being. This fold designates Burns's paradoxical home in literary history: diverging at once from shape and number, Burns uncannily "is" and (or precisely because he) "is not"; iconically visible, Burns nevertheless does not "count" in academic circles.[10]

* * *

As unusual as this mathematical matrix may seem as a way of formulating Burns's legacy, it actually accords with a more conventional narrative about his place in history. Burns enjoyed immense popularity almost from the instant his *Poems, Chiefly in the Scottish Dialect* was published in July 1786. Then, in the decades following his death in 1796, he became something of an icon. A series of editors, critics, and biographers elevated Burns into a national symbol and then into something even more global and abstract. A key figure here was James Currie, who in 1800 published a popular edition of Burns's work replete with a life of the poet portraying Burns as the emblem of a noble but expiring Scottish peasantry. This image would take more elaborate visual form later in the nineteenth century in such volumes as *Views in North Britain, Illustrative of the Works of Robert Burns* (1805); *The Poems,*

Letters and Land of Burns (1838); and *Tweed's Tourist Guide to the Land of Burns* (1878). Replete with beautiful images of open—and sometimes hauntingly empty—landscape, the poet came to personify an idealized past and an idyllic though largely deserted Scottish scene, a sanctuary of feeling inflated to the status of a genius loci. Heralded in his own era as the plowman-poet, Burns now became the symbol of a vanishing laboring class and the oracle of supposedly timeless human values. Societies and clubs sprang up all over the world in Burns's name and to honor his memory.[11] Scholars translated his Scots dialect into dozens of languages—including English.[12] He became in some ways the world's best-known and most beloved literary figure.[13]

And yet, despite all this, or perhaps because of it, Burns's reputation precipitously declined in academic circles after the early decades of the twentieth century. Murray Pittock has documented the virtual disappearance of Burns from scholarly journals, university press books, and literary anthologies after the 1930s, remarking that "[t]he sheer strangeness of this [withdrawal] is visible on a number of levels." For example, Burns's poetry exists in more than fifty languages, he acquired a significant following after the 1930s in places like Russia and China, and his work and legacy annually help generate hundreds of millions of pounds in tourism.[14] The reasons for Burns's relative eclipse in scholarly consciousness thus have more to do with the evolution of the field of Romanticism, Pittock argues, than with Burns. They partly involve the drift of literary theory from Britain to the continent and especially to Germany—a process hastened, ironically, by late nineteenth- and early twentieth-century Scottish intellectuals, who, Cairns Craig reminds us, "played key roles in the translation of German ideas for the English-speaking world" via editions of Kant, Hegel, and Heidegger.[15] Neither a seer like Blake nor a brooder like Wordsworth (hence, bearing little existential resemblance to later oracles like Nietzsche or Walter Benjamin), Burns devolved to the status of an uncanny artifact, an unclaimed relic, Pittock's "strangeness [made] visible."[16] I say this because, in its frequency of popular citation (for example, "Auld Lang Syne") but relative estrangement from scholarly commentary—in the way it began inciting repetition without paraphrase—the Burnsian canon became a poem unto itself.

Of course, that begs the age-old question of what poetry is. And it is a familiar but, here, peculiar answer to that question within Burns's work—*ut pictura poesis*, conceived as an evocatively geometric phenomenon—that is the subject of this chapter. Currie invokes this trope in his *Life of Robert*

Burns, juxtaposing it with the type of rational thinking traditionally associated with the sciences, including geometry:

> The maxim of Horace, *ut pictura poeisis*, is faithfully observed by these rustic [Scottish] bards, who are guided by the same impulse of nature and sensibility which influenced the father of epic poetry, [Homer.] . . . By this means the imagination is employed to interest the feelings. When we do not conceive distinctly, we do not sympathize deeply in any human affection; and we conceive nothing in the abstract. Abstraction, so useful in morals, and so essential in science, must be abandoned when the heart is to be subdued by the powers of poetry or eloquence. . . . Generalization is the vice of poets whose learning overpowers their genius; of poets of a refined and scientific age.[17]

Currie's observation devolves on a set of eighteenth-century commonplaces, most obviously in the Ossianic proximity between Scotland's "rustic bards" and Homeric "nature." The passage also draws a familiar if problematic distinction between such poets and those "of a refined and scientific age," effectively separating "enlightenment" from "romance" and thus implicitly reiterating Adam Smith's apothegm that "Prose is naturally the Language of Business; as Poetry is of pleasure and amusement."[18] As we discussed in Chapter 3, such partitions rarely sustain themselves in the overlapping traditions of Scottish Romanticism and the picturesque. And so it is here. The comparison with Smith seems especially fitting because Currie's larger point concerns the concept of sympathy, of which Smith is the Enlightenment's most famous theorist. We can only sympathize, Currie argues, with what we "conceive distinctly," with conception here involving feeling as much as visual perception (corresponding with Joseph Addison's definition of sight as "a more delicate and diffusive kind of Touch"[19]). "Abstraction," meanwhile, consists of cognition without sentiment, in form(ality) without passion—that is, in something like geometric figure. Burns makes a similar assertion in a 1788 letter: "Men of grave, geometrical minds . . . may cry up reason as much as they please; but I have always found an honest passion, or native instinct, the trustiest auxiliary in the warfare of this world."[20] "Passion"—sympathy—trumps bare reason.[21]

But Burns's own poetic picture is, unsurprisingly, more nuanced. We catch a glimpse of how this is so in his epistolary invocation of deity in

February 1793: "O thou, wisest among the Wise, meridian blaze of Prudence, full-moon of Discretion, & Chief of many Counsellors!—How infinitely is thy puddle-headed, rattle-headed; wrong-headed, round-headed slave indebted to thy supereminent goodness, that from the luminous path of thy own right-lined rectitude thou lookest benignly down on an erring Wretch, of whom the zig-zag wanderings defy all the powers of Calculation, from the simple copulation of Units up to the hidden mystery of Fluxions!"[22] Here, God is the personification of geometry (or of "right-lined rectitude"), with the poet "an erring Wretch" whose "zig-zag wanderings defy all powers of Calculation," whether arithmetical or fluxional. But by this logic, the poet is actually "geometric" along the lines established by Scottish mathematicians like Robert Simson and Colin Maclaurin, who conceived of fluxions geometrically precisely because shape compensated visually for what algebra could not justify philosophically. Accordingly, the poet is known by a God who "lookest benignly" on what "def[ies] . . . Calculation," anticipating Badiou's point about how the numerical riddle, introduced by the "infinite series" of the calculus (Burns's "hidden mystery of Fluxions"), redounded even onto simple arithmetic (Burns's "simple copulation of Units"). This means the poet sets geometry not only against "calculation" but also against itself: he is no "right-lined" Euclidean but rather a "zig-zagging" *late* Euclidean whose images, like those on Keats's Grecian Urn, tease one out of thought. In other words, Burns introduces a distinction between geometry and poetry that he himself deconstructs.

How does this affect our understanding of Burns and Burns of the complex late classicism of the Scottish Enlightenment? More broadly still, how does Burns affect the *picture* of literary history that Moretti tries to capture by way of geometry? I will argue that, like the picturesque "clumps" and "belts" of which Uvedale Price writes and that we discussed in Chapter 3, the work and legacy of Burns elucidate a series of "figures" that engage our powers of perception while taxing those of understanding. In effect, Burns personifies the graphs through which Moretti seeks to defamiliarize literary history but in such a way that they open reflection to the complications that Badiou introduces into that paradigm. Burns thus takes the triangulation for which Smith's concept of sympathy is famous—the relationship between subject, object, and impartial spectator—and converts that triangle into a wedge that opens up a different way to see poetry and the past.

Strangeness Visible

Contrary to appearances, poetry and mathematics are in some ways isomorphic disciplines. True, poetry is the traditional home of figurative language, while mathematics, as a language of strict logic, tendentiously evades tropes altogether. A circle, for example, is not a metaphor for objects in the world but rather an invention of the mind, equivalent to its own definition as "a plane figure bounded by a single curved line, called the circumference, which is everywhere equally distant from a point within, called the centre."[23] But this means that in each we experience a coincidence of word and thing: to speak poetically or to define a shape is to create the thing one describes; pure figuration is (also) the banishment of all figures.

To conceive of poetry in this way is to sketch how Burns, one of the world's most popular poets, could also have become strangely (in)visible in literary history—how, that is, such a celebrated and influential figure could also have effectively been taken out of time, converted into an "abstraction" of Scotland. Perhaps fittingly—"poetically"—Burns's favorite poet, the brilliant Robert Fergusson, a luminary of the vernacular revival in Scots poetry, had commented on another Scottish abstraction twenty years earlier. Here, the abstraction was mathematics, specifically fluxions. In 1765, not yet fifteen though beginning his university education, Fergusson composed an "Elegy, On the Death of Mr. David Gregory, late Professor of Mathematics in the University of St. Andrews." Adopting the folksy Habbie stanza that Burns would later make famous, the young pupil ironically mourned the respected teacher's death in a broad Scots dialect melding high and low, serious and ribald.[24] The third of the poem's seven stanzas is especially telling:

> He could, by *Euclid* prove lang sine
> A ganging *point* compos'd a line;
> By numbers too he cou'd divine
> When he did read,
> That *three* times *three* just made up nine;
> But now he's dead.[25]

As the references to Euclid and the "ganging" (or "moving") point indicate, Fergusson was speaking here of Gregory's ability to elucidate Newtonian calculus.[26] Gregory was the namesake of his uncle, the renowned David Gregory, who, elected to the chair of mathematics at the University of Edinburgh in 1683, was among the first university teachers in Britain to take up Newtonian thought. Even after Gregory left Edinburgh in 1691, obtaining with Newton's help a Savilian professorship of astronomy at Oxford, Newtonianism continued to flourish in Scotland, acquiring traction among Scottish Episcopalians in the 1690s as a rationalized form of resistance to the dogmatic enthusiasm of the Presbyterian majority.[27]

By the mid-1720s, Newtonianism was embraced in Scottish universities by Presbyterian and Episcopalian, Whig and Tory. But Fergusson's stanza does not encrypt a triumphalist history of Scottish Newtonianism. For one thing, the poet situates his reference to fluxions within a comic elegy accentuating the futility of such learning: "But now he's dead." This is where Fergusson's poem thus retrospectively configures two national myths. One pertains to Scottish geometry, which, according to George Davie, would, like Gregory, fall dead after the eighteenth century, when Scottish universities began adopting the English model of disciplinary specialization and thus largely renounced their traditional philosophical commitment to general education. The effect was to widen a gulf dividing the arts from the sciences that geometry had always helped bridge. The second myth speaks to the idea of enlightenment, or to the power of general education, to improve individuals' circumstances.[28] Hence, Davie remarks, his aim in writing *The Democratic Intellect* was "to restore life and meaning to the dimming legend of the 'Metaphysical Scotland' of 'the lad o' pairts,'" or upwardly mobile commoner trained in Enlightenment thought.[29]

Here, Davie implicitly conjures not only Fergusson but Burns, the romantic exemplar of this cultural ideal. Burns received no university education, but he was schooled by a tutor in the classics, including in geometry. The philosopher and mathematician Dugald Stewart would later inform Currie that Burns "was well instructed in Arithmetic, and knew something of practical Geometry, particularly of Surveying."[30] In his famous biographical letter to John Moore in 1787, Burns described having spent one summer "on a smuggling [coast] a good distance from home at a noted school, to learn Mensuration, Surveying, Dialling, &c. in which [he] made good progress."[31] As Nigel Leask reminds us, these skills would serve Burns in future years when he began work as an exciseman and found himself responsible for measuring volumes of liquor, molasses, and other commodities.[32] But in that same letter to Moore—the same paragraph, in fact—Burns also begins having fun with his geometrical training: "I went on with a high hand in my Geometry; till the sun entered Virgo, a month which is always a carnival in my bosom, [and] a charming Fillette, who lived next door to the school overset my Trigonomertry [*sic*], and set me off in a tangent from the sphere of my studies" (1:140). Here, light-heartedly adopting a mathematical conceit, Burns attributes his "zig-zag" nature to sexual energies, rendering risqué the abstractions of polite learning. He strikes a similarly playful note in his song "Caledonia," which concludes with this Fergussonian (that is, comically contorted and yet also lyrically poignant) analogy:

> Thus bold, independent, unconquer'd and free,
> Her bright course of glory for ever shall run;
> For brave Caledonia immortal must be,
> I'll prove it from Euclid as clear as the sun:
> Rectangle-triangle, the figure we'll chuse,
> The upright is Chance and old Time is the Base;
> But brave Caledonia's the Hypothenuse,
> Then, Ergo, she'll match them, and match them always.—[33]

The figure is contorted, gangly, and self-consciously absurd. Nevertheless, the song appeals to Euclid to demonstrate the immortality of a nation whose endurance or distinct identity, after the 1707 Union with Britain, had become less certain or at least less distinct—viscerally evident, certainly, but conceptually a little less clear.

In "Caledonia," then, geometry is a concrete tool that lends shape to an elusive concept. But in other Burns poems, geometry takes subtler and less reassuring forms. For instance, the "strangeness visible" to which Pittock calls our attention (and for which geometry is a crucial eighteenth-century medium) is the theme of one of Burns's most popular poems, "To a Louse." My aim over much of the rest of this chapter is to elucidate the challenge this poem presents to reflection, with the dimensions of that challenge cast in mathematical as well as literary terms.

But before taking stock of what the poem brings, strangely, to view, let's begin with a close reading. If Wordsworth's "Tintern Abbey" is one of the late eighteenth century's great poems about the fertile rapport between the senses and the imagination (or between what the mind "half create[s] / And what perceive[s]"[34]), then Burns's didactic apostrophe is certainly one of the period's signature pieces about their dysfunction. Opening with an exclamatory burst as the poet, seated in a church service, spies a louse atop a young woman's ostentatious headwear, it is the poet's imagined relation to what he sees that gradually comes most luridly into focus:

Ha! whare ye gaun, ye crowlan ferlie!
Your impudence protects you sairly:
I canna say but ye strunt rarely,
          Owre *gawze* and *lace*;
Tho' faith, I fear ye dine but sparely,
On sic a place.

Ye ugly, creepan, blastet wonner,
Detested, shunn'd, by saunt and sinner,
How daur ye set your fit upon her—
          Sae fine a *Lady*!
Gae somewhere else and seek your dinner
          On some poor body.[35]

The invective is lively, but its repellant counsel is Swiftian and unsettling. It would be easier to regard as straightforwardly sarcastic the poet's declaration that the creeping scourge belongs with the lower classes were it not for the jocularity of the poet's insults, which take the form of flyting, a Scottish tradition of poetic hazing indicative of a rival's esteem. As is, then, the rhetorical fillip doubles as an acknowledgment of the parasite's fine taste. In this respect, the silent foil tacitly reflects the poet's desire by lodging itself "Below the fatt'rels [or ribbon-ends] . . . / O' *Miss's bonnet*" (20, 24, Burns's emphasis) in intimate proximity to the desired object. But in its pretentiousness, the vermin also bears a mimetic relation to its gaudy host ("right bauld ye set your nose out" [25]), rendering its—and our—desire all the more complex in its simultaneous tendencies toward sustenance, sex, and status. The woman, meanwhile, seems oblivious to the drama unfolding atop her head, noticing neither the critter nor the effect its presence is having on others seated nearby. And so the poetic word, which is either dumb or falling on deaf ears, proceeds from louse to lady:

O Jenny dinna toss your head,
An' set your beauties a' abread!

Ye little ken what cursed speed
The blastie's makin,
Thae *winks* and *finger-ends*, I dread,
Are notice takin! (37–42)

The attention Jenny garners—leering contempt, droll commentary, and a parasitic dinner guest—cannot be what she had intended.

The poem's folksy vernacular and lilting rhythms (accentuated with feminine rhymes) lend it the gentle quality of Horatian satire and partly blunt the cruder features of the scene. But the poet casts a pall over the spectacle of human folly with sobering allusions to economic inequality and even slavery: if the louse were to choose "some beggar's haffet squabble" more proper to its station, it might "creep, and sprawl, and sprattle / Wi' ither kindred, jumping cattle," presumably fleas; more odiously, it might set up residence "In shoals and nations" and "thick plantations" like the usurious traders who subsist on the labor of others (13–14, 16, 18). Burns composed the poem, pointedly, during the period when he was preparing to immigrate to Jamaica and work as a bookkeeper and assistant overseer on a sugar plantation sustained by slave labor. But to render these associations explicit and to forge a link between human misery and the production of such luxuries as "Miss's fine *Lunardi*," her hat, "fye! / [The poet] daur [not] do't" (35–36). This would require a capacity for circumspection we do not possess, or so the poet tells us. Human opacity is an observable fact, he believes (albeit opaquely, since he too is human), which incites him to conclude with this plea to a god unknown:

O wad some Pow'r the giftie gie us
To *see oursels as ithers see us*!
It wad frae monie a blunder free us,
An' foolish notion:
What airs in dress an' gait wad lea'e us,
An' ev'n Devotion! (43–48)

Burns lifts his theme from a passage in Smith's *Theory of Moral Sentiments* asserting that "self-deceit, this fatal weakness of mankind, is the source of half the disorders of human life. If we saw ourselves in the light in which others see us, or in which they would see us if they knew all, a reformation would generally be unavoidable. We could not otherwise endure the sight."[36]

To be sure, these lines apply as liberally to the poet as they do to the lady given that his prolonged gaze (and fraternity with the noxious "wonner") betrays more carnal desires. Indeed, we might well ask ourselves who exactly the parasite is in this poem, since the louse seems more intent on strutting "[o]wre *gawze* and *lace*" than in dining upon its host. Of course, Jenny displays little interest in feasting on the word of God, either: if she could see herself and her infested accessory as the poet beholds her in it, and if people generally were capable of unstinting self-reflection, they would free themselves from pious pretenses as readily as the churchgoers who embrace worship as the prelude to sexual intercourse—"Houghmagandie"—in Burns's poem "The Holy Fair."[37]

Fittingly, although with significant interpretive consequences, the poet seems not to recognize the voraciousness of his own gaze: he cannot see himself as his readers see him. Rather, in philosophizing about how we are creatures of impulse, the poet himself speaks impulsively. Burns's poem thus performs the conundrum that a limited capacity for reflection presents for our conception of human nature. If we are creatures of impulse rather than understanding, of instinct rather than reason, then we resemble the nature over which we lord. We may not exactly be vermin, no matter how much some lice resemble some poets or some ladies, but to exalt ourselves above the natural creation on the basis of a rational faculty we do not fully possess would be an inhuman—which is to say, an irrational, un-self-reflective—gesture. Conversely, to explain our inhumanity—to take stock of ourselves as the creatures we "really" are—would be to rationalize our irrationality, a problematic and in some ways contradictory endeavor. We are thus caught between the categories through which we define our being: our humanity attests to our inhumanity and vice versa.

This paradox, often mediated for us today through environmental and posthumanist criticism (which portrays humans as creaturely beings), was a centerpiece of Scottish Enlightenment moral philosophy. Decades before James Burnett, Lord Mondboddo notoriously likened human language to that of primates, Smith, David Hume, Francis Hutcheson, and others were already identifying passion rather than (and even set against) reason as the driving force behind familial and civic societies, national and religious identities, and arts and the wealth of nations.[38] Burns's poem takes up the conflicted logic of such first principles through the incongruous passions motivating its mouthpiece—sympathy and concupiscence, on the one hand, and indignation and stoic resolve on the other. But if passion motivates thought, as Hutcheson and his followers suggest, then it also fuels an explanatory volume like Smith's *Theory of Moral Sentiments*. This places philosophy, a deliberative discipline, in a tenuous position even as it enables poetry to burrow its way "below the fatt'rels" of the problem. For, in syncopating moral reflection to the pulsations of musical speech, the poem yokes together rationality and sensibility as a union of opposites. This is not to say, however, that the poem's speaker is in full possession of the dialectic he initiates: indeed, failing fully to grasp the irony of his own lament—failing to see himself as others see him—he obscures and even undercuts his own observations and thus acts as a louse in the Enlightenment imaginary, a parasite attesting to the flaw in the reason he upholds.

Hence, in brilliantly orchestrating a paradox, Burns's poem enacts a crisis on which moral philosophy prospectively flounders. But this also means that the poem beguiles its own commentary. For one thing, when the louse "bauld[ly] . . . set[s its] nose out" (25), it evokes the critics in Burns's verse "Epistle to John Lapraik" who "cock their nose" and utter falsehoods, accentuating the parasitical relation of criticism to poetry.[39] But also, and more perplexingly, criticism recapitulates the rationalizing position the poem undercuts when it makes sense of the tensions the latter exploits. In explicating the sinuous reasoning of the poem's contortions—basically, in explaining why the poem's irrationality is, after a fashion, rational—criticism lends itself an invisible hand, reprises Smith's universalizing judgment (that people cannot see themselves as others see them), and thus inadvertently becomes the poem's object of scrutiny. In the Burnsian fun house, critics are beings more gazed upon than gazing; in reading carefully, they misread themselves.

And yet, in warping the mirror of criticism, "To a Louse" reflects the discipline of geometry, which famously purported to square irrational quantities (for example, through the sketching of ratios). In this respect, geometry assumed something of a poetic function in eighteenth-century Scotland. As we have discussed in previous chapters, geometry was a language of figures, an exercise of perception as well as reason and a prominent oracle of infinitesimal being(s)—for example, of the infinitely small (and, in George Berkeley's view, parasitic) numbers whose quantities, irreducible to whole numbers, lacked any ontological foundation. Burns's poem effectively literalizes Berkeley's concerns, bringing them into our line of vision. As Robert Heron would rhapsodize in his elegiac 1797 *Memoir of the Life of the Late Robert Burns*, Burns welded sentiments to images, such that "[y]ou actually see what he describes: you more than sympathize with his joys: your bosom is enflamed with all his fire: your heart dies away within you, infected by the contagion of his despondency."[40] But as "To a Louse" illustrates, what we "actually see" is also that we fail to see—and, hence, that vision itself poses a problem that philosophy essentially fails to address. Nevertheless, taking Heron's encomiastic (and widely shared) enthusiasm at face value, and bearing in mind our discussion of Burns's legacy earlier in the chapter, we might say that Burns crystallizes a *condordia discors* between poetry and geometry around the idea of clarity. Burns converts sympathy, or at least the relation between poetic agents (poet, louse, and lady), into something like shape, lending form to amorphous structures of feeling. As "To a Louse" attests, these forms were most compelling to the degree that they orchestrated contradiction, expressed the inconceivable, and traced fractious, un-whole figures of being, which is precisely where geometry begins to play the role of something like a supplement.

Line, Surface, Solid: Poetry by Other Names?

It is that supplement that I wish to address here by reflecting on the legacy of one of Burns's Enlightenment predecessors, Robert Simson. In some ways, Simson, like Robert Fergusson, is a powerful if uncanny precursor to Burns in that he lends both voice and form to overlapping Scottish philosophical traditions (metaphysics and common sense), helping to articulate a national culture from which he nevertheless remains detached. (Simson rarely figures, for instance, into discussions of Scottish Enlightenment luminaries.) As such, Simson constitutes an Archimedean point from which much can be seen even as it falls outside the normative boundaries of perception. Simson thus delimits the position later occupied by Burns, whose legacy, as Pittock portrays it, has become wholly incommensurate with his material contributions to literary history. If Burns is the overlooked "wonner" in *The Norton Anthology of English Literature*, then Simson and the mathematical tradition of which he is part help us conceptualize the modern paradox, the fold or "fatt'rel," between what *appears* and what *counts*—between Moretti's shape and Badiou's number—that makes Burns newly compelling in our era of distant reading.

Simson assumed the position of chair of mathematics at the University of Glasgow in 1711, retired a half-century later in 1761, and died in 1768. In 1797, John Robison, one of Simson's former students, composed a substantive biography of Simson for the third edition of the *Encyclopaedia Britannica.* Robison was expert in mathematics and also an experienced writer. After completing his MA at the University of Glasgow in 1756, Robison had traveled the continent, held the mathematics chair at the Imperial Sea Cadet Corps of Nobles at Kronstadt, and then in 1773 assumed the chair of natural history at the University of Edinburgh. He was a man of wide learning and a notoriously vivid imagination. The same year that his essay on Simson appeared in the *Encyclopaedia Britannica,* Robison also published one of the most elaborate political tracts of the late 1790s, a massive tome entitled *Proofs of a Conspiracy against all the Religions and Governments in Europe,* a paranoid account—allegedly based on firsthand knowledge—of how freemasons, in concert with such secret societies as the Illuminati, were plotting the downfall of Western civilization. Fanning flames of terror that were spreading from France, the book went through four editions within a year of its publication. Professing to explain the causes of the French Revolution, Robison's *Proofs* told a dire, sensationalized story of the degradation of the modern world.

That worldview and, in places, its rhetorical structures inflected Robison's biography of Simson. Markman Ellis observes that "in the late eighteenth century, the practices of secret association overlapped with the practices of secret interpretation, especially with esoteric forms of arcane knowledge."[41] In Robison's account of Simson, geometry shares a kind of expressive kinship with the dark arcana propagated by secret societies, but of Simson in particular, Robison paints the portrait less of a government conspirator than of an eccentric genius who graced and was eventually consumed by the discipline to which he had devoted his life. When Simson was a student at the University of Glasgow, Robison tells us, he "acquired in every walk of science a stock of information, which . . . would have done credit to a professional man in any of his studies. He became, at a very early period, an adept in the philosophy and theology of the schools," or in the study of metaphysics, "and was [also] able to supply the place of a sick relation in the class of oriental languages, was noted for historical knowledge, and [was] one of the most knowing botanists of his time."[42] Like many young men, Simson was originally slated to enter the ministry, but it "was during his theological studies . . . that mathematics took hold of his fancy" (504).

It gradually becomes clear that this defining moment seizes Robison's imagination as much as it does Simson's, serving in his biography as a romance of origins for the balance of Simson's career. This self-reflexive quality in Robison's *Encyclopaedia* article, unlocking the mystery of Simson's life as the moment when Simson himself purportedly finds the key to his life's work, is at once consummately Romantic—accounting for an organic relation between its subject matter and its own production or for the lyric coincidence of speaker and object—and also suggestively geometric. Robison tells us that Simson "felt a dislike [for] the Cartesian method of substituting symbols for operations of the mind, and still more was he disgusted with the substitutions of symbols for the very objects of discussion, for lines, surfaces, solids, and their affections" or items related to these figures (504). "Lines, surfaces, [and] solids" functioned here as things in themselves, the conjunction of sign and referent, the imagination become real—poetry in Euclidean form.

The allure of such figures would eventually prove harmful to Simson, Robison asserts.

> It was during [Simson's] theological studies, as preparatory for his entering into orders, that mathematics took hold of his fancy. He used to tell in his convivial moments how he amused himself when preparing for exercises for the divinity hall. When tired of vague speculation, in which he did not meet with certainty to reward his labours, he turned up a book of oriental philology, in which he found something which he could discover to be true or false, without going out of the line of study which was to be of ultimate use to him. Sometimes[, however,] even this could not relieve his fatigue. He then had recourse to mathematics, which never failed to satisfy and refresh him. For a long while he restricted himself to a very moderate use of the cordial, fearing that he would soon exhaust the small stock which so limited and abstract a science could yield; till at last he found, that the more he learned, a wider field opened to his view, and scenes that were inexhaustible. (504)

Geometry in this passage bears the status of a "cordial," constituting a disciplinary counterpart to the "convivial moments" in which Simson would later share his story. Robison draws a soft equivalence between the two, if not substantively then narratively, even (we would say) psychologically. Initially, geometry provided Simson with a pick-me-up in moments of "fatigue"; however, as Robison will later regretfully observe, Simson began resorting to it more and more heavily, as though geometry itself were a form of intellectual dissipation.

This makes Simson a prototype for the image that began circulating about Burns—that he was a man undone less by vulgar profligacy than by his own inclinations, his own genius. Burns had died in 1796, and the following year (when Robison published his biography of Simson as well as his *Proofs of a Conspiracy*), Robert Heron issued his *Memoir of the Life of the Late Robert Burns* explaining the poet's demise. "[T]he enticements of pleasure too often unman our virtuous resolution, even while we wear the air of rejecting them with a stern brow. We resist, and resist, and resist; but, at last, suddenly turn and passionately embrace the enchantress." Such had been Burns's fate in Edinburgh, reportedly, where he succumbed to "convivial excess," Dionysius incarnate.[43] This was the story, now discredited (and vigorously disputed in the early nineteenth century even by those, like J. G. Lockhart, who were hardly Burns enthusiasts), that Currie, a physician, would canonize when his own *Life of Burns* appeared three years later.[44]

But in a strange way, Robison implies, it was Simson's story first. Strange, because the retiring, recondite Simson was in some ways the antithesis of the waggish poet, not his uncanny double. That they would be linked at all through a common narrative structure suggests that this paradigm, the unreformed prodigal, was already inscribed into the Scottish Enlightenment (and indeed, far more broadly), making Burns the product of a culture industry: Scotland's poet and geometer absorbed into a national *mythos* of biblical proportion. Simson gradually devolved, Robison tells us, from a promising young student of diverse interests and talents into something of an eccentric pedant. He remarks that Simson's "veneration . . . for the ancient geometry was carried to a degree of idolatry" (504); that Simson was "fastidious" in his prosecution of arcane subjects (506); that his zeal in defending Euclid and Apollonius amounted to a "superstitious palaeology" (or dogmatic study of antiquities [507]); that his "disgust . . . at the artificial and slovenly employment on subjects of pure geometry . . . hindered him from even looking at the most refined and ingenious [algebraic] improvements of . . . Euler, D'Alembert, and other eminent masters" (508); and that Simson's life, "convivial moments" aside, was "more abstracted than [that of] any other person from the ordinary occurrences of life, and even the ordinary topics of conversation" (508). A quick glance at Simson's considerable library confirms this quality of quotidian abstraction: it contained one copy of Pascal's *Pensées* but multiple translations of Euclid; a slender volume by Longinus on the sublime but many more by mathematicians—a dozen editions of Newton's works, four of Humphry Ditton's, six of John Napier's, five of John Wallis's, and so on.[45] In his leisure, Simson might pick up Plato but was more likely to turn to Apollonius, or to Archimedes instead of Aristotle, or to Isaac Barrow before Francis Bacon. The library's contents reaffirm the story Robison wishes to tell of a man in whom polite learning morphed into something more extreme in its intensity and "abstraction." The image conforms to what Burns wrote in his epistle "To James Smith" of men "Far seen in *Greek*, deep men o' *letters*" who "Hae thought they had ensur'd their debtors, / A' future ages," and yet, "Now moths deform, in shapeless tatters, / Their unknown pages."[46]

Robison's tale of what might have been—of potential unrealized, of greatness cut short—would become a standard view of Simson. In 1812, fifteen years after the publication of the *Encyclopaedia* essay, William Traill, one of Simson's students who later assumed a professorship of mathematics at Marischal College, Aberdeen, crafted a similar biographical portrait of his mentor. For Traill, Simson was an eccentric figure, part Immanuel Kant, part James Macpherson. Like Kant, Simson was given to "fixed and regular habits," such that while Kant famously strolled through Königsberg at the same hour every day, so the walks "in the squares or garden of the College" at the University of Glasgow "were all measured by [Simson's] steps."[47] At the same time, Traill (like Robison) recognized Simson's wide veneration as the restorer of ancient geometry (Traill 17; Robison 507) even as, in Traill's mind (as in Robison's), Simson's reconstructions were not always literal as much as poetic, "expressive of the notions . . . entertained by the ancients" (45). In other words, and in line with the *Ossian* skeptics, Simson's Euclid was as much the product of Simson's "inventive genius" (73) as of his careful research.[48]

So, Macpherson's Ossian, Currie's Burns, Simson's Euclid—the primitive, the pastoral, the classical: these were all figures of uneven development, which was itself, as a model for the passage of time, a cousin of Newtonian fluxions. But Robison, in complaining that Simson's geometric fixation actually blunted intellectual progress, lighted upon a fortuitous image evocative of Burns. And I wish to transition here from a discussion of Simson to a reconsideration of Burns's poetry as a contiguous disclosure of complexity rending the veneer of classical form. The problem with Simson's brand of classical geometry, Robison observed, is that it "appears to restrain us in the application of the knowledge we have already acquired" in other mathematical pursuits. And, "disgusted with the tedious, and perhaps indirect path, by which we must arrive at an object which we see clearly over the hedge, and which we could reach by a few steps, of this security of which we are otherwise perfectly assured," we feel inclined to bypass the critical exercise of geometry altogether (507). Robison's complaint here is with the "tedious" proofs of geometry and with the impediments it imposes in our ability to calculate "object[s] which we see clearly over the hedge" in algebra. Forty years later, the Scottish philosopher William Hamilton would return to this image in defending the phenomenological and poetic aspects of precisely this type of deliberative practice:

> The mathematical process in the symbolical [or algebraic] method is like running a railroad through a tunnelled mountain; that in the ostensive [or geometric] like crossing the mountain on foot. The former carries us, by a short and easy transit, to our destined point, but in miasma, darkness and torpidity; whereas the latter allows us to reach it only after time and trouble, but feasting us at each turn with glances of the earth and the heavens, while we inhale the pleasant breeze, and gather new strength at every effort we put forth.[49]

Geometry here takes the form of pastoral absorption, of the cumulative experience of nature; it does so, moreover, at a moment (for Hamilton, in the mid-nineteenth century) when the railroad began compressing the phenomenological distance between remote locations, seeming to collapse time and space. Most striking here is the abundance of metaphors and the multisensory quality of the experience they elicit. Hamilton blends the perception of shapes and diagrams with the "pleasant breeze" of nature, metaphysically linking vision ("glances") to a Romantic promenade.

Hamilton's pastoral defense of geometry links (ideas we associate with) Simson to (ideas we associate with) Burns. But Hamilton's nature is not exactly Burns's. Hamilton portrays mathematics in terms of an implicitly geometric principle of *adaequatio*: different tracks, one destination. Burns, meanwhile, was a laureate of inadequacy or of things that do not fully reconcile with one another. His well-known poem "To a Mouse" dramatizes the irremediable failure of formal congruity to unify disparate entities. The poem's subtitle, "On turning her up in her Nest, with the Plough," reveals that the poet has been etching furrows, tracing lines in the soil, when the accident occurs. As he pauses to watch the creature scurry, he reflects on the irreconcilability not only of man and mouse but also of the whole and the fragmentary:

> Wee, sleeket, cowran, tim'rous *beastie*,
> O, what a panic's in thy breastie!
> Thou need na start awa sae hasty
>   Wi' bickering brattle!
> I wad be laith to rin an' chase thee,
>   Wi' murd'ring *pattle*![50]

Burns's virtuosity is on full display here, both in the rapid pace of his language after the initial line (in mimicry of the rodent's panicked scuttle) and in his manipulation of a stanzaic form and dramatic setup that belong to a long tradition of Scottish verse.[51] But the poem is also a product of its era: critics observe that the mouse's relative voicelessness (its "bickering brattle" never preempts the poet's speech) makes it more of an object than a subject, even an allegorical one, and the plowman's distantiated appraisal of nature evokes the ethos of the picturesque (in which peasants serve as window dressing) more than it does the polyvocal inclusivity of a Scottish precursor like Robert Henryson.[52] Looking forward, we may even discern the outlines of Heidegger's ascription of a "world" to humans that animals lack or to poets that simple peasants lack.[53]

Burns's plowman thus establishes a proximity to the natural world that he complicates with that same gesture. The poet underscores this move in the final two stanzas:

> But Mousie, thou art no thy-lane,
> In proving *foresight* may be vain:
> The best laid schemes o' *Mice* an' *Men*
>   Gang aft agley,
> An' lea'e us nought but grief an' pain,
>   For promis'd joy! [ll. 37–42, Burns's emphases]

The plowman intuits or else projects some significant points of kinship with the rodent: each "schemes" for a better life and suffers disappointment at the hands of fate, like plundering by those who claim the land by force or legal ownership. Leask, who makes this last point, discerns a further trace of geniality between man and mouse in the poem's diction, "softened by sibilance and diminutives" like "Mousie."[54] However, the "fellow-mortal[s]" (l. 12) do not share similar states of being:

Still, thou art blest, compar'd wi' *me*!
The *present* only toucheth thee:
But Och! I *backward* cast my e'e,
  On prospects drear!
An' *forward*, tho' I canna *see*,
  I *guess* an' *fear*! [ll. 43–48, Burns's emphases]

The poem concludes by drawing these essential contrasts: the mouse dwells in the present, whereas human existence suspends itself between past and future; the mouse inhabits a world of objects—straw and soil—while humans occupy a realm of haunting absences and pseudo-presences; the mouse's existence is tangible, the poet's atmospheric; the mouse is an organism of earth, as is the plowman, although he is also a creature of heaven or, more properly, of the "environment" as that which literally environs or surrounds him, spiriting him away from what is materially at hand.[55] His "Och!" marks a point of contact and disjunction, amplifying Rousseau's cry of nature, the "primitive" ejaculation of sentiment that connects humans to nature even as it foreshadows a "civilized" tendency toward linguistic abstraction.[56] This displacement, in fact, ruins the plowman's ontological integrity and converts his existence into a fraction, into something less than "one."

"To a Mouse" thus inverts the dilemma we encounter in "To a Louse." The latter, again, presents being as the distribution of complexity, that is, as the multiplication of airs and identities, parasites and spectators: the poet plays the part of observer, moralist, and lech; Jenny adopts the roles of fashionista, femme fatale, fool, and food; the louse is at once a lowly pest, an emblem of upwardly mobile affect (in "stick[ing its] nose out" atop the hat), and a figure of the hungry poet. By contrast, the plowman in "To a Mouse" experiences his own existence as diffuse, sundered from self-presence by cares of past and future, whittled by circumstance into the fragment of a whole. Irreducible to a mere "one" in the first instance, comprising something less than "one" in the second: in each case, the poet comes to seem as creaturely as the critter he addresses. Un-"whole" but manifestly evident as a complex figure, the poet is unknowable to himself.

Of Lice and Men

Giving voice to multitudes and to ghosts of the departed (in effect, anticipating Walt Whitman by way of "Ossian" Macpherson), Burns's complementary poems craft images of poets beside themselves, both more and less than themselves. Unable to become "one" and severing connections they might otherwise foster (with nature and others) on account of their instability, Burns's poets are implicitly fractious because they are fractioned (if they are not—as irrationals—incapable even of that). This makes them consummate case studies for Smith's theory of sympathy, which synthesized wholes from fragments. Purporting to explain how and why societies form, the idea of sympathy was born, Ian Duncan argues, from the impulse "to maintain a collective, neutral, abstract field of insensibility," a kind of impersonal grid, for "a civil society fearful of the potential violence of individual passions."[57] To this end, Smith conceived of society in harmonious, proportional, and, we will see, implicitly geometric terms. He contends that the sympathy-seeking subject "must flatten . . . the sharpness of" his feeling's "natural tone, in order to reduce it to harmony and concord with the emotions of those who are about him." Such "flatten[ing]" "not only lowers [this feeling] in degree, but, in some measure, varies it in kind." And while these two sentiments, the one that motivates the subject to seek sympathy and the other into which it evolves, "will never be unisons, they may be concords, and this is all that is wanted or required."[58] Terms like "degree," "unison," and "concord" conjure classical mathematics, but Smith is attempting to forge something more modern. Along the lines of Newtonian fluxions, sympathy sublates ("infinitesimal") differences into (graphable) points of convergence, thus converting a riot of divisive feelings into a series of orderly, generally progressive social operations.

The dialogues with Smith in the "Louse" and "Mouse" poems are self-conscious: Burns jotted passages from *The Theory of Moral Sentiments* into a commonplace book.[59] But Burns also imagined himself as much the victim as the beneficiary of the sentimental economy, especially of the vagaries of desire that fueled commerce and transmuted farming in places like his native Ayrshire from ventures of subsistence into speculation—enterprises at which he and his family repeatedly lost.[60] Accordingly, Burns's poems are as much about the failure as the role of sympathy, insinuating themselves into the residual space Smith underscores in distinguishing "unison," or oneness, from "concord," or convergence. And it seems significant here that the question with which Smith grapples resembles the one haunting eighteenth-century practitioners of calculus: how is one to account for irrational remainders, be they infinitesimals or quanta of personal sentiments?

Not coincidentally—he was a keen defender of Newton's and also a product of the Scottish university system (specifically the University of Glasgow)—Smith envisions sympathy geometrically. Driven by the impulse to resolve complexity through clarity and, to that extent, channel the affect of geometry, Smith writes of the geometric "proportion or disproportion" of our private feelings (18) and of the virtues of perspective (110). Although critical of his mentor Francis Hutcheson's notoriously algebraic calculations of moral conduct (323–27) and intent on distinguishing moral reasoning from strict applications of mathematical logic, Smith nevertheless speaks favorably of "[t]he two greatest mathematicians that [he] ever [has] had the honour" to know, Simson and Matthew Stewart (124).[61] But, analogously to fluxions, the shapes Smith traces are not static but rather the products of moving points in a teeming society.

Accordingly, sympathy inheres in the moving lines of the gaze, with the relation between subjects mediated by Smith's famous "impartial spectator," to which I will return below. What this means is that Smith is essentially delineating a social plane whose emergent shape brings its elements into relation with one another while still keeping them distinct. And so, and as we discussed in Chapter 2, while sympathy is often imagined by way of an implicit algebra in which one thing stands in for another (x for y; feelings of compassion in the place of the original sentiment), we might more accurately describe these relations as flows of imaginative energy across distances that trace complex social figures: subject, object, impartial spectator. In other words, sympathy operates both figuratively and metonymically as well as symbolically and metaphorically; its relations operate through a logic of contiguity as well as (or alongside) one of displacement. In Burns's poems, these complex sympathetic networks—poet, louse, and lady; plowman and plowed—not only undercut any possibility of metaphorical union (of *this* swallowed up in *that*) but also distend themselves into warped shapes indicative of the dispersal of the types of energies (libidinal and existential) Smith's model strives to contain. This is especially the case in "To a Louse," where the players are distributed beings, multiples tending in more than one direction simultaneously. Such relations dispel the illusion of simple equivalence and, with it, the ideology of pure exchange. One thing cannot simply stand in the place of another because one thing is not one thing.

The poem thus enunciates itself, as we discussed near the outset of this chapter, in the gap between shape and number, the unity of form and the complexity of multiples. But the paradox the poem presents to moral philosophy meets with a rather different outcome when we read it alongside a far-reaching 1735 thought experiment by the Swiss mathematician Leonhard Euler. Inspired by an urge to articulate if not fully resolve the tensions between algebra and geometry, Euler wrote that "[i]n addition to that branch of geometry which is concerned with magnitudes, and which has always received the greatest attention, there is another branch, previously almost unknown, which Leibniz first mentioned, calling it the geometry of position," or *geometria situs* (also referred to as *analysis situs*).[62] Euler illustrates this new geometry through his famous example of the seven bridges of Königsberg—seven bridges connecting four land masses and a recreational puzzle mathematicians posed about whether it would be possible to walk around the city crossing each bridge only once, with the *flâneur* ideally returning to the point from which he or she started. Rather than trying to work through each possible route separately (a strategy corresponding to the "method of exhaustion," a precursor to calculus for determining the area of a curved shape), Euler simplified the problem by relating the number of land masses to the number of bridges and by creating a formula for how these relationships would operate: "If there are more than two areas to which an odd number of bridges lead, then such a journey is impossible. If, however, the number of bridges is odd for exactly two areas, then the journey is possible if it starts in either of these two areas. If, finally, there are no areas to which an odd number of bridges lead, then the required journey can be accomplished starting from any area."[63] Early nineteenth-century mathematicians would further refine Euler's invention by reducing the land masses to an abstract set of vertices and the bridges to lines or edges. Basically, they converted the map of a place into an abstract network graph. And in doing so, they laid the foundations for modern graph theory and topology, which translate the relation between points into an array of malleable shapes.

It is unlikely, to be sure, that Burns knew anything about the puzzle of the seven bridges of Königsberg or, more generally, about Leibniz's and Euler's geometry of position. Even renowned geometers like Maclaurin, Simson, and Stewart, who were mentioned alongside Euler in eighteenth-century mathematical encyclopedias, do not discuss *geometria situs* directly.[64] However, all three implicitly empathized with Euler in desiring to extend the scope of geometry. Provocatively, so does Smith. He conceives of the impartial spectator, a linchpin of his theory (as a reflexive operation in the mind of the subject, a way of "see[ing] ourselves as others see us"), as what makes it possible to "relate[] to [oneself] in [one's] proper shape and dimensions" (134). Geometry constitutes the metaphorical foundation of Smith's famous figure. But the *geometry of position*, or something analogous to it, animates its inner logic. I say this because, in a manner evocative of the puzzle to which Euler responds, Smith deduces sympathy from the relations between differential positions, specifically those occupied by the seeker of sympathy, the object (or observer) of his desire, and the privileged vantage point of the impartial spectator. Smith's model, in other words, is one of directed triangulation, with the seeker first gazing at the observer from whom he seeks sympathy, then at the impartial spectator (from whom he acquires the proper social comportment), then, through that mediation, back at himself. It is not the players alone but their position that is central.

But a problem emerges in Smith's matrix. The sympathy seeker's view, as Smith has it, is effectively split: she reflects only in a refracted way, one position by way of the other (the spectator's), converting her perspective into a trope, a "seeing *as*." (Such imaginative projections mark the plowman's speech in "To a Mouse": "I *doubt na*, whyles, but thou may thieve"; "*Thou saw* the fields laid bare an' wast" [13, 25, my emphasis].) What is more, a structural imbalance distorts this economy of sentimental gazing inasmuch as the observer, the one from whom the seeker desires sympathy, is actually the least observant of the three parties. This is because the seeker of sympathy sees both the observer and the impartial spectator (imagining herself, moreover, through their eyes), and the impartial spectator regards both the subject and the observer (if not literally, then as an abstracted position from which all is hypothetically visible). But Smith has the observer seeing only the spectacle of the sympathy seeker and thus failing to emulate the seeker by not taking cues from the impartial spectator. Hence, whereas the seeker discovers a model for how to act, the observer has no correspondent paradigm for how to perceive. This means that the fact of observation is taken for granted even as it appears subordinated to a system of substitutive relations—in essence, exemplifying Simson's concerns regarding the displacement of geometry (or Hamilton's "ostensive" pastoral) with the "symbolic" operations of algebra. Therefore, in both seeker and observer, we uncover a crisis of perspective and thus of moral philosophy: the seeker's gaze is split, and the observer's is literally unreflective (or unable to see itself). If Smith were to revise "To a

Mouse" on the basis of the relations he sketches in *A Theory of Moral Sentiments*, he would have the self-divided plowman seeking emotional solace from the self-possessed but purely instinctive and un-self-reflective rodent.

Burns's poem, of course, is more nuanced than that, and "To a Louse" is more complex still. A late nineteenth-century illustration of "To a Louse" by the Scottish painter William Small captures the split between the gaze and the gazing subject (see Figure 6). Though supposedly railing against the louse, the poet's eyes seem to hold the lady in view and tell a more amorous story. Small's image, in other words, highlights an important ambiguity inscribed into the poem, which complicates the poet's position. Looking to Jenny but addressing the louse, the poet exhibits something far from Smith's "unison" and only a strange form of "concord." So the three (or, in their complexity, $3n$) parties—poet, louse, and lady—bear an affective if not wholly sympathetic relationship with one another: their relations are proximal but not harmonious.

Small's illustration divulges the formal complexity at work in Burns's poem. Just as important, it highlights how the poem generates such literary effects as ambiguity and complexity of character (as a function of distributed, compounded subjectivity) not only through its rhetoric but also through its referents—that is, through the relations between its objects. And in that respect, such an image helps explain how "To a Louse" delineates and describes an elaborate economy of meaning while circumventing Smith's prototype of human relations, the concept of sympathy. Burns presents us with a portrait of failed sympathy but also fashions an alternative. "To see oursels as ithers see us," as Smith would have us do, is to engage in an act of reading: it is to arrive at meaning through a transposition of registers—signs for referents (what Simson called "symbolic" cognition). "To a Louse," however, presents us less with substitutions than with networks, placing pressure on the weaknesses—mathematical as well as moral—of Smith's design and hence on the latter's concept of human nature and civil society (or space of social relations). The Burnsian network of poetic objects, looping around each other and forging a virtually infinite plenitude of relations, suggests that we already are the "ithers" whose sympathy we crave.

This is where Burns's poem resonates with the work of Michel Serres. For Serres, topology, the evolutionary product of Euler's geometry of position, is *the* great model of modern existence. This becomes especially evident, for Serres, in the case of historiography. This is because history technically constitutes a closed set of circumstances that, nevertheless, acquires different

Figure 6. *The Complete Works of Robert Burns* (Philadelphia: Gebbie and Co., 1886). L. Tom Perry Special Collections, Harold B. Lee Library, Brigham Young University, Provo, Utah.

meanings—different shapes—depending on how we sketch its formal relations. Similarly to interpretive practices involving big data (in which new input variables produce new textual/topological shapes), topology as Serres imagines it generally refutes the causalities of grand narratives, accommodating instead the conviction that history might always be configured otherwise, scaled up or down to reveal new structures of relation—and, with them, new forms of being.[65] History thus represents our recomposition (narrative but also artisanal, a crafting) of the past through a redesigning of its elements: "History is the locus of full causes without effects, immense effects with futile reasons, strong consequences from insignificant causes, rigorous effects from chance occurrences."[66] The past consists of a protean field of relations whose agents function as shape-shifters, or forces that rearrange the configuration of the past and thus the meaning we make of it.

Serres likens these shape-shifters to parasites. By way of exposition, he recounts, as a topological fable, Aesop's narrative about the country and city rats who feast on the leftovers of the tax farmer's table. As Serres tells it, the city rat benefits from the country rat, who has invited him to the farmer's residence, and the farmer, like the pests (and like the beneficiaries of the invisible hand in Smith's theory), "regale[s him]self at the expense of" others. All three are parasites. But they are not alone: "[W]e know that the feast is cut short. The two companions scurry off when they hear a noise at the door. It was only a noise, but it was also a message, a bit of information producing panic: an interruption, a corruption, a rupture of information. Was the noise really a message? Wasn't it, rather, static, a parasite? A parasite who has the last word, who produces disorder and who generates a different order" (3). Why is the noise also a parasite? In French, *bruit parasite* is the term for "static," and here, in this example, it breaks up a preexisting condition, feasting, as it were, on the nervous meal of the gorging rodents. But this intrusion, *any* intrusion, alters the presiding state of affairs and hence the topological shape of the situation. Such disruptions are perpetual and inexorable, such that "[w]e parasite each other and live amidst parasites," Serres remarks. "Which is more or less a way of saying that [parasites] constitute our environment. We live in that black box called the collective; we live by it, on it, and in it" (10). This makes for a chaotic state of existence, an intensification of what Smith theorized by way of sympathy. But here, existence consists less of shared sentiments than of "[p]oints and lines, beings and relations" (10) in perpetual flux. Parasitic mutation inhabits "all beings," Serres claims; it is a tale "[o]f lice and men" (7).

Of lice and men: a rich pun. And while it may refer to Steinbeck's *Of Mice and Men* (which appeared in France as *Des Souris et des Hommes*), it more likely alludes to the French translations of Burns's famous poems.[67] Through it, Serres effectively mock-canonizes Burns as the bard less of historical Scotland than of modern being imagined as a condition of continuous deformation. This is a variation on Pittock's argument concerning Burns's "strange visibility," the poet's distortional shapes (once anthologically expansive, now contracted) relative to the literary canons in which he is only partly included. More specifically, it introduces a distinction between shape-shifting and shape, between the process and product of literary form.

Consider, in "To a Louse," the implication of the poet's inability to see himself. More literally, think of the disjunction between what the poet says—that Jenny exhibits moral failings—and what the poem implies (as suggested in the final stanza)—that the sympathy that binds us also eludes us. The threat of social disarray takes the form of a detachment of the poet's vision from the poem he articulates. And yet, the poem is inseparable from that voice, meaning that the poem "is" and "is not" simultaneously: it exists in ironic relation to itself. In essence, we might say (after Serres) that the poem feasts on itself or behaves parasitically relative to itself. But this means it never takes a single form or, rather, that the form that *appears* is never the only one that is possible. For when we follow the *poet's* logic, we miss the *poem's* rationale. And when we keep the poem in view (the full constellation of nodes, as it were, and their relation to each other), we distance ourselves from the poet and the "path" or "paths" on which he sends us. "To a Louse" thus illustrates the aporia between performative and constative language that Paul de Man theorized—the split between what a poem says and does or between the elements of which it consists and the event it comprises in its enunciation. This bifurcation, de Man obliquely concludes, gives language "the appearance of a history," a perpetually unfolding drama between what happens (the performative) and the recursive structures from which such linguistic events are fashioned (the constative).[68]

Serres, however, calls this "history" shape-shifting. He emphasizes, in other words, the perpetually "strange visibility" of history's *almost* literal unfolding. And that helps explain why Burns's poem and perhaps the Burnsian canon are important for the sympathetic exchange they short-circuit. This story becomes more powerful, I am suggesting, when perceived against the backdrop of eighteenth-century geometry, which figured as a discipline, science, propaedeutic, and cultural figure. This is true when understood relative not only to the eighteenth century proper but also to the puzzle of distant reading. I have not attempted a quantitative analysis of Burns's poetry, but I have tried to show how the dynamics of shape and number on which such reading—such *seeing*—are predicated informed the philosophical debates in which both geometry *and* some of Burns's best-known poems figured. Burns was no geometer, true. But his carefully crafted identity (and subsequent reputation) as Scotland's national poet and the recrudescence there (both uncanny and shrewdly canny) of some perplexing formal and philosophical conundrums reveal the wide reach not only of sympathy but also of geometry in the culture of the Scottish Enlightenment. This has been my point in arguing that there was something poetic about Simson's biographical legacy and something mathematical about Burns's poems. And the disclosure of how these two things relate to each other constitutes a kind of recovery effort that is a standard feature of many literary histories. But the mathematical inflections of recovery—of Moretti's distant reading, Badiou's mathematical ontology, Serres's shape-shifting topologies, and so on—shows us why Burns's case and those of his contemporaries become important not only *in* history but *to* it.

PART III

Locus: Measuring the Scottish Enlightenment Across History

Locus: 1a. Place in which something is situated, locality. . . . 3. *Math.* The curve or other figure constituted by all the points which satisfy a particular equation of relation between coordinates, or generated by a point, line, or surface moving in accordance with any mathematically defined conditions.

—*Oxford English Dictionary*

CHAPTER 5

The Newtonian Turn/Turning from Newton: James Thomson's Poetic Calculus

Isaac Newton's impact on modernity is well documented and perhaps unparalleled. Citing the influence of his work on the applied as well as the theoretical sciences, Margaret C. Jacob calls Newton the driving force behind "the making of the industrial west."[1] But assessing Newton's literary legacy is more complicated. There are, to be sure, direct connections. In her 1963 book *Newton Demands the Muse*, Marjorie Hope Nicolson shows how widely Newton's ideas from the *Opticks* permeated eighteenth-century poetry.[2] And, of course, there is the converse argument to be made for Newton's "negative influence"—the case that literature began shaping itself in opposition to the scientific and industrial ideology that Newton enunciated and later personified, with Keats famously pledging "[c]onfusion to the memory of Newton" for "destroy[ing] the poetry of the rainbow."[3] Raymond Williams makes the broader claim that the narrowing of the definition of literature from educated discourse to creative or imaginative writing was "in part a major affirmative response, in the name of an essentially general human 'creativity,' to the socially repressive and intellectually mechanical forms of a new social order: that of capitalism and especially industrial capitalism," which is precisely where Jacob locates Newton's impact. According to this schematic, literature emerged as a reaction against the instrumentalizing of modern life, the principles of Newtonian science giving rise to what C. P. Snow famously dubbed "the two cultures debate."[4]

In recent decades, trends toward interdisciplinarity and the disclosure of the creative exigencies of scientific thinking have considerably opened the borders between the "two cultures" and the way they shape our perception of the past. Hence, today, Robert Markley locates seventeenth- and eighteenth-century literary and scientific discourses within a more encompassing crisis of representation that alternatively stenciled and erased boundaries not only between, say, novels and natural philosophy but also between Newton and the "Newtonianism" of followers who often undercut or grossly distorted his work under the auspice of promoting it.[5] John Bender takes the further step of showing how Newton's theories feigned the types of hypotheses that Newton himself professed to disdain, weaving unprovable narratives about the nature of matter in motion (for example, gravity) and thus implicating "science" within a modus operandi of "fiction."[6] In terms more familiar to the history of science, one might say with I. Bernard Cohen that Newton rendered the universe discursive by "introduc[ing] mathematical analysis into the study of nature in a . . . new and particularly fruitful way," deploying processes of "simplification and idealization" that translated contingent empirical phenomena into systemic form.[7] As Richard Westfall remarks, such translations enabled Newton to arrive at conclusions on the basis of his system of analysis rather than on direct observation; hence, Newton was able to argue that "forces . . . reveal motions, not motions forces."[8] Such imaginative élan inspires Frank Durham and Robert D. Purrington to label Newton "astounding" in his "inventiveness."[9] By this reckoning, the real question may not concern Newton's impact on literature but rather literature's impact, or the impact of literary (that is, of inventive, discursive) thinking, on Newton.

The influence of this creative, literary Newton took hold in the "long" Scottish Enlightenment. It inspired David Hume, for example, to import principles of Newtonian science into moral philosophy, where he transformed them into a psychological physics of forceful passions. A century later, it motivated scientists like William Thomson (Lord Kelvin) and James Clerk Maxwell to mimic Newton's universalizing gesture in supplanting the latter's theory of force with a new physics of energy.[10] To some degree, Newtonianism in Scotland replicates the positions we sketched above. For example, did Newton directly influence Scottish literature? Yes, if we take seriously not only poems celebrating Newton (for example, by Allan Ramsay: "The God-like *Man* now mounts the sky") but also the literary recrudescence there of Newtonian ideas (like fluxional calculus in David Mallet's long 1728 poem *The Excursion*: "with transport I survey / This firmament, and these her rolling worlds, / Their *magnitudes*, and *motions*").[11] Did Newton also exert a "negative" (or romantic) influence on Scottish literature? Yes, perhaps most vividly in the primitivist ethos of the *Ossian* phenomenon, though with even greater poignancy in the anti-Enlightenment affect of Gaelic poets like Alasdair Mac-Mhaighstir Alasdair and Donnchadh Bàn Mac-an-t-Saoir (that is, Alexander MacDonald and Duncan Bàn Macintyre), who equated the "improving" sciences with the deterioration of bardic culture.[12] And did Scottish literati also go so far as to suggest, with Bender, that science is another form of narrative? Yes, most famously in Hume's ascription of causal reasoning to the workings of fiction, which we discussed in Chapter 2.

For all these congruities, Scotland's strong geometric tradition adds a different dimension to literary Newtonianism. As we have seen, geometry involved not only a discipline but also, and more broadly, an encompassing logic of *figure* uniting form and symbol, eye and ear, present and past. Forged in an ambivalent relationship with algebra, Newtonian geometry extended itself into the domain of the literary or literally figurative realm in which forms became shapes of mind and nature, shapes of being. This is the imaginative place where Scott's reflexive (or non-Euclidean) historicism, the perspectival aesthetics of the picturesque, and Burns's complex (creaturely) brand of poetry were all conceived. It also makes up a crucial aspect of James Thomson's nature poems, which are the principal subject of this chapter.

The Seasons helped initiate a new literary aesthetic in the eighteenth century. Often interpreted as part of a "sublime" or inward turn away from Alexander Pope's bouncing oratories, Thomson's verse might also be understood as an evocatively fluxional enterprise—a Newtonian effort to construct figures over a widening abyss of symbolic reference. Indeed, Newton's model and its penchant for abstract but true-to-life shapes helps explain the strange merger of the empirical and the ideal in *The Seasons*, the poem's power to place us in a landscape of rich but geographically unrecognizable details.

> Moist, bright, and green, the Landskip laughs around.
> Full swell the Woods; their every Musick wakes,
> Mix'd in wild Concert with the warbling Brooks
> Increas'd, the distant Bleatings of the Hills,
> The hollow Lows responsive from the Vales,
> Whence blending all the sweeten'd Zephyr springs.[13]

These lines, immediately preceding a reference to Newton in *Spring* (originally published in 1728), situate us in a rural locale that is dense with sensations (visual, sonorous, olfactory) and poetic modes (descriptive, pastoral, georgic) but is nowhere locatable as such. "Landskip" here is a kind of Platonic abstraction, an inflation of nature into idealized form. It amounts, we will see, to a virtual geometric exercise that departs from Newton in the very act of emulating him, much as Newton broke with Descartes. *The Seasons* then becomes, we might say, the pseudo-geometry of a pseudo-geometry. It illustrates the logic and strangeness of the Scottish mathematical enterprise, one that, as we will see in Chapter 6, imparted its legacy in the arts and sciences in later modernity.

It was in large part the strangely inorganic quality of abstract, geometric figure, the obtrusion of the visible, to which Wordsworth and Keats objected in eighteenth-century poetry. They complained in particular that the Newtonian conception of nature vandalized a certain exercise of the imagination, detaching observation from visceral experience and "[u]nweav[ing] the [poetic] rainbow" in the process.[14] Of course, Romantic literature teems with "monstrous" forms that were the products of the poetic engagement with science, often born of impulses to revise Newtonian mechanics.[15] One medium of this revisionist impulse was the science of vitalism, "the theory that life is generated and sustained through some form of non-mechanical force or power specific to and located in living bodies." Catherine Packham, who observes that vitalism "marked the transitional period between the rejection of earlier [i.e., Newtonian] mechanical models and the formalism of the modern sciences of life," identifies vitalist themes in the work of such Romantic writers as Coleridge, Mary Shelley, Ann Radcliffe, and others.[16] While she traces vitalist thought to the theoretical and experimental labor of Scottish thinkers like the poet John Armstrong, the physician Robert Whytt, and the philosophers David Hume and Adam Smith, we might draw a distinction between the Scottish-influenced branch of English Romanticism and Scottish Newtonians like Thomson. Vitalists perceived Newton as a mechanist, whereas for Thomson, Newton also remained a metaphysician, uniting moral and natural philosophy; hence, while the vitalists viewed Newton as part of the "old" science of material forces, he retained for many Scots a reputation as a touchstone of critical thinking and even, possibly, otherworldly truth—a nature beside nature, as it were.[17]

And, crucially, there was an additional discrepancy, a formal one. Vitalists and Romantic poets imagined life as an organic addendum to a clockwork universe, a "one" exceeding the "voided" or empty status of mere matter. But Thomson associated poetic vitality (if not vital*ism*) less with the transcendence of science through poetry, and hence less with an imaginative compensation for the loss of an experientially immediate world, than with the union of ones and zeroes, moral and natural philosophy. Newton's fluxional calculus, we recall, involved its own drama of ones and zeroes in the form of prime and ultimate ratios—constructs calculating the origin and cessation of motion. As we discussed in Chapter 2, Berkeley objected to the flagrantly imaginary quality of these constructs, these "ghosts of departed quantities" that, in geometric shape, granted form and thus conceptual substance to inexistent quantities. But these shapes were hardly incidental to Newton's fluxions, as Niccoló Guicciardini has argued; they functioned instead as dynamic, empowering metaphors, transporting the mathematician across the chasm dividing irrational from whole numbers and thus constituting a meaning in themselves as much as an illustration of an analytical process. Newton thus perceived in *figure*—geometric-*qua*-literary—the form of the cosmos as well as the lineaments of his own concepts.

This fact bears implications not only for the mathematical sciences but also for our understanding of the "Scotch metaphysics" relative to the "English Romantics." What Wordsworth and Keats shared was a conviction that imagination necessarily supplements the abstractions of science, whereas for the Scottish geometers, imagination (literally, the power to compose diagrammatic images and the imprint in those images of the shapes, or habits, of thought) was immanent to the very process of abstraction.[18] Hence, whereas the logic of Romantic supplementarity might present itself as a dialectical antithesis to instrumental reason, Newtonian geometry in Enlightenment Scotland tells a story of the mind's harmonious relation to its tools as well as its environment. Such attunement may strike us as ironic when we reflect, for example, on the barbaric afterimage of progress in the industrialized slum heaps of nineteenth-century Glasgow, the offspring of Newtonian innovations. But if we juxtapose these images with those of the Celtic Revival in early twentieth-century Edinburgh, or if we think about Art Nouveau and, with Murdo Macdonald, about the "sensitivity to the exactness of proportion" in these designs—designs that derived from "the practical geometrical tradition of Glasgow engineering"—then we arrive at a fuller picture not only of the Scottish Enlightenment but also of an artistic ideal that connects the Enlightenment even with its imagined antitheses, like modernism and the avant-garde.[19] What I mean to suggest is that the Scottish tradition bypasses a certain Romantic ideology of the compensatory nurturing power of rocks, and stones, and trees. This is one important reason why Thomson's nature seems so different from Wordsworth's. For Thomson, geometry was an instrument of nature, not the image of its opposite.

My aim over the next two chapters is to convey some of the logic and history of this tradition by tracing a trajectory that leads from Thomson's *Seasons* and Scottish philosophy to Edgar Allan Poe's brilliant and bizarre poetico-scientific treatise *Eureka* and, from there, into the early (or, if you will, long) twentieth century. Newton, we will see, functions in this tradition not only as a luminary of the "improving" sciences but also as a poet whose failings resulted partly from his reticence in pursuing the very logic of figure he made available. If to Keats Newton was an icon of mathematical science, then to Thomson he was something of a Romantic genius.

Newton's Poetic Genius

In his prize-winning 1764 essay on the subjects of natural and moral philosophy, Kant declared that a true science of metaphysics must replicate Newton's achievement in natural philosophy. Metaphysics, that is, must ascertain the rules underlying our experience much as Newton intuited the laws governing nature.[20] Kant famously set forth these rules, or at least some of them, in his 1781 opus *The Critique of Pure Reason*, asserting Newtonian models of space and time as the foundational categories of all cognition. One hundred years later, critics like Henri Bergson would turn Kant's assertion against him, arguing that Kant had conflated Newtonian space with all spatiality whatsoever, a tenuous move given the nineteenth-century emergence of non-Euclidean, postclassical spaces.[21]

Kant serves as an important hinge opening onto the Scottish Enlightenment and Newton's classical physics, on one end, as well as, on the other, the theory of modern aesthetics in the work of such neo-Kantians as Georg Simmel.[22] This situates him, evocatively, in the niche we have called late Euclideanism. As we have seen, one of the principal sites of late Euclideanism was fluxional calculus, which fused algebra with geometry and converted geometric figures into emblems of motion or flux. And in subtle but important ways, fluxions informed Kantian philosophy from its early stages in the 1760s all the way through the three Critiques in the 1780s and early 1790s. Kant drew heavily on geometry, which is not to say that his critical program was overtly mathematical: Kant actually (albeit somewhat erroneously) distinguished philosophy's "analytical" qualities from the "synthetic" operations of mathematics. I say "erroneously" because fluxions, for example, possessed both an analytical and a synthetic component. But Kant reasoned that while philosophy reflects on the world as it is given to us, mathematics constructs its realities in the process of defining them. Straight lines, say, correspond with their own definition as the shortest distance between two points. Such a mental operation accords a special "intuitive" role to geometry, Kant believed, as the basis by which such things as straight lines even appear to the mind in the first place. For Kant, one "sees" mathematical concepts against a spatial backdrop: the "figure" of the line, that is, appears against a "ground" of space.[23] And space, for Kant (and, with it, *anything* that appears to the understanding), involves a temporal dimension in the process of its own formation: space is the backdrop of the line, but the line's delineation is the becoming-time of space. Newtonian calculus provided Kant with an important precedent here, for fluxions presented space as a temporal construction of the line: "Lines are described," Newton declared, "by a continual motion of Points."[24] Newton thus traced the horizons of the Kantian process of cognition and, with it, the metaphysical critique as well as the instrumental elaboration of science.

Kant turned increasingly to the intuitive properties of geometry in his critical philosophy.[25] And yet, Newton's presence there is mostly implicit: he factors into Kant's conception of the categories of space and time in the *Critique of Pure Reason* (1781), but it is not until the *Critique of Judgment*, published nearly ten years later (1790), that Kant mentions Newton by name. He does so in his discussion of genius, which in turn occurs within the framework of the "Analytic of the Sublime," where Newton's calculus insinuates itself into Kant's thinking in subtle but important ways. Take the notions of "magnitude" and "maxima," which designate the degree of fluctuation (or change in speed) and the greatest value taken by a function. "Estimation of magnitude," Kant writes, "by means of numerical concepts (or their signs in algebra) is mathematical; estimation of magnitudes in mere intuition (by the eye) is aesthetic." The latter (the "aesthetic") essentially underwrites the former inasmuch as it sets the bounds, the backdrop, against which algebraic numbers and their measurements acquire meaning. In this way, "all estimation of the magnitude of objects . . . is ultimately aesthetic," which is to say, geometric: without space and the synthetic activity of the mind, algebraic quantities would have no meaning.[26] And yet, Kant continues, while

> there is not maximum for the [numerical] estimation of magnitude (inasmuch as the power of numbers progresses to infinity), yet for the aesthetic estimation of magnitude there is indeed a maximum.

> And regarding this latter maximum I say that when it is judged as [the] absolute measure beyond which no larger is subjectively possible . . . then it carries with it the idea of the sublime and gives rise to that emotion which no mathematical estimation of magnitude by manner of numbers can produce. (107)

Kant envisions the sublime, in other words, as marking the limit of the mind's ability to experience magnitude. Newton's calculus, we recall, converted sequences of irrational numbers into sets of graphable points; in Kant's terms, it transformed infinitesimal units "beyond which no larger" or more discriminating denominator was possible into the "aesthetic" image of a moving line. In Kant's concept of the sublime, these constructs clarify the process of thought even as they also serve as the index of what escapes it.

Kant thus fashions the sublime through an analogy with Newton's fluxions. But Kant also affiliates the sublime with the work of art. Sublime forms may resemble nature, he says, but they are mental operations, much as "the vast ocean heaved up by storms" is evocatively though not technically sublime (99). The sublime belongs, rather, to the order of freedom in which the mind engages with the world and adds something to the measure of its experience. Art, Kant says, is one such "production through freedom," a "power of choice that bases its acts on reason" (170). This makes the creation of art a moral activity that nevertheless has "the *look* of nature" (174, Kant's emphasis). Art thus follows from the same order of reasoning as the sublime, which is a moral category to the extent that it ultimately reveals "that the mind has a power surpassing any standard of sense" (106) and is therefore an active agent in the world and not merely a passive receptacle of sensations.

Sublimity as philosophy, sublimity as calculus, sublimity as art: Kant's associative logic paints a mixed picture of this axial category. Inflated into a sign of freedom, the sublime serves as the guarantor of cognitive authority legitimizing the philosophical reconstruction of nature. And yet, because sublimity also operates in a manner akin to art, Kant must conceptualize art as a "free" enterprise operating outside all governing (philosophical and mathematical) concepts. Accordingly, Kant appeals to the idea of genius as that outside-the-box "talent . . . that gives the rule to art" or that, in sublime fashion, reveals a work's (or a philosophy's) integrity after the fact. At its inception, however, genius "cannot describe or indicate scientifically how it brings about its products" (174, 175). Indeed, "genius must be considered the very opposite of the spirit of imitation" or of any rote activity (176, Kant's emphases deleted). And this, in turn, explains why Newton, alas, is no genius—but also, beguilingly, why he is:

> one can indeed learn everything that Newton has set forth in his immortal work on the principles of natural philosophy [i.e., the *Principia*], however great a mind was needed to make such discoveries; but one cannot learn to write inspired poetry, however elaborate all the precepts of this art may be, and however superb its models. The reason for this is that Newton could show how he took every one of the steps he had to take in order to get from the first elements of geometry to his great and profound discoveries. . . . But no Homer or Wieland can show how his ideas, rich in fancy and yet also in thought, arise and meet in his mind; the reason is that he himself does not know, and hence also cannot teach it to anyone else. In scientific matters, therefore, the greatest discoverer differs from the most arduous imitator and apprentice only in degree, whereas he differs in kind from someone whom nature has endowed for fine art. (176–77, Kant's emphases deleted)

Newton's status here is curious and complex. For starters, Kant's claim that, unlike Homer or Wieland, Newton could demonstrate the steps he took in making his discoveries is historically suspect. Margaret C. Jacob and Larry Stewart rehearse the tale that "[h]istorians often repeat . . . about Newton being spotted by a couple of students in the lanes of Cambridge before he moved to London. One undergraduate says to the other, 'There goes the man who wrote that book that no one can understand.'"[27] Robin Valenza remarks that "historians have turned up fewer than ten individuals who likely mastered the *Principia* in its entirety before Newton's death" but adds that Newton purposely cultivated this aura of obscurity as a way of keeping his work from being dragged through the muck of public debate.[28] As such, demonstration was something of a labile activity in the Newtonian corpus. But the historical accuracy of Kant's reference aside, what comes to the fore here is Newton's ambiguity within the Kantian system. We have seen that Newtonian calculus helps Kant synthesize the categories of cognition as well as the schematics of the sublime. And yet, what Kant identifies with "art," or with "Homer" rather than "Newton," is seemingly the very principle for which Berkeley took Newton to task. Newton erred, Berkeley argued, in inflating irrational quantities into measurable wholes and converting them into coherent edifices or into shapes as the illusion of substance. But what Kant associates with sublimity and with art as "moral" categories is that very quality—the (geometric) abstraction from experience and the "free" imitation of nature at the point at which the understanding (or the grasp of the infinite or of infinitesimals) fails. And to the extent that Kant is able to theorize this dynamic only because of Newton's groundbreaking innovations, Newton effectively becomes the "genius" or "poet" who enables Kant to play the part of "philosopher."

Kant's conflicted, even contradictory reflections on the repeatability of Newtonian science would leave a lasting impact on our conception of art as a lightning flash of inspiration, an artifact of pure serendipity. It contributed significantly to our understanding of the Romantic repudiation of Newton as a "mechanical" thinker.[29] But the Newtonian poetics of Kant's argument also open onto the Scottish Enlightenment, where the discussion of genius was heavily tinged by the "Homeric" pretentions of Macpherson's *Poems of Ossian*.[30] William Duff, the Presbyterian minister who was one of the first philosophers of genius, expounded in 1767 on this link between Macpherson and Homer. The "Works of Homer and Ossian" prove that "in the early periods of society, original Poetic Genius will in general be exerted in its utmost vigour," while it "will seldom appear in a very high degree in cultivated life."[31] The comparison between Ossian and Homer (and, indeed, the Ossian phenomenon itself) grew out of Thomas Blackwell's influential lectures on Homer, which the young James Macpherson attended at Marischal College, Aberdeen, and which Kant effectively reprises in making Homer Newton's counterpoint.[32] While Kant never refers directly to Ossian, his early *Observations on the Feeling of the Beautiful and Sublime*, published in 1764 during the initial wave of the Ossian sensation, strikes similar chords in its descriptions of deserts, ghosts, and melancholy.[33]

The logic of primitive genius itself derived from the so-called battle of the books in the late seventeenth and early eighteenth centuries, which posed the question of whether experience or learning—the proximity to pure, untrammeled nature or the perspective acquired from cultivation in the arts—produced better poetry.[34] In a move I deem symptomatic of Scottish geometry, Duff collapsed this distinction: to stand on the shoulders of giants and thus to gaze more clearly into the heavens does not preclude a closeness to nature any more than philosophical reflection—which is at one remove from the direct experience of objects—forbids us from having an experience of cognition. Relative to our discussion above of the English-Romantic rejection of the "mechanical" Newton, culture—abstraction, figure, even diagram—is natural to man. So it was that Duff regarded Newton as "an original Genius of the first rank" (119). Duff's foil, provocatively, was Colin Maclaurin, who, despite being the most rigorous advocate of Newton's calculus in Europe (even impressing the likes of mathematical philosophers like Jean le Rond d'Alembert), "did not possess that compass of imagination, and that depth of discernment, which were necessary to discover the doctrines of the Newtonian system" (75, Duff's emphases deleted).

"[I]magination" and "discernment," "compass" and "depth": Duff's reference to Newton evokes the rhetoric of exploration and adventure that characterized the pioneering work on calculus in the seventeenth century.[35] Indeed, fluxions were "sublime" before Kant ever got to them. Humphry Ditton labeled them a "Sublime Invention" in his 1705 *Institution of Fluxions*; John Rowe proclaimed in the 1757 *Introduction to the Doctrine of Fluxions* that "[o]f all the Mathematical Sciences, the *Doctrine of Fluxions* is the most extensive and sublime." Most provocatively, Maclaurin himself described fluxions as "a sublime geometry" in his 1748 *Account of Sir Isaac Newton's Philosophical Discoveries*.[36] "Sublimity" in these cases did not signify a fully conceptualized moral-philosophical system on the order of Kant's, but it did forge the association between Newton and the far reaches of nature on which Kant would later capitalize. But just as important, we come here to a crucial historical inversion: for Duff, Newton is Homeric (or Ossianic), whereas Maclaurin, at least in Kantian terms, is more Newtonian. In other words, Duff saw Newton as (what Kant would call) a poet, whereas Newtonians like Maclaurin were something less, something poet-like without being poetic, mere translators of the Newtonian word. As we saw with Robert Simson's "Ossianic" perspective onto Euclid, these geometers purported to be creative adaptors of the Newtonian system, making them the oracles of a poetry without poets, the purveyors of a bardic culture of everyday life.[37]

Even Newton occasionally affected something of the poet, at least by Kant's schematic terms. He assumes a science-*cum*-poetry position in the "General Scholium," his famous coda to the *Principia*. There, he invokes God as the "pantocrat" or "Universal Ruler" from whose "true dominion it follows that [he] is a living, intelligent, and most perfect [being]. He is eternal and infinite, omnipotent and omniscient." However natural these qualities may seem in a notionally universal being, they nevertheless lead Newton into conceptual difficulties given that God is at least partly exempt from the universe he has created: "In him are all things contained and moved; yet neither affects the other: God suffers nothing from the motion of bodies; bodies find no resistance from the omnipresence of God. It is allowed by all that the Supreme God exists necessarily; and by the same necessity he exists always and every where. Whence also he is all similar, all eye, all ear, all brain, all arm, all power to perceive, to understand, and to act; but in a manner not at all human, in a manner not at all corporeal, in a manner utterly unknown to us."[38]

In this metaphysical supplement to his natural philosophy, Newton elicits anthropomorphic categories he instantly retracts: God is "all eye . . . ear . . . brain . . . arm . . . power to perceive, to understand, and to act" but not in any human way. The rhetoric is antiphrastic, apophatic (in denying what it asserts)—or rather, in Newton's own terminology, it is allegorical: "by way of allegory, God is said to see, to speak, to laugh, to love, to hate, to desire, to give, to receive, to rejoice, to be angry, to fight, to frame, to work, to build; for all our notions of God are taken from the ways of mankind by a certain similitude, which, though not perfect, has some likeness" (442). In other words, to characterize God and metaphysically explain nature is to adopt the strategy of the poet, employing metaphors to create a concrete image of what otherwise would elude the imagination altogether. In this concluding section of the *Principia*, Newton plays the part of Homer, or perhaps Milton, justifying the ways of God to man.

In a famous essay on the "Newtonian synthesis," that convergence of mathematics and experimental philosophy in Newton's thought, Alexander Koyré ascribes such complex reconciliations to Newton's "genius—not *skill*." Newton's greatest innovation, he says, was in geometrizing space, substituting an abstract grid for "the concrete . . . place-continuum of pre-Galilean physics and astronomy." This was effectively a *poetic* gesture in that it extended (or metaphorically connected) this geometrized grid to experimental science, thus installing a new framework and methodology by which we process information. But it was generative and not simply mimetic. For, crucially, Koyré elaborates, the Newtonian system hinged on *nothing*—on gravity as an attractive (but inexplicable) force, an emptiness drawing everything into itself even as it fostered an elaborate explanatory system. "The introduction of the void was a stroke of genius and a step of decisive importance. It is this step that enabled Newton to oppose and unite at the same time . . . the discontinuity of matter and the continuity of space." "The corpuscular structure of matter . . . formed a firm basis for the application of mathematical dynamics to nature. It yielded the *fundamenta* for the relations expressed by space," the yang and yin of experimental science and mathematics. However, Koyré continues, "by substituting for our world of quality and sense perception, the world in which we live, and love, and die, another world—the world of quantity, of reified geometry," the Newtonian synthesis gave rise to "a world in which, though there is place for everything, there is no place for man." Newton "estranged" from science "the world of life"; in explaining the orderly motions of the planets, his genius only further accentuated the erratic, irrational behavior of humankind, thus sundering science from humanity (and, as the "two cultures" critics would have it, from the humanities).[39]

And so, if Newton was a poet in the sense that he opened the heavens and helped spawn a remaking of the earth (bearing in mind the etymology of "poetry" from the Greek *poeisis*, or "making"), he also, by that same gesture, severed humans from their traditional place in the cosmos, in nature, and with themselves. Newton's innovations thus laid the groundwork for the paradox Burns formulated in "To a Louse," which we discussed in Chapter 4: through these inventions, we behold many things more clearly but risk losing sight of ourselves. This corresponded with the concern Simson expressed about Newtonian mathematics, that it was more symbolic, more algebraic, than geometric—and, as such, Simson believed, it obscured what it purported to explain. Newton introduced an irrationality (of number—of infinite series—but also of free-thinking philosophy) he could neither resolve nor contain. Newton thus delineated a problematic, even paradoxical space for poetry, which now entered a world that was full but empty, clear but uncertain. Drawing upon but displacing the metaphysical function of geometry as the foundation of thought, Newton's "poetry" conjured the need for figures other than its own.

Thomson's Newtonian Figures

That Newton's genius simultaneously eliminated and empowered poetry is a paradox that James Thomson takes up in his poems. Newton was a source of ongoing interest and even inspiration for Thomson. After leaving Scotland for London, he taught briefly at Watts Academy, a school that promulgated Newtonian thought, in 1726. Then, when Newton died in March 1727, Thomson temporarily suspended his labor on *The Seasons* (having just completed *Summer* and commencing work on *Spring*) and began composing one of his most acclaimed works, the *Poem Sacred to the Memory of Sir Isaac Newton*, which he published that May. Extolling Newton as the "belov'd / Of Heaven" and the "first of men," Thomson's encomium attests to the currency of Newtonian thought in the British imaginary.[40] The poem also displays the effects of Thomson's university education in Edinburgh, where he studied *The Principia* under such enthusiastic Newtonians as Robert Stewart and where Newton's influence had permeated even subjects like moral philosophy.[41]

For Thomson, this influence extended to poetry. In his elegy, Thomson casts Newton in the role of a primordial deity, a kind of muse:

> Have ye not listen'd while He bound the *Suns*,
> And PLANETS to their spheres!. . .
> . . . [He] sat not down and dreamt
> Romantic schemes, defended by the din
> Of specious words, and tyranny of names,
> But bidding his amazing mind attend,
> And with heroic patience years on years
> Deep searching, saw at last the SYSTEM dawn,
> And shine, of all his race, on him alone. (17–18, 23–29)

Although adorned in the leaden robes of elegiac bombast, Thomson's Newton is clearly a genius in the "Homeric" sense of originality and invention: "our SOLAR ROUND / First gazing thro', he by the blended power / Of GRAVITATION and PROJECTION saw / The whole in silent Harmony revolve" (39–42). No mere observer of nature, however acute his "gaz[e]," Newton also brought something to nature, "blend[ing]" observation with theories of celestial motion. He expressed the laws that allowed nature to be, and to the extent that this was an imaginative synthesis of observation and imagination, the *Poem Sacred* becomes not only an encomium to science but also a self-reflexive celebration of poetry. As Shaun Irlam notes, Thomson, a poet, bestows the title of *poietes*—"maker"—on Newton.[42]

But the poet tempers his enthusiasm when he considers the effects of Newtonian poetry on more conventional verse like his own. He articulates this concern, however, in the form of apparently unstinting praise: Newton

> . . . took his ardent flight
> Thro' the blue Infinite; and every STAR,

> Which the clear concave of a winter's night
> Pours on the eye, or astronomic tube,
> Far-stretching, snatches from the dark abyss,
> Or such as farther in successive skies
> To fancy shine alone, at his approach
> Blaz'd into SUNS, the living centre each
> Of an harmonious system: all, combin'd,
> And rul'd unerring by that single Power
> Which draws the stone projected to the ground. (57–67)

Newton's genius follows the path of poetic "fancy" into the cosmos but then goes much further, "Blaz[ing]" nebulous and merely fanciful images "into SUNS," or virtual realities, by imbuing them with the explicative power of gravity. This occult force functions as the ultimate poetic metaphor or Newtonian "allegory," linking concrete phenomena with abstract powers and common stones with the furthest rings of Saturn. Thomson's Newton thus enacts Joseph Addison's 1712 observation in *The Spectator* No. 420 that "there are [no writers] who more gratifie and enlarge the Imagination, than the Authors of the new Philosophy," or the new science, "whether we consider their Theories of the Earth or Heavens, the Discoveries they have made by Glasses [i.e. by telescopes and microscopes], or any other of their Contemplations on Nature."[43] Even more directly, he anticipates Adam Smith's remarks in the "Essay on the History of Astronomy," written in the early 1750s. "The imagination," Smith says, once "felt a gap, or interval, betwixt the constant motion and the supposed inertness of the Planets," spawning an idea that "there must be a connecting chain of intermediate objects to link together these discordant qualities." Kepler, Descartes, and others failed to wrap their minds around this prospect. However, the "superior *genius* and sagacity of Sir Isaac Newton . . . made the most happy, and, we may now say, the greatest and most admirable improvement that was ever made in philosophy" with his theory of gravity, "a principle of connection" or cosmic metaphor "which completely removed all the difficulties the imagination had hitherto felt in attending to" the intricacies of motion.[44] In Newton, that is, "fancy" became truth, actuality; poetic figures took life as science.

This is a process of poetic animation or personification by which Thomson anoints nature Newtonian. He does so, however, within the context of an encomium that, we will see below, is not without its reservations concerning the stifling effects of Newtonian thought. In other words, Thomson worries about the effects of Newtonian personification.[45] This is a point worth underlining, for Thomson is widely remembered as one of the eighteenth century's serial personifiers, not as one of its critics.[46] In his *Elements of Criticism* (1762), for example, Lord Kames labels Thomson "licentious" in his frequent recourse to the trope.[47] But Thomson actually crafts a position similar to Kames's own: for each, personification is a *figure* that, like Newton's geometric calculus, tenuously straddles a void or gap separating image from concept, trope from meaning.[48]

For Kames, personification accentuates the subtle difference between image and emptiness or what is partly present and mostly absent. The poet who employs personification, he says, aspires "to afford conviction . . . of life and intelligence" to its objects of description (2:538); in other words, he imbues these objects with "ideal presence," a modality of thought that brings imaginary or nonexistent entities to life. Kames associates "ideal presence" with the theater, which, like personification, "bestow[s] sensibility and voluntary motion upon things inanimate" (1:71, 2:533). A mathematical analogy, however, embeds itself within the theatrical one. Its presence is subtle rather than overt, but it negotiates ideal presence through broad categories that had defined the cultural and philosophical parameters of geometry. Ideal presence consists, Kames says, of an "intuition" or "waking dream . . . into which reflection enters not" (1:68) and thus passes momentarily for a perception extrapolated from our experience. This moment of virtual reality is important to the degree that it underscores the ambiguity of the perception. Its logic is parallel to that of geometric objects, which derive (Hume, John Leslie, and others tell us) from our experience but then take a more abstract form as mathematical shapes. Such shapes are at once material and ideal, "real" in the sense of realism, which resembles but thus sets itself against the real as such. So it is with ideal presence, which Kames distinguishes "from real presence on the one side, and from reflective remembrance on the other" (1:68). Unlike an actual experience, whether present or recollected, ideal presence conjures "the idea of a thing I never saw, raised in me by speech, by writing, or by painting" (1:68). Ideal presence is thus in Kantian terms an *aesthetic* reality, occupying a middle ground between the concrete and the abstract, in the place reserved by Scottish intellectuals for the geometric interface of mind and world, physics and metaphysics. (Attesting to the impact of geometric reasoning on the Scottish imaginary, Kames names his *Elements* after Euclid's.)

Accordingly, geometric calculus presents a truer and more wide-ranging analogy for personification than does the theater, for calculus appeared to reconcile figure and idea (or content and expression) but not—as mathematicians and philosophers contended—in a wholly resolved or satisfying way. The important point for Kames, after all, is not that the personified figure is insufficiently real or true to life but that it seems to belong to a different order of experience: translated into terms of the mathematical debates we have been discussing, the (geometric) figure does not fully coincide with the (algebraic) operation it purports to represent. Hence, Kames remarks that personification signifies an "agitation" and "failure" of the illusion of ideal presence; it amounts less to a "waking dream" than to a dream at the fitful moment of waking, introducing a gap between representational objects and real ones (2:534, 535).[49]

This disjunction, integral to the very logic of representation, foreshadows (or, rather, belongs to a body of work that influenced) the Kantian notion of the sublime.[50] And for Kames, Newtonian thought illustrated this fraught principle; as such, it was practically the personification of personification itself, a roadblock to cognition as much as an instrument of it. "As the progress of arts and sciences toward perfection is greatly promoted by emulation, nothing is more fatal to an art or science than to remove that spur, as where some extraordinary genius appears who soars above rivalship." This, we have seen, was Thomson's concern regarding Newton, a concern that Kames converts into a creative hypothesis: "Mathematics seem to be declining in Europe: the great Newton, having surpassed all the ancients, has not left to the moderns even the faintest hope of equalling him; and what man will enter the lists who despairs of victory?"[51] A sublime phenomenon located at the limits of the understanding, Newton's thought exhibits ideal presence at the point at which the latter begins to decompose. The mathematical analogy is again useful here: Newtonian science illustrates (geometric) clarity at the moment of the latter's occlusion into the realm of the grand but unimaginable, the essence of the sublime.

What I am describing here is the mathematico-philosophical version of the hinge Thomson identifies in the *Poem Sacred* between Newton's "poetry" and his own. In "Blaz[ing]" the vision of traditional poets "into Suns," Newtonian science more than provides the measure for poetic intuition; it divides conventional poetic fancy from truth and thus marginalizes the poetry it ostensibly inspires. For example, in describing how Newton "To the charm'd eye educ'd the gorgeous train" of colors in the rainbow (101), Thomson asks whether any poet "ever . . . image[d]" or imagined "aught so fair" (119). The answer, the poet clearly implies, is no; such virtuosity, by dint of its sheer brilliance, casts ordinary poetry into shadow. Newton's is a "sublime" poetics that ventures into forests where the eye cannot follow.

What remains to a poet like Thomson, then, is to describe the experience of obscurity. Fittingly, shade is precisely where Thomson's *Summer* (the poem he concluded prior to composing the *Poem Sacred*) opens as the poet seeks refuge from the sun:

> From brightening Fields of Ether fair disclos'd,
> Child of the Sun, refulgent SUMMER comes,
> In pride of Youth, and felt thro' Nature's Depth . . .
> . . . .
> Hence, let me haste into the mid-wood Shade,
> Where scarce a Sun-beam wanders thro' the Gloom.[52]

"Shade" here is phenomenological as well as descriptive; it captures the poet's experience generally and not only the peculiarities of his movements in this particular instance:

> Come, *Inspiration*! from thy Hermit-Seat,
> By Mortal seldom found: may Fancy dare,
> From thy fix'd serious Eye, and raptur'd Glance
> Shot on surrounding Heaven, to steal one Look
> Creative of the Poet, every Power
> Exalting to an Ecstasy of Soul. (15–20, Thomson's emphasis)

What the poet seeks from "Inspiration" is what Newton so rapturously enjoyed—an exalting gaze of the heavens. But unlike Newton, who in the *Poem Sacred* "Blaz[es]" Fancy "into *Suns*," the poet here, in his shade, will cast only a fanciful "Glance" at the "surrounding Heaven": his muse dwells not in the stars but in a "Hermit-Seat" at the nether reaches of the *human* world, where Koyré says Newton failed to go. For Thomson, Newton is something more and hence also less than a poet: he overwhelms the imagination and thus disrupts the cognitive rhythms by which we coordinate perception with reflection.

The mathematical analogy animates Thomson's conceit as it does Kames's. Thomson's concerns were not expressly geometric, but poetry and geometry each "measured" (as Heidegger would say) the fading light of the modern era.[53] "Welcome, kindred Glooms!" With that apostrophe in the opening stanza of *Winter* (5), the first of the "seasonal" poems to appear in print (1726), Thomson captured the ethos of the emergent "graveyard school." Traditionally, critics have tended to follow Joseph Warton's lead in interpreting this credo as a salvo against Alexander Pope.[54] Its melancholy bespeaks what John Sitter memorably labeled a kind of "literary loneliness." Formally, such verse marked an inward turn away from satirical commentary and from the discourse of history, which increasingly became the substance of prose fiction.[55] And yet, as Thomson's *Poem Sacred* indicates, Newton plays an important symbolic role here, as well. This is a significant point, for while the sometimes scintillating effect of Pope's couplets are seen to have incited a reactionary descent into sublime obscurity (in, for example, Thomas Parnell's "Night-Piece on Death" and Edward Young's *Night Thoughts*), Newtonian thought furnished an example of geometric *poiesis*, or figure making, struggling to clarify an already extant murkiness. Hence, while the traditional narrative about the mid-century turn from Pope presents poetry in terms of algebraization—a proliferation of auto-referential symbols amid an atmosphere of obscurity—Thomson instead attempts something like Newton's fluxions, tracing figures among the shadows.

* * *

Thomson's poetic challenge was therefore to make like Newton or to be even more Newtonian than Newton in clarifying this new obscurity or in converting abstractions into images. Two tropes seem most aptly to characterize that operation. One, we have seen, is personification, which not only attributes human qualities to abstract entities but also, in Kames's view, foregrounds the tension between clarity and obscurity. The other would be metalepsis, which denotes the metonymical substitution of one word for another word that is also a metonym and that more broadly implies a collapsing of tropes into one another, a riot of figures. One famous example is found in the scene of Christopher Marlowe's *Doctor Faustus* when Mephistopheles conjures Helen of Troy, prompting Faustus to ask, "Is this the face that launched a thousand ships?"[56] Helen's "face" refers to the "thousand ships" of the Grecian army, which itself refers to the Grecian state: the image thus constitutes a figure within a figure. Metalepsis in *The Seasons* involves a more literal collapsing of figures—poetic and diagrammatic—in the poem's conceit to present a sweeping view of natural objects and even of the earth itself in its annual passage around the sun. This mobile perspective renders our experience of the seasons into a trope or figure of Newtonian calculus, which in turn mathematically expresses an astronomic process. In this respect, *The Seasons* functions as the poetic complement to a mathematical practice that is already, itself, a figure of nature (in what is "every Day seen in the motion of Bodies," Newton tells us).

Thomson's poem is thus the figure of a figure, the vision of a vision. This principle extends even to the layout of *The Seasons*, with prefatory summaries providing overviews of the poem's compounded (or meta-visionary) prospects. Consider, for example, Thomson's announcement in the introductory "Argument" of *Summer* that his poem will furnish the reader with a "View of . . . the torrid Zone," an extensive scene that necessarily commands a position from high above the field of vision: "Plains immense / Lie stretch'd below, interminable Meads, / And vast Savannahs, where the wandering Eye, / Unfixt, is in a verdant Ocean lost" (690–93). These exalted views, pervading each of the four poems, repeatedly yield to more intimate tableaux "beneath primeval Trees" (716) or to one of the poem's ubiquitous catalogs—like the enumerations of fowl and foliage in *Spring* or great men and grand rivers in *Summer*. In their own way, these catalogs reveal the workings of a metaphorically fluxional poetics, for they evoke a sense of number that seems virtually infinite without being "whole." The poet *might* identify every observable facet of nature (for example, crocus, daisy, violet; blackbird, bullfinch, linnet: items he actually mentions) in the same way that he *might* count to a thousand but does not. (Where, for instance, are azaleas, rhododendrons, and marigolds or grouses, gulls, or corncrakes, all of which "belong" to the corner of nature he verbally paints but are missing in the poem?) Instead, in making these lists, he appeals to nature's "Infinite Numbers" and "Innumerous" creatures (*Spring* 553, 608). To this extent, poetic counting, like calculus, sets a "limit" to its available data in order to portray a general likeness to objects. Scenes in nature thus resemble points along a graph: our ability to move past the specter of the infinite or microscopic is what permits our passage to other objects. We behold nature in its entirety only because we partly "void" it or disregard its infinite (or infinitesimal) details.[57]

This one-eye-closed approach to nature thus conjures in poetic fashion the crisis of irrational numbers that rendered traditional geometry so appealing to Scots like Robert Simson in the first place. The philosophical riddle surrounding these numbers prevented the practitioners of calculus from rendering the discipline fully rigorous until Louis-Augustin Cauchy formulated a new theory of limits in the 1820s. According to C. H. Edwards, "The device that enabled [Cauchy] to 'reconcile rigor with infinitesimals' was a new definition of infinitesimals that avoided the infinitely small *fixed* numbers of earlier mathematicians. Cauchy defined an infinitesimal . . . or *infinitely small* quantity . . . to be simply a variable with zero as its limit."[58] He thus restricted the converging properties of a given sequence to the terms provided by that sequence, effectively defining all available terms. This would have appeased Berkeley to the degree that "number" became a self-conscious artifice as opposed to a supposed index of actual existence. Maclaurin and his contemporaries, by contrast, were still essentially working on the analogical model likening complex numbers to geometric proportions (that is, presenting *images* of wholeness, of being, in the place of formal or logical solutions like Cauchy's).[59] In other words, Maclaurin and his peers were trafficking in a kind of mathematical metalepsis: their diagrams were figures of irrational numbers that were themselves figures of ontologically insoluble (but empirically measurable) masses of statistical being.

To be sure, mathematics and poetry (or mathematics and philosophy) are discrete disciplines possessing their own narratives of development. My aim here is not to conflate the particularities of these histories but instead to divulge how Thomson and the geometers often worked within similar—symmetrical—aesthetic and epistemic frameworks. For example, Thomson's habit of varying our perspective (taking us from, say, distant "Aspiring Cities" buried by earthquakes and "Mountains in the flaming Gulph" to "nearer Scene[s]" at home [*Summer* 1100–2]) essentially reiterates the point that John Keill, the Scot who was the first person to lecture on Newton at Oxford, made in his 1721 *Introduction to the True Astronomy*: "That we may have a more Distinct knowledge of the Fabrick of the *World*, and that the admirable Beauty of the Universe, and the harmonious Motions of the Bodies therein contained may be more easily understood, it will be requisite that that Divine and immense Fabrick should not be observed from one Point or Corner only: . . . to have a true and just Notion of the World, we must suppose it to be observed, in different Situations and Distances."[60]

Thomson literalized Keill's vision. In doing so, and given the impossibility of voyaging to Archimedean points at the edge of the universe, he converted the premise articulated in Keill's treatise into an aesthetic manifesto or Euclidean space probe—a desideratum for "suppose[d]" observation—defending the logic of poetic fancy as the visual complement to Newtonian science. Purporting to justify Newton, Keill thus effectively anticipated *The Seasons*. Indeed, what Keill declared in the preface to his lectures, that astronomy "for the certainty of its Demonstrations is not inferiour to *Geometry*; its usefulness is manifold, and the Amplitude of its *Subject* is so large that it comprehends nothing less than the World itself" (ii–iii, Keill's emphases), he might also have claimed for Thomson's poetry. Each aspired to the status of "earth measurement"—*geo-metria*—in an encompassing sense, not only of nature but also of metaphysics, with the aim of imparting "at last a distinct Knowledge of this Immense Palace of *God Almighty*" (17, Keill's emphasis) or, as Thomson put it, of gaining "The Heights of Science and of Virtue" (*Summer* 1741).

But for all its philosophical aspirations, and to borrow a phrase from Edwin Muir, there is a "curious emptiness" that resides at the heart of Thomson's poem or that inheres in the abstract portraits of nature that appear there. The measure of this emptiness may be found partly in the poem's cadences, the "numbers" of its famously orotund diction, its more-than-Miltonic *blank* verse. Lighting specifically on the poet's "numbers, his pauses, his diction," Samuel Johnson speaks to this point, remarking that Thomson "thinks in a peculiar train, and . . . always as a man of genius. . . . The reader of *The Seasons* wonders that he never saw before what Thomson shews him, and that he never yet has felt what Thomson impresses." And yet, at the same time, Thomson "may be charged with filling the ear more than the mind," such that he beguiles us for what is not there (but should be) and dazzles us for what is (even though it occasionally seems, upon reflection, to be "nothing").[61]

Johnson's view of Thomson is a more appreciative analog of Berkeley's take on Newton: *The Seasons*, like the fluxions, are a wilderness of hallucinatory forms and haunting voids. And, while Berkeley's Newton conjures "the Ghosts of departed Quantities," Thomson's poet ventures onto spectral terrain of his own:

> Still let me pierce into the midnight Depth
> Of yonder Grove, of wildest largest Growth:
> That, forming high in Air a woodland Quire,
> Nods o'er the Mount beneath. At every Step,
> Solemn, and slow, the Shadows blacker fall,
> And all is awful listening Gloom around. (*Summer* 516–21)

"Quire[s]" are collections of leaves, usually meaning parchment, hence designating writing as well as foliage. The "Depth[s]" whose "Grove[s]" we "pierce" here, then, are objects of speech as much or more than of sense; we cannot see them, certainly not outwardly, given the "midnight . . . Shadows" in which they lurk. The poetic cadences, "Solemn, and slow," evoke a kind of aural "black[ness]" that awakens imagination. But what exactly does the poet expect us to see at this "midnight" hour? The scene is more visionary than visual; it confounds eye and mind via pulsations that enter through the ear. This helps explain why the climactic "all" of the passage takes the catachrestic form of a personified "awful listening Gloom," a rapturous image of moody density, of the inconceivable accorded a kind of vague and visceral shape.

Thomson frequently resorts to personification in moments when he shifts from natural description to philosophical explication. As Kames theorized, it often marks the point at which Thomson's figures begin to lose themselves in labyrinths of their own recursion. The "awful listening Gloom" of the visionary "Depth," for instance, represents the logical outcome and also the breakdown of a series of figures in the poem commingling light and darkness. *Summer* opens in "Shade," as we have seen, and it eventually imagines God dwelling in a similar abode: "How shall I . . . attempt to sing of HIM, / Who, LIGHT HIMSELF, in uncreated Light / Invested deep, dwells awfully retir'd / From mortal Eye, or Angel's purer Ken" (175–79)? The deity, a shade-dwelling (deeply "Invested") source of light, is the animating agent behind the sun, whose "strong, attractive Force, / As with a Chain indissoluble," binds together the planetary "System" (97–99). The sun, the source of natural light, is thus also the effect of a hidden—divine—source of luminescence. This places God in the poet's position, removed from a planetary body that he (that is, God and poet) illuminates in turn (whether through the creative or merely the descriptive word—or through what Coleridge differentiated as primary or secondary imagination[62]).

And this raises the specter of Newton, whose work and suite of associations in Thomson's verse effectively stitches together the divine and the secular in the figure of Thomson's deific poet. I say this because Thomson refers to the summer sun as the "INFORMER of the planetary Train," but this in turn conjures Thomson's image of Newton in *Poem Sacred* as the one who binds together the universe within a system not of nature but of diagrammatic imagination. Without Newton's "quickening Glance," as with the sun's, the "cumbrous Orbs," the planets, "Were brute unlovely Mass, inert and dead. . . . / How many Forms of Being wait on thee! / Inhaling Spirit!" (105–6, 108–9). The sun "Inhal[es]" its vitality from God and breathes life into the universe, but it also derives meaning from Newton who, in *The Seasons*, takes life from the poetic word.

In effect, Thomson reprises a puzzle here to which Pope gives expression in his "Epitaph. Intended for Sir Isaac Newton, In Westminster Abbey." There, Newton more than rivals this poetic privilege; he personifies it: "Nature, and Nature's Laws lay hid in Night. / God said, *Let Newton be!* and All was *Light*."[63] The couplet recapitulates the third verse of the creation story in Genesis—"And God said, Let there be light: and there was light"—but it also divides nature from the divine, physics from metaphysics. Pope assumes the position of God: he is the one whose word proclaims light, who turns on the light(s); Newton, by contrast, is "Let . . . be," a product of the divine creation. However, the metaphorical union of Newton with brilliance (Newton comes to "be" and nature suddenly appears) makes Newton an enlightener of a different variety. This is because, on one hand, as an emblem of light, Newton effectively translates "Nature, and Nature's Laws" into the human form of mathematical equations, explaining the elements in the set of the divine creation. But on the other hand, Newton can account neither for nature's origins nor for his own since, Pope says, that is a function of metaphysics, of what "God said"—an oral original that precedes its own translation. Hence, Newton is "Newton" only to the extent that he is also (in Kant's terms) "Homeric": he cannot "show how his ideas . . . arise and meet in his mind" (*Critique of Judgment* 177). By the terms of Kant's analysis ("In scientific matters . . . the greatest discoverer differs from the most arduous imitator and apprentice only in degree, whereas he differs in kind from someone whom nature has endowed for fine art"), Pope's Newton is both a scientist *and* a poet.

As in Pope's "Epitaph," Newton in *The Seasons* occupies the place of the sun, serving as an "effect" of God and poet but also as a "cause" of our understanding of that effect (that is, of the natural world). Newton is thus a metaleptic emblem in his own right, a conjunction of many figures—physical, metaphysical, poetic. Newton connects nature to deity, poetry to the divine. The "awful listening Gloom" of the later passage in *Summer*, which the poet subsequently describes as "the Haunt of Meditation . . . / The Scenes where antient Bards th'inspiring Breath, / Extatic, felt" (522–24) and where they "Convers'd with Angels, and immortal Forms" (525), is therefore an emblematic site at which nature collapses into its expressive portrayal.

It represents an abstract point at which poetry becomes "real" or at which ideas take shape as verse. In that way, it is a poetic complement to fluxions—or perhaps the other way around.

Thomson's Poetic Calculus: Measuring the "Seeds . . . Innumerous"

Thomson partly composed *The Seasons* in Newton's shadow, and he creatively adapted his poem to the exigencies of Newton's example. But he occasionally wandered into "midnight Depth[s]" he likely had no idea he was entering. Take, for example, one of the more overtly "Newtonian" passages in the poem. As *Summer* nears the close of day and the fulsome "Gloom" once again descends, the poet turns his gaze from the "faint erroneous Ray / Glanc'd from th'imperfect Surface of Things" (1687–88) "to Heaven," where, "[a]mid the radiant Orbs, / That more than deck, that animate the Sky" (1693, 1703–4), he beholds a majestic wanderer:

> Lo! from the dread Immensity of Space
> Returning, with accelerated Course,
> The rushing Comet to the Sun descends;
> And as he sinks below the shading Earth,
> With awful Train projected o'er the Heavens,
> The guilty Nations tremble. But, above
> Those superstitious Horrors that enslave
> The fond sequacious Herd, to mystic Faith
> And blind Amazement prone, th'enlightened Few,
> Whose Godlike Minds Philosophy exalts,
> The glorious Stranger hail. (1706–16)

Thomson is referring here to a well-known philosophical debate in which Newton was implicated. Comets, orbiting bodies moving in a contrary direction to the planets, were a key exhibit for Newton in disproving the Cartesian theory of vortices, the currents of fine matter that supposedly swept the planets along their celestial course. In the context of this passage, an understanding of the Newtonian theory of motion distinguishes "th'enlightened Few" from "the fond sequacious [or uninventive, unoriginal] Herd" who tremble at the sublime messenger sent "from the dread immensity of Space." The

"Few" who understand the nature of comets thus not only designate the West with respect to the Rest but, more pointedly, Britain and Newton relative to the "guilty Nations" on the Continent and especially the followers of Descartes and Leibniz.

The gravitational force explaining planetary motion was, as a matter of physics, largely resolved by the 1720s, when Thomson was composing *The Seasons*; however, the metaphysical implications of Newton's theory remained very much in play. Leibniz, who subscribed with Descartes to the theory of the universe as a plenum of vortices driving the planets along a current of ether, criticized Newtonian gravity as action at a distance, an idea converting a universe dense with God's presence into a vacuum traversed by matter. In his contentious correspondence with the Newtonian defender Samuel Clarke, Leibniz complained that Newton "admits empty space, besides matter; and . . . according to his notions, matter fills up only a very small part of space." For his own part, by contrast, Leibniz maintained that "the more matter there is, the more God has occasion to exercise his wisdom and power." Hence, as Leibniz saw it, Newton's doctrine of empty space severed celestial bodies from contact with God, and to argue otherwise was tantamount to either contradiction or Spinozist pantheism: "Space, according to Sir Isaac Newton, is intimately present to the body contained in it, and commensurate with it." But does God dwell in such emptiness, or is he intrinsic to it? If we say that he does or that he is, then "[d]oes it follow from thence, that space perceives what passes in a body; and remembers it, when that body is gone away?" If so, then space is not empty, and if not, then God is flawed. This struck Leibniz as philosophically unsound and as occult in its animation of the void.[64]

This philosophical disagreement makes the dispute over calculus more than simply a function of who got there first. Leibniz's grievance with fluxions stemmed in part from the fact that the model assisted Newton in calculating motion in empty space. Or, as Newton saw it, fluxions putatively enabled one to account for the deviation of bodies off the straight course instituted by God. Fluxions help us to understand the speed and degrees of divergence and also how God regenerates the state of nature from time to time. As we discussed in Chapter 2, fluxions thus helped establish the course and even the concept of history, human and providential. Comets provided Newton with one such example of divine replenishment. They not only disproved Cartesian vortices but also restored vapors to planets whose minerals were "spent upon vegetation and putrefaction."[65] Numerous Scots—David

Gregory, Keill, Maclaurin—took up wide-ranging, philosophical defenses of Newton's theory of comets.[66] Thomson's comet operates to similar effect in *Summer*: it "work[s] the Will of all-sustaining Love . . . shak[ing] / Reviving Moisture" from its "huge vapoury Train" (1724–26). Hence, Thomson's appeal to the comet as a "glorious Stranger" amounts to a Gregory- and Keill- and Maclaurin-like defense of Newton from his continental critics.

And yet, at key moments, Thomson's poem appears to uphold the continental reasoning it tacitly condemns, even when it articulates and defends Newtonian thought. Take, for instance, the most explicitly Newtonian excerpt in any of *The Seasons*, the famous passage in *Spring* that describes the rainbow and the way in which "awful [i.e., awe-inspiring] Newton" reveals "The various Twine of Light" from out of the "white mingling Maze" (p. 12, ll. 208, 211–12):

> Meantime refracted from yon eastern Cloud,
> Bestriding Earth, the grand ethereal Bow
> Shoots up immense; and every Hue unfolds,
> In fair Proportion, running from the Red,
> To where the Violet fades into the Sky.
> Here, awful NEWTON, the dissolving Clouds
> Form, fronting on the Sun, thy showery Prism;
> And to the sage-instructed Eye unfold
> The various Twine of Light, by thee disclos'd
> From the white mingling Maze. Not so the Swain,
> He wondering views the bright Enchantment bend,
> Delightful, o'er the radiant Fields, and runs
> To catch the falling Glory; but amaz'd
> Beholds th'amusive Arch before him fly,
> Then vanish quite away. (203–16)

Nature "unfolds" the rainbow "[i]n fair Proportion," but Newton "disclos[es]" its secrets; nature figures, Newton explains. In its way, the episode reprises the passage in the *Poem Sacred* in which Newton "Blaz[es] into Suns" the fanciful images that flit before the poet, here represented by the benighted "Swain."

What follows this disclosure, however, is less Newtonian, if indeed it is Newtonian at all:

Then spring the living Herbs, profusely wild,
O'er all the deep-green Earth, beyond the Power
Of Botanist to number up their Tribes:
Whether he steals along the lonely Dale,
In silent Search; or thro' the Forest, rank
With what the dull Incurious Weeds account,
Bursts his blind Way; or climbs the Mountain-Rock,
Fir'd by the nodding Verdure of its Brow.
With such a liberal Hand has Nature flung
Their Seeds abroad, blown them about in Winds,
Innumerous mix'd them with the nursing Mold,
The moistening Current, and prolifick Rain. (222–33)

The poem diverts us from the rainbow to a vast field of vision, transporting the eye with the botanist as he traverses dales, forests, and mountains. But the task confronting us is less that of perception than of comprehension as we must somehow measure these infinite prospects. This was the challenge that calculus was devised partly to resolve. Thomson implicitly underscores the connection to calculus by invoking the specter of numbers we cannot fathom, both irrational and infinite (or infinitesimal). The botanist attempts to "rank" and "account" for the various floral species, but nature's sheer profusion, its "liberal Hand," makes this an impossible exercise, flinging the "Innumerous" seeds into the "Winds" where they "mix[]" with soil, currents, and rain and eventually recede from view into an unbounded expanse. Hence, what at first seems countable ascends into virtual infinity. Ralph Cohen argues that this sublime image reflects Thomson's theology, which holds that a "sensuous, creative nature beyond the ability of man even to catalog is the consequence of the fall of man"—that mortality, limiting us to place and time, hampers our ability to comprehend the full extent of God's creative design.[67] But Cohen's lapsarian point is also an implicitly mathematical one, for conceptual tools like infinite series in calculus reinscribe our fallen condition even as they compensate for it: they enable us to formulate simulacra of what we cannot see but thus downgrade the epistemic authority of experience (or, in Thomson's case, of natural description).

In effect, this passage in *Spring* poetically presents something like the quandary of "infinitely small" particles or infinitesimals. At the strictly "aesthetic" level, as Kant might have said, Newton purported to resolve this problem by reducing such increments to zero and according them the appearance of geometry. Leibniz, by contrast, integrated infinitesimals into his differential calculus and then illustrated the process through graphs that segmented curves into a series of tiny straight lines, thus highlighting the algebraic artifice by which one calculates the area under a curve. At the level of appearance and not mathematics, Newton's figures corresponded (comparatively speaking) with nature and Leibniz's with art. For his part, Thomson appears to take a comparatively Newtonian line, dissolving the "Innumerous" seeds into "nursing Mold" and other natural elements as the eye sweeps along its course. However, if we consider the passage more intently, its trajectory of vision traces a complicated image, for the poem affixes "motion" to substances—"Dale," "Forest," "Mountain-Rock"—whose serial articulation makes our perspective less fluid than saccadic, jumping from location to location, each momentarily holding our attention through its corresponding description. While it is true, as John Sitter argues, that "the scene unfolds sequentially," the poetic gaze does not flow across the landscape as much as it subtly marks a series of points connecting and differentiating its aggregate parts.[68] What we behold, then, is less an encompassing "nature" than a sequence of dale-forest-rock (or, in other catalogs, crocus-daisy-violet). The poem therefore presents movement as more rectilinear than curvilinear—a product of the (affectively Leibnizian) artifice of its arrangement. But in creating figures for these movements—in converting the points on his poetic grid into "dales" and "forests" and "rocks" and in personifying the puzzle of incomprehensible numbers in the dazzled botanist—Thomson also takes Newton's place as the illustrator of an otherwise sublime, obscurely technical process. Hence, while the *Poem Sacred* elegiacally celebrates Newton as the enlightener par excellence, *The Seasons* crafts a more complex image of Newton's legacy. Rhapsodizing on the ambiguities within the Newtonian system—disclosing the dark matter in Newton's particles of light—the poem effectively turns Newtonian metaphysics into an oracle of the human mysteries Koyré accused Newton of occluding. It also opens the door to an aesthetics Kant would barely have recognized, as we will see in Chapter 6.

* * *

The finer points of Leibnizian and Newtonian mathematics were, of course, well beyond Thomson's expertise, let alone his aims in *The Seasons*. But he does anticipate a debate in Scottish thought between David Hume and

Thomas Reid that conscientiously engaged Newtonian science and its metaphysical implications. We discussed in Chapter 2 how, later in the 1730s, the decade when *The Seasons* first appeared in its entirety, Hume imported Newton into moral philosophy in *A Treatise of Human Nature* (1739–40). He did so partly by pursuing to their logical conclusion the implications of empirical science, segmenting our experience of objects into a discrete set of impressions. He even adopted the language of fluxions in describing the mind as "a bundle or collection of different perceptions, which succeed each other with an inconceivable rapidity, and are in a perpetual *flux* and movement."[69] In effect, Hume proffered a fluxional calculus in the Thomsonian mold, an expository flow across a set of points. But Hume underscores the gaps between these points, arguing that the identities we fashion—of objects and ourselves—are *mere* figures without substance. In Hume's world, as in Berkeley's (whom Hume greatly esteemed early in his career), what we confront are less things in themselves than the fictions of our imagination, the products of human art.

The ensuing debate between Hume and Reid reprised dynamics that Thomson had illustrated, though not conceptualized, in the Newtonian passage from *Spring*. For starters, Hume's *Treatise* resembled Thomson's poetic calculus in turning Newton's logic into the aesthetic form of its continental antithesis. Although nominally skeptical, Hume's subversive critique of reason evoked Cartesian idealism, the self-evidence of an unassailable "I" as the bedrock of thought, in according ideality to impressions as the elemental particles of cognition that mediate between the mind and its world. Indeed, what grants these impressions their ideal status is Hume's refusal to subject them to the same withering (and essentially deconstructive) analysis that he applies to the category of the understanding. Instead, he essentially takes them on (poetic) faith: "All the perceptions of the human mind resolve themselves into two distinct kinds, which I shall call IMPRESSIONS and IDEAS. The difference betwixt these consists in the degree of force and liveliness, with which they strike upon the mind," with impressions being the more vivid of the two (49). "Liveliness" was a feature to which John Dryden had appealed in the seventeenth century in defining drama as "a just and lively image of human nature."[70] And it was the theater, notably, to which Hume compared the fluctuating or fluxional mind: "The mind is a kind of theatre, where several perceptions successively make their appearance" (301).

Hume was quick to qualify his analogy, asserting that the "comparison of the theatre must not mislead us" and that it was "the successive perceptions" of the mind only—their flux—he wished to emphasize (301). But Reid argued that Hume erred in placing his faith in the notion of "impressions" in the first place, as though they were one of Newton's chimerical figures of which Berkeley was so critical. As Reid saw it, all our perceptions, impressions included, are (in the manner of Thomson's seeds) "so mixed . . . by habits, associations, and abstractions, that it is hard to know what they were originally."[71] If we think about this issue in terms of Thomson's passage in *Spring*, it would appear that Hume plays the botanist to Reid's nature, attempting vainly to conceptualize a cognitive process that so "mixes, compounds, dissolves, evaporates, and sublimes" its materials that they eventually "put on a quite different appearance" from whatever may once have been their impetus (Reid, *Inquiry* 99). Or, reflecting back onto *The Seasons* from the standpoint of Scottish philosophy, perhaps it would be more accurate to say that Thomson's passage on the "living Herbs" takes a Humean tactic to illustrate Reid's point: the botanist *cannot* enumerate or even produce an adequate image of the organisms constituting an "Innumerous" nature any more than Hume can number the impressions making up an idea. Each fails in his task because, for Thomson as for Reid, perception is irreducibly complex and cannot be winnowed down (or, in what amounts to the same thing, idealistically inflated) to the status of impressions. While it may reside at the seat of consciousness, it resists further analysis or explanation. But for that reason, perception, and hence figure—geometric, poetic—becomes a primary *phenomenological* quality of objects. By emphasizing this fact, a poet like Thomson, a geometer like Maclaurin, and a philosopher like Reid become more Newtonian than Newton himself, taking the "appearance of nature" (by which Newton partly justified his method) more literally than the inventor of fluxions.

By the terms we discussed in Chapter 3, these are all "picturesque" projects to the extent that they explore the limits of geometric (or figural, "evident") constructs. This was particularly the case with Reid, as we will see in Chapter 6. Indeed, these experiments in visual and verbal form, the strangeness of their shapes, also help explain why the next logical step in the poetic-Newtonian direction to which Thomson pointed would prove to be one of conceptual and formal (r)evolution, an imaginative basis of a more modern aesthetics.

CHAPTER 6

A Long and Shapely Eighteenth Century

The story I am telling in this book concludes with a set of Scottish Enlightenment ideas that made (and mutated) their way into the nineteenth and early twentieth centuries. I leave off with a 1934 poem. But I can best get to that place by beginning from a point located outside that chronology. Most readers familiar with *1984* know that George Orwell chose the title for his dystopian novel by inverting the final two digits of the year he completed it, 1948. Written largely during Orwell's stay on the Scottish Hebridean island of Jura, the novel's defamiliarized projection of its own moment was a fitting emblem for a book given to dire speculation about a world coming unglued: this was the era, after all, when Hiroshima, Nuremberg, and Berlin became descriptive categories as well as place names. Then, in 1984, Jean-François Lyotard inverted and thus reiterated Orwell's gesture, identifying 1948 as a watershed moment from which to assess the present.[1] As his vehicle of critique, he chose the giant, vertical-stripe canvases of the abstract expressionist Barnett Baruch Newman and an essay Newman published in 1948, entitled "The Sublime Is Now."

Why was Lyotard, in 1984, so interested in what Newman was thinking in 1948? The short answer is that Newman's aesthetic helped Lyotard frame his own poetics of figuration. This was a model of mind and reading that Lyotard had developed in the late 1960s and that he was newly elaborating in a series of essays in the mid-1980s—"The Sublime and the Avant-Garde," "The Dream-Work Does Not Think," "Figure Foreclosed"—as an alternative to the virtually monolithic equation of French theory with the linguistic heritage of Ferdinand de Saussure. As Lyotard saw it, the priority accorded to Saussure and the play of signification in (post)structuralist theory derived largely from Lacan's dictum that "the unconscious is structured like a language," an assumption Lyotard believed was predicated on a partial misreading of Freud. Theorists, Lyotard observed, mistakenly reduced language to the rules of discourse, a procedure ignoring the mind's tendency to equate words with images and, by extension, objects (in, for instance, the work of dreams, one of Freud's examples being his own reverie of a botanical monograph binding plant specimens among its pages[2]). The language of objects comprises a rhetoric of visual figure, Lyotard contended, which operates according to a logic of designation rather than signification: it modulates words and things instead of signifiers and signifieds. To overdetermine language as discourse forecloses this immediate relation to objects; it displaces magic—the conversion of word into thing—with science and the primitive—the innocent, the open, the childlike—with the modern.[3] Therefore, with respect to the legacy of this displacement in literary theory (that is, with the reduction of language to symbols or, in essence, to a series of algebraic displacements), it ensures the hegemony of the same through a rubric of "difference." Real difference, Lyotard argued, consists of something other than the play of signifiers.

Newman's aesthetic helped Lyotard make this case. The dramatic vertical stripes of the large canvases portrayed an emergent figuration from out of a sea of (bare) atmosphere, (mere) noise. Lyotard labeled these stripes "events," which he set against "thought." Continental philosophy, particularly French theory, has circled repeatedly around this opposition. For Lyotard, events consist of occurrences that are "infinitely simple, but can only be approached through a state of privation" in which normative patterns of thinking do not take hold. We never see an event coming; if we did, it would not be an event. "That which we call thought must be disarmed" if an event is to occur because "[t]hought works over what is received, it seeks to reflect on it and overcome it," reducing its singularity to preformed matrices of meaning.[4] "Thought" here assumes the role of the Freudian ego or of "discourse," mediating our relation to the external world, whereas events denote incidents that consciousness cannot anticipate or predetermine. They are, rather, "what dismantles consciousness, what deposes consciousness, what consciousness cannot formulate, and even what consciousness forgets in order to constitute itself" as normative in the first place (197).

Newman qualifies this aesthetic as *sublime*, Lyotard says, because sublimity is the traditional rubric of the event. And Lyotard sets out his own analysis of "dismantle[d] consciousness" by way of this rubric, divulging in Kant's

Critique of Judgment the loopholes disjoining the impulse toward critique from the doctrines of philosophy (or the "event" of thinking from the concepts mediating it).[5] Lyotard traces this dynamic back to a treatise composed by Kant's precursor, Edmund Burke, in *A Philosophical Enquiry into the Origin of Our Ideas of the Sublime and Beautiful* (1757). For Burke, sublimity denotes obscurity; its temporal correlative is an occluded future, an inability to discern the course of gathering circumstances. This obscurity incites in us an anxious "feeling that nothing might happen" (Lyotard 198), which is precisely the "privation" that makes any occurrence an event. To dwell in a state of sublimity is to experience repeatedly (and almost compulsively) the anxiety of nothingness followed by the almost painful ecstasy of an encounter. This temporal component of sublimity, this modulation of experience, is important to Lyotard. In Kant's "Analytic of the Sublime," he says, time "signifies an inability to synthesize" a particular form through its containment "within 'a single moment' "; time means that shape, perpetually in flux, is never present in or to itself.[6] This harrows the artist, who must always await the next note, line, color, or word of inspiration without fully grasping the meaning of his or her own work. And this is a *historical* as well as a *temporal* phenomenon. "Between the seventeenth and eighteenth centuries in Europe this contradictory feeling" of expectation and emptiness "was christened . . . by [this] name of the sublime. It is around this name that the destiny of classical poetics was hazarded and lost . . . and that romanticism, in other words, modernity, triumphed."[7]

This was a paradoxical modernity, however: it represented at once a vast sea of general experience—a monochromatic state of things, as it were—while also naming the dramatic experience of incipient figure (in Newman's case, the vertical stripe) that announces a break from that state. In Newman's work, the stripe denotes revitalized, "disarmed" consciousness and thus recasts previous thought as mere "discourse." However, and this is where the dynamic Lyotard describes becomes most interesting for my purposes, it does so precisely by converting time into a figure, a line; it makes time appear, as it were, and in that spirit it operates geometrically. But Newman renders overt an important fact that is only implicit in, say, Newton's fluxions, which is that geometric shapes here (lines and squares) do not represent Euclidean mastery as much as the point at which shape begins to morph into something strange, something literally—"sublimely"—inconceivable. Newman's, like Newton's, is a late if not entirely non-Euclidean moment.

Lyotard's essay brings into relief a few of the implications of the story I have been telling about the late Euclidean qualities of Scottish Enlightenment geometry. Scottish thought's geometric orientation shares with Lyotard a dynamic concept of figure that opens onto an alternative vector of modern experience, a different way of measuring the world (*geo-metria*). The cultural labor of eighteenth-century Scottish geometry represented other (Lyotard might say "nondiscursive") habits of understanding and also connected a deeper set of (metaphysical) traditions to creative rearrangements of the past by an emergent and self-consciously postclassical public sphere. The first four chapters of this book discussed facets of these relationships (for example, the different ways to conceive of narrative in Scott's work or of Burns's exploration of human irrationalities). Chapter 5 was a little different in that it focused primarily on the poetry of James Thomson and its engagement of the quandaries of Newton's legacy within the boundaries of the eighteenth century. This chapter essentially unfolds from that one, showing how the "commonsensical" position that *The Seasons* anticipates projects a compelling trajectory through subsequent cultural and intellectual history. This chapter thus begins where the last one leaves off, taking up one important branch of Thomas Reid's thought in the eighteenth century, proceeding to contemporaries of Scott's who refashioned "common sense" for later modernity, and then showing how those ideas made their way into the twentieth century. There, they inflected aspects of both the continental avant-garde and Scottish modernism. The latter represents a somewhat sketchy tradition that has been portrayed by some scholars as too parochial to qualify as a true modernism—an international, experimental movement. While recent work has largely overturned this characterization, the mottled status of Scottish modernism actually fits with my argument concerning the "long" Enlightenment, which condensed lengthy spans of affective time—classical, romantic, and precociously postclassical—into the form of geometric figures that ranged across a breadth of disciplines and media.

The Poe(tics) of Common Sense

The divergence from Euclid in mathematics was accompanied by a distortion of Euclid in the arts. This would become most evident in the West in the nineteenth and early twentieth centuries, with Riemannian spaces and avant-garde experiments with spatial form. That said, *divergence* and *distortion* did not happen simultaneously—or, if they did, their relationship was not always obvious. One of the most vivid examples of this phenomenon is Reid's "geometry of visibles" from his 1764 *Inquiry into the Human Mind on the Principles of Common Sense*. We discussed this idea briefly in the Introduction and then again in Chapter 1. Composed as a thought experiment in support of the thesis that our senses collectively attest to the existence of an external world, the geometry of visibles divulges how conclusions drawn on the basis of a single sense can lead us astray. "Supposing the eye placed in the centre of a sphere, every great circle of the sphere will have the same appearance to the eye as if it was a straight line," even though it is actually curved and "even when it . . . returns [and closes] into itself."[8] In this scenario, "[i]f two lines be parallel . . . they cannot both be straight" (148)—a proposition that ventures into the non-Euclidean territory of spatial curvature. Reid did not intend to walk that particular path, and yet, he claims that his experimental geometry is "not less true nor less evident than the propositions of Euclid," meaning that the "visibles" he presents to us are not exactly Euclidean either (148). What is more, Reid proceeds from here into speculation on multi-dimensional spaces, connecting all this to the praise—and critique—of Newton.

A point worth underscoring is that Reid undertook his "geometry of visibles" as part of a larger critique of idealism, specifically of Berkeley and Hume, which means he employed geometry against the grain of its own eighteenth-century reputation as the reflex of idealist philosophy—the idea of perfect forms apprehensible only to the rational mind. Such idealism was the view taken from an influential branch of Newtonian thought; in the early eighteenth century, for example, the English scholars Richard Bentley and Samuel Clarke appealed to Newton's geometry as a metaphysical (and, as they saw it, unassailable, deductive) basis of moral judgment.[9] But in Scotland, geometry did not transcend as much as complement experience: it was what a later generation would call an aesthetic exercise, bearing as much in common with the early aesthetic philosophy of Lord Shaftesbury and Francis Hutcheson as with Bentley and Clarke.[10] Geometric shapes, that is, bear the traces of the tangible experience from which they are born and that they help distill; shapes rearrange the mass of impressions in a manner conducive to reflection.[11] Reid likewise remarked that "[w]hat is said about the non-existence of the objects of geometry . . . is rather too strongly expressed," elaborating that such objects are "modifications" of common perceptions of "length, breadth, and thickness."[12]

Reid's ideas concerning geometry suggest that for Scottish Enlightenment geometers and those who drew upon their work, the traces of nature informed even extreme abstractions from it (like the "geometry of visibles"). We might also infer that theirs was a modified rather than a neoclassicism, for they undertook their thought experiments under the banner of Euclid. This point goes mostly unnoticed in intellectual and cultural history given the reputed conservatism of Scottish geometry vis-à-vis continental algebra. Not coincidentally, this is largely the reputation of Thomson's descriptive poetry relative to that of such Romantic poets as William Wordsworth. According to Fred Wilson, the image of a classical, Newtonian Thomson became a normative antithesis for the Romantic poets and especially for Wordsworth, who repudiated Newtonian thought by rooting poetry in the experience of place and time rather than in abstract universals.[13]

Once again
Do I behold these steep and lofty cliffs,
That on a wild secluded scene impress
Thoughts of more deep seclusion; and connect
The landscape with the quiet of the sky.[14]

These famous Wordsworthian lines contemplate nature from a particular locale "a few miles above Tintern Abbey," whereas the passage on the Newtonian rainbow in *Spring* gazes down at the earth from an abstract, elevated position.[15] This leads, however, to a curious inversion evocative of Reid's critique of residual idealism in Hume. For Thomson imagines (with John Keill) a synthesis of landscape and sky, physics and metaphysics, while Wordsworth's version of that union actually propagates an idealizing dialectic between sterile geometry (the vision of "a landscape to a blind man's eye" [25]) and material experience. In situating himself in the landscape, Wordsworth thus divorces geometric from putatively human reality—the type of bifurcation that, according to Alexander Koyré, Newton hastened but that Newton's Scottish defenders denied.[16]

However, the picture is actually more nuanced still. In examining the illustrations that appeared in the multiple eighteenth-century editions of Thomson's *Seasons*, Sandro Jung has noted that the elaborate allegorical prints, which were designed by the renowned English architect William Kent and initially appeared in the volume, eventually gave way to a series of "sentimental, pathetic, and tragic" representations of particular scenes anticipatory of Wordsworth's own professed aesthetic.[17] And yet, even this Wordsworthian aesthetic was not entirely what it appeared to be. Alice Jenkins observes that Wordsworth's *A Guide through the District of the Lakes in the North of England* (1810) places its readers in positions of spectatorial eminence that replicate the presumed distance of Keill's geometer.[18] Hence, *The Seasons* in some ways were (at least by the terms of subsequent literary history) more "Wordsworthian" than Wordsworth. What is more, Scottish mathematicians like Robert Simson had already long taken to denouncing the sterile abstractions of Newton's calculus in the latter's reduction of geometry to algebra; this is one reason why Colin Maclaurin, for example, went to such exhaustive lengths to translate fluxions back into geometric form. Thomson's personifications performed a similar operation, converting a host of abstract concepts into more tangible figures—literary diagrams, as it were. Thomson's was less a distancing than a domesticating operation.

Hence, in its way, Thomson's "Newtonian" poetry was actually "Romantic" *avant la lettre*.[19] Or, better said, Thomson and the Scottish geometers effectively undercut from the outset the compensatory relationship between imagination and experience, poetry and science—Homer and Newton—that would eventually render compulsive the dialectic of enlightenment and romance. Indeed, and as Reid foresaw, the literary sublation of science essentially displaced a concept of experience inclusive of mind and world with one predicated on the conviction of their divergence. The pabulum of Romantic genius would thus find its eventual and ironic apotheosis not only in the Romantic "symbol" but also in Duchamp's *Fountain* (the urinal he converted into an art installation), an all-too-vivid (indeed, parodic) image of worldly filth that purportedly inspired the impulse toward transcendence in the first place.

Reid's subversion of idealism, meanwhile, inspired a different trajectory. In his 1883 Balfour Lectures at the University of Edinburgh, Andrew Seth presented Reid's thought as the forgotten philosophical alternative to the idealism of Descartes and Kant (and Hume), which differentiated world from mind, perception from reflection. The key to Reid's philosophy, Seth argued, is that it does not consider perception as a thing in itself but rather embeds it in a "temporal and spatial environment" such that perception becomes "a complex of . . . relations" that are historical as well as phenomenological, rooted in a being's past as well as in its present experience.[20] In this way, Seth asserts, Reid diverted the course of Western thought. Or, at least, he might have done so if his philosophy were more widely known. But his thinking fell prey to its own principles, specifically in the way Reid's philosophy integrated itself into the Scottish university system and that system's vital role in

Scottish society. "Reid wrote no *magnum opus*, in the sense in which Kant wrote several," Seth remarks. "He had no learned class to whom he could have appealed, if he had written with the elaborate technicality of Kant. His works were addressed to the reading portion of his countrymen generally," falling under the aegis of public discourse. And while this diminishes Reid's impact within the discipline of philosophy, "it is possible that what Scottish philosophy lost in scientific precision may have been compensated for . . . by the greater influence which it has exerted upon the body of the people—an influence which has made it a factor, so to speak, in the national life" (129). Indeed, Common Sense became the overarching philosophy of the Scottish university system in the eighteenth century as the logic of a multifaceted assemblage of disciplines. And while one of the precepts of Common Sense philosophy is its irreducibility (no discipline devolves directly on another, just as perception is not a function of, say, "impressions" or "ideas"), the Common Sense insistence on the *relations* between things—and the shapes or configurations these disciplinary relations trace among themselves—accorded a special place to geometry within that pedagogical system.[21]

We may dispute Seth's claims concerning the absence of a "learned class" in eighteenth-century Scottish society, but we should not lose sight of his main point. In defending common sense, Seth was differentiating a tradition in Scottish thought from the pervasive idealism of Romantic philosophy. This would become even clearer in the Balfour Lectures that Seth delivered four years later, in 1887, subsequently published as *Hegelianism and Personality*. While praising Hegel for the rigor of his thinking, Seth attacks what we would label Hegel's "ideological" conflation of objects with an idealized conception of their purpose.[22]

And yet, the Common Sense tradition bore a wide circumference in its own right. By Seth's era, it had expanded well beyond philosophy, encompassing aspects of theology and, significantly, nineteenth-century physico-theology (a descendant of the philosophy Thomson employs in *The Seasons*). While Hume had brought physico-theology into partial disrepute for its defense of creative design (a position that would seem even more tenuous after Darwin), philosophers in the Common Sense tradition deployed physico-theology against the vestiges of idealism. In 1817, for example, Thomas Chalmers, a prominent Scottish churchman, published his *Discourses on the Christian Revelation, Viewed in Connection with the Modern Astronomy*, expounding the position that "infidels" cannot disprove Christianity on the basis that "God would not lavish such a quantity of attention on so insignificant a field" as a single earth in a boundless universe. His strategy here was to deploy skepticism against itself, much as Reid had done against Hume. After all, Chalmers wondered, "How do infidels know that Christianity is set up for the single benefit of this earth and its inhabitants? How are they to tell us, that if you go to other planets, the person and the religion of Jesus are there unknown to them?" Significantly, Chalmers declares, Newton would never have claimed as much: "with a justness which reigns throughout all his inquiries, [Newton] saw the limit of his own understanding, [and] would [not] venture himself beyond it."[23]

That said, and as we have already seen with Thomson, Maclaurin, and Reid, Newton served less as an exemplum of moral restraint in the Scottish tradition than as an impetus for new ideas. In the late 1830s, John Pringle Nichol, Regius Professor of Astronomy at the University of Glasgow, invoked Newton's authority in inflating the commonsensical principle of irreducibility into a cosmic theory. He proclaimed that to gaze into the heavens with the benefit of a telescope was to behold not only world upon world but also the formation of still others: "nay, who can tell" in gazing upon nebulae and "bygone worlds—the fossil relics that mark the early progress of our own planet"—whether this matter may not bear within itself "the germs, the producing powers, of that LIFE, which in coming ages will bud and blossom, and effloresce, into manifold and growing forms, until it becomes fit harbourage and nourishment to every varying degree of intelligence, and every shade of moral sensibility and greatness!" For Nichol, as for Chalmers (as for Robert Stewart, Thomson's teacher at the University of Edinburgh—and for Thomson himself), Newton was a moral philosopher as well as a scientist. He displayed "the modesty of all great minds" when he declared that, relative to the universe, he was "but a child standing on the shore of the vast undiscovered ocean, and playing with a little pebble which the waters have washed to [his] feet."[24] But "modesty" was less in play here than imaginative speculation, "the vast undiscovered ocean" to which Newton turned our gaze.

Nichol's *Views of the Architecture of the Heavens* (1837), Robert Chambers's *Vestiges of the Natural History of Creation* (1844), and other works from the Scottish Common Sense tradition extended their influence into nineteenth-century America, where they left a deep imprint on Edgar Allan Poe. Poe, in turn, would leave a powerful mark on a broad swathe of nineteenth- and twentieth-century modernisms. "The Murders in the Rue Morgue," for example, often cited as the first modern detective story, opens with a credo that Reid employs against Hume: "The mental features discoursed of as analytical are, in themselves, but little susceptible of analysis."[25] We cannot, that is, reduce cognition to elemental impressions. But it is in *Eureka*, Poe's prose-poem-qua-philosophical-treatise (qua-literary-hoax), that Nichol, Chambers, and Reid perhaps rear their heads most significantly.[26] There, Poe orchestrates a grand cosmic thesis that echoes the work of these precursors: "My general proposition . . . is this:—*In the Original Unity of the First Thing lies the Secondary Cause of All Things, with the Germ of their Inevitable Annihilation.*"[27] Such unifying gestures (bringing together primary with secondary causes, origins with ends) are consistent with Scottish Enlightenment metaphysics and geometry, taking upon themselves the task of reconciling reason with perception, truth with "evidence." That "*[t]he Body and the Soul walk hand in hand*" (54, Poe's emphases) is a precept that is true of the universe, Poe argues, and also of his essay, which fuses scientific principles with a theory of literary creation. In each case, universal and rhetorical, Poe brings conflicting but complementary forces into play—one a function of gravitational attraction and the other "a repulsive influence" that he identifies "now as heat, now as magnetism, now as *electricity*" (27, Poe's emphasis). "The development of Repulsion (Electricity) must have commenced . . . with the very earliest particular efforts at Unity," he speculates, enabling him to reason that these "two Principles Proper, *Attraction* and *Repulsion*—the Material and the Spiritual—accompany each other, in the strictest fellowship, forever" (53–54, Poe's emphases).

In merging attraction and repulsion into a single theory (after the manner of Reid's senses: a single strand of the theory would lead us astray), Poe fuses categories that would diverge in the later nineteenth century. This was part of a major revision of the relationship between force and electricity in the work of the Scottish physicists William Thomson (Lord Kelvin—a student of Nichol's at the University of Edinburgh) and James Clerk Maxwell, who displaced the Newtonian model and built a crucial bridge to Einstein's theory of relativity.[28] However, the most important bridge in *Eureka* may be one that leads backward in history, rather than forward. Poe seems to have taken a cue here from the Scottish physicist David Brewster, whose biographical work *The Martyrs of Science: The Lives of Galileo, Tycho Brahe, and Kepler* (1841) introduces a qualitative relationship on which Poe would expound. According to Brewster, "When we consider [Kepler] . . . as the discoverer of the three great laws which bear his name, we must assign him a rank next to that of Newton." As the creator of the model within which Newton worked, Kepler bears the hallmarks of genius: "The history of science does not present us with any discoveries more original, or which required for their establishment a more powerful and vigorous mind." And, in an image reminiscent of Adam Smith's in "The History of Astronomy," which we discussed in Chapter 5, Brewster claims that "[t]he splendid discoveries of Newton sprung immediately from those of Kepler, and completed the great chain of truths which constitute the laws of the planetary system."[29]

Poe's assessment of Kepler and Newton expands on Brewster's contentions: "Newton deduced [his physics] from the laws of Kepler. Kepler admitted that he *guessed*—these laws whose investigation disclosed to the greatest of British astronomers that principle, the basis of all (existing) physical principle, in going behind which we enter at once the nebulous kingdom of Metaphysics. Yes!—these vital laws Kepler *guessed*—that is to say, he *imagined* them" (15, Poe's emphases). The juxtaposition is a familiar one in Kantian terms. Kepler is the agent of imagination, of genius, in whose wake Newton follows. Kepler experiences a flash of inspiration; Newton crafts logical deductions. Kepler is Homer and Newton is, well, Newton.[30] And yet, as in so many other broadly "literary" works we have analyzed in previous chapters, Newton's presence makes itself felt in *Eureka* in the form of a geometric calculus that functions as the imaginative medium of Poe's literary experiments, the elaborate analogies by which he conjoins the "evidence" of natural philosophy with the workings of the imagination. "Now, distinctness—intelligibility, at all points, is a primary feature in my general design. . . . All are alike, in facility of comprehension, to him who approaches them by properly graduated steps" (17). These are "steps," we recall, by which Kant differentiates poetry from science, Homer from Newton. And Poe himself calls these steps "our road to the Differential Calculus" of nature's laws: "The plots of God are perfect. The Universe is a plot of God" (89). More specifically, the universe is poetic *and geometrical*, a divine orchestration of "the poetical instinct of humanity . . . which the Soul, not only of Man but of all created beings, took up, in the beginning, from the *geometrical* basis of the Universal radiation" at the origin of all things (89, Poe's emphasis).

This is what Poe seeks not only to explain but also to emulate; as Peter Swirski asserts, "*Eureka* casts the poet as a unifying agent, able to encompass all experience through the process of intuitive synthesis."[31] For Poe, as for Scottish Enlightenment literati, and perhaps most poignantly for Thomson (as we discussed in Chapter 5), Newton enables but also partly impedes this project. Poe appeals on this point to Nichol, "the eloquent author of 'The Architecture of the Heavens,'" in making the case that Newton is insufficiently geometric: Newton's great law of gravity "has not the aspect of an ultimate *principle*; which always assumes the simplicity and self-evidence of those axioms which constitute the basis of Geometry" (cited in Poe 35, Poe's emphasis). For Poe, then, as for Nichol and his Scottish forebears, Newton's theory, while formative, remained at once too empirical and too algebraic—it was too given to matter, on one hand, and to derived symbols, on the other. And what Poe envisioned, as Thomson had a century earlier, was a more expansive theory of figure, a conception in which poetry and the universe are one.

This idea would carry forward into nineteenth-century France, where *Eureka* influenced a group of writers we now identify with Symbolism and the movements that followed. Charles Baudelaire translated Poe's treatise and disseminated it widely, bringing Poe to the awareness of René Ghil, Charles Morice, Paul Valéry, and others. Especially significant to these writers were Poe's quasi-geometric ideas concerning "the value of intuition for scientific discovery, and the affinity between consciousness and the cosmos."[32] These ideas complemented the influence of Scottish geometry proper on, among others, Michel Chasles, professor at the École Polytechnique and the Sorbonne and a defender of Simson's theory of Euclid's porisms.[33] They also would make a deep impression on the young Walter Benjamin, who assimilated nineteenth-century French thought—and the residual implications of Newtonian geometry—into his own work. We find one especially provocative example in the concluding section of Benjamin's 1928 essay "One-Way Street," where Benjamin reflects on the dialectical distinction of modernity from earlier periods via the ancients' "absorption in a cosmic experience scarcely known to later periods." This premodern experience is one of universality, of unity between individuals, society, and outward circumstances in a grand symphony of nature. The "waning" of this collectivist ontology, meanwhile,

> is marked by the flowering of astronomy at the beginning of the modern age. Kepler, Copernicus, and Tycho Brahe were certainly not driven by scientific impulses alone. All the same, the exclusive emphasis on an optical connection to the universe, to which astronomy very quickly led, contained a portent of what was to come. The ancients' intercourse with the cosmos had been different: the ecstatic trance. For it is in this experience alone that we gain certain knowledge of what is nearest to us and what is remotest to us, and never of one without the other. This means, however, that man can be in

> ecstatic contact with the cosmos only communally. It is the dangerous error of modern men to regard this experience as unimportant and unavoidable, and to consign it to the individual as the poetic rapture of starry nights. It is not; its hour strikes again and again, and then neither nations nor generations can escape it.[34]

Benjamin's notion of "the ecstatic trance" as a mode of cosmological experience evokes Nietzsche's concept of the Dionysian in *The Birth of Tragedy*.[35] But it also finds a precedent in the exuberance of *Eureka*. And here, as in Poe's essay, Kepler is the one helping to usher in a new age. But Benjamin is also critical of the (Kantian—indeed, the Keplerian) genius that separates modern astronomers from their predecessors. This is why early modern astronomy functions for Benjamin as the threshold of modernity: it is the place from which to view not only the heavens but also the undivided cosmos of human experience. To this extent, Newton is a compelling, albeit spectral, presence in Benjamin's argument. For in the Scottish tradition that informs *Eureka*, as we have seen, Newton represented the prospective perpetuation of the type of unified experience that began to erode with Kepler, Copernicus, and Brahe. It was Newton, after all, who in the *Principia* tendentiously translated calculus—the "new science"—back into the form of classical geometry.[36] And while the Romantic image of geometry exemplifies the overrationalizing, abstractly ocular engagement of the universe of which Benjamin is critical, it also represents (in Poe and his precursors) the cohesion of mind and world that Benjamin celebrates. This is all the more true because of the logical, Newtonian steps Kant criticized—steps by which geometry binds us (by dint of Newtonian "reciprocity," Poe believes) to the universe and to each other. Hence, for Benjamin, if Kepler brings us to the threshold of modernity, then Newton implicitly acts as the window onto the experience we lose in the process. Kepler is revolutionary, Newton (merely) restorative; Kepler is comparatively Romantic, whereas Newton is more neoclassical—or, relative to the tradition out of which this idea genealogically unfolds, Newton is more *commonsensical*.

Celtic Modernism

By the early twentieth century, arguments concerning the origins and nature of cognition that were once identified with Common Sense had largely migrated into the emergent field of phenomenology. But aspects of the subject that bore on the relationship of art to the understanding and on the broad reach of aesthetic figure (for example, into the sciences) informed not only the work of Poe and, from there, the European avant-garde but also a sprouting branch of Scottish modernism. This was a protean movement for contemporaries unsure of how to situate their work relative to that of peers on the continent or of luminaries in their own national tradition, and it remains a contested category in the field of Scottish literary studies.[37] Significantly, this movement negotiated a space for itself in nature as the latter had been formulated by the disciples of Reid.

This was most evident in the Celtic Revival and the Arts and Crafts movements. Each drew upon the principles and designs of traditional Celtic art, with its swirling, recursive lines, embedding its figures in complex whorls of cosmic and cultural unity. In Margaret Macdonald's 1902 painting *The Heart of the Rose*, for example (see Figure 7), the swirling lines that draw the female figures together into a kind of communion also comprise both a rose and a womb (or perhaps a cradle) for the child. The image thus unites contemporaries and generations, nature and nurture, binding discrete entities together into an aesthetic ecosystem.

Patrick Geddes, perhaps most widely remembered as an urban planner, provided much of the intellectual impetus for this movement in his late nineteenth-century revival of a vernacular architecture promoting new styles in light not only of a culture's traditions but also of its environmental conditions—its "nature" as well as its "history." One of Geddes's signature achievements was his creation of the short-lived journal *The Evergreen* in 1895. Taking its title from Allan Ramsay's eighteenth-century collection of vernacular poems and appearing in seasonal installments ("Spring," "Summer," "Autumn," "Winter," with the epigraph "Four seasons fill the measure of the year; / There are four seasons in the mind of man"), *The Evergreen* collated poems and stories alongside scholarly essays and original artwork. Duncan Macmillan remarks that "[t]he visual make-up of *The Evergreen* is unambiguously modern even though it includes Celtic elements." Many of its images are flat in the mode of Cézanne or composed after the manner of "a vigorous art-nouveau."[38] A guide to the murals published in Geddes's 1896 venture *The Interpreter* evokes—or, rather, anticipates—Wassily Kandinsky's landmark 1912 essay "On the Problem of Form." With the murals and their borders, "line and colour [are] woven into patterns, changing as they go. . . . [Each is] expressible only in [the artist's] medium of line and colour, like a

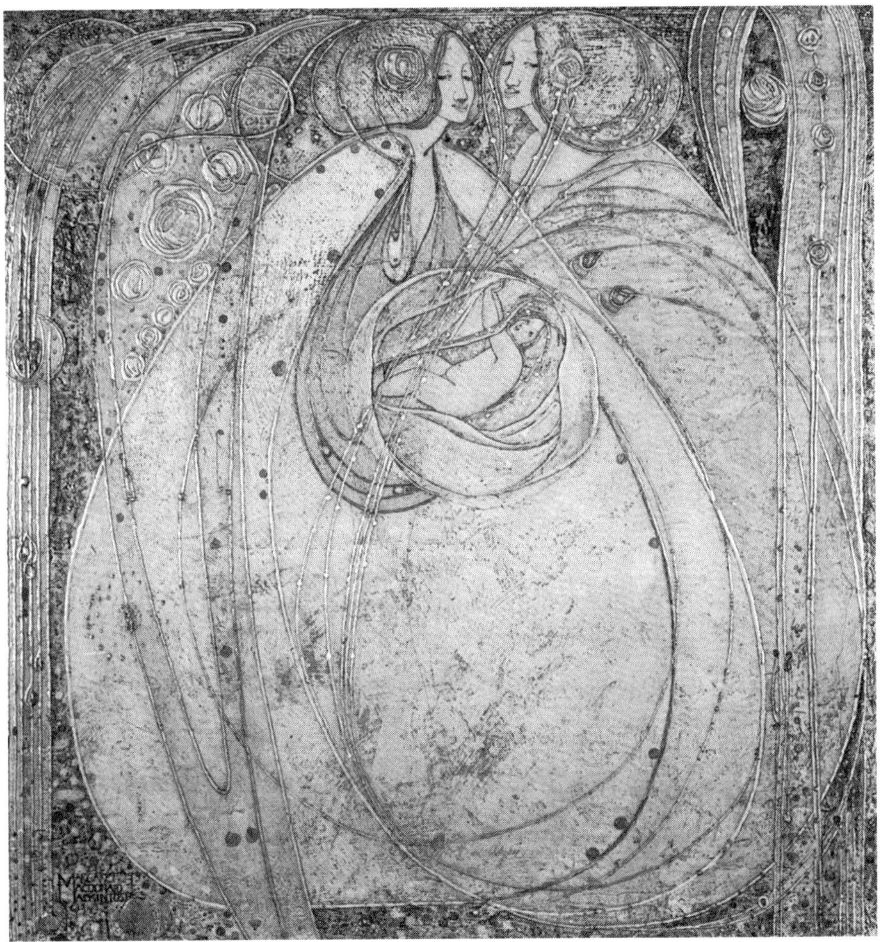

FIGURE 7. Margaret Macdonald, *The Heart of the Rose*. Reproduced from Timothy Neat, *Part Seen, Part Imagined: Meaning and Symbolism in the Work of Charles Rennie Mackintosh and Margaret Macdonald* (Edinburgh: Canongate, 1994).

chord of music."[39] Accordingly, the focus of *The Evergreen* was persistently on the fusion of elements—local and distant, contemporary and historical, aesthetic and scientific—almost as a philosophical embodiment of the involutions, the circuitous but recursive designs, of Celtic art.[40] *The Evergreen* called this principle, simply, "nature." In the introductory "Proem" of the inaugural issue, W. (that is, William) Macdonald and J. Arthur Thomson (a naturalist who, in the tradition of the nineteenth-century physico-theologists, wished to unify science with religion) proclaimed "the seasonal rhythm of the earth" as "the ultimate system in which we live." This system reconciles modern "Decadence" (of "clever writers . . . eager for the distinction of decay") and rotting industrial conditions with an avant-gardiste conviction of regeneration: "Nay, already we seem to see, against the background of Decadence, the vaguely growing lines of a picture of New-Birth."[41]

This translation of history—or the passage of time, the perpetual onset of modernity—into nature, or organically "growing lines," connects *The Evergreen*, its experimental artistic and social philosophy, and its Celtic Revival ethos to the philosophical tradition of geometry that had attained such cultural vibrancy in the Scottish Enlightenment. Fittingly, one of Geddes's associates in the Edinburgh School of Sociology, Victor Branford, contributed an article to the first issue of *The Evergreen* linking the journal's innovative vision to a geometric program:

> Francis Galton [the English polymath and half-cousin to Charles Darwin] has taught us how to measure the strength of a nation: that is, how to construct a curve, reflecting the development of those things which make for progress in physique. Some one will, in course of time, show us how to measure the mental and emotional, the intellectual and spiritual life. Then a mathematician will show us how to connect the hand curve, the mind curve, and the heart curve into one composite graphic. That curve, when we get it, will be the first line of the science of history. (85)

Geddes's vision here, Branford implies, is not, *stricto sensu*, mathematical. It bespeaks, rather, a "central idea" that his biographer Helen Meller notes throughout his work, which is that "social processes and spatial form are intimately related." Geddes had studied in Paris in the 1870s and had imbibed the *esprit de géométrie* that characterized "an enlightened pursuit of reason." At the same time, Geddes "set his face resolutely against mathematical quantification," particularly "algebraic formulation," believing instead in the integration of mathematics into a wider ecology of thought and life.[42] Hence, Geddes's curves evoked the kinds of symmetrical shapes that the German biologist Ernst Haeckel and Geddes's successor at the University of Dundee, D'Arcy Wentworth Thompson, famously attributed to nature and that informed Art Nouveau and other avant-garde movements.[43] As with James Thomson's ambiguously Newtonian lines in *The Seasons*, the aesthetic geometry conjured by Geddes purportedly reconciled poetry with science and human life with the furthest reaches of the universe. This was the tenor, moreover, of the stargazing philosophy attributed to Newton by Poe (following Brewster, Chalmers, and Nichols) and, implicitly, Benjamin. And it would soon become the driving aesthetic principle of the most influential of all the Scottish modernists, Hugh MacDiarmid.

A fractious but galvanizing force in Scottish culture in the 1920s (and for much of the next fifty years), MacDiarmid articulated a personal credo through the oracle of his landmark long 1926 poem, *A Drunk Man Looks at the Thistle*, who declares his determination to "aye ['always'] be whaur / Extremes meet."[44] MacDiarmid adapted this motto from G. Gregory Smith's distillation of a "Caledonian Antisyzygy" (or back-and-forth divagation between contrary impulses) as the cardinal feature of the Scottish literary tradition, thus converting—*pace* the "Drunk Man" and the "Thistle"—a negative image of the nation into a badge of honor.[45] But MacDiarmid's profession not only embraced a stereotype, it also literalized a shape, specifically the jagged, zigzagging lines associated with the Vorticism movement and the images promulgated in Wyndham Lewis's *Blast* magazine from 1914 to 1915. MacDiarmid appealed to a "Scottish Vortex" as "a movement with designs to generate a whirlpool of creative activity" across multiple avant-garde movements and even disciplines—art, literature, philosophy, quantum physics, and more.[46] His own poetry was rife with these diverse references. Later, in the 1940s, MacDiarmid would invoke poetry itself "As the integration of all the rich parts / Uncovered by the separate disciplines," thus looking to join codified knowledge to all that lay beyond.[47] His was a nationalist literary project patterned after the example of visual form. He even appealed to "the significance of sound *and shape*" of the Scots language from which he crafted his early poetry.[48]

In conceptualizing this project, MacDiarmid drew substantively from the example of Geddes while in some ways radicalizing—by modernizing—Geddes's vision.[49] *The Evergreen* would serve as a model for *The Scottish Chapbook*, a magazine MacDiarmid (in his given name of Christopher Murray Grieve) created in the early 1920s; Scott Lyall claims that Geddes's multidisciplinary prototype would prove "valuable to MacDiarmid as a Scottish rebel within the specialised educational establishment" of Britain.[50] At the same time, MacDiarmid loathed the insularity of the Celtic Revival and the Ossianic image of glorious defeat. Hence, the movement he propounded was no mere, inward-looking "Scottish Renaissance" but was instead a self-conscious modernism connecting Geddes's ideal of integrated disciplines in the service of social regeneration to radical concepts taking shape on the Continent.[51]

In fact, it was the example of these other schools of thought that fueled MacDiarmid's appreciation of Geddes and the Celtic Idea. Correlatively with the primitivism that inspired surrealists, expressionists, and others (as an emblem of the primal energies associated with the unconscious or the pure forms of nature), MacDiarmid imagined "Gaeldom [as] a way back beyond the Renaissance which had drained Western culture of its imaginative energy, to a classicism flowing directly from the 'Ur-motives' of the race."[52] It was this notion that spurred MacDiarmid in the early 1930s to promote a Scottish equivalent to the fascism that was inciting so much nationalist fervor in Italy and Germany.[53] But it also lent a distinctive, if sometimes blunted edge to his vision of a multidisciplinary poetry. MacDiarmid had always been fascinated by the sciences, prompted initially by the wonders of mathematics and astronomy.[54] His lengthy 1930 poem *To Circumjack Cencrastus* cited a remark of Paul Valéry's that "we can detect 'nationality in Algebra even,'" a position that had defined the Scottish literati's defense of Newton during the eighteenth century.[55] To that point, *A Drunk Man Looks at the Thistle* had cited "The words o' Plato when he said, / 'God o' Geometry is made,'" and a later work, "Poetry and Science," would merge algebra and geometry in its epigraph: "Science is the Differential Calculus of the mind, / Art is the Integral Calculus; they may be / Beautiful apart, but are great only when combined."[56]

That Poe- (and Reid-) like fusion becomes poignantly evident in one of MacDiarmid's greatest poems, "On a Raised Beach" (1934). He composed the poem after he had left Montrose, on the east coast of Scotland, for London and then Liverpool before returning to London and eventually moving to Whalsay in the remote northern reaches of Shetland. During this time, his first wife, Peggy Skinner, left him and took with her the couple's two children. Lonely and depressed, MacDiarmid began rethinking his poetic convictions, coming to the conclusion that he needed (like the nineteenth-century German poet Heinrich Heine, he claimed) to renounce writing in the (Scots) vernacular for a different type of poetry, one more able to navigate (and manipulate) the vocabulary of science.[57] Personally and artistically, then, MacDiarmid found himself reckoning with the elemental facets of his existence. His new neighbors in Whalsay worried that he might be suicidal; creatively, however, what confronted him in his new home was Kandinsky's ideal of pure forms and an ecstatic image of a primordially unified Scotland.

This vision came to him, however, in geological form, specifically in the shape of Shetland's two-billion-year-old rocks. As Catherine Kerrigan observes, these

> rocks are covered with only a thin layer of topsoil which, with the severe winds which buffet the islands, is often reduced to a minimum, making it impossible for anything to take root there. . . . MacDiarmid pointed out that those things which give the pleasure of movement to the senses, "trees and running water," are absent in [that] still and sparse landscape, but, he recalled, "one quickly gets accustomed to that, and appreciates that, even if trees and singing streams could be introduced, they would be no improvement; they would simply make the Shetlands like other places we know, whereas, without them, the Shetlands are complete in themselves. . . . [T]he infinite beauties of the bare land and the shapes and colours of the rocks which first of all impress one with a sense of sameness and next delight one with a revelation of the endless resources of Nature albeit in subtler and less showy or sensational forms than we are accustomed to appreciate in regions of more profuse development."[58]

These "shapes and colours"—their geometric form, geological substance, and phenomenological power to generate impressions—are the subject of "On a Raised Beach." But little of this is immediately evident in the poem's first few lines:

> All is lithogenesis—or lochia,
> Carpolite fruit of the forbidden tree,
> Stones blacker than any in the Caaba,
> Cream-coloured caen-stone, chatoyant pieces,
> Celadon and corbeau, bistre and beige,
> Glaucous, hoar, enfouldered, cyathiform,
> Making mere faculae of the sun and moon.[59]

The technical-geological language here is practically foreign: lithogenesis (the process whereby rocks are formed), carpolite (fossilized or petrified fruits, nuts, or seeds), caen-stone (a light-colored limestone used for building), and other words are hardly familiar to the lay reader. MacDiarmid accentuates them with other recondite terms thrown in for good measure: lochia (a term related to childbirth), Caaba (the shrine of Mecca), cyathiform (cup-shaped), and more. I use the term "good measure" self-consciously, for Nancy K. Gish insightfully remarks that MacDiarmid combines "rare and technical words with a strong cadence and musical effects [which create] an unusual fusion of uncertainty and ease. . . . The passage is in stressed, alliterative verse, with mainly four stressed lines in two balanced phrases. The lists of unknown adjectives becomes almost chant-like, so that each word holds a kind of fascination."[60] Kerrigan adds that the passage possesses a kind of mimetic, reflexive quality, with the "seemingly fragmented pile of words" serving as "the linguistic equivalent of the stones on the beach." The effect is one of defamiliarization, of an elemental encounter with the coarse matter of language, such that "perception dulled by habit is suddenly made fresh again. MacDiarmid is using language in much the same way that modern movements in the visual arts, like Cubism, created a deliberate displacement of form in order to refocus attention on the dynamics of space itself."[61]

Kerrigan's observation reiterates the point we made above that MacDiarmid drew extensively from the example of avant-garde art.[62] But, in concert with the larger argument of this chapter and book, he did even more than that, engaging in a mode of literary production whose experimentation with form took its place in a long line (pun intended) of Scottish literature.

Consider the reflexive movements and shapes created by the poet's meditations. After taking note of the beach's geological features in the poem's opening section, the poet pauses to reflect on the stillness of the scene around him. He does so by comparing two sets of minimalist motions, one by a bird and the other by the rocks themselves.

> Nothing has stirred
> Since I lay down this morning an eternity ago
> But one bird. The widest door is the least liable to intrusion,
> Ubiquitous as the sunlight, unfrequented as the sun.
> The inward gates of a bird are always open.
> It does not know how to shut them.
> That is the secret of its song. (146, ll. 32–38)

The passage alludes to William Blake's famous question in *The Marriage of Heaven and Hell*: "How do you know but ev'ry Bird that cuts the airy way, / Is an immense world of delight, clos'd by your senses five?"[63] MacDiarmid's poet does not pose this question directly as much as assume the bird's unrestrained sensuality: its "inward gates . . . are always open." But so are those of the rocks—gapingly so, unthinkably so:

> I look at these stones and know little about them,
> But I know their gates are open too,
> Always open, far longer open, than any bird's can be,
> That every one of them has had its gates wide open far longer
> Than all birds put together, let alone humanity,
> Though through them no man can see,
> No man nor anything more recently born than themselves
> And that is everything else on the Earth. (147, ll. 40–47)

The linguistic register has shifted significantly from the poem's opening lines, renouncing geological arcana in favor of discursive (but still measured, musical) reflections on the existential limits of human experience, of what "no man can see." The stones, like the bird, are conduits to nature, to truth, but more bird-like than any fowl they wing themselves through time to origins no other creature can fathom. They move—develop, change, take and lose and reacquire form—just as the bird, albeit more slowly and with infinitely greater duration. This is why the poet, seeking answers to the core mysteries of existence, "must begin with these stones the way the world began" (147, l. 58).

In essence, MacDiarmid appears to anticipate a version of what today we call speculative realism. Quentin Meillassoux, Graham Harman, and other revisionist ontologists contend that "[r]ocks, trees, and stars have other destinies besides haunting knowledge as a dark residue ungraspable by human categories" or, in other words, that objects in the world have existences independent of a subject's consciousness of them.[64] For a speculative realist, if a tree falls in the forest and nobody is there to hear it, the question of whether it produces sound is only the reflex of a Western philosophical tradition obsessed with and hence distracted by human experience. Sound represents only the subject's experience of a tree. But as Meillassoux observes, "Empirical science is today capable of producing statements about events anterior to the advent of life as well as consciousness," and the challenge is therefore to conceptualize a world without ourselves or our thought processes in it.[65] The paradox is that if we are to understand the world and universe on their terms, we must do so without ourselves present; we must learn to think an absence.

This is the poet's task in "On a Raised Beach." As he acknowledges in the lines we cited above, through the ancient stones he encounters there, "no man can see, / No man nor anything born more recently than themselves / And that is everything else on the earth." Indeed, "We are so easily baffled by appearances / And do not realise that these stones are one with the stars. / It makes no difference to them whether they are high or low" (148, ll. 96–98). This is why MacDiarmid's poem, he tells us, unlike Eliot's *The Waste Land*, "is no heap of broken images" (150, l. 166), no hand-wringing reflection on the dereliction of modern society. If Eliot's landmark poem presents a tradition collapsing under its own weight, obsessed with the gravity of its own belatedness, then MacDiarmid's poem radically dismisses that problem as an existential trifle—human, all-too-human.

> What happens to us
> Is irrelevant to the world's geology
> But what happens to the world's geology
> Is not irrelevant to us.
> We must reconcile ourselves to the stones,
> Not the stones to us. [151, ll. 215–20]

This reconciliation is what the poem dramatizes, producing what MacDiarmid's peer and fellow poet Iain Crichton Smith calls a "visionary illumination" at the point of confrontation between man and mineral.[66] The stones orchestrate our confrontation with the Thing Itself.

The hinge on which speculative realism turns is one that opens onto the tradition whose lineage after Reid we have traced in this chapter (from Chalmers and Nichol to Poe and Benjamin and from there to Scottish modernism). That hinge is what Meillassoux labels "Hume's problem" or the quandary that ensues from Hume's famed deconstruction of causal reasoning in *A Treatise of Human Nature*. There, Hume contended that we cannot know what will happen simply on the basis of our observation of what has happened in the past. It was this claim that eventually motivated Kant to devise a theory of cognition asserting that causality may not be necessary to objects but that it is so *for us*—that without it we could not arrive at full self-consciousness—and that we can never supersede this mental process. Kant's reasoning introduced what Meillassoux calls "correlationism," the idea that we only have access to things to the degree that we can think them.[67] But Hume enables a different type of thought process, Meillassoux claims, one that is best expressed in Georg Cantor's mathematical theory of the transfinite. This theory holds that "the (quantifiable) totality of the thinkable is unthinkable."[68] This is because, for Cantor, there is no absolute set of all sets, no absolutely quantifiable totality, making any designation of reality merely one possible set among others. Hence, one cannot posit, as Kant did, a law of necessity that supersedes aleatory experience. We are thus thrown back onto Hume's argument that there is no causal necessity to physical laws (for, logically speaking, they might be otherwise), which then makes it possible to formulate universes on non-metaphysical grounds—universes of which we are not "necessarily" a part. In the terms presented by "On a Raised Beach," Hume enables a proper—or at least a possible—reckoning with the stones.

In a 1961 lecture at Edinburgh University, MacDiarmid hailed Hume as "Scotland's greatest son."[69] In "On a Raised Beach," however, it is not Hume's course of reasoning the poet follows as much as Reid's. Recall our discussion concerning Hume's and Reid's shared notion regarding geometric shapes—namely, that they represent abstractions of our concrete experience of nature. For Hume, such experience roots geometry in ephemeral impressions, whereas Reid understands the process of mathematical refinement whereby we modify "things we dayly perceive by our senses" to mean that "complex geometrical conceptions of cycloids and other curves, are only artificial compositions of more simple notions which are common to the vulgar. Hence, a man of ordinary capacity finds no difficulty in understanding the definitions of Euclid."[70] In other words, Euclidean shapes personify for Reid the operations of common sense.[71]

The different inferences Hume and Reid draw from similar ideas concerning geometry help explain the difference between the analogies each makes to the theater—analogies that bear upon speculative realism. For Hume, famously, "[t]he mind is a kind of theatre, where several perceptions successively make their appearance; pass, re-pass glide away, and mingle in an infinite variety of postures and situations."[72] Because everything is rooted in experience, and because experience is ever changing, any truth we glean on the basis of that experience is ephemeral. But for Reid, "[t]he processes of Nature, in perception by the senses, may . . . be conceived as a kind of drama, wherein some things are performed behind the scenes."[73] The mind is not the sum total of all that appears "on stage" or in experience. And so, while Meillassoux discerns the recrudescence of Hume's rationale in set theory and concludes on that basis that no particular set of impressions exhausts the possibility of other sets, Thomas Chalmers and John Pringle Nichol—Reid's disciples—effectively render contingent the very theory of contingency. Without discrediting the power of science to reframe our perceptions of ourselves and the universe, we cannot nullify the existence of an absolute—for the theistic Chalmers and Nichol, for example, the presence of a Creator—that in turn potentially reframes the meaning of our speculations. Contingency endures in this latter, commonsensical formulation, but it itself becomes uncertain, as does the "realism" the latter sanctions.

"On a Raised Beach" anticipates the effect of Meillassoux's reading of Hume to the degree that it portrays the human world as contingent, but it also fancies, with Reid and his followers, the notion of absolutes. The stones are one such absolute. The poem about the stones is another; in fact, it models itself on them. Reflecting the conviction we cited above that "We must reconcile ourselves to the stones, / Not the stones to us," the poet labels "an emotion chilled . . . an emotion controlled" and proclaims such coldness "the road leading to certainty, / Reasoned planning for the time when reason can no longer prevail" (149, ll. 125–27). This resembles speculative realism in its appeal to a world beyond the reach of humanity, except that MacDiarmid's poem fancies less a realm of nonhumanity than one of a transformed humanity at the "stony limits" of existence.[74]

> I must get into this stone world now.
> Ratchel, striae, relationships of tesserae,
> Innumerable shades of grey,
> Innumberable shapes,
> And beneath them all a stupendous unity. (149, ll.149–53)

So it is that the poet imports dozens of geological terms into his verse like so many stones on a beach. The terms do not acquire a metaphorical function, not really: "ratchel" (a Scots term for broken stone), "striae" (the streaks or furrows of a column), and "tesserae" (fragments of a mosaic) might serve as figures for the layering or scattering of unfamiliar lexical pebbles throughout the poem, but at their point of contact—of reading—they merely comprise a momentary impediment to the understanding. The poem makes them its own metrically and thematically, but their initial unfamiliarity creates a gap between reading and comprehension. "This is no heap of broken images," true, but the recondite language produces effects similar to Eliot's tangle of junkyard (that is, Waste Land) allusions.

The stones themselves, then, are not the object of the poem as much as the impetus of a set of phenomenological effects. As Catherine Kerrigan puts it, the "stones are [a] fundamental reality and that is why it is important to know them, not simply in the objective way provided by geological knowledge, but by experiencing them as part of our humanity."[75] They represent the bedrock, as it were, of the worlds we create—the limits but also the foundations of possibility. "These stones go through Man, straight to God, if there is one. / What have they not gone through already? / Empires, civilisations, aeons. Only in them / If in anything, can His creation confront Him" (150, ll. 179–82). In that respect, the stones do not evoke Hume's notion of contingency as much as Reid's idea of common sense as the cornerstone of consciousness.

It thus seems fitting here that in the passage in which the poet professes his need to merge with the stones ("I must get into this stone world now"), he appeals not only to geology but also to geometry, invoking the "Innumerable shapes" that together constitute a "stupendous [metaphysical] unity." As we discussed in Chapter 1, Reid extolled geometry for presenting a clear relation between signs and objects and thus for bringing mind and world—poet and rocks on a raised beach—into close proximity with one another. Not that this makes MacDiarmid's poem geometric in any conventional sense of the term: rather, the "Innumerable shapes" of the unthinkably ancient stones conjure the excerpt in Thomson's "Spring" in which the botanist fails to number "the living Herbs, profusely wild," a passage we related to the unresolved quandaries of fluxional calculus and to Thomson's poetic modification of Newtonian thought. Perhaps an even better analogue for MacDiarmid's mind-teasing poem is thus Reid's "geometry of visibles," in which a straight line makes contact with itself.

This figure, perhaps better than any other, exemplifies MacDiarmid's own determination to be "whaur extremes meet." I say this because Reid's line represents the unification of a point with itself as the outcome not of metaphysical harmony but rather of a tendency toward self-differentiation (as the point converts to a line and moves perpetually further from its own place of origin). It is, in its way, an emblem of the "Caledonian Antisyzygy" to which MacDiarmid was so drawn. It joins the antipodes of realism and fantasy that G. Gregory Smith underscored in formulating that trope (being at once the expression of sound logic but also the product of a bizarre but true-to-life sci-fi fantasy about an eyeball dwelling at the center of a spherical world), and it defends common sense while defying conventional wisdom about the nature of straight lines. Relative to MacDiarmid, it foreshadows the ambition of the poet in "On a Raised Beach" to connect "the beginning and end of the world" through the stones (151, l. 231), and the stones, in turn, function as virtually monadological entities by which the poet unites the motions and shapes of his own thoughts with those of nature.[76]

At the turn of the twenty-first century, the journalist Neal Ascherson would replicate MacDiarmid's gesture: "Staring into the Scottish landscape, I have often asked myself why . . . bracken, rocks, man and sea are at some level one. Sometimes this secret seems about to open, like a light moving briefly behind a closed door. In writing about birds and stones whose 'inward gates' are open, MacDiarmid came as near as one can to finding the answer."[77] But what MacDiarmid sought was not only the mystery of nature but also something on the order of a "Gaelic Idea" that would radicalize the "Revivalist" ambitions of Patrick Geddes. For MacDiarmid, this "Idea" was more explicitly avant-gardiste than it had been for Geddes (being motivated partly by the example of an international avant-garde), but for each, it involved the fusion of the deep past with an as-yet-unrealized future. Whereas the poet in T. S. Eliot's *Four Quartets* had lyrically remarked that "In my beginning is my end," for Reid and the Scots, that trajectory was reversed: only in the end, at the limits of existence—at the conclusion of a process of lineation, whether geometric or artistic, from a position on a raised beach, beside stones—might one contemplate and rediscover one's beginnings.[78]

Late—and Later—Euclideanism

In the terms with which we began this chapter, Reid's geometry and MacDiarmid's poem, spanning nearly the entire duration of Scotland's Age of Union, comprise provocative instances of what Lyotard calls figuration. Figures—tropes but also and especially more elemental forms, like diagrams—diverge from the rational, predetermined set of meanings that Lyotard labels "thought."[79] The latter operates under the rubric of discourse, a category to which figure "does violence. . . . At the margin of discourse [figure] is the density within which what I am talking about retires from view; at the heart of discourse[, figure] is its 'form.'"[80] As with Barnett Newman's dramatic vertical stripes, figure designates the rupture from a particular system of thought even as it implicitly opens the space for a new set of possibilities. Figure exceeds the thought whose horizons it traces.

The tension between figure and discourse amounts to a drama of conception and, perhaps more fundamentally, of perception, of the conditions by which thought becomes apparent to us. Since the eighteenth century, the diagram has served as a medium of this drama. For John Bender and Michael Marrinan, the diagram functioned as a technology whereby encyclopedists could "concretize process[es]" of emergence and understanding, "represent[ing] complex processes uncovered by scientific investigations or instantiated by mechanical inventions."[81] And the complexities of network technologies and theories have given new life to diagrams in the twentieth and twenty-first centuries. For Anna Munster, diagrams are "inflection[s] of potential movement" that help us conceptualize how operational forms, protean creatures of information in perpetual flux, come into and then pass out of particular configurations. Diagrams, that is, present us with images, "*dispositifs*," of a network at a given moment in time even as their purely provisional character accentuates the fluidity of what they illustrate.[82] Diagrams thus help Munster theorize a posthuman condition, given that human existence is now thoroughly bound up in network society. Where MacDiarmid thus contemplated the unimaginable durability of stones, Munster tries to seize on the ephemerality of flickering ones and zeroes. To lend this operation some heft, she takes up a phenomenological history of the diagram that begins where the one presented by Bender and Marrinan leaves off, starting with William James and Charles Sanders Peirce and continuing through Gilles Deleuze's and Félix Guattari's *Thousand Plateaus* and beyond. Of particular interest is the dialectic she initiates between the diagram and the *dispositif* (or "apparatus"), that is, between the pure potentiality of relations and "an actualization of the concrete network," for it reanimates Lyotard's pas de deux between figure and discourse or between thought as it begins to congeal and thought after it has calcified.[83] For Lyotard, this was a philosophical and, crucially, historical problem, with the "sublime" and the "avant-garde" operating in both the eighteenth and twentieth centuries.

Such formulations would incur the derision of Fredric Jameson, who views Lyotard as "a quintessential modernist" obsessed with the "New" (or with what Lyotard, in "The Sublime and the Avant-Garde," describes as "the intensification of being that the event brings with it").[84] Jameson is patently skeptical of such queries into "the" nature of experience, advising instead that readers "search out the concealed ideological narratives at work in all seemingly non-narrative concepts, particularly when they are directed at narrative itself."[85] In other words, "Always historicize!"[86] And it is true that, on its surface, Lyotard's exploration of figure—the countertype to an explanatory model of narrative, like Jameson's, which corresponds more readily to "discourse"—is not a historicist undertaking. But this is true *only* on its surface. For my argument in this book has been that the exploration of "figure," or of the shapes of thought, has a history. Scottish Enlightenment literati were profoundly interested in the historicity—the temporality if not the "history" per se—of shape, its fluxional unfolding from point to line and beyond. With Reid's example and legacy in view, we might say that Scottish geometers broadly conceived—Simson and Maclaurin, yes, but also Thomson and Scott and many others—articulated less a history of phenomenology than a phenomenology of history, an examination of history's forms, its lines of progress. In this they anticipated or at least laid some of the conceptual terrain for a literary history like Wai Chee Dimock's, which is taken with the "spatialized image[s]" that deep time makes of literary history, the "loops of relations" and "whirling, percolating, clumping shapes" that obtain when we follow the logic and reticulated associations of literary texts. Hers is a geometric history, but "a geometry of what loops around, of what breaks off, [of] what is jagged."[87] She appeals directly to Benoit Mandelbrot's fractals, though her language of "loops" and "clump[s]" is strikingly resonant with the picturesque and hence, for us, with the poetics of late Euclideanism. Commensurate in some ways with what Raymond Williams calls a structure of feeling, geometry here, in literary studies, represents an experience of something of which we have as yet no corresponding concept.[88] It is an "old" language put to "new" measures. In that respect, it is also a relic, like the stones that prompted MacDiarmid to the deepest and hence, Dimock would say, most circuitous form of reflection.

Affectively, what Dimock and Lyotard articulate is the desire for a different way of imagining the contours of the present—specifically, of how we think now and of how we do history. As diverse as the ends of their critical projects may be, each turns, evocatively or expressly, to geometry as a way to lend concrete form to that desire. Franco Moretti has done the same thing, as we have seen, and even more overtly.[89] These collective and ultra-modern (if not modern*ist*) investments in geometric figure, however novel they may seem in the context of Western, European, English, or American literary history, were actually hardwired into the Scottish Enlightenment and its legacy. And that makes the relatively mundane permutations of what Andrew Seth called "the Scottish philosophy"—common sense—significant well outside the boundaries of Scotland.

This chapter has shown how that philosophy permeated later intellectual history, bypassing some of the more conventional developments one associates with Romanticism. But really, the larger lesson here does not concern the particular influence of geometrically inflected Scottish thinking as much as the way such thought enables us to reconceptualize a host of more general cultural phenomena in the eighteenth century and after. Hence, while George Davie, whose dynamic study *The Democratic Intellect* partly inspired this one, has made the case that Adam Smith influenced Jean-Paul Sartre through the concept of sympathy, and hence that it is not only the idealist tradition but also that of common sense that has left its mark on modern consciousness, my point is ultimately a little different.[90] Scottish thought has influenced the West, yes, but just as important is the set of paradigms it bequeaths us still to think and that stand potentially to reformulate the relationship between distant reading and mathematical ontology, deep time and fractal poetics, "discourse" and "figure," and much more. Indeed, it incites us to apprehend modern thought in a multitude of forms, of shapes, in energetic reconfiguration.

NOTES

INTRODUCTION

1. Jameson, *The Political Unconscious*, 9.

2. *Distant Reading*, 48, original emphasis.

3. Jockers, *Macroanalysis*, 7.

4. Anne Burdick, Johanna Drucker, Peter Lunenfeld, Todd Presner, and Jeffrey Schnapp, *Digital Humanities*, 42.

5. Ibid., 43.

6. *Graphs, Maps, Trees*, 56.

7. For Bernard Stiegler, a "tool is, before anything else, memory." See *Technics and Time*, 254; cf. Jerome McGann, "Philology in a New Key," 335–36.

8. See Plotnitsky, "Algebras, Geometries and Topologies of the Fold."

9. Quoted in Judith Bailey Slagle, *Joanna Baillie*, 67–68.

10. Judith Bailey Slagle, ed., *The Collected Letters of Joanna Baillie*, 760.

11. Alexander Pope spurned such fancy, conjuring the image for his *Dunciad*: "Mad *Mathesis* alone was unconfin'd; / Too mad for mere material chains to bind, / Now to pure Space lifts her extatic stare, / Now running round the Circle, finds it square." *The Poems of Alexander Pope*; cf. "Squaring the Circle."

12. The phrase is Slagle's in *Joanna Baillie*, 68.

13. Plato, *The Republic*, 759.

14. *A Series of Plays*, 21.

15. Ibid., 325.

16. This point was played up in the way the piece was staged. See Catherine B. Burroughs, *Closet Stages*, 127–29.

17. Baillie, *The Family Legend*, xi.

18. Gamer, *Romanticism and the Gothic*, 139. Gamer's point more particularly concerns the tension in Baillie's plays between the outward effects of the supernatural and their natural habitat in the minds of certain characters.

19. "Scottish literary history describes rhythms of continuity, change, and disjunction quite different from the English model to which it has been subordinated. Against that English model, Scotland could only loom as an intermittent, shadowy anachronism, a temporal as well as spatial border of Romanticism. In Scotland, 'Classical' and 'Romantic' cultural forms occupy the same historical moment and institutional base, rather than defining successive stages or periods." Ian Duncan, Leith Davis, and Janet Sorensen, "Introduction," 3 (1–19).

20. This continuity is most evident in the label "Scottish Renaissance," which has long defined early twentieth-century Scottish literature. But see Margery Palmer McCulloch's revision of this history, *Scottish Modernism and Its Contexts, 1918–1959*.

21. Pascale Casanova contends that "[t]he internal configuration of each national space," created during the eighteenth and nineteenth centuries, "precisely mirrors the structure of the international literary world as a whole." *The World Republic of Letters*, 108.

22. The "modernism" to which I refer here is primarily literary and philosophical, influenced by mathematics, certainly, but not mathematical modernism per se. On the latter, see Jeremy Gray, *Plato's Ghost*.

23. Phillip E. Wegner, *Imaginary Communities*, 24–25, emphases deleted.

24. *The Democratic Intellect*, 109.

25. Alexander Broadie, *The Scottish Enlightenment*, 203.

26. On Ferguson's epithet, see Andrew Blaikie, *The Scots Imagination and Modern Memory*, 29–30 (cf. 29–52).

27. *An Essay on the History of Civil Society*, 220, my emphasis.

28. As Hewitt explains, the term is sociological in origin, but Hewitt employs it to undercut "the separation between literary and lived experience that disciplined thought between the Romantic era and our own time." *Symbolic Interactions*, 25.

29. See Husserl, *The Crisis of European Sciences and Transcendental Phenomenology*, 33ff.

30. *A Treatise of Human Nature*, 99–100. In his later *Enquiry Concerning Human Understanding*, Hume defends geometric reasoning against the assertions of "matters of fact" to which he elsewhere subjects all knowledge. Upholding this distinction in the *Enquiry*, Hume asserts that geometrical propositions "are discoverable by the mere operation of thought, without dependence on what is anywhere existent in the universe. Though there were never a circle or triangle in nature, the truths demonstrated by Euclid would for ever retain their certainty and evidence." *An Enquiry Concerning Human Understanding*, 71.

31. Reid here reaffirmed the assertion of his countryman John Keill that "wherever [a] Spectator resides, he will . . . be in the Center of his own view" and will "look upon [any scene] as placed in the Surface of a Sphere, which has the Eye for its Center." *An Introduction to the True Astronomy*, 19.

32. See Ian Duncan, *Scott's Shadow*, 119–35.

33. "Account of the Life and Writings of Adam Smith, L. L. D.," in Adam Smith, *Essays on Philosophical Subjects*, 294.

34. *The Letters of Walter Scott*, quoted in Penny Fielding, *Scotland and the Fictions of Geography*, 91.

35. See Fielding, *Scotland and the Fictions of Geography*; Gidal, *Ossianic Unconformities*; Buckland, *Novel Science*; Duncan, "The Trouble with Man"; Shields, *Sentimental Literature and Anglo-Scottish Identity, 1745–1820*; Gottlieb, *Feeling British*; and McLane, *Balladeering, Minstrelsy, and the Making of British Romantic Poetry*.

36. Chai, *Romantic Theory*, xv. An anonymous reader of my manuscript more familiar than I with the intricacies of mathematical history points out that the real issue here is whether it is possible to determine in advance whether a polynomial equation, not just any equation, is solvable by radicals.

37. Ibid., xvi, 146.

38. Badiou credits Galois with effectuating a formal revolution in mathematics that potentially bears upon politics: "What is at stake for [Galois] is . . . nothing less than a new definition of algebra, which replaces the central consideration of calculations, whose terms are

numbers, with the consideration of structures, whose terms are operations. That is why Galois brings forth a *new body* in the field of mathematics: the body that he names 'group'" and that enables philosophers like Badiou to reconceptualize not only an important moment in history but also the mechanics of how history itself, as a "group" of incidents and "structure" of relations, may even be said to happen in the first place. *Logics of Worlds*, 460–61, Badiou's emphases.

39. Jenkins, *Space and the "March of Mind,"* 4.

40. Ibid., 24.

41. Bender and Marrinan, *The Culture of Diagram*, 23.

42. Meli, *Thinking with Objects*, 9–10.

43. See especially Robert Crawford, ed., *The Scottish Invention of English Literature.*

44. See Bachelard, *The Poetics of Space*, and Moretti, *Graphs, Maps, Trees.*

CHAPTER 1

1. "Manifesto of Futurism," 284.

2. See Margaret C. Jacob, *Scientific Culture and the Making of the Industrial West*, esp. 1–11.

3. *The Human Condition*, 261. Susan Strehle concurs: "Modernism remains, in its way, faithful to Newton's vision. . . . The picture of reality emphasizes its own composed nature, to be sure, but it composes according to Newtonian principles. . . . The modernist becomes the maker of a clockwork universe." *Fiction in the Quantum Universe*, 17.

4. "Avant-Garde and Kitsch," 8.

5. Louis Menand, "The Pound Error."

6. Specifically, Kant directed his essay at a remark by Johann Friedrich Zöllner, who asked, "What is enlightenment? This question, which is almost as important as: *What is Truth*? should have been well answered before one begins to enlighten!" Hudson, "What Is the Enlightenment?" 163 (163–74). Subsequent references will be cited in the text.

7. As Horkheimer and Adorno put it, "The more extensively [they] pursued [their] task, the clearer it became that . . . [they] had set [them]selves nothing less than the discovery of why mankind, instead of entering into a truly human condition, is sinking into a new kind of barbarism." *Dialectic of Enlightenment*, xi. Cassirer's tone was more conciliatory: "More than ever before, it seems to me, the time is again ripe for applying such self-criticism to the present age, for holding up to it that bright clear mirror fashioned by the Enlightenment. Much that seems to us today the result of 'progress' will to be sure lose its luster when seen in this mirror; and much that we boast of will look strange and distorted in this perspective." Cassirer, *The Philosophy of the Enlightenment*, xi.

8. In America, Hudson says, "versions of the Enlightenment have become virtually Bismarkian in their confidence in the epochal definition and the eschatological promise of history," particularly among conservatives, which is why "anti-Enlightenment philippics" have become virtually de rigueur in the liberal arts. "[W]e are all familiar with the glib line rehearsed by politicians and editorialists that [9/11] marked the attack of a 'civilization' that had not experienced an 'Enlightenment' on one that had." "What Is the Enlightenment?" 172–73.

9. Hudson remarks that both Stirling and Caird evoked the term somewhat ironically and as part of a more wide-ranging defense of metaphysics—a fact that will become important to my argument. See Hudson, "What Is the Enlightenment?" 165.

10. The title of Arthur Herman's well-publicized book is telling in itself: *How the Scots Invented the Modern World: The True Story of How Western Europe's Poorest Nation Created Our World & Everything in It* (also called *The Scottish Enlightenment: The Scots Invention of the Modern World*).

11. Scott's use of the term occurs in the context of his appreciative analysis of the impact of the Scots Irish philosopher Francis Hutcheson, whom Scott calls "a Philosopher of the Enlightenment in Scotland. While the expression—*Aufklärung*—is a commonplace in accounts of German and French Philosophy of the last century, it has seldom, if ever, been used in reference to this country; yet the remarkable output of metaphysical and ethical works, already noticed, would lead one to expect some exponent of a popular philosophy which aided in preparing the way for Hume and subsequent thinkers from 1740 onwards." William Robert Scott, *Francis Hutcheson*, 257–58. On the gradual emergence of interest in the Scottish Enlightenment in the twentieth century, see Cairns Craig, *Intending Scotland*, 77–82.

12. This argument of Craig's may be found in his book *Intending Scotland*, esp. pp. 77–144. For a classic account of Scotland's purported nineteenth-century decline, see George Davie, *The Democratic Intellect*, esp. xi–xx. David Craig makes a similar point: "The glorification of Scotland's 'Golden Age,'" the eighteenth-century Enlightenment, "does not explain the cultural impasse which followed: the use of the native language became embarrassed, poetry ran shallow and dried up, the novel was provincial from the start, many of the most original minds emigrated. Hence the historian is left calling Victorian culture in Scotland 'strangely rootless' . . . whereas a more critical sense of the 18th century would have seen that this same sort of disintegration was already visible even in the best Scots poetry and in the way the language was being used." *Scottish Literature and the Scottish People, 1680–1830*, 13, Craig's emphases deleted.

13. Craig, *Intending Scotland*, 103. Subsequent references will be cited in the text.

14. In the center of Glasgow, for instance, "there was an accumulated mass of squalid wretchedness which was probably unequalled in any other town in the British dominions," a scene that "concentrated everything wretched, dissolute, loathsome and pestilential." T. M. Devine, *The Scottish Nation*, 334 (333–50).

15. Robert Clyde recounts this transformation in *From Rebel to Hero*.

16. Muir, *Scott and Scotland*, 11.

17. See Elazar Barkan and Ronald Bush, eds., *Prehistories of the Future*, especially the essays by Vincent Crapanzano (on Durkheim), Christopher Herbert (on Frazer), and Nancy Perloff (on Gauguin).

18. "The existing monuments" of a literary tradition "form an ideal order among themselves, which is modified by the introduction of the new (the really new) work of art among them. The existing order is complete before the new work arrives; for order to persist after the supervention of novelty, the *whole* existing order must be, if ever so slightly, altered." Eliot, "Tradition and the Individual Talent," 15 (13–22). See Muir's dire account of his experience in Glasgow in *An Autobiography*, 81–121.

19. Eliot, "Was There a Scottish Literature?" quoted in Margery Palmer McCulloch, ed., *Modernism and Nationalism*, 9 (7–10). Cairns Craig makes the persuasive case that Eliot himself may have coopted the work of the Scottish professor of English literature, Herbert Grierson, who enunciated the logic of a "dissociation of sensibility" not only by reference to John Donne but also the Scottish poets Byron and Burns. I am indebted to Cairns Craig and his paper "Tradition and the Individual Editor: Professor Grierson, Modernism and National Poetics,"

which makes up a chapter of Craig's forthcoming book on the influence of Scottish professors of literature on the emergent consciousness of British modernism.

20. I am referring to Speirs's *The Scots Literary Tradition* (1940), Craig's *Scottish Literature and the Scottish People, 1680–1830* (1961), Daiches's *The Paradox of Scottish Culture* (1964), and Simpson's *The Protean Scot* (1988). For an overview of these and other texts, see Gerard Carruthers, *Scottish Literature*, ch. 1.

21. See *The Break-Up of Britain*, 102–5, 92–96.

22. Andrew Blaikie quotes Hugh MacDiarmid's poem *In Memoriam James Joyce* in stating of Scottish modernism that "Our ideal ethnological method / May fairly be called the ecological one." See Michael Grieve and W. R. Aitken, eds., *The Complete Poems of Hugh MacDiarmid*, 788, and Blaikie, *The Scots Imagination and Modern Memory*, 110–11; cf. Scott Lyall on MacDiarmid's "eco-Marxism" in *Hugh MacDiarmid's Poetry and Politics of Place*, 122. Nairn cites MacDiarmid (in his proper name of Christopher Murray Grieve) on the complexity of Scotland's "organic" national consciousness as the epigraph to ch. 3 of *The Break-Up of Britain* (see 115).

23. Nairn acknowledged in 1997 that he had underestimated the resilience of Scottish nationalism two decades earlier in his landmark book, *The Break-Up of Britain*. See *Faces of Nationalism*, 179–81.

24. I am referring to the two decades between the failed devolution referendum of 1979 and Scotland's reestablishment of a parliament in 1998, as well as to the role "letters"—literature and culture—played in stoking national consciousness. For reflections on this process, see Caroline McCracken-Flesher, ed., *Culture, Nation, and the New Scottish Parliament*.

25. Craig, cited in Craig Beveridge and Ronnie Turnbull, *Scotland After Enlightenment*, 7.

26. Key texts here include (but are by no means limited to) Alexander Broadie's *The Tradition of Scottish Philosophy* (1990), Duncan Macmillan's *Scottish Art* (1990), John Purser's *Scotland's Music* (1992), and, in literary studies, Cairns Craig's four-volume edited set *The History of Scottish Literature* (1987) and his monograph *Out of History* (1996), Robert Crawford's *Devolving English Literature* (1992), and Douglas Gifford and Dorothy McMillan's edited collection *A History of Scottish Women's Writing* (1997). Craig Beveridge and Ronald Turnbull produced two books (*The Eclipse of Scottish Culture* [1989] and *Scotland After Enlightenment* [1997]), which took polemical aim at the very idea of a nineteenth-century Scottish decline.

27. See Murray Pittock, *The Road to Independence?* esp. 17–22.

28. Frank, *The Idea of Spatial Form*, 11. Subsequent references will be cited in the text. Frank partly based his work on Worringer's *Abstraction and Empathy* (1908) a study of the relationship between naturalistic and nonnaturalistic painting styles over several centuries, and Hulme's "Romanticism and Classicism" (1911).

29. Frank discusses these critics in *The Idea of Spatial Form*, xi, 69–106.

30. See Muir, *The Structure of the Novel*, esp. 62–87. Muir also speaks disparagingly in this book about Scott ("His heroes and heroines are wooden and unreal. The action has almost always an artificial origin" [35]), thus foreshadowing *Scott and Scotland*.

31. Frank underscores this point in his discussion of Worringer and Hulme, who perceived modernist trends as palimpsests of sedimented history. See *The Idea of Spatial Form*, 53–64.

32. Woolf, "Mr. Bennett and Mrs. Brown," 320.

33. See Manning, *Fragments of Union*, 15–16.

34. Scott, *Waverley*, 340. T. M. Devine observes in particular that the 1760s seem "to have been a defining watershed because from then on Scotland began to experience a social and economic transformation unparalleled among European societies of the time in its speed, scale and intensity." *The Scottish Nation*, 107.

35. On the statistical valences of conjectural history relative to Scottish literature, particularly the work of John Galt, see Mary Poovey, *A History of the Modern Fact*, esp. ch. 5.

36. Stewart, "Account of the Life and Writings of Adam Smith," 293.

37. Maclaurin, *Treatise of Fluxions*, 1.

38. I quote here from a popular seventeenth-century pamphlet by John Hawles, *The English-Man's Right*, on the law of evidence. See my discussion of this principle in *The Ruins of Experience*, 25–34 (31).

39. "Essay on Romance," 160–62.

40. Hume, *An Enquiry Concerning Human Understanding*, 64. On ballad culture, see Maureen N. McLane, *Balladeering, Minstrelsy, and the Making of British Romantic Poetry*; on Scott's adoption of Hume's theories, see Ian Duncan, *Scott's Shadow*, esp. ch. 5. We will attend more rigorously to this idea in Chapter 2.

41. Newton, for example, "claimed that the geometrical analysis of the ancients was superior to the algebraic of the moderns in terms of elegance and simplicity." Niccolò Guicciardini, *Isaac Newton on Mathematical Certainty and Method*, 15.

42. See, generally, Howard Gaskill, ed., *The Reception of Ossian in Europe*.

43. *The Life and Letters of James Macpherson*, 45.

44. Stafford, *The Sublime Savage*, 26, 27.

45. Betty Ponting, "Mathematics at Aberdeen, Developments, Characters and Events, 1717–1860," quoted in Niccolò Guicciardini, *The Development of Newtonian Calculus in Britain 1700–1800*, 97.

46. Stafford, *The Sublime Savage*, 30.

47. Blackwell, *Proofs of the Enquiry into Homer's Life and Writings, Translated into English*, 4, 76, my emphasis.

48. Alexander Broadie, *The Scottish Enlightenment*, 203.

49. Reid, *An Inquiry into the Human Mind on the Principles of Common Sense*, 118; quoted in Stafford, *The Sublime Savage*, 32.

50. Blair, *Lectures on Rhetoric and Belles Lettres*, 275.

51. Stafford, *The Sublime Savage*, 32–33; Macpherson, *A Dissertation*, 49.

52. Macpherson, *A Dissertation*, 48.

53. Blair, *A Critical Dissertation on the Poems of Ossian*, 378.

54. Macpherson, *Fragments of Ancient Poetry*, 9.

55. Duncan, "The Pathos of Abstraction," 49.

56. Robert Crawford explores the link between Ossianic and modern, Eliot- and Pound-imagined "fragments" in *The Modern Poet*, 62–69.

57. Simson, *The Elements of Euclid*, Preface (no pagination).

58. Simson, "Preface" (no pagination).

59. Playfair, *On the Origin and Investigation of Porisms*, 18.

60. Blanchot, *The Infinite Conversation*.

61. Pittock, "Historiography," 260 (258–79).

62. Niccoló Guicciardini provides an example from the world of mathematics: "Newton was keenly aware of [the] asymmetry between modern algebraic analysis and geometrical synthesis and tried hard to recover and extend the analytical geometrical process of discovery to

curvilinear figures. But this did not lead him to recover the unity between analysis and synthesis that, he was convinced, characterized the mathematical practices of the ancients. What he obtained was a series of interesting results in projective geometry," a concept that distends Euclidean space. *Isaac Newton on Mathematical Certainty and Method*, 386.

63. See the Introduction for my discussion of the "diagrammatic" poetics evoked by John Bender and Michael Marrinan in *The Culture of Diagram*.

64. Newton, *The Method of Fluxions and Infinite Series* (1736), quoted in Guicciardini, *The Development of Newtonian Calculus in Britain 1700–1800*, 57.

65. Glissant, *The Poetics of Relation*, 33.

66. I refer in this latter instance to the volume compiled by Tore Frängsmyr, J. L. Heilbron, and Robin E. Rider on the impact of geometry and mathematical abstraction on Enlightenment scientific and cultural practices. See Frängsmyr, Heilbron, and Rider, eds., *The Quantifying Spirit in the Eighteenth Century*.

67. "Foucault and the Eclipse of Vision," 281.

68. Dimock, *Through Other Continents*, 2.

69. See Alexander Koyré, "The Significance of the Newtonian Synthesis," 60, and Foucault, *The Order of Things*, 71–76.

70. Nobody has examined the complexities of vision during the Enlightenment more rigorously than Stafford. I refer here to a distinction she draws in *Voyage into Substance*. In her more recent work, she analyzes how images "lay down tracks that affectively activate our eyes and mind." And yet, even as they "stamp us with the marks and textures of the phenomenal world," they themselves derive from a "distributed network" of sensory and cognitive functions, such that our most basic (and/or rational) perceptions are born from a sensual orgy of riotous impressions. *Echo Objects*, 11, and "The Remaining 10 Percent," 41.

71. For an exemplarily extensive analysis of such relations and the challenge they pose to historicism, see Susan Manning, *Poetics of Character*, 3–55.

72. *The Fourth Dimension and Non-Euclidean Geometry in Modern Art*, 40–41. The three Poincaré books to which Henderson refers are *Science and Hypothesis* (1902), *The Value of Science* (actually published in 1905), and *Science and Method* (1908). I am grateful here to the work of Alice Jenkins, Melanie Bayley, Daniel Brown, and other participants in the "Literature and Mathematics" conference at the University of Glasgow in May 2011 for helping me flesh out my understanding of the "new" mathematics in the nineteenth century.

73. "Henri Poincaré, Marchel Duchamp and Innovation in Science and Art," 130.

74. Henderson, *The Fourth Dimension and Non-Euclidean Geometry in Modern Art*, 33.

75. On the implication of Duchamp's readymades in the new mathematics, see Craig Adcock, "Conventionalism in Henri Poincaré and Marcel Duchamp." For a more detailed discussion of Duchamp's implication in the new geometries, see Henderson, *The Fourth Dimension and Non-Euclidean Geometry in Modern Art*, 117–63.

76. *Farewell to an Idea*, 213–15.

77. *Science and Hypothesis*, 50, emphases deleted. Michael Friedman argues that Kant's geometric error isn't Euclideanism per se—Euclidean geometry is a "convention" like any other—but rather the confusion between "pure" and "applied" geometry or between geometry as a system of logic and as an actual index of the material world. See *Kant and the Exact Sciences*, ch. 1.

78. *Critique of Pure Reason*, 25.

79. *Science and Hypothesis*, 50.

80. "The Foundation and Manifesto of Futurism," 286.

81. Florian Cajori, "Attempts Made During the Eighteenth and Nineteenth Centuries to Reform the Teaching of Geometry," 182.

82. Neal, *From Discrete to Continuous*, 46, 6; cf. 115–37.

83. *Mathematics*, 44; cf. pp. 123–26. For a fuller history of these innovations, see Henk J. M. Bos, *Redefining Geometrical Exactness.*

84. Euclid, *The Thirteen Books of the Elements*, 155.

85. Jeremy Gray takes up the history of these questions in *Ideas of Space.*

86. For an overview of the Islamic navigation of the parallel postulate, see Carl B. Boyer, *A History of Mathematics*, 242–44.

87. Quoted in Marvin Jay Greenberg, *Euclidean and Non-Euclidean Geometries*, 125.

88. Reid, *An Inquiry into the Human Mind on the Principles of Common Sense*, 147–48.

89. Broadie, *The Scottish Enlightenment*, 206.

90. Reid, *An Inquiry into the Human Mind on the Principles of Common Sense*, 149.

91. Neal, *From Discrete to Continuous*, 9.

92. Richards, *Mathematical Visions*, 4, 2.

93. See John E. Lesch, "Systematics and the Geometrical Spirit," and Robin E. Rider, "Measure of Ideas, Rule of Language."

94. " 'Now, what I want is, Facts. . . . Facts alone are wanted in life.' " So says Gradgrind, possessed of a sternly geometric "square forefinger . . . square wall of a forehead . . . [and] square coat, square legs, [and] square shoulders." Dickens, *Hard Times*, 5.

95. Fontanelle, *Eloge de Neuton*, cited in Hall, *Isaac Newton*, 59.

96. Quoted in Hall, *Isaac Newton*, 79.

97. The mathematical scholars James M. Henle and Eugene M. Kleinberg assert that "[t]he history of modern mathematics is to an astonishing degree the history of the calculus. The calculus was the first great achievement of mathematics since the Greeks and it dominated mathematical exploration for centuries. The questions it answered and the questions it raised lay at the heart of man's understanding not only of geometry and number, but also space and time and mathematical truth. . . . The methods it developed gave the physical sciences an impetus without parallel in history, for through them natural science was born." *Infinitesimal Calculus*, 3.

98. Guicciardini, *Isaac Newton on Mathematical Certainty and Method*, 179, 216. Subsequent references will be cited in the text.

99. Newton, "Quadrature of Curves," 141, Newton's emphasis.

100. *Philosophers at War*, 161, 134.

101. *Never at Rest*, 721.

102. Boyer, *A History of Mathematics*, 414.

103. *Symbols, Impossible Numbers, and Geometric Entanglements*, 242–43.

104. Keill, "A Preface, Shewing the *Usefulness* and *Excellency* of this work," no pagination.

105. On the "classical" tradition in Scottish education, see Davie, *The Democratic Intellect*, 169–200, and Craig Beveridge and Ronnie Turnbull, *Scotland After Enlightenment*, 135–52.

106. Playfair's axiom is far simpler: "Given a line and a point not on it, at most one parallel to the given line can be drawn through the point."

107. *Walter Scott and the Limits of Language*, 22.

108. Campbell, *The Philosophy of Rhetoric*, cited in Lumsden, *Walter Scott and the Limits of Language*, 24.

109. In exposition of this principle in Hume's work, Lumsden cites the essays "The Sceptic" and "Of the Standard of Taste." She builds here on arguments by Cairns Craig, Ian

Duncan, and especially Susan Manning, who "draws a direct parallel between Hume's philosophy and what we might describe as 'postmodernism'" (17; cf. 16–19).

110. See Hume, *A Treatise of Human Nature*, 49–73 (esp. 57–60); cf. Cairns Craig, *Associationism and the Literary Imagination*, 1–39 (esp. 8–10). Claudia Brodsky Lacour undertakes an extensive analysis of the implications for signification of the relationship between geometry and algebra in *Lines of Thought*.

111. See Virginia Spate, *Orphism*, esp. ch. 1 ("Mystical Orphism," 9–59) and the discussion of *Newton's Discs* on 126–28.

CHAPTER 2

1. "Scott's shadow," Ian Duncan calls this heritage—one that impacted the future and also helped shape our perception of the past. See *Scott's Shadow*, esp. 3–45.

2. See Davie, *The Democratic Intellect*, chs. 6 and 7, and *The Scotch Metaphysics*, ch. 1, and Craig, *Intending Scotland*, ch. 6.

3. See Lukács, *The Historical Novel*, 30–63, and Jameson, *Postmodernism, or, The Cultural Logic of Late Capitalism*, 404–5. For James Chandler, commenting on historicism at century's end, Scott is at once modern and romantic—or modern-*because*-romantic—for not only exhibiting but also, in some way, instantiating such consciousness as a critical reflex. See *England in 1819*, ch. 2.

4. "Walter Scott's Romantic Postmodernity," 119. McGann says Scott's fiction shares less with Jamesian realism than with works like Flann O'Brien's *At-Swim Two Birds*, Italo Calvino's *If on a Winter's Night a Traveler*, Thomas Pynchon's *Gravity's Rainbow*, and Alasdair Gray's *Lanark*.

5. See Langan, "Understanding Media in 1805." Subsequent references will be cited in the text. Cf. Kittler, *Discourse Networks, 1800/1900*. For a larger and more recent study that addresses Scottish Romantic literature (especially ballads and poetry) in light of media studies, see Maureen N. McLane, *Balladeering, Minstrelsy, and the Making of British Romantic Poetry*.

6. McGann, "Visible and Invisible Books," 297; "Dialogue and Interpretation at the Interface of Man and Machine," 99.

7. Scott, *Guy Mannering*, 241.

8. See Mandelbrot, "How Long Is the Coast of Britain?" in *The Fractal Geometry of Nature*, 25–33.

9. See Hogarth, *The Analysis of Beauty*.

10. *The Antiquary*, 72. I am grateful to Miranda Burgess for bringing this passage to my attention.

11. Judith V. Grabiner shows "how Maclaurin applied 'the Newtonian style' to areas ranging from the actuarial evaluation of annuities to the shape of the earth." See "Newton, Maclaurin, and the Authority of Mathematics," 841.

12. At least, this is how Richard Westfall sees it. He remarks that Newton's later protestations against Descartes's methods have created the false impression that the *Principia* is primarily a geometric work. In actuality, the Euclidean aspects of that work "lay mostly on the surface. . . . [T]hought patterns of the calculus," and hence of algebra, are what drive Newton's masterpiece "behind the façade of classical geometry." *Never at Rest*, 379, 424. But see Niccoló Guicciardini's protestations in note 20.

13. Newton, "Quadrature of Curves," 141, emphases deleted.

14. So claimed Newton's nephew, John Conduitt. See Rupert Hall, *Isaac Newton*, 79, Conduitt's emphasis.

15. See Alex D. D. Craik, "Geometry Versus Analysis in Early 19th-Century Scotland."

16. Maclaurin introduces his definitive two-volume treatise on calculus by remarking that "[g]eometry is valued for its extensive usefulness, but has been most admired for its evidence," drawing upon the etymology of evidence as lucidity. *A Treatise of Fluxions*, 1.

17. Playfair, "Dissertation," 42–43; I refer here to Pater's "Conclusion" to *The Renaissance*, 186–90.

18. In this respect, fluxions presented an even more sophisticated model than Joseph Priestley's fascinating but comparatively rigid depiction of the flow of time in his 1769 *New Chart of History*.

19. The novel corresponds in this respect with the relatively recent fad of timelines, crafted by Joseph Priestley and others, which Ted Underwood discusses in *Why Literary Periods Mattered*, 58–62. Scott's innovation in *Guy Mannering*, I am suggesting, is a more ductile illustration of that principle.

20. On Scott's deployment of such narrative structure relative to other (British and German) Romantics, see Paul Hamilton, *Metaromanticism*, ch. 5.

21. The place of calculus in the *Principia* is a subtle and historical source of debate. See Niccolò Guicciardini, *Isaac Newton on Mathematical Certainty and Method*, 235–57 (esp. 252–54).

22. Although he was no mathematician himself, Scott was well aware of Scottish innovations in mathematics and sciences. And while Scott's personal library did not contain Maclaurin's books, Scott did own the work of Maclaurin's son, Lord Dreghorn, a lawyer like Scott. I am grateful to Alison Lumsden for this information.

23. On the dynamics of Manet's painting, see Thierry de Duve, "How Manet's *A Bar at the Folies-Bergère* Is Constructed." Michel Foucault addresses this same issue in *Manet and the Object of Painting*, 72–79.

24. "History is . . . not a temporal notion, it has nothing to do with temporality, but it is the emergence of a language of power out of a language of cognition." "Kant and Schiller," 133.

25. One is reminded here of the young Walter Benjamin's observations concerning the difference between "reflection and positing" in German Romanticism. Reflection in "Fichte, Schlegel, Novalis, and Schelling," Benjamin remarked, was irreducible to "the realm of experience," functioning instead as the mind's way of mediating that experience, of framing it. But the seemingly infinite regression of the act of reflection (that is, the experience of seeing, then thinking on the meaning of that experience, then thinking on the thinking on the meaning of that experience, etc.) inspired dreams of an "absolute reflection" that would return to the status of experience, though this time in ultimate form as a moment of higher vision—of trope become figure. See "The Concept of Criticism in German Romanticism," 121.

26. Hardie, *John Pettie*, 171.

27. For a larger, art-historical argument to this effect, see John Morrison, *Painting the Nation*, esp. 1–18.

28. Nairn, *The Break-Up of Britain*, 104.

29. Scott underscores this point in person of the Edinburgh lawyer Pleydell, the eventual executor of justice on Harry's behalf. We meet Pleydell in the midst of a weekly burlesque in which he plays the part of "the Scottish monarch" (205). With this carnivalesque introduction to "the law," Scott sends up the Union of Crowns and Parliaments that had cost the Scots,

respectively, their king and independence. Scott does not necessarily wish to change history, but he shows here that "history" has had garish consequences in Scotland.

30. Scott, *Waverley*, 283.

31. On the logic of the chronotope in Scott, see especially Chandler, *England in 1819*, 127–51, and Saree Makdisi, *Romantic Imperialism*, 70–99.

32. Ian Baucom, *Specters of the Atlantic*, 45. Subsequent references will be cited in the text. Baucom here takes up Lukács's *The Historical Novel* (1937), Jameson's *Marxism and Form* (1971), and Chandler's *England in 1819* (1998).

33. As he puts it, "If the eighteenth century manifests itself in crucial respects as the century of the typical and the average . . . [then] the key to that contract, moment, mode of speculation, and speculative epistemology is that procedure by which value detaches itself from the life of things and rearticulates itself in the novelistic theater of the typicalizing imagination" (106).

34. Gallagher, *Nobody's Story*.

35. Baucom borrows here from Giovanni Arrighi's *The Long Twentieth Century* (1994). Gallagher, another important source for Baucom, had made a similar move concurrently with Arrighi: "Instead of assuming the labor theory of value on which the Marxist understanding rests, [novelistic] rhetoric stresses that value is an effect of exchange, not production. . . . Indeed, [eighteenth-century novels'] authors commonly figured their labor as the accumulation of credit rather than the production of property" (*Nobody's Story*, xxi–xxii).

36. I refer here to Benjamin's famous declaration in his "Theses on the Philosophy of History": "There is no document of civilization which is not at the same time a document of barbarism" (*Illuminations*, 256). Slavoj Žižek plays an equally important role in Baucom's argument, particularly in his reflections concerning the emptiness of the modern category of the human subject—of the "nobodies" wrought by the representational engine of high finance (though not of the slaves, who count as less than "nobody" and who therefore fall outside the scope of this particular void). See Žižek's discussion of this principle by way of the French Revolution in *Tarrying with the Negative*, 27–29.

37. Baucom refers here to Duncan's argument in *Modern Romance and Transformations of the Novel*, esp. 6–9.

38. In his 1755 *Dictionary of the English Language*, Samuel Johnson defined the imagination as "the power of forming ideal pictures; the power of representing things absent to one's self or others." I will return to this point in Chapter 3.

39. *Transactions of the Royal Society of Edinburgh*, Appendix, 69. See Stewart, *The Distance of the Sun from the Earth Determined, by the Theory of Gravity*.

40. *Transactions of the Royal Society of Edinburgh*, 57–58.

41. In a difference discipline, the Scottish biologist, mathematician, and classicist D'Arcy Wentworth Thompson pioneered a study of nature on similar terms—*On Growth and Form in Shapes*, published in 1917. Philip Balls calls it "the first formal analysis of pattern and form in nature," the prototype of modern morphology. See Ball, *Nature's Patterns*, 1:6.

42. Clark, *Farewell to an Idea*, 7, 9.

43. Kandinsky, for example, wrote a famous treatise entitled *On the Spiritual in Art* (1912), and of geometry specifically, Mondrian averred that "[t]hroughout the history of culture, art has demonstrated that universal beauty does not arise from the particular character of the form, but from the dynamic rhythm of its inherent relationships, or . . . from the mutual relations of forms. . . . Geometrical forms being so profound an abstraction of form may be regarded as neutral; and on account of their tension and the purity of their outlines they may even be

preferred to other neutral forms" (quoted in Herschel B. Chipp, ed., *Theories of Modern Art*, 350–51).

44. Badiou, *Number and Numbers*, 1–3. Subsequent references will be cited in the text.

45. On the growing impact of multiplicity as a cultural principle in the era of emergent colonialism, see Stephen Greenblatt, *Marvelous Possessions*; on the complexities of this principle relative to the category of gender, particularly in the eighteenth century, see Felicity A. Nussbaum, *Torrid Zones*, esp. 194–210.

46. Rotman, *Signifying Nothing*, 27.

47. Gallagher too appeals to Rotman: see *Nobody's Story*, xv n.6. Technically, zero became an "empty" number standing in for the operation of *all* numbers or for the *system* of numbers that is not itself a number (and hence which, technically, is void, "zero"). The void, that is, assumed the place of the medium through which we think numbers in the first place. Such "empty" operations become normative, Rotman explains, once we move from simple arithmetic to equations with more complex variables. "In expressions like $x + 1 = y$, $2x + 3y - z = 0$, and so on, the letter signs enter into full arithmetical relations with number signs: multiplying them, being added to them, being numerically compared to them, being substituted for them, and generally being treated as if they *were* number signs according to a common syntax. Perceived externally, this unitary syntax comes apart, since variables are not of course number signs; on the contrary, they are signs which meta-linguistically indicate the possible, but not the actual, presence of number signs" (*Signifying Nothing*, 31–32, Rotman's emphasis).

48. *Badiou*, 65, Hallward's emphasis.

49. *Mathematics*, 201.

50. "The modern instance of this movement attests to the void and the infinite as materials for the thinking of Number. Nevertheless, none of these concepts can be inferred from experience, nor do they propose themselves to any intuition, or submit to any deduction, even a transcendental one. None of them amounts to the form of an object, or of objectivity. These concepts arise from a *decision*, whose written form is the axiom; a decision that reveals the opening of a new epoch for the thought of being qua being." *Number and Numbers*, 212, Badiou's emphasis.

51. Ibid., 7, emphases deleted.

52. Kline, *Mathematics*, 127.

53. Scott, *The Letters of Sir Walter Scott*, 1:174. On Playfair's influence on Scott and his world, see Adelene Buckland, *Novel Science*, esp. 33–55.

54. Smith, *The Theory of Moral Sentiments*, 10.

55. See, most paradigmatically, "From Restricted to General Economy."

56. Berkeley, *The Analyst*, 59. For a helpful overview of Berkeley's argument and the *Analyst* controversy, see Douglas M. Jesseph, "Editor's Introduction," 111–55.

57. Berkeley, *The Analyst*, 59.

58. He asked, for example, "whether the Diagrams in a Geometrical Demonstration are not to be considered, as Signs of all possible finite Figures, of all sensible and imaginable Extensions or Magnitudes of the same kind." *The Analyst*, 77. In his *Principles of Human Knowledge* (1710), Berkeley speaks somewhat contemptuously of such "amusing geometrical paradoxes" as the infinite divisibility of finite extension, which leads to the type of thinking on display with the infinitesimals. Such paradoxes have a "direct repugnancy to the plain common sense of mankind, and are admitted with so much reluctance into a mind not yet debauched by learning." Berkeley, *Principles of Human Knowledge and Three Dialogues*, 80.

59. As a facet of what she calls "The Newtonian Enlightenment," Margaret C. Jacob observes that "the new science . . . offered a radically altered picture of nature. Science made nature lawful, and as the definition of creation changed so too did the human conception of the Creator. . . . A vision of order and harmony, God's work, replaced biblical texts and stories, God's word. But in the hands of freethinkers science also permitted the first articulation of a coherent universe without any creator." *Scientific Culture and the Making of the Industrial West*, 74.

60. "As time passes the original divine order declines due to material friction and interactions (which cause loss of motion in the material world) and the indulgence of souls in idolatry (which remove humanity from its direct connection with the Lord and Master). God then periodically repairs and restores the original and pure state of creation with the assistance of material agents, like comets. . . . Newton's method of fluxions and his later geometrical methods in the *Principia* . . . capture and reveal the most fundamental truth about the mechanism of perception and the natural decline of all processes in Nature." Ayval Ramati, "The Hidden Truth of Creation," 419, 422.

61. *A Treatise of Fluxions*, 244. Subsequent references will be cited in the text.

62. In his "Essay on Romance," Scott traces something similar, discerning in traditional narratives the emblem of both history and the passage of time, the composite forming an idealized shape of the nations who recount them: Italy, Spain, France, Britain, and so on. See *The Miscellaneous Prose Works of Walter Scott*, 129–216.

63. In his private correspondence, Maclaurin remarked that "[t]he Method of fluxions was the boasted production of the past age, & notwithstanding the emptiness, darkeness, confusion nay direct impossibilitys & contradictions which [Berkeley] pretends to discover in its foundations, I shall not be afraid to apply to it what was said of Homer's Iliad that it is preciosissimum humani animi opus, the most noble production of the humane Understanding." Recipient not stated, *The Collected Letters of Colin Maclaurin*, 427. Such "Understanding" is a function not only of logic but also of the evident (or visible) correlation between reason and perception, as Maclaurin asserts in his large volume on Newton: "As our *analysis* of the system [of nature] must be founded upon the real figures, magnitudes and motions, of the bodies of which it is composed; so we shall have an excellent instance of the method of proceeding by *analysis* and *synthesis*," which is to say, deductively and inductively, "if we describe in what manner we are enabled, from the apparent phaenomena, to deduce an account of the real; without the knowledge of which our enquiries into the powers or causes that operate in nature must be doubtful or erroneous." *An Account of Sir Isaac Newton's Philosophical Discoveries*, 222.

64. In a well-known passage about the eighteenth century, John Barrell remarks that "[a]s society itself becomes more various, and as the abilities of those who compose it become proportionately more limited, the ability of each link in a productive chain . . . to see, to *comprehend* the range and organization of activities necessary to its survival and progress, is impaired, and this is perceived as a political problem, as a threat to social coherence, and one which is proposed to be solved either by the provision of compensatory education, or by its deliberate non-provision, according to whether it appears to the proposer that social unity is best guaranteed by an attempt to teach an understanding of its principles, or to conceal them." *English Literature in History, 1730–80*, 29, Barrell's emphasis.

65. This is the type of process I analyze elsewhere—the paradoxical devaluation of experience precisely as a function of its extension through science. See *The Ruins of Experience*, esp. the Introduction and ch. 1.

66. "The Structure of *Guy Mannering*," 109. Subsequent references will be cited in the text.

67. Duncan, *Modern Romance and Transformations of the Novel*, 130.

68. *Scott's Shadow*, 136. Subsequent references will be cited in the text.

69. *A Treatise of Human Nature*, 146. Subsequent references will be cited in the text.

70. *The Political Unconscious*, 13, Jameson's emphasis.

71. But see, for example, Donald L. M. Baxter, "Hume on Infinite Divisibility" and, most helpfully, Dale Jacquette, "Hume on Infinite Divisibility and Sensible Extensionless Indivisibles."

72. George Davie, *The Scotch Metaphysics*, 3.

73. Ibid., 12. Subsequent references will be cited in the text.

74. Scott, *Waverley*, 340. Subsequent references will be cited in the text.

75. I am grateful to Ian Duncan for reminding me of this passage relative to the larger issue of the fluxional valences of Scott's historical fiction.

76. John O. Hayden, who edited the 1970 volume *Scott: The Critical Heritage*, says that Scott's "popularity and critical reputation" began declining around 1885 and that most of the attention he received after that period was scholarly rather than creative. See *Scott*, 20.

77. *The Historical Novel*, 13, 14. Subsequent references will be cited in the text.

78. Muir, *Scott and Scotland*, 13. Subsequent references will be cited in the text.

79. Pascale Casanova likens the task of criticism to a kind of geometric detective work, specifically to the discovery of a "figure in the carpet," the Jamesian metaphor for the discernment of a formal principle that lends shape to a particular literary work or, for Casanova, to a body of works, a "world republic of letters." *The World Republic of Letters*, 1.

Chapter 3

1. *Scottish Journey*, 243. Subsequent references will be cited in the text.

2. *Scott and Scotland*, 11–12. Subsequent references will be cited in the text.

3. *We Moderns*, 104, 176. Muir was still appealing to the bidirectionality of time in the late 1930s, stating that before World War I, "everything seemed to be making for progress," but that "various events after the War [had] clearly tak[en society] backwards." Muir, *The Present Age from 1914*, 25.

4. "Avant-Garde and Kitsch," 5–6.

5. In a 1944 lecture on Scott delivered at the University of Edinburgh, Muir reiterated the association between Scott's work and effects widely associated with modernism, attesting that "after re-reading" Scott, he "experience[s] the full shock of his imagination." "Walter Scott," 65.

6. See *Mapping an Empire*.

7. On this "cosmography" relative to coastal surveillance, see Charles W. J. Withers, "The Social Nature of Map-Making in the Scottish Enlightenment, c. 1682–c. 1832." Of the overtly geometric layout of Edinburgh's New Town, Charles McKean observes that "the approved plan . . . was a larger and more sophisticated variation of the plans for the hundreds of new rural towns and urban suburbs founded in Scotland between 1735 and 1800." "Twinning Cities," 47.

8. *Scottish Art*, 79.

9. *An Essay on the Picturesque, as Compared with the Sublime and the Beautiful*, 25, 61.

10. I refer here to the discussion of *Guy Mannering* in Chapter 2.

11. *The Quarterly Review*, 36 (569). I am grateful to my colleague Nick Mason for bringing this essay to my attention. On Price's influence on Scott, see George Dekker, *The Fictions of Romantic Tourism*, ch. 6.

12. The account of this tour, which Scott called a "diary," is found in John Gibson Lockhart's *The Life of Sir Walter Scott*, 158–324. I cite specific passages in the chapter.

13. Scott, *Waverley*, 104–5.

14. Glendening, *The High Road*, 174.

15. The Derrida essay to which I am referring is "Freud and the Scene of Writing."

16. Pittock, *Scottish and Irish Romanticism*, 192, 190.

17. Katie Trumpener calls Macpherson's *Ossian* an "echo chamber." See *Bardic Nationalism*, 70. Cf. Burke, *A Philosophical Enquiry into the Origin of Our Ideas of the Sublime and Beautiful*, 149–61.

18. Dorothy Wordsworth recounts the visit she and William made to Ossian's Hall in terms at once rapt and amused. Before viewing the falls, she and William were "conducted into a small apartment, where the gardener desired us to look at a painting of the figure of Ossian, which, while he was telling us the story of the young artist who performed the work, disappeared, parting in the middle, flying asunder as if by the touch of magic, and lo! we are at the entrance of a splendid room, which was almost dizzy and alive with waterfalls, that tumbled in all directions. . . . We both laughed heartily." *Recollections of a Tour Made in Scotland*, 173–74.

19. Lyotard, *The Postmodern Condition*, 78.

20. "I shall call modern the art which devotes its 'little technical expertise,' as Diderot used to say, to present the fact that the unpresentable exists." A sublime painting, "[a]s painting . . . will of course 'present' something though negatively; it will therefore avoid figuration or representation. It will be 'white' like one of Malevitch's squares; it will enable us to see only by making it impossible to see; it will please only by causing pain." *The Postmodern Condition*, 78.

21. *The Beautiful, the Sublime, and the Picturesque in Eighteenth-Century British Aesthetic Theory*, 186.

22. Gilpin, "On Picturesque Beauty," 3. Subsequent references will be cited in the text.

23. Price, *An Essay on the Picturesque, as Compared with the Sublime and the Beautiful*, 46, 18, 17. Subsequent references will be cited in the text.

24. Richard Payne Knight, responding to Price in 1805, insisted further on this point that the picturesque is a quality of art—and criticism—rather than nature: "[T]he great and fundamental error, which prevails throughout [Price's] otherwise able and elegant *Essays on the Picturesque*, is seeking for distinctions in external objects, which only exist in the modes and habits of viewing and considering them." Knight thus locates in the mind what Price (through Burke) locates in objects. Price "unfortunately suffered himself to be misled by the brilliant, but absurd and superficial theories of" Burke's *Inquiry*. See *An Analytical Inquiry into the Principles of Taste*, 196.

25. *The Order of Things*, 133.

26. *The Fractal Geometry of Nature*, 1.

27. *Inquiry into the Picturesque*, 93.

28. "Nine Revisionist Theses on the Picturesque."

29. Ibid., 89, 85.

30. Leslie, *Elements of Geometry, Geometrical Analysis, and Plane Trigonometry*, vi. Subsequent references will be cited in the text.

31. On Playfair's importation of algebraic techniques into traditional geometry—in opposition to the practices of Robert Simson, Matthew Stewart, and others—see William Christie, *The Edinburgh Review in the Literary Culture of Romantic Britain*, 154–58; cf. Amy Ackerberg-Hastings, "Analysis and Synthesis in John Playfair's 'Elements of Geometry.'"

32. On Playfair's disagreement with Leslie, see Richard Olson, "Scottish Philosophy and Mathematics, 1750–1830."

33. See *The Democratic Intellect*, 130–31. I am grateful to Murdo Macdonald for reminding me of this passage.

34. "Imperial Landscape," 5.

35. I am thinking, for example, of William Combe's Dr. Syntax, the eponymous hero of a series of satirical adventures for which the celebrated English painter Thomas Rowlandson supplied the illustrations. See Combe's 1812 poem *The Tour of Dr. Syntax in Search of the Picturesque*.

36. *Space and the "March of Mind,"* 62, 77–78.

37. See Ibid., 68–77.

38. Panofsky, *Perspective as Symbolic Form*, 27, 30. Subsequent references will be cited in the text.

39. Pierre Bourdieu invokes Panofsky in his discussion of Flaubert relative to experimentation in fine art: "As Manet will do later, Flaubert abandons the unifying perspective taken from a fixed and central point of view in favour of what one could call, with Panofsky, an 'aggregated space', meaning a space made of juxtaposed pieces and without a privileged point of view." *The Rules of Art*, 112.

40. *Critique of Judgment*, 106. On the Kantian basis of Panofsky's philosophy, see Mark A. Cheetham, "Theory Reception."

41. Robinson, *Inquiry into the Picturesque*, 17.

42. Adam Ferguson, for example, remarked in 1767 that "the earliest and latest accounts collected from every quarter of the earth, represent mankind as assembled in troops and companies," such that a man's "disposition to friendship or enmity, his reason, his use of language and articulate sounds, like the shape and the erect position of his body, are to be considered as so many attributes of his nature." *An Essay on the History of Civil Society*, 9.

43. "Rarely did [Adam] have time to expend on the mechanical task of making the elaborate and exquisite final drawings that carry his name." *Robert Adam and Scotland*, nonpaginated Introduction.

44. Rowan, *Designs for Castles and Country Villas by Robert and James Adam*, 15. I am grateful to my student Danielle Hurd for uncovering this reference.

45. *Robert Adam and Scotland*, nonpaginated Introduction.

46. Ibid., entry 31. Tait adds that this painting was Adam's "visual statement of the theme of [the Scottish painter] Allan Ramsay's *A Dialogue on Taste*" of 1762. See especially Ramsay's discussion of the architectural move from Egypt to Rome to the Goths, *Eighteenth Century Collections Online*, 35ff (http://find.galegroup.com.erl.lib.byu.edu/ecco/infomark.do?&contentSet=ECCOArticles&type=multipage&tabID=T001&prodId=ECCO&docId=CW124617947&source=gale&userGroupName=byuprovo&version=1.0&docLevel=FASCIMILE).

47. Duncan, Davis, and Sorensen, "Introduction," 3.

48. See Pittock, *Scottish and Irish Romanticism*, 4, 12 (cf. 9–14); see also Jerome McGann, *The Romantic Ideology*.

49. These include the "development of a separate public sphere . . . the inflection of genre towards a distinctively national agenda of selfhood . . . the use of hybrid language and

variable register reflective of multilingual societies," and others. See *Scottish and Irish Romanticism*, 7; cf. Pittock, "Introduction," esp. 2–5.

50. *Humphry Clinker*, 276–77.

51. *Antiquities and Scenery of the North of Scotland*, 1, 3.

52. *Scottish Scenery*, 44.

53. "The Solitary Reaper," 659.

54. Michasiw, "Nine Revisionist Theses on the Picturesque," 94. Earlier in the essay, Michasiw discusses how the picturesque theories of Price and Richard Payne Knight adopted a more Wordsworthian, Romantic line (see 87).

55. *Observations on a Tour Through the Highlands*, 1:10–11, 68.

56. *Letters on a Tour Through Various Parts of Scotland, in the Year 1792*, 228, 255, 257–58. Peter Manning divulges that the source of the poem is probably Thomas Wilkinson's manuscript *Tours to the British Mountains*. See *Reading Romantics*, ch. 11.

57. On Wilkie, see Nicholas Tromans, *David Wilkie*.

58. See especially Ann Bermingham, *Landscape and Ideology*, 65–66; cf. Barrell, *English Literature in History, 1730–80*.

59. Womack, *Improvement and Romance*, 68–69, 62.

60. *Burt's Letters from the North of Scotland*, 157.

61. *Capital*, 890.

62. See Eric Richards, *The Highland Clearances*, esp. chs. 8–11.

63. I analyze Marx's logic more extensively in *The Ruins of Experience*, chs. 3 and 4.

64. Burke, *A Philosophical Enquiry into the Origin of Our Ideas of the Sublime and Beautiful*, 36; see Žižek, *The Sublime Object of Ideology*.

65. *Scottish and Irish Romanticism*, 190.

66. The Scottish geologist James Hutton made a similar (and, in its era, radical) case regarding topography, which consisted of the residues of earlier stages of the earth's existence. See especially his 1788 treatise *Theory of the Earth*.

67. On the subtle form of this engagement in Macintyre's work in particular, see my essay "Gaelic Poetry's Province of Stone."

68. Johnson, *A Dictionary of the English Language*, no pagination.

69. *An Enquiry Concerning Human Understanding*, 64.

70. James M'Nayr, *A Guide from Glasgow to Some of the Most Remarkable Scenes in the Highlands of Scotland, and to the Falls of Clyde*, 242–43.

71. I am grateful to Matthew Grenby for his striking remarks on this passage when I presented it as part of my talk, "Franco Moretti and the Picturesque: A Long View of 'Distant Reading,'" at the Centre for Eighteenth-Century Studies at the University of York in June 2011.

72. *The Monk*, 275.

73. *A Journey to the Western Islands of Scotland*, 73.

74. See Andrews, *The Search for the Picturesque*, 3.

75. Ibid., 200, 206.

76. *Observations Made During a Tour Through Parts of England, Scotland, and Wales*, 4–6.

77. I refer here to Hanway, *A Journey to the Highlands of Scotland*; Schaw, *Journal of a Lady of Quality*; Murray, *A Companion and Useful Guide to the Beauties of Scotland*; and Grant, *Essays on the Superstitions of the Highlanders of Scotland*.

78. Hussey, *The Picturesque*, 4–5.

79. *The Historical Novel*, 31, 33.

80. *The Break-Up of Britain*, 114, 115, 116.

81. "Walter Scott's Romantic Postmodernity," 113–29.

82. Duncan, Davis, and Sorensen, "Introduction," 3.

83. Adorno, *Aesthetic Theory*, 4.

84. On the embattled relation of Johnson to all things Ossianic, see Thomas M. Curley, *Samuel Johnson, the* Ossian *Fraud, and the Celtic Revival.*

85. *Graphs, Maps, Trees*, 56, emphases deleted.

86. Hence, when Moretti recounts the painful stupor he once felt in trying to explain why all Italian box office hits during a particular decade were comedies, "a problem for which [he] had absolutely no solution" (26), he essentially reanimates Kant's familiar formula: "[What happens is that] our imagination strives to progress toward infinity, while our reason demands absolute totality as a real idea, and [the imagination,] our power of estimating the magnitude of things in the world of sense is inadequate to this idea." Kant, *Critique of Judgment*, 106.

87. On the relationship between technology and the sublime, see David E. Nye, *American Technological Sublime.*

88. *Scottish Journey*, 114. There was, moreover, a picturesque quality to Muir's Glasgow in the way it unapologetically presented its own unpresentability: "A slum is a poor quarter in which the people no longer take the trouble to keep up appearances. . . . All that respectable society conceals is openly displayed. Language has a flat and commonplace obscenity; knowledge, however vile, is frankly expressed; passions and hatreds let themselves go" (117).

89. *An Autobiography*, 289.

90. While it is the eighteenth-century associations that most interest me here, Andrew Blaikie reads Muir's thinking here as symptomatic of the early twentieth-century drama of modernist alienation, "exceptionally well articulated through the projection of [Muir's] personal discontents onto the national scale." See *The Scots Imagination and Modern Memory*, 153.

91. Virilio, *The Aesthetics of Disappearance*, 101. See my discussion of this phenomenon in the context of representations of the Highlands in *The Ruins of Experience*, ch. 6 (esp. 162–68).

92. The Scottish Highlands have long conjured such associations, as I argue in *The Ruins of Experience* (see esp. 1–15).

CHAPTER 4

1. See Gottlob Frege's discussion of this problem in his 1844 study, *The Foundations of Arithmetic*, and Badiou's own commentary on it in *Number and Numbers*, 16–23. Subsequent references to Badiou's book will be cited in the text.

2. Badiou observes that "[t]he Greek thinkers of number related it back to the One, which, as we can still see in Euclid's *Elements*, was considered not to be a number. From the supra-numeric being of the One, unity is derived. And a number is a collection of units, an addition" (7). Locke adds that "[a]mongst all the *Ideas* we have . . . there is none more simple, than that of *Unity*, or One." And simple ideas, he says, are those that are "united" and that are "simple and unmixed." See *An Essay Concerning Human Understanding*, 119.

3. See, in particular, Paul de Man's discussion of this point in "The Epistemology of Metaphor."

4. One might tell a much longer story about this philosophical crisis, which goes back to Pythagoras. For a succinct but helpful overview, see Arkady Plotnitsky, *The Knowable and the Unknowable*, 117–40 (esp. 118–20).

5. We might think here of Ernest Renan's contention that nations represent the point at which the spirit of a people intersects with the people's determination to constitute a particular social structure or at which character takes form. See Renan, "What Is a Nation?" 52–54.

6. See esp. Badiou, *Being and Event*, 23–30, 38–51.

7. Plato, *The Republic*, 757.

8. See John MacQueen, *Complete and Full with Numbers*, esp. 20–37.

9. I refer here to Henry Mackenzie's famous remark in *The Lounger*, December 9, 1786. See *Robert Burns*, 67–71.

10. This may be changing with the spate of work on Burns out of Glasgow University. Nevertheless, Murray Pittock, who directs the Arts and Humanities Research Council–funded Global Burns Network there, remarked to me that this mathematical paradox corresponds especially neatly to the reception of Burns in eighteenth- and early nineteenth-century Germany, where Burns was seen "as both an individual avatar of Schlegel's progressive universal poetry and . . . [as] the (almost) disembodied voice of the undifferentiated tradition. [Burns] is both an author and not an author," which "is one of the paradoxes that enables him to be the bard who speaks for all & the bardie of intensely individuated locality." Private correspondence, May 27, 2009.

11. Ann Rigney discusses the centenary commemoration of Burns in "Embodied Communities." Christopher Whatley and Murray Pittock take a broader view of Burnsian commemoration in the nineteenth century in "Poems and Festivals, Art and Artefact and the Commemoration of Robert Burns, c. 1844–c.1896."

12. The earliest reviews of Burns's 1786 *Poems, Chiefly in the Scottish Dialect* played up the pastoral singularity of the poet's voice. The anonymous October 1786 review in the *Edinburgh Magazine* did so by way of an image of figure and ground and, more specifically, of form against obscurity: the poems' "author is . . . a striking example of native genius bursting through the obscurity of poverty and the obstructions of laborious life." In the famous review published two months later dubbing Burns the "Heaven-taught ploughman," Henry Mackenzie complained that the poetic voice was rather too conspicuous: "Even in Scotland, the provincial dialect which Ramsay and [Burns] have used, is now read with a difficulty which greatly damps the pleasure of the reader; in England it cannot be read at all, without . . . reference to a glossary." Quoted in Low, *Robert Burns*, 64, 69.

13. For material evidence of the enthusiasm he inspired, see the catalog of materials searchable from the website "Robert Burns: Inventing Tradition and Securing Memory, 1796–1909." Accessed March 11, 2015.

14. Pittock, *Scottish and Irish Romanticism*, 145.

15. Craig is writing of a tradition that runs "from Sir William Hamilton and Thomas Carlyle in the 1820s to Edward Caird and William Robertson Smith in the 1870s and 80s" and that includes James "Hutchison Stirling's *The Secret of Hegel* in 1865 [and] the major English editions of Hegel, Kant and Heidegger produced by William Wallace, Norman Kemp Smith and John Macquarrie." Craig, *Intending Scotland*, 131.

16. Even in the field of Scottish studies, Burns is something of an enigmatic figure. See my review essay, "The End of Biographies?"

17. Currie, *Works of Robert Burns*, 319–21.

18. Smith, *Lectures on Rhetoric and Belles Lettres*, 137.

19. Addison, "*The Spectator* No. 411," 387.

20. "Capt Richard Brown," March 7, 1788, *The Letters of Robert Burns*, 1:257.

21. Nigel Leask underscores the importance of Currie to Burns's reputation, observing that Currie's edition became "the main portal through which Burns's life and poetry reached the Romantic and nineteenth-century reader," shaping the perceptions of Burns by a host of luminaries, "including Wordsworth, Coleridge, Lamb, Scott, Hogg, Moore, Jane Austen, Byron, Shelley, Keats, and Hazlitt." See Leask, *Robert Burns and Pastoral*, 276–77.

22. "William Nicol," February 20, 1793, *The Letters of Robert Burns*, 2:183.

23. *Oxford English Dictionary*, http://www.oed.com.erl.lib.byu.edu. Accessed August 15, 2011.

24. Matthew Simpson addresses the historical context of Fergusson's elegy in his essay "Robert Fergusson and St Andrews Student Culture," 21–39.

25. *The Poems of Robert Fergusson*, 1, original emphases.

26. See John MacQueen, *Progress and Poetry*, 57–58.

27. See John Friesen, "Archibald Pitcairne, David Gregory and the Scottish Origins of English Tory Newtonianism, 1688–1715"; Anita Guerrini, "The Tory Newtonians"; and Christina M. Eagles, "David Gregory and Newtonian Science," 216–25.

28. For a fuller record of the circulation of texts and knowledge in eighteenth-century Scotland, see Mark R. M. Towsey, *Reading the Scottish Enlightenment*. Towsey documents the wide reach not only of Burns's poetry but also of Fergusson's, remarking that "imaginative literature and history sat side by side on eighteenth-century bookshelves in celebrating and commemorating the cultural identity of the Scottish nation," including the two myths of which Davie writes, "as its distinct political identity was fast receding from memory" (41).

29. *The Democratic Intellect*, 106.

30. Currie, *The Works of Robert Burns*, 151. Stewart appended an anecdote of passing a winter evening with Burns. "My friend [Archibald] Alison," author of the esteemed *Essay on the Nature and Principles of Taste* (1790), "was the only other in the company. I never saw [Burns] more interesting. A present which Mr. Alison sent him afterwards of his *Essays on Taste*, drew from Burns a letter of acknowledgement, which I remember to have read with some degree of surprise at the distinct conception he appeared from it to have formed, of the several principles of the doctrine of *association*" (151–52, original emphases). In this letter, Burns tells Alison that "except Euclid's Elements of Geometry, which [he] made a shift to unravel by [his] father's fire-side, in the winter-evenings of the first season [he] held the plough, [he] never read a book which gave [him] such a quantum of information & added so much to [his] stock of ideas." *The Letters of Robert Burns*, 2:71–72.

31. "Dr. John Moore," August 1787, *The Letters of Robert Burns*, 1:140. Subsequent references will be cited in the text.

32. Burns was an exciseman from late 1791 through the end of his life in 1796 and was, like all tax collectors, instructed in square and cube roots, conics, and spheres, which were used to measure the contents of casks and barrels. *Robert Burns and Pastoral*, 250. Leask's source here is John Brewer, *The Sinews of Power*, 105–6.

33. *The Poems and Songs of Robert Burns*, 458–59. Subsequent references will be cited in the text. Penny Fielding discusses this geometrical reference very insightfully in "Burns's Topographies," 176–77.

34. William Wordsworth, "Lines Written a Few Miles Above Tintern Abbey," 115, ll. 107–8.

35. *The Poems and Songs of Robert Burns*, 193–94, ll. 1–12.

36. Smith, *The Theory of Moral Sentiments*, 158–59.

37. Gerard Carruthers analyzes the "kinky" quality of Burns's religious poetry in "Burns and Publishing," esp. 9–13.

38. Monboddo makes these claims in his voluminous work *Of the Origin and Progress of Language* (1773–92) For a reassessment of the alternative relation of Scottish Enlightenment theories of passion relative to the iconic value of reason, see Michael L. Frazer, "John Rawls."

39. *The Poems and Songs of Robert Burns*, 85–89, l. 55.

40. Heron, *A Memoir of the Life of the Late Robert Burns*, 49–50.

41. Ellis, "Enlightenment or Illumination," 82.

42. "Simson, Robert," *Encyclopaedia Britannica*, 17:504. Subsequent references will be cited in the text.

43. Heron, *A Memoir of the Life of the Late Robert Burns*, 27, 38.

44. Currie believed Burns to be "too much enamoured" of "gaiety and dissipation" (*The Works of Robert Burns*, 194), but Lockhart decried this view as "false. . . . [H]is aberrations of all kinds were occasional, not systematic." Lockhart, *Life of Robert Burns*, 295.

45. From *An Alphabetical Catalogue of Dr Robt. Simsons Books*, no pagination.

46. "To James Smith," 110, ll. 44–48.

47. Traill, *Account of the Life and Writings of Robert Simson, M.D. Late Professor of Mathematics at the University of Glasgow*, 75. Subsequent references will be cited in the text.

48. An undated, unsigned biographical essay on Simson in the University of Glasgow Special Collections asserts that Simson's "reputation rests chiefly on his 'restorations,' or, as they might more properly be called, 'reconstructions,' of the Greek geometers." MS Gen 146/31.

49. William Hamilton's 1838 *Letter to the Provost*, quoted in Davie, *The Democratic Intellect*, 127.

50. *The Poems and Songs of Robert Burns*, 127, ll. 1–6, Burns's emphases. Subsequent references will be cited in the text.

51. On the form of Burns's poem in light of traditional conventions of Scottish poetry, see Douglas Dunn, "'A Very Scottish Kind of Dash.'" On the dramatic quality of the poem, see Edwin Morgan, "A Poet's Response to Burns," 8.

52. On the relationship of the poem to sentimental culture and society more generally, see Carol McGuirk, *Robert Burns and the Sentimental Era*, 7–10, and David Perkins, "Human Mouseness." The Scottish tradition from which Burns wrote is rich in poems featuring speaking animals. On this point, see Robert L. Kindrick, "Robert Burns and the Tradition of the Makars," 91–107.

53. I am referring here to Heidegger's famous postulate that "[a] stone is worldless. Plant and animal likewise have no world; but they belong to the covert throng of *a surrounding*"—an environment, as it were—"into which they are linked. [A] peasant woman, on the other hand, has a world because she dwells in the overtness of beings" (Heidegger, "The Origin of the Work of Art," 170, my emphasis). The peasant woman, like the plowman poet, is capable of reflection on what things "are": men and mice, houses and grain. To this extent, nature "belongs" to the workers of the land who assume dominion over it. For exemplary discussions of the violence inscribed into this position, see Jacques Derrida, *Of Spirit*, 47–57, and Giorgio Agamben, *The Open*. Thomas Crawford makes a more sympathetic case for the poet's rapport with the mouse: "Burns sees the mouse as she really is: the outer and inner nature of the beast, her 'inscape,' as Hopkins would have called it." *Burns*, 165.

54. *Robert Burns and Pastoral*, 161.

55. It is on such a basis that Laurence Buell draws an ideological distinction between "environment" and "ecology" in *The Future of Environmental Criticism*, 140–41.

56. See Rousseau, "Essay on the Origin of Languages," 247–48.

57. Duncan, "The Pathos of Abstraction," 45.

58. *The Theory of Moral Sentiments*, 22.

59. On the influence of Smith on Burns, see Robert Crawford, *The Bard*, 132, 135, 315.

60. On Burns's persistent financial anxieties, both while composing "To a Mouse" and then upon his initial poetic success, see Crawford, *The Bard*, 200–202, 299–300; on his father's financial struggles, see 26–30.

61. Although suspicious of mathematically neat arguments concerning moral fitness, Hutcheson himself propounded a series of mathematical formulae, to wit: "The *Quantity of Love* toward any Person is in a compound Proportion of the apprehended *Causes of Love* in him, and of the *Goodness of Temper* in the Observer. Or $L = C \times G$." Hutcheson, *An Essay on the Nature and Conduct of the Passions and Affections, with Illustrations on the Moral Sense*, 189. Smith added the lines about Simson and Stewart in 1790 to the sixth edition of *The Theory of Moral Sentiments*.

62. "The Solution of a Problem Related to the Geometry of Position," in Norman L. Biggs, E. Keith Lloyd, and Robin J. Wilson, *Graph Theory*, 3, emphases deleted. The Leibnizian letter to which Euler refers is cited by Brian Hopkins and Robin J. Wilson, "The Truth About Königsberg," 201. Hopkins and Wilson's article is the most useful exposition of what Euler imagined with his "geometry of position" as it applies to the problem of the "seven bridges" that I address in the text.

63. Quoted in Wilson and Hopkins, "The Truth About Königsberg," 205–6.

64. See, for instance, Charles Hutton, *Mathematical Tables*, 118.

65. The most rigorous exposition of this topological principle is probably furnished by Sha Xin Wei, *Poiesis and Enchantment in Topological Matter*.

66. *The Parasite*, 20. Subsequent references will be cited in the text. For a useful discussion of topology, especially as it relates to Serres, see Steven Connor, "Topologies, Michel Serres and the Shapes of Thought."

67. Serres's original line in the French reads "*Cela est vrai du pou comme des hommes.*" Serres, *Le Parasite*, 14.

68. De Man, *Allegories of Reading*, 131 (see 119–31).

CHAPTER 5

1. I quote here from the title of Jacob's book, *Scientific Culture and the Making of the Industrial West*. See esp. the Introduction and ch. 4 ("The Newtonian Enlightenment").

2. See Marjorie Hope Nicolson, *Newton Demands the Muse*.

3. *The Autobiography and Memoirs of Benjamin Haydon*, 269; cf. M. H. Abrams, *The Mirror and the Lamp*, 303–12.

4. Williams, *Marxism and Literature*, 50; cf. Snow, *The Two Cultures*, esp. 1–22.

5. See *Fallen Languages*, esp. 178–215. Markley's examples include William Whiston, John Theophilus Desaguliers, Henry Pemberton, and, among the Scots, Maclaurin, John Keill, and George Cheyne.

6. See "Enlightenment Fiction and the Scientific Hypothesis."

7. *The Newtonian Revolution*, 15.

8. Westfall, *Force in Newton's Physics*, 445.

9. "Newton, Nonlinearity and Determinism," 208.

10. See David B. Wilson, *Seeking Nature's Logic*, esp. chs. 1 and 6.

11. See Ramsay, *An Ode to the Memory of Sir Isaac Newton*; Mallet, *The Excursion*, 22, my emphases. Magnitude applied to fluxions is the name for an infinitely little quantity; hence, "magnitudes and motions" refers to the progress of a point via tiny, incremental movements. Last, on the resonance between Newton's work and the seventeenth-century Scottish tradition, see John MacQueen, *Progress and Poetry*, 17–31.

12. On Mac-Mhaighstir Alasdair, see MacQueen, *Progress and Poetry*, 79–80; on Mac-an-t-Saoir, see my book, *The Ruins of Experience*, 153–62.

13. Thomson, *Spring*, *The Seasons*, 12, ll. 197–202.

14. See Keats, "Lamia," 431, l. 237.

15. See, for example, Denise Gigante's discussion of Keats's "rainbow-sided" creature, "The Monster in the Rainbow."

16. Packham, *Eighteenth-Century Vitalism*, 1–2.

17. Newton figures, for example, in the nineteenth-century Scottish scientist David Brewster's speculative 1854 discussion of life on other planets, *More Worlds than One*. On the Scottish vitalists, see Packham, *Eighteenth-Century Vitalism*, 25–51.

18. This helps explain, for example, Maclaurin's physico-theological view of Newton as the architect of a system mediating "between ideal forms and 'avowed imperfections' . . . between a knowable physical world and the 'unfathomable' existence of God. . . . Newtonian philosophy accurately reflects an aesthetically and theologically constructed nature." Markley, *Fallen Languages*, 194.

19. Macdonald, *Scottish Art*, 144.

20. "When the method, according to which the greatest possible in this species of cognition can be attained, is established, and the nature of this conviction well introspected, an immutable precept of method instead of the perpetual inconstancy of the opinions and sects of the schools, must unite the men of reflection in the like endeavours; in the same manner as Newton's method in natural philosophy altered the licentiousness of the physical hypotheses to a sure procedure according to experience and to geometry." "An Inquiry Concerning the Perspicuity of the Principles of Natural Theology and of Moral," 341.

21. See Bergson, *Matter and Memory*, esp. ch. 4.

22. Simmel, a renowned sociologist, became interested in the early twentieth century in the cognitive—Kantian—categories through which we organize our sense impressions. In Expressionism in particular, he argued, these categories project themselves onto the work of art: "The meaning of Expressionism is that the inner emotions of the artist are manifest in the work exactly as he experiences them; his emotions are continued, extended in the work. . . . [T]he image on the canvas represents an immediate condensation of inner life." "The Conflict of Modern Culture," 16.

23. See Michael Friedman, *Kant and the Exact Sciences*, esp. 55–95, and Philip Kitcher, "Kant and the Foundations of Mathematics," 28–33.

24. Newton, "Quadrature of Curves," quoted in Friedman, *Kant and the Exact Sciences*, 74.

25. See Ofra Rechter's discussion of how Kant insisted in the three *Critiques* on "the assurance . . . of seeing something with one's own eyes," intuitively, ostensively, in "The View from 1763," 25.

26. Kant, *Critique of Judgment*, 107. Subsequent references will be cited in the text. Kant further draws upon the language of calculus in referring to "numerical series progressing to infinity." See 107, 108.

27. *Practical Matter*, 13.

28. *Literature, Language, and the Rise of the Intellectual Disciplines in Britain, 1680–1820*, 58.

29. Hans-Georg Gadamer reads into the Romantic tradition the contradictions embedded into Kantian aesthetic philosophy and its appeal to genius in *Truth and Method*, esp. 30–60.

30. Norbert Waszek paints a broad picture of the Scottish Enlightenment's influence on German thought in "The Scottish Enlightenment in Germany, and Its Translator, Christian Garve (1742–98)."

31. *An Essay on Original Genius*, 286. Subsequent references will be cited in the text.

32. Blackwell repeatedly refers to Homer as a "genius" and often in the modern (or Romantic) sense of dynamic originality. "If Homer . . . came into the World, in *such* a Country, and under *so propitious* an Aspect of Nature, we must . . . enquire, what Reception he met with upon his Arrival; in what Condition he found things, and what Dispositions they must produce in an exalted Genius, and comprehensive Mind." See *An Enquiry into the Life and Writings of Homer*, 10; cf. 71, 119, and 162, Blackwell's emphases. Blackwell even makes "genius" a three-line item in his index.

33. See *Observations on the Feeling of the Beautiful and Sublime*; cf. Wolf Gerhard Schmidt, "'Menschlichschön' and 'Kolossalisch,'" 192–93.

34. As Joseph M. Levine explains, this "battle" devolved in part on the disciplinary division "between imitation and scholarship, rhetoric and philology," and, most portentously, "literature and history." A schism eventually opened within history between "narrative," on one hand, and "philology and antiquities," on the other, thus implicitly affiliating the literary dimensions of genius with the ancients rather than the moderns. *The Battle of the Books*, 2, 414.

35. According to Amir Alexander, for such pioneers of calculus as Bonaventura Cavalieri, the new analysis "was a mysterious undiscovered land, which promised precious gems and marvels to the mathematician who would penetrate to its hidden recesses." *Geometrical Landscapes*, 183.

36. Ditton, *An Institution of Fluxions*, nonpaginated dedication "To the Learned and Ingenious Mr. Benjamin Moreland"; Rowe, *An Introduction to the Doctrine of Fluxions*, v, Rowe's emphases; Maclaurin, *An Account of Sir Isaac Newton's Philosophical Discoveries*, 8.

37. Alexander Gerard, professor of divinity at King's College, Aberdeen, composed an argument similar to Duff's in his 1774 *Essay on Genius*. True genius, Gerard argued, draws on the faculty of "judgment" as well as "fancy," which is why Newton was such an exemplar: he displayed "the nicest judgment, as well as the most comprehensive imagination," conducting his experiments on light, for instance, "in such a manner that every succeeding one should conform and extend the conclusions to which the previous ones had given life" (*An Essay on Genius*, 82, 87, 93). For Gerard, "Genius is . . . [quite simply] the power of invention, either in science or in the arts, either of truth or of beauty" (318). Hence, contrary to Kant's concept, which divides such step-by-step procedures from poetry, Gerard imagined that Homer and Newton followed the same modus operandi. Maclaurin had actually made a similar point thirty years earlier, professing that "they who understand all [fluxions'] advantages will not think it an extravagant exaggeration if We should apply to it with respect to the speculative sciences what was said of old of a Work of Genius of another kind [i.e., Homer's] that was styl'd

pretiosissimum humani animi opus," a "precious work for humankind" ("Recipient Not Stated," *The Collected Letters of Colin Maclaurin*, 435). Maclaurin is believed to have composed this letter in 1734 or 1735.

38. *The Principia*, 440–41. Subsequent references will be cited in the text.

39. Koyré, "The Significance of the Newtonian Synthesis," 59, 60, 65, 72, Koyré's emphasis. In calling Newton a "genius," Koyré was following in the footsteps not only of Gerard and other Scottish philosophers but also of the English mathematician John Colson, who, in his 1736 preface to Newton's *Method of Fluxions and Infinite Series*, praised Newton for finding "an accurate and habitual knowledge of . . . Mathematical Principles of a superior kind . . . which, assisted by his great Genius and Sagacity . . . enabled him to become so compleat a Master in the higher Geometry, and particularly in the Art of Invention." Newton, *The Method of Fluxions and Infinite Series*, xx (ix–xxiii).

40. *Liberty, The Castle of Indolence*, pp. 1–14, ll. 72–73, 76.

41. Thomson's biographer, James Sambrook, remarks that Thomson's tutor, Robert Stewart, "taught astronomy according to Newton's system and taught it in such a way as to demonstrate religious truths" (*James Thomson, 1700–1748*, 52). On the influence of Thomson's education in Newtonianism on his poetry, see Hilbert H. Campbell, *James Thomson*, 17, and Herbert Drennon, "James Thomson's Contact with Newtonianism and His Interest in Natural Philosophy." Alan Dugald McKillop extends this discussion of Newton's "moral" influence to a consideration of other Scottish intellectuals like Francis Hutcheson. See *The Background of Thomson's Seasons*, 30, and also Harro Maas, "Where Mechanism Ends." Robert Stewart's name may be found among the subscribers to Pemberton's *A View of Sir Isaac Newton's Philosophy* (1728), and late in his life, Thomson subscribed to Maclaurin's *Account of Sir Isaac Newton's Philosophical Discoveries* (1748).

42. Irlam identifies Newton as an example "of the kind of visionary wisdom that the poet [i.e. Thomson] seeks to emulate." Irlam, *Elations*, 115.

43. "*The Spectator* No. 420," 350. Ann Stewart Balakier and James J. Balakier argue that Addison's essay provides the link between Thomson and Newton. See "The Addisonian Connection Between James Thomson's *The Seasons* and Sir Isaac Newton's *Principia*," esp. 70–71.

44. Smith, "Essay on the History of Astronomy," 91, 98, my emphasis.

45. On Newton's own penchant for personification in his explication of the laws of motion, see James J. Paxson, "The Allegory of Temporality and the Early Modern Calculus," 43–44.

46. For reactions to personification in *The Seasons*, see Ralph Cohen, *The Art of Discrimination*, 315–80. Kevis Goodman connects this impulse toward personification, toward the fixing of essences through observation, to the privilege Thomson's poem accords to sight. See *Georgic Modernity and British Romanticism*, 38–39.

47. Kames, *Elements of Criticism*, 548. Subsequent references will be cited in the text.

48. This gap not only evokes the relationship between geometry and algebra but also obtains between "thing" and "person," making it a prototypically (albeit problematically) *modern* figure. On this relationship between person and thing, as well as between Bruno Latour and Samuel Johnson (a stranger conjunction than Thomson and Kames), see Heather Keenleyside, "Personification for the People."

49. "In contradistinction to real presence, ideal presence may properly be termed *a waking dream*; because, like a dream, it vanisheth the moment we reflect upon our present situation." *Elements of Criticism*, 68.

50. See Steven Knapp, *Personification and the Sublime*, esp. 66–97.

51. *Sketches of the History of Man*, 1:105; cf. 1:155 and 2:421. Not coincidentally, Kames also fancied himself an opponent of Newton's, at least relative to the Newtonian theory of inertia. See David B. Wilson, *Seeking Nature's Logic*, 83–89.

52. *Summer*, *The Seasons*, 58, ll. 1–3, 9–10. Subsequent references are to line numbers and will be cited in the text.

53. "In poetry there takes place what all measuring is in the ground of its being. . . . To write poetry is measure-taking, understood in the strict sense of the word, by which man first receives the measure for the breadth of his being." At the same time, Heidegger specifies, "This measure-taking . . . is no mere geo-metry . . . no [mere] science." ". . . Poetically Man Dwells . . .," 219.

54. Dedicating his 1756 poetic manifesto *An Essay on the Writings and Genius of Pope* to Edward Young, the author of the melancholic *Night-Thoughts* (1742–45), Warton praises Thomson as a poet of "strong and copious fancy" who "enriched poetry with a variety of new and original images, which he painted from nature itself, and from his own actual observations." In this respect, Thomson is Newtonian. But "he is equally to be praised, for impressing on our minds the effects" or moods of these scenes, and in this way, Thomson's work does more than merely describe nature empirically. *An Essay on the Writings and Genius of Pope*, 42, 47.

55. "For [Adam] Ferguson, as for Hegel, history begins once myth and poetry have been cleared away. History is prose. And the poets would seem to agree," Sitter remarks. "Whether by decision or default, from the 1740s on, most of the younger poets avoid direct historical treatment of the events of their day, even of their century. We can best appreciate how fundamental a shift occurs here by recalling that one of the deepest connections we can find between Dryden and Pope . . . is the shared sense of the poet's role as historian of his own times." Sitter, *Literary Loneliness in Mid-Eighteenth-Century England*, 83.

56. *Doctor Faustus*, 190.

57. For a more detailed discussion of the problem of number in *The Seasons*, see Jessie Leatham Wirkus, "Number, Newtonianism, and Sublimity in James Thomson's *The Seasons*," 5–9, 18–23.

58. Edwards, *The Historical Development of the Calculus*, 310 (cf. 308–22).

59. The so-called Maclaurin Series, for example (which Maclaurin modified from the early eighteenth-century English mathematician Brook Taylor), deployed a fixed number of terms to approximate a function or "to derive sufficient conditions for the existence of local maxima and minima" (Edwards 291). But the series did not formally redefine these terms as much as suggest they were *like* whole numbers. To this end, Maclaurin claims that Newton employed analogies. For example, "[a]fter having established the principle of the universal Gravitation of Matter . . . when he is not able to demonstrate the causes of . . . phaenomena . . . he endeavours to judge of them, by *analogy*, from what he had found in the greater motions of the system; a way of reasoning that is agreeable to the harmony of things, and . . . approved by the observation and judgment of the best philosophers." *An Account of Sir Isaac Newton's Philosophical Discoveries*, 20–21 (mistitled 21–20), Maclaurin's emphasis.

60. Keill, *An Introduction to the True Astronomy*, 16–17, Keill's emphasis. On the oscillation between macroscopic and microscopic perspectives in *The Seasons*, see Kevis Goodman, *Georgic Modernity and British Romanticism*, esp. 56–66.

61. Johnson, "Thomson," 298–300.

62. See Coleridge, *Biographia Literaria*, quoted in H. J. Jackson, ed., *Samuel Taylor Coleridge*, 313.

63. "Epitaph," 808, Pope's emphases.

64. "Mr. Leibnitz's Second Paper," 16, 17.

65. *Principia*, 429. Domenico Bertolini Meli discusses this idea in the context of the general reception of Newton's and Leibniz's respective theories of calculus, calling attention to the relationship between the organic quality of "vegetation and putrefaction" and the alchemical bent to Newton's thinking. See *Equivalence and Priority*, 191–96 (192 n.1). On the theological significance of fluxions, see Ayval Ramati, "The Hidden Truth of Creation." Ann Stewart Balakier and James J. Balakier note that Thomson draws from a range of sources on comets: Newton, certainly, but also Edmond Halley, John Flamsteed, and even Milton. See "The Addisonian Connection Between James Thomson's *The Seasons* and Sir Isaac Newton's *Principia*," 74.

66. On the defense of Newton's theory of comets by David Gregory and John Keill, see David B. Wilson, *Seeking Nature's Logic*, 42–46.

67. *The Unfolding of* The Seasons, 30.

68. Sitter, *Literary Loneliness in Mid-Eighteenth-Century England*, 178. Richard Westfall reminds us that Newton manipulated the concepts of time, speed, and motion in his theory of fluxions in order to supersede the doctrine of points. See *Never at Rest*, 126–34.

69. *A Treatise of Human Nature*, 300, my emphasis. Subsequent references will be cited in the text.

70. *An Essay of Dramatic Poesy*, 42.

71. Reid, *An Inquiry into the Human Mind on the Principles of Common Sense*, 99. Subsequent references will be cited in the text.

Chapter 6

1. Lyotard attests to his interest in Orwell's *1984* in "Gloss on Resistance," 87–97. There, Lyotard muses—geometrically—on "extend[ing] the line of the body in the line of writing" (96).

2. Freud, *The Interpretation of Dreams*, 316–19.

3. Lyotard had pursued this line of thought in the early 1970s in *Discours, Figure* before continuing it in "The Dream-Work Does Not Think" (1983), "Figure Foreclosed" (1984), and "The Sublime and the Avant-Garde" (1984), all of which are included in *The Lyotard Reader*. For an extended meditation on Lyotard's concept of infancy, see Christopher Fynsk, *Infant Figures*.

4. Lyotard, "The Sublime and the Avant-Garde," in *The Lyotard Reader*, 197. Subsequent references will be cited in the text.

5. For Lyotard's reflections on Kant, see *Lessons on the Analytic of the Sublime*, esp. 1–8: "System and Feeling." Subsequent references will be cited in the text.

6. *Lessons on the Analytic of the Sublime*, 22, emphases deleted.

7. "The Sublime and the Avant-Garde," 198–99, emphases deleted.

8. *An Inquiry into the Human Mind on the Principles of Common Sense*, 147. Subsequent references will be cited in the text.

9. See especially Clarke, *A Discourse Concerning the Unchangeable Obligations of Natural Religion and the Truth and Certainty of the Christian Religion*, 5–11, where Clarke enunciates the idea that moral judgment should proceed from a rational basis of pure relations.

10. Hutcheson extols the "Beauty" of Euclid, fluxions, and Newton's theory of gravity—he even applies "mathematical Calculation to moral Subjects"—while maintaining that our sense of beauty is a faculty unto itself and not derivative from higher mathematical realities. See *An Inquiry into the Original of Our Ideas of Beauty and Virtue*, 36–38, 134.

11. Hume, recall from Chapter 2, contends that "[w]hatever can be conceiv'd by a clear and distinct idea necessarily implies the possibility of [its] existence." *A Treatise of Human Nature*, 64, 91.

12. "Letters to Dr James Gregory," 77.

13. Wilson, "Wordsworth and the Culture of Science," 332.

14. Wordsworth, "Lines Written a Few Miles Above Tintern Abbey," 112, ll. 4–8.

15. "Where Wordsworth records a deeply felt experience of a definite and particular place, Thomson [uses] images and impressions of places for their capacity to yield a generic or universal impression." Wilson, "Wordsworth and the Culture of Science," 335.

16. In *The Prelude*, this dichotomy becomes more complex. I am thinking of the dream in Book V prompted by a meditation "On Poetry, and geometric Truth," illustrated by way of the difference between a shell and a stone. While the poem links the two as "knowledge that endures," it idealizes the shell as a fusion of poetry and geometry, or as a higher geometry truer to the latter's reputation of holding "acquaintance with the stars, / And wed[ding] man to man by purest bond / Of nature undisturb'd by space or time." Poetry thus reaffirms geometry but only by sublimating its Newtonian variant. *The Thirteen Book Prelude*, 1:164–65, ll. 64–65, 104–6. See Theresa M. Kelley, "Spirit and Geometric Form," esp. 565.

17. Jung, "Visual Interpretations, Print, and Illustrations of Thomson's *The Seasons*, 1730–1797," 25.

18. See *Space and the "March of Mind,"* 68–77. Actually, "Wordsworth confusedly attempts to use both kinds of image," the geometrically abstract and the empirically particular, and this accords his account an ambiguous relation to the information it both conveys and organizes (75).

19. This certainly became Thomson's reputation in the mid-nineteenth century, when he became best known as a precursor to Wordsworth et al. Significantly, however, one of Thomson's most avid emulators was Byron, who himself was pursuing a different aesthetic. See R. R. Agrawal, *Tradition and Experiment in the Poetry of James Thomson*, 215–52.

20. Seth, *Scottish Philosophy*, 42. Subsequent references will be cited in the text.

21. See George Davie, *The Democratic Intellect*, chs. 6 and 7; cf. Susan Manning, "'Whether Utility or Pleasure Be the Principal Aim in View,'" 4.

22. "I would dissuade no one from the study of Hegel. His aim is so great that the mere effort to keep pace with him strengthens the thews [or habits] of the mind. . . . It is Hegelianism as a system, and not Hegel, that I have attacked." *Hegelianism and Personality*, 241–42.

23. Chalmers, "Astronomical Discourses," 124, 126. The renowned physicist David Brewster articulated a similar argument in his 1854 treatise *More Worlds than One*, citing Newton's declaration that God is able to "make worlds of several sorts in several parts of the universe." *More Worlds than One*, 93.

24. Nichol, *Views of the Architecture of the Heavens*, 138, 24.

25. Poe, *The Complete Tales and Poems*, 141.

26. On the status of Poe's essay as a hoax, see Susan Manning, "'The Plots of God Are Perfect,'" 235–37. On the influence of Scottish common sense on nineteenth-century America, see Susan Welsh, "The Value of Analogical Evidence," 3.

27. Poe, *Eureka*, 7, Poe's emphasis. Subsequent references will be cited in the text.

28. On the emergence of this new energy physics and its relation to the aesthetics of modernism, see Cairns Craig, "Identifying Another Other," 293–98. In her survey of modernity, Hannah Arendt ascribes "the dissolution of matter into energy," whose study Kelvin and Maxwell initiated, to the breakdown of common sense and the displacement of geometry with algebra (Arendt, *The Human Condition*, 282). In Scotland, however, the story is more nuanced: Maxwell, for example, was an acclaimed geometer as a young student, and his contemporary, the physicist Peter Guthrie Tait, claimed that Maxwell "preferred always to have before him a geometrical or physical representation of the problem in which he was engaged . . . [a]fterwards, when necessary, translating them into symbols." Quoted in Martin Goldman, *The Demon in the Aether*, 36. On Maxwell's precocious feats as a young geometer, see Basil Mahlon, *The Man Who Changed Everything*, 13–15.

29. Brewster, *The Martyrs of Science*, 237.

30. Susan Manning discerns in Poe's treatise an attitude of "towering condescension towards Newton" and also Pierre-Simon Laplace, "'mere' mathematicians" by comparison with Kepler ("'The Plots of God Are Perfect,'" 238). Alexander Schlutz agrees: "Without the 'vital laws' discovered by Kepler, claims Poe's letter writer, Newton, confined to the dead ends of inductive and deductive reasoning, would have been unable to postulate anything of true import." "Purloined Voices," 219.

31. *Between Literature and Science*, 65.

32. See Reino Virtanen, "Poe's *Eureka* in France from Baudelaire to Valéry," 223.

33. See Davie, *The Democratic Intellect*, 151.

34. "One-Way Street," 1:486.

35. Nietzsche associates Dionysus with intoxication as well as ecstasy. See *The Birth of Tragedy*, esp. sections 1 and 2.

36. Or so some scholars argue. See my discussion of the different positions taken relative to this issue by Richard Westfall and Niccolò Guicciardini in Chapter 2.

37. Margery Palmer McCulloch makes a compelling if somewhat nontraditional case for the status of early twentieth-century Scottish literature as a modernism, while Patrick Crotty reminds readers that the term these writers chose for themselves was that of the "Scottish Renaissance"—a description McCulloch finds too insular. See McCulloch, *Scottish Literature and Its Contexts, 1918–1959*, esp. 1–8, and Crotty, "Review of *Dear Grieve*."

38. Duncan Macmillan, *Scottish Art*, 298 (see 292–99).

39. Quoted in Murdo Macdonald, "Celticism and Internationalism in the Circle of Patrick Geddes," 73. Similarly, Kandinsky writes that "a line . . . freed from the aim of designating a thing and function[ing] as a thing itself [achieves] inner resonance . . . and acquires its full inner strength." "On the Problem of Form," in Chipp, ed., *Theories of Modern Art*, 164.

40. The idea for *The Evergreen* was hatched not only by Geddes but also by William Sharp (pen name Fiona Macleod), who suggested the title *The Celtic World*.

41. "Proem," *The Evergreen*, 9–11. Subsequent references will be cited in the text.

42. Meller, *Patrick Geddes*, 1, 32, 45. This distinguishes Geddes's vision from the Marxian version of this schematic, which is essentially algebraic in that it converts the flowing line of history into a series of leaps from one point or phase of social existence to another after the manner of a grand differential equation. Marxian theorists like Franz Borkenau (Benjamin's contemporary) and Richard W. Hadden attributed this very process of mathematical abstraction to the division of labor and "the capitalist mode of exchange, which reduces all commodities to uniform, numerical 'values.'" Amir Alexander, *Geometrical Landscapes*, 207; more generally, see Hadden, *On the Shoulders of Merchants*.

43. See Macdonald, "Celticism and Internationalism in the Circle of Patrick Geddes," 69; cf. Philip Ball's discussion of D'Arcy Wentworth Thompson's pioneering study *On Growth and Form in Shapes* in *Nature's Patterns*, 6–15 passim.

44. *A Drunk Man Looks at the Thistle*, in *Hugh MacDiarmid*, 30, ll. 141–42. Subsequent references are to this edition.

45. The reference from which Smith's influential (and notorious) formulation was taken in *Scottish Literature*, 4.

46. Scott Lyall, *Hugh MacDiarmid's Poetry and Politics of Place*, 35.

47. From *The Kind of Poetry I Want*, quoted in *Hugh MacDiarmid*, 215.

48. Kenneth Buthlay, "Hugh MacDiarmid (11 August 1892–9 September 1978)," 214, my emphasis; *Dictionary of Literary Biography Complete Online* (http://go.galegroup.com.erl.lib.byu.edu/ps/retrieve.do?sgHitCountType=None&sort=RELEVANCE&docType=Biography&prodId=DLBC&tabID=T002&searchId=R1&resultListType=RESULT_LIST&searchType=BasicSearchForm&contentSegment=¤tPosition=1&searchResultsType=MultiTab&inPS=true&userGroupName=byuprovo&docId=GALE%7CEMYCJC340123634&contentSet=GALE%7CEMYCJC340123634). Accessed June 10, 2013.

49. On MacDiarmid's genuine, if ambivalent, appreciation of Geddes, see Julian Hanna, "Manifestoes at Dawn."

50. Lyall, *Hugh MacDiarmid's Poetry and Politics of Place*, 45; cf. Catherine Kerrigan, *Whaur Extremes Meet*, 142.

51. See Margery Palmer McCulloch, *Scottish Modernism and Its Contexts, 1918–1959*, 96–97 and 5–6; cf. Duncan Glen, *Hugh MacDiarmid (Christopher Murray Grieve) and the Scottish Renaissance*, 57.

52. Stephen Maxwell, "The Nationalism of Hugh MacDiarmid," 212.

53. Although versions of this sentiment were expressed in more than one place, the most vivid articulation of this view is found in MacDiarmid's essay, "The Caledonian Antisyzygy and the Gaelic Idea": "Scottish nationalists . . . ought to consider carefully the principle which Hitler and his National Socialists in Germany oppose to Marxism. Hitler's 'Nazis' wear their socialism with precisely the difference which post-socialist Scottish nationalists must adopt. Class-consciousness is anathema to them, and in contradistinction to it they set up the principle of race-consciousness." In *Selected Essays of Hugh MacDiarmid*, 70.

54. MacDiarmid's biographer, Alan Bold, recounts an experience when the young Christopher Grieve and a friend "turned up at school, on the evening of 18 February 1910, to listen to a talk by Peter Ross, Principal Teacher of Mathematics at Broughton. Author of a textbook on algebra, Ross was a vivacious character who had become engrossed in astronomy. . . . Grieve must have been enraptured by the lecture. He began to see the space between the stars as profound with meaning." *MacDiarmid, Christopher Murray Grieve*, 53.

55. On this passage, see Kenneth Buthlay, "The Scotched Snake," 150.

56. *A Drunk Man Looks at the Thistle*, 104, ll. 2405–6, and "Poetry and Science," in *Hugh MacDiarmid*, 196. MacDiarmid converts into poetic form the phrase of the scientist and occasional poet Ronald Ross. See Carey, *Eyewitness to Science*, 212.

57. See "Hugh MacDiarmid, 1892–1978" (http://www.poetryfoundation.org/bio/hugh-macdiarmid). Accessed June 10, 2013.

58. Kerrigan, *Whaur Extremes Meet*, 188–89. Kerrigan is quoting from MacDiarmid's essay, "Life in the Shetland Islands."

59. "On a Raised Beach," in *Hugh MacDiarmid*, 146, ll. 1–7. Subsequent references will be cited in the text.

60. Gish, *Hugh MacDiarmid*, 168–69.

61. Kerrigan, *Whaur Extremes Meet*, 198.

62. Margery Palmer McCulloch shows that MacDiarmid not only borrowed from Lewis's *Blast* but also from "[Ezra] Pound's Imagist credo," which "was primarily an attempt to capture in language-based poetry the instantaneous effect available in the visual arts." *Scottish Modernism and Its Contexts*, 32.

63. These lines may be found in "A Memorable Fancy" from *The Marriage of Heaven and Hell*, plates 6–7.

64. Harman, "Realism Without Materialism," 55.

65. *After Finitude*, 9.

66. Smith, "MacDiarmid and Ideas, with Special Reference to 'On a Raised Beach,'" 161.

67. See the chapter "Hume's Problem" in *After Finitude*, 82–111.

68. Ibid., 104. See 103–11.

69. MacDiarmid, *David Hume*. In this lecture, MacDiarmid cites his poem "Third Hymn to Lenin" in reference to "Divers geometries—Euclidean, Lobatchewskyan, Riemannian" as emblematic of the "scientific spirit" that Hume personifies (8).

70. "Letters to Dr James Gregory," in *The Works of Thomas Reid*, 1:77.

71. As Reid puts it in his *Inquiry into the Human Mind on the Principles of Common Sense*, "A mathematician cannot prove the truth of his axioms, nor can he prove anything, unless he takes them for granted. We cannot prove the existence of our minds, nor even of our thoughts and sensations." *The Works of Thomas Reid*, 130.

72. Hume, *A Treatise of Human Nature*, 301.

73. Reid, *Inquiry into the Human Mind on the Principles of Common Sense*, 187.

74. *Stony Limits and Other Poems* is the title of the collection in which "On a Raised Beach" appeared.

75. *Whaur Extremes Meet*, 206.

76. Nancy Gish observes that "On a Raised Beach" and the other poems in *Stony Limits* consist of MacDiarmid's mind in a series of motions and shapes. See *Hugh MacDiarmid*, 161.

77. Ascherson, *Stone Voices*, 26.

78. The Eliot line serves as both opening and refrain in "East Coker." See *Four Quartets*, 23.

79. Lyotard proposes, in effect, that "thought" forecloses the multitude of possibilities stemming from the ludic quality of language. But even Wittgenstein, who analyzes language games, appeals to a similar logic as Lyotard in describing how these games work. One must, he says, "*look* and *see* whether there is anything common to all" games. "For if you look at them you will not see something that is common to *all*, but similarities, relationships, and a whole series of them at that. To repeat: don't think, but look!" *Philosophical Investigations*, 27.

80. Lyotard, "The Dream-Work Does Not Think," in *The Lyotard Reader*, 19.

81. *The Culture of Diagram*, 7–8.

82. Munster, *An Aesthesia of Networks*, 24.

83. Ibid., 37.

84. Jameson, *A Singular Modernity*, 4; Lyotard, "The Sublime and the Avant-Garde," 198.

85. *A Singular Modernity*, 6. Jameson is particularly grinding his axe against Lyotard's oft-cited book *The Postmodern Condition*, which characterizes that "condition" as a skeptical attitude toward "grand narratives." See *The Postmodern Condition*, xxiii–xxv.

86. Jameson, *The Political Unconscious*, 9.

87. Dimock, *Through Other Continents*, 3, 2, 76.

88. See Williams, *Marxism and Literature*, 131.

89. Perhaps symptomatically, Dimock invokes Moretti's historical model for the purpose of playing up its shortcomings, eliding the methodological—geometric—similarity that perhaps brings Moretti to mind in the first place. See "Critical Response I," esp. 621–22.

90. See Davie, *The Scotch Metaphysics*, 6.

BIBLIOGRAPHY

Abrams, M. H. *The Mirror and the Lamp: Romantic Theory and the Critical Tradition.* Oxford: Oxford University Press, 1953.

Ackerberg-Hastings, Amy. "Analysis and Synthesis in John Playfair's 'Elements of Geometry.'" *The British Journal for the History of Science* 35, no. 1 (2002): 43–72.

Adcock, Craig. "Conventionalism in Henri Poincaré and Marcel Duchamp." *Art Journal* 44, no. 3 (1984): 249–58.

Addison, Joseph. "*The Spectator* No. 411." *The Commerce of Everyday Life: Selections from* The Tatler *and* The Spectator, ed. Erin Mackie. Boston: Bedford/St. Martin's, 1998.

———. "*The Spectator* No. 420." *Eighteenth-Century English Literature*, ed. Geoffrey Tillotson, Paul Fussell Jr., and Marshall Waingrow. San Diego: Harcourt Brace Jovanovich, 1969.

Adorno, Theodor. *Aesthetic Theory.* Trans. Robert Hullot-Kentor. Minneapolis: University of Minnesota Press, 1997.

Agamben, Giorgio. *The Open: Man and Animal.* Trans. Kevin Attell. Stanford, CA: Stanford University Press, 2004.

Agrawal, R. R. *Tradition and Experiment in the Poetry of James Thomson.* Salzburg: Institut für Anglistik und Amerikanistik, 1981.

Alexander, Amir. *Geometrical Landscapes: The Voyages of Discovery and the Transformation of Mathematical Practice.* Stanford, CA: Stanford University Press, 2002.

An Alphabetical Catalogue of Dr Robt. Simsons Books. University of Glasgow Special Collections. Ms. Ea5-y.4.

Andrews, Malcolm. *The Search for the Picturesque: Landscape Aesthetics and Tourism in Britain, 1760–1800.* Aldershot: Scolar, 1989.

Arendt, Hannah. *The Human Condition.* Chicago: University of Chicago Press, 1958.

Arrighi, Giovanni. *The Long Twentieth Century: Money, Power, and the Origins of Our Times.* London: Verso, 1994.

Ascherson, Neal. *Stone Voices: The Search for Scotland.* London: Granta, 2002.

Bachelard, Gaston. *The Poetics of Space: The Classic Look at How We Experience Intimate Places.* Trans. Maria Jolas. Boson: Beacon, 1964.

Badiou, Alain. *Being and Event.* Trans. Oliver Feltham. London: Continuum, 2005.

———. *Logics of Worlds: Being and Event 2.* Trans. Albert Toscano. London: Continuum, 2009.

———. *Number and Numbers.* Trans. Robin Mackay. Cambridge: Polity, 2008.

Baillie, Joanna. *The Family Legend: A Tragedy.* New York: Garland, 1976.

———. *A Series of Plays.* Ed. Donald H. Reiman. Vol. 1. New York: Garland, 1977.

Balakier, Ann Stewart, and James J. Balakier. "The Addisonian Connection Between James Thomson's *The Seasons* and Sir Isaac Newton's *Principia*." *University of Dayton Review* 19, no. 2 (1988): 69–77.

Ball, Philip. *Nature's Patterns: A Tapestry in Three Parts*. Vol. 1. Oxford: Oxford University Press, 2009.

Barkan, Elazar, and Ronald Bush, eds. *Prehistories of the Future: The Primitivist Project and the Culture of Modernism*. Stanford, CA: Stanford University Press, 1995.

Barrell, John. *English Literature in History, 1730–80: An Equal, Wide Survey*. London: Hutchinson, 1983.

Baucom, Ian. *Specters of the Atlantic: Finance Capital, Slavery, and the Philosophy of History*. Durham, NC: Duke University Press, 2005.

Baxter, Donald L. M. "Hume on Infinite Divisibility." *History of Philosophy Quarterly* 5, no. 2 (1988): 133–40.

Bender, John. "Enlightenment Fiction and the Scientific Hypothesis." *Representations* 61 (1998): 6–28.

Bender, John, and Michael Marrinan. *The Culture of Diagram*. Stanford, CA: Stanford University Press, 2010.

Benjamin, Walter. "The Concept of Criticism in German Romanticism." Trans. David Lachterman, Howard Eiland, and Ian Balfour. *Walter Benjamin: Selected Writings*, ed. Marcus Bullock and Michael W. Jennings. Vol. 1. Cambridge, MA: Harvard University Press, 2004.

———. "One-Way Street." *Walter Benjamin: Selected Writings*, ed. Marcus Bullock and Michael W. Jennings. 4 vols. Cambridge, MA: Harvard University Press, 1996.

———. "Theses on the Philosophy of History." *Illuminations*, trans. Harry Zohn. New York: Schocken, 1968.

Bergson, Henri. *Matter and Memory*. Trans. Nancy Margaret Paul and W. Scott Palmer. New York: Zone Books, 1991.

Berkeley, George. *The Analyst; or, A Discourse Addressed to an Infidel Mathematician*. London: Printed for J. Thomson, 1734.

———. *Principles of Human Knowledge and Three Dialogues*. Ed. Howard Robinson. Oxford: Oxford University Press, 1999.

Bermingham, Ann. *Landscape and Ideology: The English Rustic Tradition, 1750–1840*. Berkeley: University of California Press, 1986.

Beveridge, Craig, and Ronnie Turnbull. *The Eclipse of Scottish Culture: Inferiorism and the Intellectuals*. Edinburgh: Polygon, 1989.

———. *Scotland After Enlightenment: Image and Tradition in Modern Scottish Culture*. Edinburgh: Polygon, 1997.

Biggs, Norman L. E., Keith Lloyd, and Robin J. Wilson. *Graph Theory: 1736–1936*. Oxford: Oxford University Press, 1976.

Blackwell, Thomas. *An Enquiry into the Life and Writings of Homer*. New York: Garland, 1970.

———. *Proofs of the Enquiry into Homer's Life and Writings, Translated into English*. London, 1747.

Blaikie, Andrew. *The Scots Imagination and Modern Memory*. Edinburgh: Edinburgh University Press, 2010.

Blair, Hugh. *A Critical Dissertation on the Poems of Ossian*. *The Poems of Ossian and Related Works*, ed. Howard Gaskill. Edinburgh: Edinburgh University Press, 1996.

———. *Lectures on Rhetoric and Belles Lettres*. Vol. 1. London: Printed for W. Strahan, 1783.

Blake, William. "A Memorable Fancy." *The Marriage of Heaven and Hell*, ed. Geoffrey Keynes. Oxford: Oxford University Press, 1975.

Blanchot, Maurice. *The Infinite Conversation*. Trans. Susan Hanson. Minneapolis: University of Minnesota Press, 1993.

Bold, Alan. *MacDiarmid, Christopher Murray Grieve: A Critical Biography*. London: John Murray, 1988.

Bos, Henk J. M. *Redefining Geometrical Exactness: Descartes' Transformation of the Early Modern Concept of Construction*. New York: Springer-Verlag, 2001.

Bourdieu, Pierre. *The Rules of Art: Genesis and Structure of the Literary Field*. Trans. Susan Emanuel. Stanford, CA: Stanford University Press, 1996.

Boyer, Carl B. *A History of Mathematics*. Rev. Uta C. Merzbach. Hoboken, NJ: Wiley and Sons, 1991.

Brewer, John. *The Sinews of Power: War, Money and the English State, 1688–1783*. Cambridge, MA: Harvard University Press, 1990.

Brewster, David. *The Martyrs of Science: The Lives of Galileo, Tycho Brahe, and Kepler*. New York: Harper, 1841.

———. *More Worlds than One: The Creed of the Philosopher and the Hope of the Christian*. New York: Robert Carter, 1854.

Broadie, Alexander. *The Scottish Enlightenment: The Historical Age of the Historical Nation*. Edinburgh: Birlinn, 2007.

———. *The Tradition of Scottish Philosophy: A New Perspective on the Enlightenment*. Savage, MD: Barnes and Noble, 1990.

Buckland, Adelene. *Novel Science: Fiction and the Invention of Geography*. Chicago: University of Chicago Press, 2013.

Buell, Laurence. *The Future of Environmental Criticism: Environmental Crisis and Literary Imagination*. Malden, MA: Blackwell, 2005.

Burdick, Anne, Johanna Drucker, Peter Lunenfeld, Todd Presner, and Jeffrey Schnapp. *Digital Humanities*. Cambridge, MA: MIT Press, 2012.

Burke, Edmund. *A Philosophical Enquiry into the Origin of Our Ideas of the Sublime and Beautiful*. Ed. Adam Phillips. Oxford: Oxford University Press, 1990.

Burnett, James, Lord Monboddo. *Of the Origin and Progress of Language*. Edinburgh: Printed for J. Balfour and T. Cadell, 1774.

Burns, Robert. *The Letters of Robert Burns*. Ed. J. De Lancy Ferguson and G. Ross Roy. 2 vols. Oxford: Oxford University Press, 1985.

———. *The Poems and Songs of Robert Burns*. Ed. James Kinsley. Vol. 1. Oxford: Oxford University Press, 1968.

———. "To James Smith." *Robert Burns: Selected Poems*. Ed. Carol McGuirk. London: Penguin, 1993.

Burroughs, Catherine B. *Closet Stages: Joanna Baillie and the Theater Theory of British Romantic Women Writers*. Philadelphia: University of Pennsylvania Press, 1997.

Burt, Edmund. *Burt's Letters from the North of Scotland*. Ed. Andrew Simmons. Edinburgh: Birlinn, 1998.

Buthlay, Kenneth. "Hugh MacDiarmid (11 August 1892–9 September 1978)." *British Poets, 1914–1945*, ed. Donald E. Stanford. Vol. 20, *Dictionary of Literary Biography*. Detroit: Gale Research, 1983.

———. "The Scotched Snake." *The Age of MacDiarmid: Essays on Hugh MacDiarmid and His Influence on Contemporary Scotland*, ed. P. H. Scott and A. C. Davis. Edinburgh: Mainstream, 1980.

Cajori, Florian. "Attempts Made During the Eighteenth and Nineteenth Centuries to Reform the Teaching of Geometry." *The American Mathematical Monthly* 17, no. 10 (1910): 181–201.

Campbell, Hilbert H. *James Thomson*. Boston: Twayne, 1979.

Carey, John. *Eyewitness to Science: Scientists and Writers Illuminate Natural Phenomena from Fossils to Fractals*. Ed. John Carey. Cambridge, MA: Harvard University Press, 1997.

Carruthers, Gerard. "Burns and Publishing." *The Edinburgh Companion to Robert Burns*, ed. Gerard Carruthers. Edinburgh: Edinburgh University Press, 2009.

———. *Scottish Literature*. Edinburgh: Edinburgh University Press, 2009.

Casanova, Pascale. *The World Republic of Letters*. Trans. M. B. DeBevoise. Cambridge, MA: Harvard University Press, 2004.

Cassirer, Ernst. *The Philosophy of the Enlightenment*. Trans. Fritz C. A. Loelln and James P. Pettegrove. 1932. Reprint, Princeton, NJ: Princeton University Press, 1951.

Chai, Leon. *Romantic Theory: Forms of Reflexivity in the Revolutionary Era*. Baltimore: Johns Hopkins University Press, 2006.

Chalmers, Thomas. "Astronomical Discourses." *Scottish Philosophical Theology, 1700–2000*, ed. David Fergusson. Exeter: Imprint Academic, 2007.

Chandler, James. *England in 1819: The Politics of Literary Culture and the Case of Romantic Historicism*. Chicago: University of Chicago Press, 1998.

Cheetham, Mark A. "Theory Reception: Panofsky, Kant, and Disciplinary Cosmopolitanism." *Journal of Art Historiography* 1 (2009): 1–13.

Chipp, Herschel B., ed. *Theories of Modern Art*. Berkeley: University of California Press, 1968.

Christie, William. *The Edinburgh Review in the Literary Culture of Romantic Britain: Mammoth and Megalonyx*. London: Pickering and Chatto, 2009.

Clark, T. J. *Farewell to an Idea: Episodes from a History of Modernism*. New Haven, CT: Yale University Press, 1999.

Clarke, Samuel. *A Discourse Concerning the Unchangeable Obligations of Natural Religion and the Truth and Certainty of the Christian Religion*. London: Printed for W. Botham, 1706.

Clyde, Robert. *From Rebel to Hero: The Image of the Highlander, 1745–1830*. East Linton: Tuckwell, 1995.

Cohen, I. Bernard. *The Newtonian Revolution*. Cambridge: Cambridge University Press, 1980.

Cohen, Ralph. *The Art of Discrimination: Thomson's "The Seasons" and the Language of Criticism*. Berkeley: University of California Press, 1964.

———. *The Unfolding of* The Seasons. Baltimore: Johns Hopkins University Press, 1970.

Combe, William. *The Tour of Dr. Syntax in Search of the Picturesque: A Poem*. London: Diggens, 1812.

Connor, Steven. "Topologies, Michel Serres and the Shapes of Thought." *Anglistik* 15 (2004): 105–17.

Cordiner, Reverend Charles. *Antiquities and Scenery of the North of Scotland*. London, 1780.

Craig, Cairns. *Associationism and the Literary Imagination: From the Phantasmal Chaos*. Edinburgh: Edinburgh University Press, 2007.

———. "Identifying Another Other." *Journal of Irish and Scottish Studies* 1, no. 1 (2007): 293–307.

———. *Intending Scotland: Explorations in Scottish Culture Since the Enlightenment*. Edinburgh: Edinburgh University Press, 2009.

———. *Out of History*. Edinburgh: Polygon, 1996.

———, ed. *The History of Scottish Literature*. 4 vols. Aberdeen: Aberdeen University Press, 1987.

Craig, David. *Scottish Literature and the Scottish People, 1680–1830*. London: Chatto and Windus, 1961.

Craik, Alex D. D. "Geometry Versus Analysis in Early 19th-Century Scotland: John Leslie, William Wallace, and Thomas Carlyle." *Historia Mathematica* 27 (2000): 133–63.

Crawford , Robert. *The Bard: Robert Burns, a Biography*. London: Cape, 2009.

———. *Devolving English Literature*. Oxford: Clarendon, 1992.

———. *The Modern Poet: Poetry Academia, and Knowledge Since the 1750s*. Oxford: Oxford University Press, 2001.

———, ed. *The Scottish Invention of English Literature*. Cambridge: Cambridge University Press, 1998.

Crawford, Thomas. *Burns: A Study of the Poems and Songs*. Edinburgh: Canongate, 1994.

Cririe, James. *Scottish Scenery: or, Sketches in Verse, Descriptive of Scenes Chiefly in the Highlands of Scotland*. London: Printed for T. Cadell, 1803.

Crotty, Patrick. "Review of *Dear Grieve: Letters to Hugh MacDiarmid (C. M. Grieve)*, ed. John Manson, and *The Edinburgh Companion to Hugh MacDiarmid*, ed. Scott Lyall and Margery Palmer McCulloch." *Scottish Literary Review* 5, no. 2 (2013): 133–36.

Curley, Thomas M. *Samuel Johnson, the* Ossian *Fraud, and the Celtic Revival*. Cambridge: Cambridge University Press, 2009.

Currie, James. *Works of Robert Burns*. Liverpool: Printed by J. M'Creery, 1800.

Davie, George. *The Democratic Intellect: Scotland and Her Universities in the Nineteenth Century*. Edinburgh: Edinburgh University Press, 1961.

———. *The Scotch Metaphysics: A Century of Enlightenment in Scotland*. London: Routledge, 2001.

De Duve, Thierry. "How Manet's *A Bar at the Folies-Bergère* Is Constructed," trans. Brian Holmes and Thierry de Duve. *Critical Inquiry* 25, no. 1 (1998): 136–68.

Dekker, George. *The Fictions of Romantic Tourism: Radcliffe, Scott, and Mary Shelley*. Stanford, CA: Stanford University Press, 2005.

De Man, Paul. *Allegories of Reading: Figural Language in Rousseau, Nietzsche, Rilke, and Proust*. New Haven, CT: Yale University Press, 1979.

———. "The Epistemology of Metaphor." *Aesthetic Ideology*, ed. Andrzej Warminski. Minneapolis: University of Minnesota Press, 1996.

———. "Kant and Schiller." *Aesthetic Ideology*, ed. Andrzej Warminski. Minneapolis: University of Minnesota Press, 1996.

Derrida, Jacques. "Freud and the Scene of Writing." *Writing and Difference*, trans. Alan Bass. Chicago: University of Chicago Press, 1978.

———. "From Restricted to General Economy: A Hegelianism Without Reserve." *Writing and Difference*, trans. Alan Bass. Chicago: University of Chicago Press, 1978.

———. *Of Spirit: Heidegger and the Question*. Trans. Geoffrey Bennington and Rachel Bowlby. Chicago: University of Chicago Press, 1987.

Devine, T. M. *The Scottish Nation: A History, 1700–2000*. New York: Penguin, 1999.

Dickens, Charles. *Hard Times*. In *Three Great Novels:* Hard Times, A Tale of Two Cities, *and* Great Expectations. Oxford: Oxford University Press, 1994.

Dimock, Wai Chee. "Critical Response I: Low Epic." *Critical Inquiry* 39 (2013): 614–31.

———. *Through Other Continents: American Literature Across Deep Time*. Princeton, NJ: Princeton University Press, 2006.

Ditton, Humphry. *An Institution of Fluxions*. London: Printed for W. Botham, 1705.

Drennon, Herbert. "James Thomson's Contact with Newtonianism and His Interest in Natural Philosophy." *PMLA* 49, no. 1 (1934): 71–80.

Dryden, John. *An Essay of Dramatic Poesy. Selected Poetry and Prose of John Dryden*. Ed. Earl Miner. New York: The Modern Library, 1969.

Duff, William. *An Essay on Original Genius*. London: Printed for Edward and Charles Dilly, 1767.

Duncan, Ian. *Modern Romance and Transformations of the Novel: The Gothic, Scott, Dickens*. Cambridge: Cambridge University Press, 1992.

———. "The Pathos of Abstraction: Adam Smith, Ossian, and Samuel Johnson." *Scotland and the Borders of Romanticism*, ed. Leith Davis, Ian Duncan, and Janet Sorensen. Cambridge: Cambridge University Press, 2004.

———. *Scott's Shadow: The Novel in Romantic Edinburgh*. Princeton, NJ: Princeton University Press, 2007.

———. "The Trouble with Man: Scott, Romance, and World History in the Age of Lamarck." *Romantic Circles Praxis*. http://www.rc.umd.edu/praxis/frictions/HTML/praxis.2011.dun can.ht ml. Accessed March 8, 2015.

Duncan, Ian, Leith Davis, and Janet Sorensen. "Introduction." *Scotland and the Borders of Romanticism*, ed. Leith Davis, Ian Duncan, and Janet Sorensen. Cambridge: Cambridge University Press, 2004.

Dunn, Douglas. "'A Very Scottish Kind of Dash': Burns's Native Metric." *Robert Burns and Cultural Authority*, ed. Robert Crawford. Iowa City: University of Iowa Press, 1997.

Durham, Frank, and Robert D. Purrington. "Newton, Nonlinearity and Determinism." *Some Truer Method: Reflections on the Heritage of Newton*, ed. Frank Durham. New York: Columbia University Press, 1990.

Eagles, Christina M. "David Gregory and Newtonian Science." *The British Journal for the History of Science* 10, no. 36 (1977): 216–25.

Edney, Matthew H. *Mapping an Empire: The Geographical Construction of British India, 1765–1843*. Chicago: University of Chicago Press, 1990.

Edwards, C. H. *The Historical Development of the Calculus*. New York: Springer-Verlag, 1979.

Eliot, T. S. *Four Quartets*. San Diego: Harcourt Brace Jovanovich, 1943.

———. "Tradition and the Individual Talent." *Selected Essays*. London: Faber and Faber, 1934.

———. "Was There a Scottish Literature?" *Modernism and Nationalism: Literature and Society in Scotland, 1918–1939*, ed. Margery Palmer McCulloch. Glasgow: Association for Scottish Literary Studies, 2004.

Ellis, Markman. "Enlightenment or Illumination: The Spectre of Conspiracy in Gothic Fictions of the 1790s." *Recognizing the Romantic Novel: New Histories of British Fiction, 1780–1830*, ed. Jillian Heydt-Stevenson and Charlotte Sussman. Liverpool: Liverpool University Press, 2008.

Encyclopaedia Britannica; or, a Dictionary of Arts, Sciences, and Miscellaneous Literature. 3rd ed. 18 vols. Edinburgh: Printed by A. Bell and C. McFarquhar, 1797.

Euclid. *The Thirteen Books of the Elements*. Trans. Sir Thomas L. Heath. New York: Dover, 1956.

Ferguson, Adam. *An Essay on the History of Civil Society*. Ed. Fania Oz-Salzberger. Cambridge: Cambridge University Press, 1995.

Fergusson, Robert. *The Poems of Robert Fergusson*. Ed. Matthew P. McDiarmid. Vol. 2. Edinburgh: William Blackwood and Sons, 1954.

Fielding, Penny. "Burns's Topographies." *Scotland and the Borders of Romanticism*, ed. Leith Davis, Ian Duncan, and Janet Sorensen. Cambridge: Cambridge University Press, 2004.

———. *Scotland and the Fictions of Geography: North Britain, 1760–1830*. Cambridge: Cambridge University Press, 2008.

Flynn, Thomas R. "Foucault and the Eclipse of Vision." *Modernity and the Hegemony of Vision*, ed. David Michael Levin. Berkeley: University of California Press, 1993.

Foucault, Michel. *Manet and the Object of Painting*. Trans. Matthew Barr. London: Tait Publishing, 2009.

———. *The Order of Things*. Trans. unnamed. New York: Vintage, 1970.

Frängsmyr, Tore, J. L. Heilbron, and Robin E. Rider, eds. *The Quantifying Spirit in the Eighteenth Century*. Berkeley: University of California Press, 1990.

Frank, Joseph. *The Idea of Spatial Form*. New Brunswick, NJ: Rutgers University Press, 1991.

Frazer, Michael L. "John Rawls: Between Two Enlightenments." *Political Theory* 35 (2007): 756–80.

Frege, Gottlob. *The Foundations of Arithmetic*. Trans. J. L. Austin. Oxford: Basil Blackwell, 1980.

Freud, Sigmund. *The Interpretation of Dreams*. Trans. James Strachey. New York: Avon, 1965.

Friedman, Michael. *Kant and the Exact Sciences*. Cambridge, MA: Harvard University Press, 1992.

Friesen, John. "Archibald Pitcairne, David Gregory and the Scottish Origins of English Tory Newtonianism, 1688–1715." *History of Science* 41, no. 2 (2003): 163–91.

Fynsk, Christopher. *Infant Figures: The Death of the "Infans" and Other Scenes of Writing*. Stanford, CA: Stanford University Press, 2000.

Gadamer, Hans-Georg. *Truth and Method*. Trans. and rev. Joel Weinsheimer and Donald G. Marshall. New York: Continuum, 1998.

Gallagher, Catherine. *Nobody's Story: The Vanishing Acts of Women Writers in the Marketplace, 1670–1820*. Berkeley: University of California Press, 1994.

Gamer, Michael. *Romanticism and the Gothic: Genre, Reception, and Canon Formation*. Cambridge: Cambridge University Press, 2000.

Garnett, Thomas. *Observations on a Tour Through the Highlands*. Vol. 1. London: T. Cadell, 1800.

Gaskill, Howard, ed. *The Reception of Ossian in Europe*. New York: Continuum, 2004.

Gerard, Alexander. *An Essay on Genius*. 1774. Reprint, New York: Garland, 1970.

Gidal, Eric. *Ossianic Unconformities: Bardic Poetry in the Industrial Age*. Charlottesville: University of Virginia Press, 2015.

Gifford, Douglas, and Dorothy McMillan, eds. *A History of Scottish Women's Writing*. Edinburgh: Edinburgh University Press, 1997.

Gigante, Denise. "The Monster in the Rainbow: Keats and the Science of Life." *PMLA*. 117, no. 3 (2002): 433–48.

Gilpin, William. "On Picturesque Beauty." *Three Essays*. London: Printed for R. Blamire, 1792.

Gish, Nancy K. *Hugh MacDiarmid: The Man and His Work*. London: Macmillan, 1984.

Glen, Duncan. *Hugh MacDiarmid (Christopher Murray Grieve) and the Scottish Renaissance*. Edinburgh: W. and R. Chambers, 1964.

Glendening, John. *The High Road: Romantic Tourism, Scotland, and Literature, 1720–1820*. New York: St. Martin's, 1997.

Glissant, Édouard. *The Poetics of Relation*. Trans. Betsy Wing. 1990. Reprint, Ann Arbor: University of Michigan Press, 1997.

Goldman, Martin. *The Demon in the Aether: The Story of James Clerk Maxwell.* Edinburgh: Paul Harris, 1983.

Goodman, Kevis. *Georgic Modernity and British Romanticism: Poetry and the Mediation of History.* Cambridge: Cambridge University Press, 2004.

Gottlieb, Evan. *Feeling British: Sympathy and National Identity in Scottish and English Writing, 1707–1832.* Lewisburg, PA: Bucknell University Press, 2007.

Grabiner, Judith V. "Newton, Maclaurin, and the Authority of Mathematics." *The American Mathematical Monthly* 111, no. 10 (2004): 841–52.

Grant, Anne. *Essays on the Superstitions of the Highlanders of Scotland.* London: Longman, 1811.

Gray, Jeremy. *Ideas of Space: Euclidean, Non-Euclidean, and Relativistic.* 2nd ed. Oxford: Clarendon, 1989.

———. *Plato's Ghost: The Modernist Transformation of Mathematics.* Princeton, NJ: Princeton University Press, 2008.

Greenberg, Clement. "Avant-Garde and Kitsch." *Clement Greenberg: The Collected Essays and Criticism,* ed. John O'Brian. Vol. 1. Chicago: University of Chicago Press, 1986.

Greenberg, Marvin Jay. *Euclidean and Non-Euclidean Geometries: Development and History.* 2nd ed. San Francisco: W. H. Freeman, 1980.

Greenblatt, Stephen. *Marvelous Possessions: The Wonder of the New World.* Oxford: Oxford University Press, 1991.

Grieve, Michael, and W. R. Aitken, eds. *The Complete Poems of Hugh MacDiarmid.* Vol. 2. London: Martin Brian and O'Keefe, 1978.

Guerrini, Anita. "The Tory Newtonians: Gregory, Pitcairne, and Their Circle." *The Journal of British Studies* 25, no. 3 (1986): 288–311.

Guicciardini, Niccolò. *The Development of Newtonian Calculus in Britain 1700–1800.* Cambridge: Cambridge University Press, 1989.

———. *Isaac Newton on Mathematical Certainty and Method.* Cambridge, MA: MIT Press, 2009.

Hadden, Richard W. *On the Shoulders of Merchants: Exchange and the Mathematical Conception of Nature in Early Modern Europe.* Albany: State University of New York Press, 1994.

Hall, Rupert. *Isaac Newton: Eighteenth-Century Perspectives.* Oxford: Oxford University Press, 1999.

———. *Philosophers at War: The Quarrel Between Newton and Leibniz.* Cambridge: Cambridge University Press, 1980.

Hallward, Peter. *Badiou: A Subject to Truth.* Minneapolis: University of Minnesota Press, 2003.

Hamilton, Paul. *Metaromanticism: Aesthetics, Literature, Theory.* Chicago: University of Chicago Press, 2003.

Hanna, Julian. "Manifestoes at Dawn: Nation, City and Self in Patrick Geddes and William Sharp's *Evergreen.*" *International Journal of Scottish Literature* 8 (2011). http://www.ijsl.stir.ac.uk/issue8/hanna. Accessed January 1, 2015.

Hanway, Mary Ann. *A Journey to the Highlands of Scotland.* London: Fielding and Walker, 1776.

Hardie, Martin. *John Pettie.* London: Adam and Charles Black, 1908.

Harman, Graham. "Realism Without Materialism." *SubStance* 40, no. 2 (2011): 52–72.

Hayden, John O., ed. *Scott: The Critical Heritage.* New York: Barnes and Noble, 1970.

Haydon, Benjamin. *The Autobiography and Memoirs of Benjamin Haydon.* Ed. Aldous Huxley. Vol. 1. New York: Harcourt Brace, 1926.

Heidegger, Martin. "The Origin of the Work of Art," trans. Albert Hofstadter. *Martin Heidegger: Basic Writings*, ed. David Farrell Krell. San Francisco: HarperCollins, 1993.

———. ". . . Poetically Man Dwells . . ." *Poetry, Language, Thought*, trans. Albert Hofstadter. New York: Harper & Row, 1971.

Henderson, Linda Dalrymple. *The Fourth Dimension and Non-Euclidean Geometry in Modern Art.* Princeton, NJ: Princeton University Press, 1983.

Henle, James M., and Eugene M. Kleinberg. *Infinitesimal Calculus.* Cambridge, MA: MIT Press, 1979.

Herman, Arthur. *How the Scots Invented the Modern World: The True Story of How Western Europe's Poorest Nation Created Our World & Everything in It*; or, *The Scottish Enlightenment: The Scots Invention of the Modern World.* New York: Crown, 2001.

Heron, Robert. *A Memoir of the Life of the Late Robert Burns.* Edinburgh: Printed for T. Brown, 1797.

Hewitt, Regina. *Symbolic Interactions: Social Problems and Literary Interventions in the Works of Baillie, Scott, and Landor.* Lewisburg, PA: Bucknell University Press, 2006.

Hipple, Walter John, Jr. *The Beautiful, the Sublime, and the Picturesque in Eighteenth-Century British Aesthetic Theory.* Carbondale: Southern Illinois University Press, 1957.

Hogarth, William. *The Analysis of Beauty.* Ed. Ronald Paulson. 1753. Reprint, New Haven, CT: Yale University Press, 1997.

Holton, Gerald. "Henri Poincaré, Marchel Duchamp and Innovation in Science and Art." *Leonardo* 34, no. 2 (2001): 127–34.

Hopkins, Brian, and Robin J. Wilson. "The Truth About Königsberg." *The College Mathematics Journal* 35 (2004): 198–207.

Horkheimer, Max, and Theordor W. Adorno. *Dialectic of Enlightenment.* Trans. John Cumming. 1944. Reprint, New York: Continuum, 1994.

Hudson, Nicholas. "What Is the Enlightenment? Investigating the Origins and Ideological Uses of an Historical Category." *Lumen: Selected Proceedings from the Canadian Society for Eighteenth-Century Studies.* Vol. 25. Kelowna, British Columbia: Academic Printing and Publishing, 2006.

Hulme, T. E. "Romanticism and Classicism." *Speculations: Essays on Humanism and the Philosophy of Art*, ed. Herbert Read. New York: Harcourt, Brace and Company, 1924.

Hume, David. *An Enquiry Concerning Human Understanding.* Ed. Antony Flew. La Salle, IL: Open Court, 1988.

———. "Of the Standard of Taste." *Essays: Moral, Political, and Literary*, ed. Eugene F. Miller. Indianapolis, IN: Liberty Fund, 1985.

———. *A Treatise of Human Nature.* Ed. Ernest C. Mossner. London: Penguin, 1969.

Husserl, Edmund. *The Crisis of European Sciences and Transcendental Phenomenology.* Trans. David Carr. Evanston, IL: Northwestern University Press, 1970.

Hussey, Christopher. *The Picturesque: Studies in a Point of View.* Hamden: Archon, 1927.

Hutcheson, Francis. *An Essay on the Nature and Conduct of the Passions and Affections, with Illustrations on the Moral Sense.* Ed. Aaron Garrett. Indianapolis, IN: Liberty Fund, 2002.

———. *An Inquiry into the Original of Our Ideas of Beauty and Virtue.* Ed. Wolfgang Leidhold. Indianapolis, IN: Liberty Fund, 2004.

Hutton, Charles. *Mathematical Tables.* London: Printed for G. G. J. and J. Robinson, 1785.

Hutton, James. *System of the Earth, 1785. Theory of the Earth, 1788. Observations on Granite, 1794. Together with Playfair's Biography of Hutton.* Darien, CT: Hafner, 1970.

Irlam, Shaun. *Elations: The Poetics of Enthusiasm in Eighteenth-Century Britain.* Stanford, CA: Stanford University Press, 1999.

Jackson, H. J., ed. *Samuel Taylor Coleridge.* Oxford: Oxford University Press, 1985.

Jacob, Margaret C. *Scientific Culture and the Making of the Industrial West.* Oxford: Oxford University Press, 1997.

Jacob, Margaret C., and Larry Stewart. *Practical Matter: Newton's Science in the Service of Industry and Empire, 1687–1851.* Cambridge, MA: Harvard University Press, 2004.

Jacquette, Dale. "Hume on Infinite Divisibility and Sensible Extensionless Indivisibles." *Journal of the History of Philosophy* 34, no. 1 (1996): 61–78.

Jameson, Fredric. *Marxism and Form: Twentieth-Century Dialectical Theories of Literature.* Princeton: Princeton University Press, 1974.

———. *The Political Unconscious: Narrative as a Socially Symbolic Act.* Ithaca, NY: Cornell University Press, 1981.

———. *Postmodernism, or, The Cultural Logic of Late Capitalism.* Durham, NC: Duke University Press, 1991.

———. *A Singular Modernity: Essay on the Ontology of the Present.* New York: Verso, 2002.

Jenkins, Alice. *Space and the "March of Mind": Literature and the Physical Sciences in Britain, 1815–1850.* Oxford: Oxford University Press, 2007.

Jesseph, Douglas M. "Editor's Introduction." *The Analyst,* De Motu *and* The Analyst. Ed. Douglas M. Jesseph. Dordrecht: Kluwer, 1992.

Jockers, Matthew. *Macroanalysis: Digital Methods and Literary History.* Urbana: University of Illinois Press, 2013.

Johnson, Samuel. *Dictionary of the English Language.* 3rd ed. Vol. 1. London: Printed for A. Millar, 1776.

———. *A Journey to the Western Islands of Scotland.* Ed. Peter Levi. New York: Penguin, 1984.

———. "Thomson." *The Lives of the English Poets,* ed. George Birkbeck Hill. Vol. 3. Oxford: Clarendon, 1905.

Jung, Sandro. "Visual Interpretations, Print, and Illustrations of Thomson's *The Seasons,* 1730–1797." *Eighteenth-Century Life* 34, no. 2 (2010): 23–64.

Kames, Lord. *Elements of Criticism.* Ed. Peter Jones. Vol. 2. Indianapolis, IN: Liberty Fund, 2005.

———. *Sketches of the History of Man.* Ed. James A. Harris. 3 vols. Indianapolis, IN: Liberty Fund, 2007.

Kant, Immanuel. *Critique of Judgment.* Trans. Werner S. Pluhar. Indianapolis, IN: Hackett, 1987.

———. *Critique of Pure Reason.* Trans. J. M. D. Meiklejohn. Buffalo, NY: Prometheus, 1990.

———. "An Inquiry Concerning the Perspicuity of the Principles of Natural Theology and of Moral," trans. unnamed. Vol. 1, *Essays and Treatises on Moral, Political, and Various Philosophical Subjects.* London: William Richardson.

———. *Observations on the Feeling of the Beautiful and Sublime.* Trans. John T. Goldthwait. Berkeley: University of California Press, 1960.

Keats, John. "Lamia." *The Complete Poems,* ed. John Barnard. New York: Penguin, 1973.

Keenleyside, Heather. "Personification for the People: On James Thomson's *The Seasons.*" *English Literary History* 76, no. 2 (2009): 447–72.

Keill, John. *An Introduction to the True Astronomy: or, Astronomical Lectures, Read in the Astronomical School of the University of Oxford.* London: Printed for Bernard Lintot, 1721.

———. "A Preface, Shewing the *Usefulness* and *Excellency* of this work." *Euclid's Elements of Geometry, from the Latin Translation of Commandine.* London: Printed for Thomas Woodward, 1733.

Kelley, Theresa M. "Spirit and Geometric Form: The Stone and the Shell in Wordsworth's Arab Dream." *Studies in English Literature* 22, no. 4 (1982): 563–82.

Kerrigan, Catherine. *Whaur Extremes Meet: The Poetry of Hugh MacDiarmid, 1920–1934.* Edinburgh: The Mercat Press, 1983.

Kindrick, Robert L. "Robert Burns and the Tradition of the Makars." *Studies in Scottish Literature* 30 (1998): 91–107.

Kitcher, Philip. "Kant and the Foundations of Mathematics." *The Philosophical Review* 84, no. 1 (1975): 23–50.

Kittler, Friedrich. *Discourse Networks, 1800/1900.* Trans. Michael Metteer and Chris Cullens. Stanford, CA: Stanford University Press, 1990.

Kline, Morris. *Mathematics: The Loss of Certainty.* Oxford: Oxford University Press, 1980.

Knapp, Steven. *Personification and the Sublime: Milton to Coleridge.* Cambridge, MA: Harvard University Press, 1985.

Knight, Richard Payne. *An Analytical Inquiry into the Principles of Taste.* London: Printed by Luke Hansard, 1805.

Koyré, Alexander. "The Significance of the Newtonian Synthesis." *Newton: Texts, Backgrounds, Commentaries,* ed. I. Bernard Cohen and Richard S. Westfall. New York: W. W. Norton, 1995.

Lacour, Claudia Brodsky. *Lines of Thought: Discourse, Architecture, and the Origin of Modern Philosophy.* Durham, NC: Duke University Press, 1996.

Langan, Celeste. "Understanding Media in 1805: Audiovisual Hallucination in *The Lay of the Last Minstrel.*" *Studies in Romanticism* 40, no. 1 (2001): 49–70.

Leask, Nigel. *Robert Burns and Pastoral: Poetry and Improvement in Late Eighteenth-Century Scotland.* Oxford: Oxford University Press, 2010.

Leibniz, Gottfried. "Mr. Leibnitz's Second Paper." *The Leibniz-Clarke Correspondence,* ed. H. G. Alexander. Manchester: Manchester University Press, 1956.

Lesch, John E. "Systematics and the Geometrical Spirit." *The Quantifying Spirit in the Eighteenth Century,* ed. Tore Frängsmyr, J. L. Heilbron, and Robin E. Rider. Berkeley: University of California Press, 1990.

Leslie, John. *Elements of Geometry, Geometrical Analysis, and Plane Trigonometry.* Edinburgh: Printed by James Ballantyne, 1809.

Lettice, John. *Letters on a Tour Through Various Parts of Scotland, in the Year 1792.* London: T. Cadell, 1794.

Levine, Joseph M. *The Battle of the Books: History and Literature in the Augustan Age.* Ithaca, NY: Cornell University Press, 1991.

Lewis, Matthew. *The Monk.* Ed. Emma McEvoy. Oxford: Oxford University Press, 1995.

Locke, John. *An Essay Concerning Human Understanding.* Ed. Peter H. Nidditch. Oxford: Clarendon, 1975.

Lockhart, J. G. *Life of Robert Burns.* Edinburgh: Constable and Co., 1828.

———. *The Life of Sir Walter Scott.* Vol. 4. London: J. B. Millet, 1839.

Low, Donald, ed. *Robert Burns: The Critical Heritage.* London: Routledge and Kegan Paul, 1974.

Lukács, Georg. *The Historical Novel.* Trans. Hannah and Stanley Mitchell. Lincoln: University of Nebraska Press, 1983.

Lumsden, Alison. *Walter Scott and the Limits of Language*. Edinburgh: Edinburgh University Press, 2010.

Lyall, Scott. *Hugh MacDiarmid's Poetry and Politics of Place: Imagining a Scottish Republic*. Edinburgh: University of Edinburgh Press, 2006.

Lyotard, Jean-François. *Discours, Figure*. Paris: Klincksieck, 1971.

———. "Gloss on Resistance." *The Postmodern Explained: Correspondence, 1982–1985*, trans. and ed. Julian Pefanis and Morgan Thomas. Minneapolis: University of Minnesota Press, 1992.

———. *Lessons on the Analytic of the Sublime*. Trans. Elizabeth Rottenberg. Stanford, CA: Stanford University Press, 1994.

———. *The Lyotard Reader*. Ed. Andrew Benjamin. Oxford: Basil Blackwell, 1989.

———. *The Postmodern Condition: A Report on Knowledge*. Trans. Geoff Bennington and Brian Massumi. Manchester: Manchester University Press, 1984.

Maas, Harro. "Where Mechanism Ends: Thomas Reid on the Moral and Animal Oeconomy." *History of Political Economy* 35, Annual Supplement (2003): 338–60.

MacDiarmid, Hugh. "The Caledonian Antisyzygy and the Gaelic Idea." *Selected Essays of Hugh MacDiarmid*, ed. Duncan Glen. Berkeley: University of California Press, 1970.

———. *David Hume: Scotland's Greatest Son*. Edinburgh: The Paperback Booksellers, 1961.

———. *Hugh MacDiarmid: Selected Poetry*. Ed. Alan Riach and Michael Grieve. Manchester: Fyfield, 2004.

Macdonald, Murdo. "Celticism and Internationalism in the Circle of Patrick Geddes." *Visual Culture in Britain* 6, no. 2 (2005): 69–83.

———. *Scottish Art*. London: Thames and Hudson, 2000.

Macdonald, W., and J. Arthur Thomson. "Proem." *The Evergreen: A Northern Seasonal*. Edinburgh: Patrick Geddes; London: T. Fisher Unwin, 1895.

Maclaurin, Colin. *An Account of Sir Isaac Newton's Philosophical Discoveries*. 1748. Reprint, New York: Johnson Reprint, 1968.

———. *The Collected Letters of Colin Maclaurin*. Ed. Stella Mills. Nantwich: Shiva Publishing, 1982.

———. *A Treatise of Fluxions*. Vol. 1. Edinburgh: T. W. and T. Ruddimans, 1742.

Macmillan, Duncan. *Scottish Art: 1460–2000*. Edinburgh: Mainstream, 2000.

Macpherson, James. *A Dissertation. The Poems of Ossian and Related Works*, ed. Howard Gaskill. Edinburgh: Edinburgh University Press, 1996.

———. *Fragments of Ancient Poetry: The Poems of Ossian and Related Works*. Ed. Howard Gaskill. Edinburgh: Edinburgh University Press, 1996.

MacQueen, John. *Complete and Full with Numbers: The Narrative Poetry of John Henryson*. Amsterdam: Rodopi, 2006.

———. *Progress and Poetry*. Edinburgh: Scottish Academic Press, 1982.

Mahlon, Basil. *The Man Who Changed Everything: The Life of James Clerk Maxwell*. Chichester: John Wiley, 2003.

Makdisi, Saree. *Romantic Imperialism: Universal Empire and the Culture of Modernity*. Cambridge: Cambridge University Press, 1998.

Mallet, David. *The Excursion*. In Samuel Johnson *The Works of the English Poets, from Chaucer to Cowper*. Vol. 14. New York: Greenwood, 1969.

Mandelbrot, Benoit. *The Fractal Geometry of Nature*. New York: W. H. Freeman, 1977.

Manning, Peter. *Reading Romantics: Texts and Contexts*. Oxford: Oxford University Press, 1990.

Manning, Susan. *Fragments of Union: Making Connections in Scottish and American Writing.* Basingstoke: Palgrave, 2002.

———. "'The Plots of God Are Perfect': Poe's *Eureka* and American Creative Nihilism." *Journal of American Studies* 23, no. 2 (1989): 235–51.

———. *Poetics of Character: Transatlantic Encounters, 1700–1900.* Cambridge: Cambridge University Press, 2013.

———. "'Whether Utility or Pleasure Be the Principal Aim in View': An Edinburgh Perspective on the Value of English Studies." *Scottish Literary Review* 1 (2009): 1–15.

Marinetti, F. T. "Manifesto of Futurism," trans. Joshua C. Taylor. *Theories of Modern Art: A Sourcebook by Artists and Critics*, ed. Herschel B. Chipp. Berkeley: University of California Press, 1968.

Markley, Robert. *Fallen Languages: Crises of Representation in Newtonian England, 1660–1740.* Ithaca, NY: Cornell University Press, 1993.

Marlowe, Christopher. *Doctor Faustus: A- and B- Texts (1604, 1616).* Ed. David Bevington and Eric Rasmussen. Manchester: Manchester University Press, 1993.

Marx, Karl. *Capital.* Trans. Ben Fowkes. Vol. 1. London: Penguin, 1976.

Maxwell, Stephen. "The Nationalism of Hugh MacDiarmid." *The Age of MacDiarmid: Essays on Hugh MacDiarmid and His Influence on Contemporary Scotland*, ed. P. H. Scott and A. C. Davis. Edinburgh: Mainstream, 1980.

McCracken-Flesher, Caroline, ed. *Culture, Nation, and the New Scottish Parliament.* Lewisburg, PA: Bucknell University Press, 2007.

McCulloch, Margery Palmer. *Modernism and Nationalism: Literature and Society in Scotland, 1918–1939.* Glasgow: Association for Scottish Literary Studies, 2004.

———. *Scottish Modernism and Its Contexts, 1918–1959: Literature, National Identity and Cultural Exchange.* Edinburgh: Edinburgh University Press, 2009.

McGann, Jerome. "Dialogue and Interpretation at the Interface of Man and Machine: Reflections on Textuality and a Proposal for an Experiment in Machine Reading." *Computers and the Humanities* 36 (2002): 95–107.

———. "Philology in a New Key." *Critical Inquiry* 39, no. 2 (2013): 327–46.

———. *The Romantic Ideology: A Critical Investigation.* Chicago: University of Chicago Press, 1983.

———. "Visible and Invisible Books: Hermetic Images in N-Dimensional Space." *New Literary History* 32, no. 2 (2001): 283–300.

———. "Walter Scott's Romantic Postmodernity." *Scotland and the Borders of Romanticism*, ed. Leith Davis, Ian Duncan, and Janet Sorensen. Cambridge: Cambridge University Press, 2004.

McGuirk, Carol. *Robert Burns and the Sentimental Era.* Athens: University of Georgia Press, 1985.

McKean, Charles. "Twinning Cities: Modernisation versus Improvement in the Two Towns of Edinburgh." *Edinburgh: The Making of a Capital City*, ed. Brian Edwards and Paul Jenkins. Edinburgh: Edinburgh University Press, 2005.

McKillop, Alan Dugald. *The Background of Thomson's Seasons.* Hamden, CT: Archon Books, 1961.

McLane, Maureen N. *Balladeering, Minstrelsy, and the Making of British Romantic Poetry.* Cambridge: Cambridge University Press, 2008.

Meillassoux, Quentin. *After Finitude: An Essay on the Necessity of Contingency.* Trans. Ray Brassier. London: Continuum, 2008.

Meller, Helen. *Patrick Geddes: Social Evolutionist and City Planner*. London: Routledge, 1990.

Meli, Domenico Bertolini. *Equivalence and Priority: Newton Versus Leibniz*. Oxford: Clarendon, 1993.

———. *Thinking with Objects: The Transformation of Mechanics in the Seventeenth Century*. Baltimore: Johns Hopkins University Press, 2006.

Menand, Louis. "The Pound Error: The Elusive Master of Allusion." *New Yorker*, June 9, 2008. http://www.newyorker.com/arts/critics/books/2008/06/09/080609crbo_books_menand. Accessed January 10, 2011.

Michasiw, Kim Ian. "Nine Revisionist Theses on the Picturesque." *Representations* 38 (1992): 76–100.

Millgate, Jane. "The Structure of *Guy Mannering*." *Scott and His Influence*, ed. J. H. Alexander and David Hewitt. Aberdeen: Association for Scottish Literary Studies, 1983.

Mitchell, W. J. T. "Imperial Landscape." *Landscape and Power*, ed. W. J. T. Mitchell. Chicago: University of Chicago Press, 2002.

M'Nayr, James. *A Guide from Glasgow to Some of the Most Remarkable Scenes in the Highlands of Scotland, and to the Falls of Clyde*. Glasgow: Printed in the Courier Office, 1797.

Moretti, Franco. *Distant Reading*. London: Verso, 2013.

———. *Graphs, Maps, Trees: Abstract Models for Literary History*. London: Verso, 2005.

Morgan, Edwin. "A Poet's Response to Burns." *Burns Now*, ed. Kenneth Simpson. Edinburgh: Canongate, 1994.

Morrison, John. *Painting the Nation: Identity and Nationalism in Scottish Painting, 1800–1920*. Edinburgh: Edinburgh University Press, 2003.

Muir, Edwin. *An Autobiography*. Edinburgh: Canongate, 1993.

———. *The Present Age from 1914*. London: The Cresset Press, 1939.

———. *Scott and Scotland: The Predicament of the Scottish Writer*. New York: Robert Speller, 1938.

———. *Scottish Journey*. Edinburgh: Mainstream, 1935.

———. *The Structure of the Novel*. New York: Harcourt, Brace and Company, 1929.

———. "Walter Scott." *Essays on Literature and Society*. Cambridge, MA: Harvard University Press, 1965.

———. *We Moderns: Enigmas and Guesses*. New York: Knopf, 1920.

Munster, Anna. *An Aesthesia of Networks: Conjunctive Experience in Art and Technology*. Cambridge, MA: MIT Press, 2013.

Murray, Sarah. *A Companion and Useful Guide to the Beauties of Scotland*. London: George Nicol, 1799.

Nairn, Tom. *The Break-Up of Britain*. Altona: Common Ground, 2003.

———. *Faces of Nationalism: Janus Revisited*. London: Verso, 1997.

Neal, Katherine. *From Discrete to Continuous: The Broadening of Number Concepts in Early Modern England*. Dordrecht: Kluwer, 2002.

Newton, Isaac. *The Method of Fluxions and Infinite Series*. London: Printed by Henry Woodfall, 1736.

———. *The Principia*. Trans. Andrew Motte. New York: Prometheus, 1995.

———. "Quadrature of Curves." *The Mathematical Works of Isaac Newton*, ed. Derek T. Whiteside. Vol. 1. New York: Johnson Reprint Corporation, 1964.

Nichol, John Pringle. *Views of the Architecture of the Heavens*. 3rd ed. Edinburgh: William Tait, 1839.

Nicolson, Marjorie Hope. *Newton Demands the Muse: Newton's* Opticks *and the Eighteenth-Century Poets*. Hamden, CT: Archon Books, 1963.

Nietzsche, Friedrich. *The Birth of Tragedy*. Trans. Walter Kaufmann. New York: Vintage, 1967.

Nussbaum, Felicity A. *Torrid Zones: Maternity, Sexuality, and Empire in Eighteenth-Century English Narratives*. Baltimore: Johns Hopkins University Press, 1995.

Nye, David E. *American Technological Sublime*. Cambridge, MA: MIT Press, 1994.

Olson, Richard. "Scottish Philosophy and Mathematics, 1750–1830." *Journal of the History of Ideas* 32, no. 1 (1971): 29–44.

Packham, Catherine. *Eighteenth-Century Vitalism: Bodies, Culture, Politics*. Houndmills: Palgrave Macmillan, 2012.

Panofsky, Erwin. *Perspective as Symbolic Form*. Trans. Christopher S. Wood. New York: Zone, 1997.

Pater, Walter. *The Renaissance*. Ed. Donald L. Hill. Berkeley: University of California Press.

Paxson, James J. "The Allegory of Temporality and the Early Modern Calculus." *Configurations* 4, no. 1 (1996): 39–66.

Perkins, David. "Human Mouseness: Burns and Compassion for Animals." *Texas Studies in Language and Literature* 42 (2000): 1–15.

Pittock, Murray. "Historiography." *The Cambridge Companion to the Scottish Enlightenment*, ed. Alexander Broadie. Cambridge: Cambridge University Press, 2003.

———. "Introduction: What Is Scottish Romanticism?" *The Edinburgh Companion to Scottish Romanticism*, ed. Murray Pittock. Edinburgh: Edinburgh University Press, 2011.

———. *The Road to Independence? Scotland in the Balance*. London: Reaktion, 2013.

———. *Scottish and Irish Romanticism*. Oxford: Oxford University Press, 2008.

Plato. *The Republic*. Trans. Paul Shorey. *Plato: The Collected Dialogues*, ed. Edith Hamilton and Huntington Cairns. Princeton, NJ: Princeton University Press, 1961.

Playfair, John. "Dissertation: Exhibiting a General View of the Progress of Mathematical and Physical Science, Since the Revival of Letters in Europe." *The Works of John Playfair*. Vol. 2. Edinburgh: Printed for Archibald Constable, 1822.

———. *On the Origin and Investigation of Porisms*. Edinburgh, 1792.

Plotnitsky, Arkady. "Algebras, Geometries and Topologies of the Fold: Deleuze, Derrida and Quasi-Mathematical Thinking (with Leibniz and Mallarmé)." *Between Deleuze and Derrida*, ed. Paul Patton and John Protevi. New York: Continuum, 2003.

———. *The Knowable and the Unknowable: Modern Science, Nonclassical Thought, and the "Two Cultures."* Ann Arbor: University of Michigan Press, 2002.

Poe, Edgar Allan. *The Complete Tales and Poems*. New York: Vintage, 1975.

———. *Eureka*. Ed. Stuart Levine and Susan F. Levine. Urbana: University of Illinois Press, 2004.

Poincaré, Henri. *Science and Hypothesis*. Trans. William John Greenstreet. London: The Walter Scott Publishing Company, 1905.

Poovey, Mary. *A History of the Modern Fact: Problems of Knowledge in the Sciences of Wealth and Society*. Chicago: University of Chicago Press, 1998.

Pope, Alexander. *Dunciad*. *The Poems of Alexander Pope*, ed. John Butt. New Haven, CT: Yale University Press, 1963.

———. "Epitaph." *The Poems of Alexander Pope*, ed. John Butt. New Haven, CT: Yale University Press, 1963.

Price, Uvedale. *An Essay on the Picturesque, as Compared with the Sublime and the Beautiful*. London: Printed for J. Robson, 1794.

Priestley, Joseph. *A New Chart of History*. London: Engraved and published for J. Johnson, 1769.

Purser, John. *Scotland's Music: A History of the Traditional and Classical Music of Scotland from the Earliest Times to the Present Day*. Edinburgh: Mainstream, 1992.

Pycior, Helena M. *Symbols, Impossible Numbers, and Geometric Entanglements: British Algebra Through the Commentaries on Newton's Universal Arithmetick*. Cambridge: Cambridge University Press, 1997.

Ramati, Ayval. "The Hidden Truth of Creation: Newton's Method of Fluxions." *The British Journal for the History of Science* 34, no. 4 (2001): 417–38.

Ramsay, Allan. *An Ode to the Memory of Sir Isaac Newton*. Edinburgh, 1727.

Rechter, Ofra. "The View from 1763: Kant on the Arithmetical Method Before Intuition." *Intuition and the Axiomatic Method*, ed. Emily Carson and Renate Huber. London: Springer, 2006.

Reid, Thomas. *An Inquiry into the Human Mind on the Principles of Common Sense. The Works of Thomas Reid*, ed. William Hamilton. Vol. 1. 1872. Reprint, Hoboken, NJ: Elibron Classics, 2005.

———. "Letters to Dr James Gregory." *The Works of Thomas Reid*, ed. William Hamilton. Vol. 1. 1872. Reprint, Hoboken, NJ: Elibron Classics, 2005.

Renan, Ernest. "What Is a Nation?" *Becoming National: A Reader*, ed. Geoff Eley and Ronald Grigo. Oxford: Oxford University Press, 1996.

Richards, Eric. *The Highland Clearances: People, Landlords and Rural Turmoil*. Edinburgh: Birlinn, 2000.

Richards, Joan. *Mathematical Visions: The Pursuit of Geometry in Victorian England*. Boston: Academic Press, 1988.

Rider, Robin E. "Measure of Ideas, Rule of Language: Mathematics and Language in the 18th Century." *The Quantifying Spirit in the Eighteenth Century*, ed. Tore Frängsmyr, J. L. Heilbron, and Robin E. Rider. Berkeley: University of California Press, 1990.

Rigney, Ann. "Embodied Communities: Commemorating Robert Burns, 1859." *Representations* 115 (2011): 71–102.

"Robert Burns: Inventing Tradition and Securing Memory, 1796–1909." http://www.gla.ac.uk/schools/critical/research/researchcentresandnetworks/robertburnsstudies/ourresearch/burns/. Accessed March 11, 2015.

Robinson, Sidney K. *Inquiry into the Picturesque*. Chicago: University of Chicago Press, 1991.

Rotman, Brian. *Signifying Nothing: The Semiotics of Zero*. Houndmills: Macmillan, 1987.

Rousseau, Jean-Jacques. "Essay on the Origin of Languages." *The First and Second Discourses, Together with the Replies to the Critics and Essay on the Origin of Languages*, trans. Victor Gourevitch. New York: HarperCollins, 1986.

Rowan, Alistair. *Designs for Castles and Country Villas by Robert and James Adam*. New York: Rizzoli, 1985.

———. "Introduction." *Robert Adam and Scotland: The Picturesque Drawings*. Edinburgh: Scottish Arts Council Gallery, 1972.

Rowe, John. *An Introduction to the Doctrine of Fluxions*. 2nd ed. London: Printed for J. Noon, 1757.

Sambrook, James. *James Thomson, 1700–1748: A Life*. Oxford: Clarendon, 1991.

Saunders, Bailey. *The Life and Letters of James Macpherson*. London: Swan Sonnenschein, 1894.

Schaw, Janet. *Journal of a Lady of Quality: Being the Narrative of a Journey from Scotland to the West Indies, North Carolina, and Portugal, in the Years 1774 to 1776*. Ed. Evangeline Walker Andrews and Charles McLean Andrews. Salem, MA: Higginson, 1997.

Schlutz, Alexander. "Purloined Voices: Edgar Allan Poe Reading Samuel Taylor Coleridge." *Studies in Romanticism* 47 (2008): 195–224.

Schmidt, Wolf Gerhard. "'Menschlichschön' and 'Kolossalisch': The Discursive Function of Ossian in Schiller's Poetry and Aesthetics." *The Reception of Ossian in Europe*, ed. Howard Gaskill. London: Thoemmes Continuum, 2004.

Scott, Sir Walter. *The Antiquary*. Ed. Nicola J. Watson. Oxford: Oxford University Press, 2002.

———. "Essay on Romance." Vol. 6, *The Miscellaneous Prose Works of Sir Walter Scott*. Edinburgh: Printed for Cadell and Co., 1827.

———. *Guy Mannering*. Ed. P. D. Garside. London: Penguin, 2003.

———. *The Letters of Sir Walter Scott*. Ed. H. J. C. Grierson. Vol. 1. London: Constable, 1932.

———. "On Planting Waste Lands." *The Quarterly Review*. Vol. 36. London: John Murray, 1827.

———. *Waverley; or, 'Tis Sixty Years Since*. Ed. Claire Lamont. Oxford: Oxford University Press, 1986.

Scott, William Robert. *Francis Hutcheson: His Life, Teaching and Position in the History of Philosophy*. Cambridge: Cambridge University Press, 1900.

Serres, Michel. *Le Parasite*. Paris: Grasset and Fasquelle, 1980.

———. *The Parasite*. Trans. Lawrence R. Schehr. Minneapolis: University of Minnesota Press, 2007.

Seth, Andrew. *Hegelianism and Personality*. Edinburgh: Blackwood, 1893.

———. *Scottish Philosophy: A Comparison of the Scottish and German Answers to Hume*. Edinburgh: William Blackwood and Sons, 1890.

Sha Xin Wei. *Poiesis and Enchantment in Topological Matter*. Cambridge, MA: MIT Press, 2013.

Shields, Juliet. *Sentimental Literature and Anglo-Scottish Identity, 1745–1820*. Cambridge: Cambridge University Press, 2010.

Simmel, Georg. *The Conflict of Modern Culture*. Trans. K. Peter Etzkorn. New York: Teachers College Press, 1968.

Simpson, Matthew. "Robert Fergusson and St Andrews Student Culture." *Heaven-Taught Fergusson: Robert Burns's Favourite Scottish Poet*, ed. Robert Crawford. East Linton: Tuckwell, 2003.

Simson, Robert. *The Elements of Euclid*. Glasgow: Printed by Robert and Andrew Foulis, 1756.

———. "Preface." *A Treatise Concerning Porisms*. Canterbury: Printed by Simmons and Kirkby, 1777.

Sitter, John. *Literary Loneliness in Mid-Eighteenth-Century England*. Ithaca, NY: Cornell University Press, 1982.

Slagle, Judith Bailey, ed. *The Collected Letters of Joanna Baillie*. Vol. 2. Cranbury, NJ: Associated University Presses, 1999.

———. *Joanna Baillie: A Literary Life*. Madison, NJ: Fairleigh Dickinson University Press, 2002.

Smith, Adam. "Account of the Life and Writings of Adam Smith, L. L. D." *Essays on Philosophical Subjects*, ed. W. P. D. Wightman and J. C. Bryce. Oxford: Clarendon, 1980.

———. "The History of Astronomy." *Essays on Philosophical Subjects*, ed. W. P. D. Wightman and J. C. Bryce. Oxford: Clarendon, 1980.

———. *Lectures on Rhetoric and Belles Lettres*. Ed. J. C. Bryce. Indianapolis, IN: Liberty Fund, 1985.

———. *The Theory of Moral Sentiments*. Ed. D. D. Raphael and A. L. Macfie. Indianapolis, IN: Liberty Fund, 1982.

Smith, G. Gregory. *Scottish Literature: Character and Influence*. London: Macmillan, 1919.

Smith, Iain Crichton. "MacDiarmid and Ideas, with Special Reference to 'On a Raised Beach.'" *The Age of MacDiarmid: Essays on Hugh MacDiarmid and His Influence on Contemporary Scotland*, ed. P. H. Scott and A. C. Davis. Edinburgh: Mainstream, 1980.

Smollett, Tobias. *Humphry Clinker*. Ed. Shaun Regan. London: Penguin, 2008.

Snow, C. P. *The Two Cultures*. Cambridge: Cambridge University Press, 1998.

Spate, Virginia. *Orphism: The Evolution of Non-Figurative Painting in Paris, 1910–1914*. Oxford: Clarendon, 1979.

"Squaring the Circle." *Wikipedia*. http://en.wikipedia.org/wiki/Squaring_the_circle. Accessed May 30, 2015.

Stafford, Barbara Maria. *Echo Objects: The Cognitive Work of Images*. Chicago: University of Chicago Press, 2007.

———. "The Remaining 10 Percent: The Role of Sensory Knowledge in the Age of the Self-Organizing Brain." *Visual Literacy*, ed. James Elkins. New York: Routledge, 2008.

———. *Voyage into Substance: Art, Science, Nature, and the Illustrated Travel Account, 1760–1840*. Cambridge, MA: MIT Press, 1984.

Stafford, Fiona J. *The Sublime Savage: A Study of James Macpherson and the Poems of Ossian*. Edinburgh: Edinburgh University Press, 1988.

Stewart, Dugald. "Account of the Life and Writings of Adam Smith." *Essays on Philosophical Subjects*, ed. P. D. Wightman, J. C. Bryce, and I. S. Ross. Oxford: Clarendon, 1980.

Stewart, Matthew. *The Distance of the Sun from the Earth Determined, by the Theory of Gravity*. Edinburgh: Printed for A. Millar, 1763.

Stiegler, Bernard. *Technics and Time*. Trans. Richard Beardsworth and George Collins. Stanford, CA: Stanford University Press, 1998.

Strehle, Susan. *Fiction in the Quantum Universe*. Chapel Hill: University of North Carolina Press, 1992.

Sulivan, Richard Joseph. *Observations Made During a Tour Through Parts of England, Scotland, and Wales. In a Series of Letters*. London: Printed for T. Becket, 1780.

Swiriski, Peter. *Between Literature and Science: Poe, Lem, and Explorations in Aesthetics, Cognitive Science, and Literary Knowledge*. Montreal: McGill-Queen's University Press, 2000.

Tait, A. A. *Robert Adam and Scotland: The Picturesque Drawings*. Edinburgh: Scottish Arts Council, 1972.

Thompson, D'Arcy Wentworth. *On Growth and Form in Shapes*. Oxford: Oxford University Press, 2009.

Thomson, James. *Liberty, The Castle of Indolence, and Other Poems*. Ed. James Sambrook. Oxford: Clarendon, 1986.

———. *The Seasons*. Ed. James Sambrook. Oxford: Clarendon, 1981.

Towsey, Mark R. M. *Reading the Scottish Enlightenment: Books and Their Readers in Provincial Scotland, 1750–1820*. Leiden: Brill, 2010.

Traill, William. *Account of the Life and Writings of Robert Simson, M.D. Late Professor of Mathematics at the University of Glasgow*. Bath: Printed by Richard Cruttwell, 1812.

Transactions of the Royal Society of Edinburgh. Edinburgh: Printed for J. Dickson, 1788.

Tromans, Nicholas. *David Wilkie: The People's Painter*. Edinburgh: Edinburgh University Press, 2007.

Trumpener, Katie. *Bardic Nationalism: The Romantic Novel and the British Empire*. Princeton, NJ: Princeton University Press, 1997.

Underwood, Ted. *Why Literary Periods Mattered: Historical Contrast and the Prestige of English Studies*. Stanford, CA: Stanford University Press, 2013.

Valenza, Robin. *Literature, Language, and the Rise of the Intellectual Disciplines in Britain, 1680–1820*. Cambridge: Cambridge University Press, 2009.

Virilio, Paul. *The Aesthetics of Disappearance*. Trans. Philip Beitchman. Boston: Semiotext(e), 1991.

Virtanen, Reino. "Poe's *Eureka* in France from Baudelaire to Valéry." *Romance Quarterly* 29 (1982): 223–34.

Warton, Joseph. *An Essay on the Writings and Genius of Pope*. London: Printed for M. Cooper, 1756.

Waszek, Norbert. "The Scottish Enlightenment in Germany, and Its Translator, Christian Garve (1742–98)." *Scotland in Europe*, ed. Tom Hubbard and R. D. S. Jack. Amsterdam: Rodopi, 2006.

Wegner, Phillip E. *Imaginary Communities: Utopia, the Nation, and the Spatial Histories of Modernity*. Berkeley: University of California Press, 2002.

Welsh, Susan. "The Value of Analogical Evidence: Poe's *Eureka* in the Context of a Scientific Debate." *Modern Language Studies* 21 (1991): 3–15.

Westfall, R. S. *Force in Newton's Physics: The Science of Dynamics in the Seventeenth Century*. London: Macdonald, 1971.

———. *Never at Rest: A Biography of Isaac Newton*. Cambridge: Cambridge University Press, 1980.

Whatley, Christopher, and Murray Pittock. "Poems and Festivals, Art and Artefact and the Commemoration of Robert Burns, c. 1844–c.1896." *Scottish Historical Review* 93, no. 1 (2014): 56–79.

Wickman, Matthew. "The End of Biographies?" *Scottish Literary Review* 2, no. 1 (2010): 159–69.

———. "Gaelic Poetry's Province of Stone: Iain Crichton Smith and the Hebridean Echoes of Paul de Man's Late Work." *Scottish Studies Review* 6, no. 2 (2005): 99–112.

———. *The Ruins of Experience: Scotland's "Romantick" Highlands and the Birth of the Modern Witness*. Philadelphia: University of Pennsylvania Press, 2007.

Wilson, Fred. "Wordsworth and the Culture of Science." *Centennial Review* 33, no. 4 (1989): 322–92.

Williams, Raymond. *Marxism and Literature*. Oxford: Oxford University Press, 1977.

Wilson, David B. *Seeking Nature's Logic: Natural Philosophy in the Scottish Enlightenment*. University Park: Pennsylvania State University Press, 2009.

Wirkus, Jessie Leatham. "Number, Newtonianism, and Sublimity in James Thomson's *The Seasons*." Master's thesis, Brigham Young University, 2010.

Withers, Charles W. J. "The Social Nature of Map-Making in the Scottish Enlightenment, c. 1682–c. 1832." *Imago Mundi* 54 (2002): 46–66.

Wittgenstein, Ludwig. *Philosophical Investigations*. Trans. G. E. M. Anscombe. Malden, MA: Blackwell, 2006.

Womack, Peter. *Improvement and Romance: Constructing the Myth of the Highlands*. Houndmills: Macmillan, 1989.

Woolf, Virginia. "Mr. Bennett and Mrs. Brown." *Collected Essays*. Vol. 1. London: Hogarth, 1966.

Wordsworth, Dorothy. *Recollections of a Tour Made in Scotland*. New Haven, CT: Yale University Press, 1997.

Wordsworth, William. "Lines Written a Few Miles Above Tintern Abbey." *Lyrical Ballads*, ed. W. J. B. Owen. Oxford: Oxford University Press, 1969.

———. "The Solitary Reaper." *William Wordsworth: The Poems*, ed. John Hayden. Vol. 1. London: Penguin, 1977.

———. *The Thirteen Book Prelude*. Ed. Mark L. Reed. 2 vols. Ithaca, NY: Cornell University Press, 1991.

Worringer, Wilhelm. *Abstraction and Empathy: A Contribution to the Psychology of Style*. New York: International Universities Press, 1953.

Žižek, Slavoj. *The Sublime Object of Ideology*. London: Verso, 1989.

———. *Tarrying with the Negative: Kant, Hegel, and the Critique of Ideology*. Durham, NC: Duke University Press, 1993.

INDEX

Images are indicated by italic page numbers accompanied by the letter *f.*

ACKNOWLEDGMENTS

I begin by inverting the convention that authors withhold expressions of gratitude to their loved ones until the concluding paragraph. My wife, Kerry, and daughters, Hadley and Elena, deserve better, having been led on a whirlwind odyssey across continents that commenced when I began working on this book. I will forever be grateful for their sense of adventure as well as their fortitude, love, and companionship.

This book has matured across several overlapping stages of my career: eighteenth centuryist, scholar of Scottish literary studies, and general humanist. It was born, fortuitously, from a line I stumbled across in Brigham Young University's Harold B. Lee Library while researching something else. And "stumbled" is probably the right word, for it took several years to find the proper footing as I ascended the face of a steep learning curve. Happily, I found others on the trail to help me stay upright and keep me from backsliding. Indeed, BYU was the perfect institution for promoting the experimental thinking this book required. In the project's early stages, when I was still an assistant and then an early associate professor, I was indebted to my colleagues, Keith Johnson and Ed Cutler, for timely suggestions and insights. I also benefited immensely from extraordinarily intelligent and gracious students (Emily Barlow, Ben Bascom, Kaila Brown, Brittany Cameron, Adam Channer, Emily Crego, Katherine Fisher, Dallin Lewis, Charisse Stephens, and Jessie Wirkus, to name only a few) who patiently endured, in the laboratory of the classroom, my efforts to solve the new puzzles I was encountering. Later, when I assumed the position of senior lecturer of Scottish literature at the University of Aberdeen (the professional honor of a lifetime), I learned from conversations with wonderful colleagues like Tim Baker, Cairns Craig, Chris Fynsk, Catherine Jones, and Ali Lumsden and from the congenial and rigorous intellectual company of Shane Alcobia-Murphy, Patrick Crotty, David Duff, Hazel

Hutchison, Wayne Price, and Thomas Rist. Once I returned to BYU to assume directorship of the BYU Humanities Center, the project finally began to come to fruition. And at this stage, I was the beneficiary of cherished friendship and perspicuous insights by my colleagues Billy Hall, Nick Mason, Brian Roberts, and Jill Rudy. Philip Snyder, chair of the English Department, was always quick to provide financial assistance and heartfelt, and deeply appreciated, moral support.

The friendships I have made at BYU since we launched the Humanities Center in 2012 are too numerous to name, and my association with more than a dozen research groups and hundreds of inspirational colleagues has been a richer intellectual and personal experience than I can possibly articulate. But three people deserve at least a halting expression of gratitude. The first is John Rosenberg, who served as dean of the College of Humanities, early visionary of the Humanities Center, and champion and supporter-in-chief of all research in the college, including mine. The second is Greg Clark, associate dean of the College of Humanities, a valued friend, and a superb example of the life of the scholar. The third is John Tanner, whose vision for BYU, which he first shared with me in 1998, has become for me something more profound than anything professional.

And, of course, I have amassed a long list of debts to people outside the ambit of my own institutions whose work, conversations, suggestions, and encouragement have fueled my thinking and buoyed my spirits. Of a list that could be much, much longer, I owe special thanks to Gerry Carruthers, Ian Duncan, Evan Gottlieb, Alice Jenkins, Caroline McCracken-Flesher, Matt Ochiltree, Murray Pittock, and Arkady Plotnitsky.

I was invited to present parts of this book as lectures at (in order) the University of California, Santa Barbara; Harvard; the University of Aberdeen; Oregon State; BYU; Glasgow University; the Centre for Eighteenth-Century Studies at York University; the University of California, Berkeley; the University of Utah; and the conference of the Consortium of Humanities Centers and Institutes in Madison, Wisconsin. I have reflected often, and with deep gratitude, on those who extended invitations to lecture and to receptive and helpful audiences who made this a better book.

Last, I must thank Jerry Singerman and his wonderful staff at the University of Pennsylvania Press, without whom this would not be a book at all. My previous experience at Penn enlightened me as to Jerry's keen judgment, standards, and professional sensibilities. This experience has taught me about his patience and friendship, for which I will always be grateful.

Parts of this book appeared elsewhere: Chapter 3 in the *Edinburgh Companion to Scottish Romanticism* (2011), Chapter 4 in *Modern Language Quarterly* 75, no. 1 (2014), and Chapter 5 in the *Journal of Scottish Thought* 2, no. 1 (2009). Many thanks to Edinburgh University Press, Duke University Press, and Aberdeen University Press for the right to republish.